Shipwrecks
of Isle Royale National Park
The Archeological Survey

D1710857

Shipwrecks
of Isle Royale National Park
The Archeological Survey

Daniel J. Lenihan
Principal Investigator
Submerged Cultural Resources Unit

Larry E. Murphy
Submerged Cultural Resources Unit

C. Patrick Labadie
Canal Park Marine Museum

Thom Holden
Canal Park Marine Museum

Jerry Livingston
Illustrations

Adapted from National Park Service publication entitled
Submerged Cultural Resources Study: Isle Royale National Park
Southwest Cultural Resources Center Professional Papers Number 8
Santa Fe, New Mexico
1987

Lake Superior Port Cities Inc.

Adapted from National Park Service, Southwest Cultural Resources Center Professional Papers Number 8 (1987)
Submerged Cultural Resources Study: Isle Royale National Park

First edition published September 1994 by

 LAKE SUPERIOR PORT CITIES INC.
P.O. Box 16417
Duluth, Minnesota 55816-0417
USA

5 4 3 2 1

Lenihan, Daniel J.
   Shipwrecks of Isle Royale National Park : / by Daniel J. Lenihan, Larry E. Murphy, C. Patrick Labadie, Thom Holden
      p.   cm.
   Bibliography, p. 205
   ISBN 0-942235-18-5
      1. Underwater archaeology – Michigan – Isle Royale National Park. 2. Shipwrecks – Michigan – Isle Royale National Park.
3. Archeological Surveying – Michigan – Isle Royale National Park. 4. Excavations (Archaeology) – Michigan – Isle Royale
National Park 5. Isle Royale National Park (Mich.) – Antiquities. 6. Navigation – Great Lakes – History. 7. Navigation –
Superior, Lake – History. I. Title.

Library of Congress Card Catalog Number 94-77712

Printed in the United States of America

   Editor: Paul L. Hayden
Designer: Stacy L. Winter
   Printer: Davidson Printing Company, Duluth, Minnesota
Front Cover Photo: Divers Toni Carrell and Larry Wiese record information at the wreck site of the *Stanley,* a wooden fish tug
      which sank in the early 1930s near Star Island, now in Isle Royale National Park. NPS photo by John Brooks.
Back Cover Photo: Recording data at the bow of the *Emperor.* NPS photo.

Acknowledgements

(From original NPS document)

Writing the acknowledgments for this report was not an easy task. The project was, by nature, a complex joint research and management venture and the list of people who provided substantial assistance to its successful completion is lengthy. First, it should be understood that Isle Royale National Park is a wilderness area in northern Lake Superior, and that cost-effective research in this Park is not feasible without the active support of the Park staff. Jack Morehead was Superintendent of Isle Royale when the project was conceived, and his expression of management concern, as well as his personal interest in seeing state-of-the-art research take place on submerged sites, was the primary reason for it happening. Doug Scovill, Chief Anthropologist of the National Park Service, and Cal Cummings, Senior Service Archeologist, provided the impetus from the cultural resources management sector of the agency necessary to generate the funding and support for the program. Stu Croll was Chief Ranger at Isle Royale during the entire period in which field activities were conducted, and his support of logistics, planning and as a sounding board for what would and wouldn't work "on the ground" at Isle Royale was invaluable. Superintendent Don Brown was not only supportive of the program, but raised some new issues emphasizing interpretation of shipwrecks to the non-diving public that have become a significant area of endeavor with the Submerged Cultural Resources Unit. Thomas Hobbs became Superintendent in 1985, and though confronted with a host of issues far different from those he experienced in Yellowstone National Park, he immediately adapted to the situation and gave us his complete support.

Others at Isle Royale who lent us continued support over the years were Ann Belleman, Carol Maass, Elen Maurer, Bruce Reed, Bruce Weber, Chuck Dale and Larry Wiese. In addition to the field assistance they rendered, Park Ranger Ken Vrana and District Ranger Jay Wells' level of commitment is best symbolized by their contributions to the writing of this report. Dave Snyder spent many hours reproducing files from the Park's office in Houghton and reviewing this report in draft. Robert Olli and Dennis Mielock of the Park maintenance staff rendered assistance in the most basic sense of the term. They scrambled to our rescue in the wee hours of the morning in 1980 to prevent our University of Wisconsin research tug from being added to the Isle Royale shipwreck population. Cliff Hannula kept our motors humming and, in association with Jay Wells, built the first "underwater mule" for use by divers in placing shipwreck mooring buoys. Lee Jameson dived with us and gave us access to maintenance division assets for our survey work whenever he could possibly justify it.

From the Midwest Regional Office, Andy Ketterson was our primary contact point; he made life easy for us in an administrative sense and found small pots of money at critical times to help us take advantage of research opportunities, such as the visit of RV *Seward Johnson* to Isle Royale. Cal Calabrese, Chief of the National Park Service Midwest Archeological Center, was supportive of the project and delegated Archeologist Mark Lynott to coordinate directly with us. Mark reviewed our preliminary and interim reports and this report in draft form and contributed on site as an instructor in a training course on "Submerged Cultural Resources, Skills and Issues" held at Isle Royale National Park.

From my own office in Santa Fe, Regional Director Bob Kerr provided his support to this and all endeavors of the Submerged Cultural Resources Unit. Bob believed in the principle of knowing your resources, whether they were dry or wet, and he provided a roof for the team and administrative support, because he felt it was "for the good of the Service." John Cook took over the Regional helm during our last year of work at Isle Royale and has continued the high level of nurture at home that allowed us to keep our energies focused on the field. Dick Sellars, Chief of our Center, not only supported us unfailingly during the five years that we devoted partial time to Isle Royale, but also visited us in the field and stoically subjected his landlubber's belly to the tortures of bouncing boats, cold and Dramamine. Larry Nordby and Jim Bradford lent their considerable archeological field talents to our project; Larry also contributed to the writing of one section of this report. Jerry Livingston, who has rendered almost all of the graphics for this report, demonstrated again and again at Isle Royale the great utility of having a diving scientific illustrator in the field. Ron Ice permitted the denuding of his archeological staff for several three-week periods during his own field season, because he believed in the importance of the Isle Royale Project, and we thank him for his forbearance.

We also benefited greatly from the input of a number of folks from the Great Lakes Region. Patrick Labadie, Director of the U.S. Army Corps of Engineers Canal Park Museum in Duluth, was a magnificent find for us because of his great knowledge of regional history and maritime material culture. Thom Holden, also of the Canal Park Museum, provided us with access to his personal files on Isle Royale shipwrecks and the benefit of his knowledge of Lake Superior maritime disasters all through the project. Ric Wright from Bowling Green State University performed an extremely helpful records search for us in the files of the Institute for Great Lakes Research. Ric has since passed away; his contributions to Great Lakes navigation research will be missed. Gerrie Noble of the Thunder Bay Historical Museum has provided useful historical information to the Park for many years. James R. Marshall gave freely of his first-hand experience regarding the salvage of the steamship *America*.

Other assistance with archival materials came from the following: Jim Delgado, Golden Gate National Recreation Area; David Hull and John Maounis of the J. Porter Shaw Library, National Maritime Museum, San Francisco; Chynoweth Collection at Michigan Technical University Archives; Penny C. Grigsby, New Mexico State Library; Ken Hall and John Vandereedt of the Judicial, Fiscal and Social Branch of the National Archives, Washington D.C.

Larry Sand, Captain of *Superior Diver*, was the charter contractor for most of our intensive field sessions. His skill and competence not only helped keep us alive, but aided measurably in the effectiveness of our operations. Scott McWilliam from Thunder Bay, Ontario, Gerry Buchanan, Duluth, Minnesota, and the late Monty Florentz are sport divers who somewhat obscure the distinction between professional and amateur maritime archeologist. They demonstrated great commitment to seeing the shipwrecks of Isle Royale inventoried and devoted many long hours of volunteer time to helping us carry out this task. We never had the opportunity to dive with Ken Merryman or Ken Engelbrecht due to scheduling conflicts, but in several long conversations they freely communicated much useful information from their extensive experience at Isle Royale wreck diving. Joe Strykowski donated his considerable photographic skills to the Isle Royale project during the 1985 field session. Mitch Kezar donated a series of slides that he obtained while working with us under contract to the National Geographic Society.

The National Geographic Society assigned a team of technicians under the able leadership of Emory Kristof to help in the documentation of *Kamloops* using Remote Operated Vehicles. Donald Shomette also contributed to this phase of the project. John Brooks spent three weeks with our team in 34-degree water, contributing his talents in underwater photography. This was a fair commitment from someone who lives and works off a boat in the Bahamas. The Harbor Branch Research Vessel *Seward Johnson* was made available to us through a NOAA Sea Grant project conducted by Michigan State University. We thank Bill Cooper, Ken Pott and Patrick Labadie for their roles in making this possible.

For information and assistance in understanding the commercial fishing, resort and mining sites at Isle Royale and the vernacular small craft we would like to thank the late Myrtle Johnson, Tim Cochrane, Ingeborg Holte, Milford Johnson Jr., Reuben Hill, Stanley Sivertson, Roy Oberg, Marge McPherren, Elvis Moe, Donald Anderson, Donald Wobrink, Phil Gale and Jim Woodward. Isle Royale concession personnel who went out of their way to help us include manager Ron Sanders. Last, but definitely not least, were the many seasonal employees at Isle Royale that gave up their lieu days to help with boating operations, participate in the diving research activities and stoke the sauna.

Barbara Stanislawski has taken the brunt of the secretarial duties involved in the typing and arrangement of this report in a finished format. In addition to the authors and contributors, various sections of this report were reviewed in draft form by the following people: Jim Bradford, James Delgado, Kevin Foster, Allen Saltus, David Snyder, Bob Krumenaker, Stu Croll, Bruce Weber, Thomas Hobbs, Jack Morehead, Don Brown, Dick Gould, Ron Ice, Cal Cummings, Mark Lynott, Patrick Martin, Joy Waldron and National Park Service Chief Historian Ed Bearss. Alice Benfer did a helpful review of the entire final draft, and Ernesto Martinez did final inking of all of the sketch maps in Chapter VI.

Daniel J. Lenihan

Table of Contents

List of Figures

List of Tables

Preface

The Submerged Cultural Resources Unit was established in 1980 to conduct research on underwater archeological sites throughout the National Park System with an emphasis on historic shipwrecks. One of the unit's primary responsibilities is to disseminate the results of research to National Park Service managers, as well as the professional community, in a form that meets resource management needs and adds to our understanding of the resource base. A report series was initiated in order to fulfill that responsibility, and the Isle Royale Study was one of the first completed.

Shortly after receiving the standard 500 copies of the document from the Government Printing Office, it became apparent that the study had considerable appeal to a readership far beyond its intended audience.

Because the Submerged Cultural Resources Unit is not in the business of writing monographs for public consumption, it was not clear how to satisfy the large number of requests for the volume which were emanating primarily from the sport diving community and Great Lakes Maritime History enthusiasts. Much of the material in the original document was inappropriate for a general audience, yet time and funds were not readily available to create a popularized version without help from outside the National Park Service. We were delighted when Mr. James Marshall of Lake Superior Port Cities Inc. offered to take the project on as a private venture. The original text and artwork were loaned to Jim minus chapters that the park superintendent or I felt would not be germane to our new target audience. Some new photos and minor additions to the text also appear.

Although most management oriented discussions have been deleted along with a chapter on non-shipwreck submerged sites, an attempt has been made to preserve the historical, archeological and resource preservation style of the volume.

History and archeology of each wreck is presented separately because that is how historical archeologists must conceptually approach such studies. Records tell one part of the story; material (shipwrecks) tells another. Both classes of information have different strengths and weaknesses, and we would not be true to the original spirit of the study to meld them.

With the changes and deletions, two authors of the original study will no longer be represented in the present volume, so I would like to recognize them here for their very significant contributions to Isle Royale shipwreck research. They are Toni Carrell and Ken Vrana.

Daniel J. Lenihan

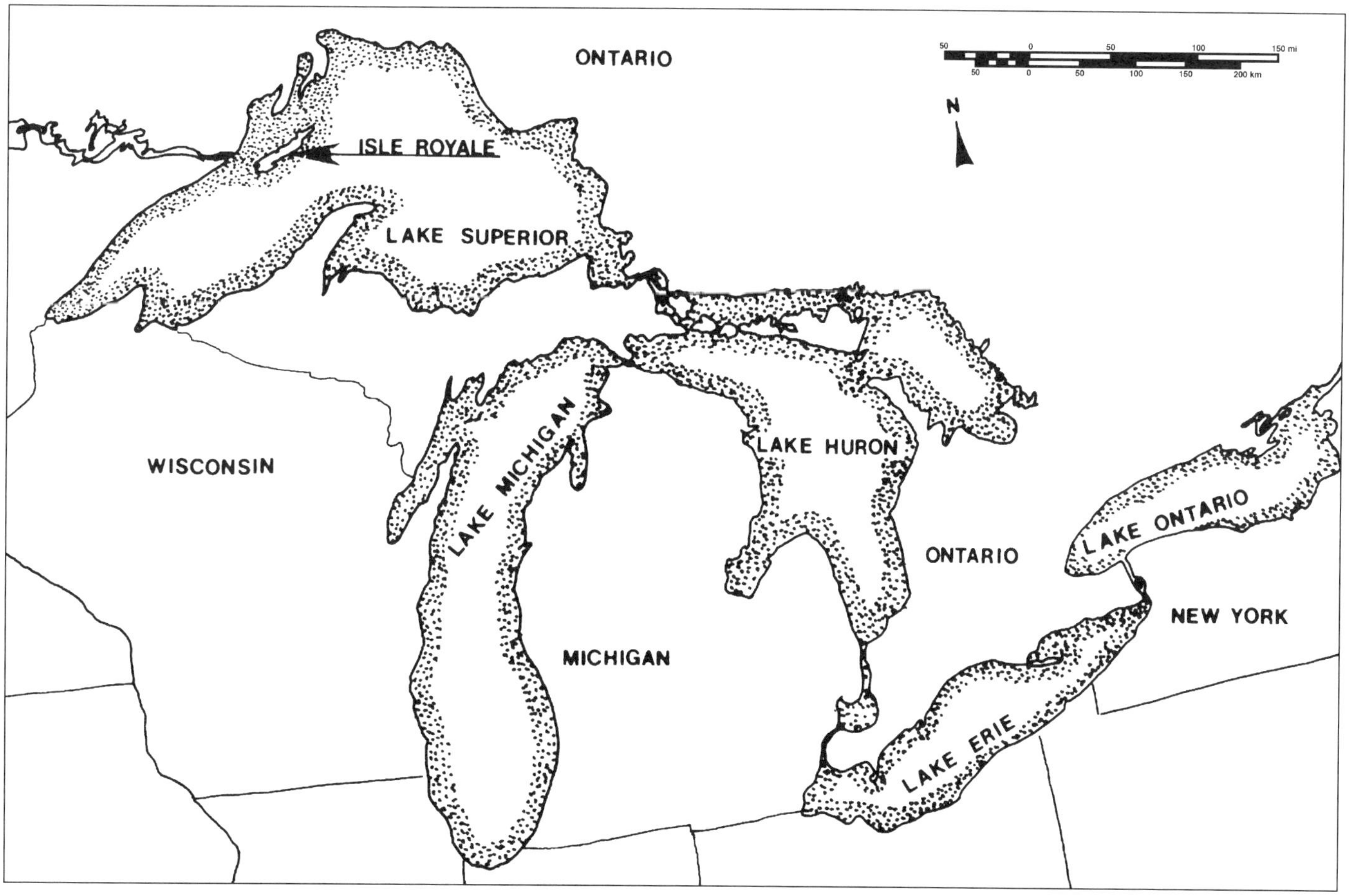

Figure 1. Isle Royale in the context of the Great Lakes Region.

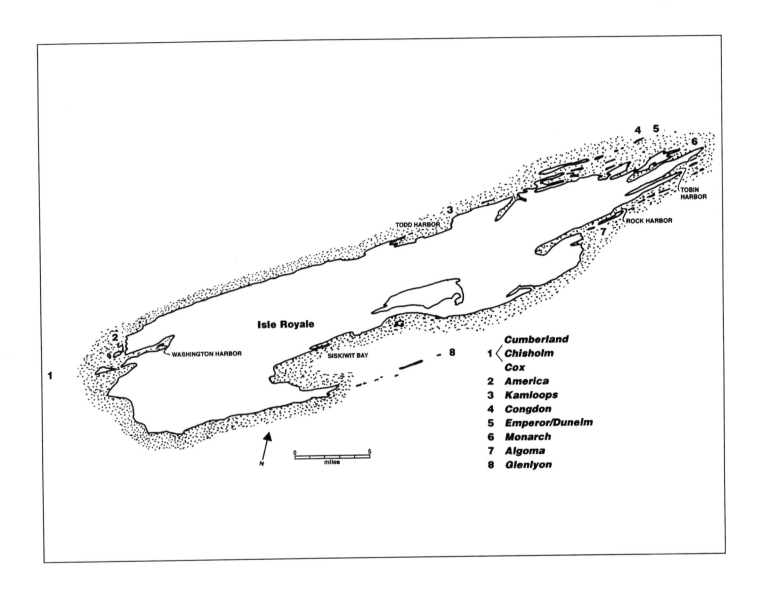

Figure 2. Isle Royale shipwrecks

Chapter I

Introduction

Isle Royale National Park was certainly not originally established for the purpose of preserving shipwrecks. It is tempting, however, to ascribe some grand scheme to the existence of such a dramatic assortment of wrecked vessels within the protected waters of a national park. The island is literally surrounded by an array of ship remains that represent many types and stages of development of maritime steam technology from the 1870s to the mid-1900s. This assortment includes passenger/package freighters, bulk freighters, a side-wheeler, wooden-hulled ships and steel behemoths more than 500 feet in length, one of which went down as recently as 1947. If one were given the opportunity of designing an underwater museum of Great Lakes marine architecture, it is likely that it would differ only slightly from what is presently within the waters of Isle Royale. Perhaps the remains of a wooden schooner to complement the steam vessels would be the most welcome addition. Even some of the local fishing craft of unique vernacular design have found their way to the bottom of the lake and have assumed the roles of diving exhibits. For the professional archeologist, the non-shipwreck underwater sites also offer an excellent opportunity for studying subsistence patterns in a lacustrine, subarctic environment; where better than a clear lake surrounding an island where the cold water conveniently preserves even the organic residues of past human behavior?

This last factor, the nature of the underwater environment around Isle Royale, contributes much to the Park's aura of being an underwater museum. The sights greeting a diver are stirring to even the most experienced and hard-to-please members of that fraternity. The more modern, intact wrecks such as *America*, *Emperor* and *Congdon* attract most of the first-timers, because they comprise a superlative underwater experience. Very few places in the world offer shipwrecks with such a "presence" in conditions that highlight the other-worldliness of the diving experience. It is possible to swim down companionways, through stateroom doors, up stairs and over engines that appear as if it would take only a head of steam to bring them back to life. Old-fashioned shoes amid the confusion of crushed bulkheads bring home the poignant personal tragedy that was experienced by so many crew and passengers and their surviv-

ing families. There is something about being there and feeling the cold water starting to creep through one's protective suit and sensing the pressure and dominance of the lake that permits an empathy with an event in history that is hard to imagine from a dry, warm perspective on land.

This unique experience is as much a part of the quality of life that should be preserved in national parks as is the beautiful, natural scenery that characterizes the island. In order to leave the historic scenes as undisturbed as possible, a totally nondestructive approach was employed in the study and recording of these remarkable underwater sites.

Underwater Archeology and the Age of Steam

Although the management concerns that prompted our inventory of submerged sites at Isle Royale are clear to most, not so the archeological import of studying steam age technology. Often, those who can relate well to underwater archeological studies of ancient sailing ships cannot understand the attention paid by archeologists to late 19th century and early 20th century steam vessel wrecks, such as the ones at Isle Royale. The questions posed in this regard are reasonable ones: aren't there plans in existence for many of those vessels, and aren't there representatives of this type of vessel still afloat? The answer to both questions is "no." In fact, there are no plans available for many of the vessels that sank at Isle Royale, and when plans do exist, they rarely deal with hull features above the waterline and/or superstructure and the modifications that were endorsed over time, which are of great importance to the archeologist studying behavioral adaptations. Likewise, only the two steel-hulled bulk freighters that are wrecked at Isle Royale have any representatives of their vessel type still afloat.

Archeologists are interested in using the material record to determine what people did, not what they think they did or said they did. In addition, much of what we need to know about past human behavior is best represented in the archeology of the mundane – the things that contemporary writers thought too obvious or insignificant to record. Thus is evidenced the complementary nature of the historic record and the archeological record, which is so exciting to those who feel that historical archeology will eventually serve as the proving ground for all anthropologically oriented archeological theory.

There is another issue regarding the documentation of steam technology that should be mentioned: the problem of myopia in the study of the recent past. Because we are closer to something in time does not necessarily mean we understand it better. This is particularly true of the last two centuries in Euroamerican affairs. Although steam engines in the most literal sense have been in existence for thousands of years in such novel forms as door closing mechanisms on ancient tombs, they were more appropriately termed "devices." It was not until the late 1700s that steam engines were used on land for doing work, and the 1800s before they saw effective utilization as a source of motive power on ships. Although historians will argue over the issue of whether Fitch or Rumsey or somebody else may have been the real "inventor" of the steamboat, it matters not a whit to the social scientist. The popular belief that Fulton invented the steamboat in 1807 serves quite well, because the steamboat *North River of Clermont* effectively ushered in the new age of maritime steam technology by succeeding in capturing the imagination of the general public.

Clermont was important because it worked, and because the fact that it worked was well marketed. Social dynamics are less keyed to historical facts than they are to a society's notion of what those facts are. Fulton's boat had good press, and Fulton had good biographers, so steam came alive in the imagination of people who had the money to build boats.

The enormous impact of steam technology on man is worth contemplating. It may put into perspective why it is such an important and difficult period of human endeavor to document in the historical and material records. It would not be an unbalanced assessment to state that man evolved from a common heritage shared by several other extant primates, learned complex manipulation of tools and symbolic thought over several million years, and in the 18th century invented the steam engine, which was followed shortly thereafter by nuclear power.

The thermodynamic forces involved in the steam engine dwarfed anything seen before and presented an unparalleled potential to the species to manipulate phenomena. The strength of thousands of beasts of burden could be harnessed in one machine that need only be fed various sorts of combustibles that were easily available. Mines could be cleared of water, tunnels dug under rivers and canals built at speeds and in places never conceived before steam use. Most important for our purpose is the fact that steam also meant cargoes of magnitudes greater size could be

moved against the wind over water.

In short order, the only limits to shipbuilding were dictated by the composition of building material of the vessels, i.e., it is difficult to make wooden ships much more than 300 feet in length that don't sag unacceptably in the middle or droop (hog) at the ends, regardless of how many engineering tricks are employed. It wasn't all quite that simple, of course. The atmospheric engine couldn't drive boats, and it took the development of adequate pressure cylinders, separate condensers and efficient boilers before steam power could be fully utilized for fast rotary motion and the full implications for steam at sea began to be realized.

The competition from sail was fierce at first, for it must be remembered that much of the creative surge of energy that typified the explosive development of steam technology was not absent from the lofts of sailmakers and shipwrights. The culmination of several thousand years of wind-ship technology was evident in the latter part of the 19th century. The most refined, most efficient and perhaps the most elegant sailing ships ever constructed were competing with steam ships into the 20th century. Mixing fire and water is an unbeatable combination, however, and man's preference for his Promethean heritage prevailed.

Research Design

There has been a considerable degree of stress generated over the issue of "proper" scientific method in the social sciences. Although there has been somewhat of a fixation on research designs in terrestrial archeology, this has not been the case in maritime archeology, where a negative reaction regarding their use is sometimes evident (e.g. Bass: 1984).

There is no doubt that useful, professional research has been carried out on underwater sites without benefit of explicit designs, but that does not excuse maritime archeologists in the

Figure 3. Generation of line drawings was a major documentation method used on the shipwreck sites. Photo by Mitch Kezar.

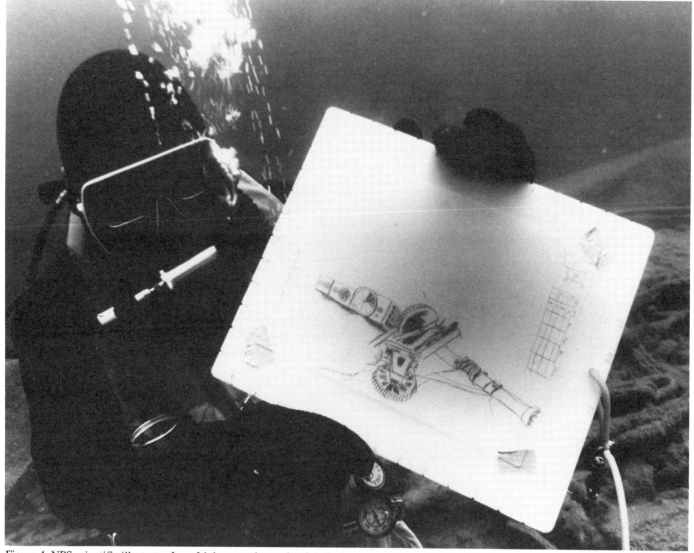

Figure 4. NPS scientific illustrator Jerry Livingston shows sketch to be incorporated into *Glenlyon* site documentation. Photo by Mitch Kezar.

public sector from meeting this basic requirement of scientific reporting. A research design is presented in this report so that the reader may know the rationale behind our field and archival activities and better understand why certain methods and techniques were selected, and others rejected. This research was paid for with public funds, and it concentrated on publicly owned resources – added reason for discussing our rationale and methods.

The research design was largely mechanistic in nature. Straightforward questions about the material record were asked and much energy was devoted to purely descriptive documentation of the sites. Our analysis and interpretation was geared toward integrating the hard data from the material record with the data from the archives.

Because American archeologists have their roots entwined more in anthropology than in history, we have consistently examined our subject matter from a social scientific perspective. In those cases in which we felt Isle Royale shipwrecks and other submerged sites were most productively viewed against a backdrop of regional or extra-regional behavioral patterns, we strived to present them in just that way. In most cases this occurred during the data evaluation process between field seasons. Cerebrating about the anthropological implications of information gleaned from the archives or from the lake bottom resulted in conclusions that are offered in the text. There is no presentation of hypotheses and test implications because it was felt that a hypothetico-deductive approach was not appropriate to this inventory. The research design formulated is a problem oriented one, however, and it represents an attempt to accommodate the best from history and social science in a cultural resources management framework. We will endeavor to make that thought process explicit for the benefit of those investigators who may follow at Isle Royale or those who have interest in similar research problems.

General Problem Statement

The objective of the field research was to obtain as much descriptive data on the underwater archeological residues as

3

possible with given equipment, time and personnel resources. This was to be accomplished using non-destructive methodology emphasizing mapping of exposed wreckage, photography, artistic perspective drawings and videotape footage. Archival work was also initiated to obtain primary source references on each vessel being investigated in the field. The literature base of the social sciences, particularly anthropology, was utilized to identify a range of broad behavioral issues that would be addressed in both the field and library components of the research activity. Following are the social, economic and technological questions that were addressed as thematic issues throughout the field research and writing of this report:

I.   What are the major environmental, social and economic attributes of the Great Lakes region that would affect the material record at Isle Royale, i.e., nature and distribution of shipwreck remains?

   A. Natural Factors: Does operation in small water bodies with the potential for severe weather influence maritime adaptive behavior? Do short wave periods, lack of sea room for maneuvering in storms, inland fog conditions and icing-over create situations that demand significantly different responses than do seaboard environments in North America? What role does Isle Royale play as a natural obstacle to shipping in Lake Superior?

   B. Cultural Factors: What effects in Great Lakes maritime activity devolve from the demands to operate in a small, highly contained shipping universe? Was the shipping activity in the lakes notably more intensive than in the rest of the nation during the steam age, and how did the demands for moving large amounts of bulk cargo (e.g. iron and grain) affect developments in ship architecture and motive technology? How do the shipwrecks of Isle Royale and associated submerged historic sites reflect any of these influences?

II. What elements of Great Lakes maritime culture represent an extension of ocean going traditions?

   A. Do technological responses to economic pressures on the Great Lakes replicate developments on the Atlantic seaboard, western rivers or post gold-rush shipbuilding activity on the West Coast?

   B. Is there a cross-fertilization of ideas, traits and behavior that can be identified between the Great Lakes, western rivers and the Atlantic seaboard?

   C. Can the technological attributes of the Isle Royale shipwreck population be used as an indicator to gauge diversity, borrowing or independent invention when compared to other ship and shipwreck studies?

III. Are there any unique characteristics to the subculture of seamen on the Great Lakes?

   A. Did the seamen on Great Lakes vessels derive from local populations that had no prior seafaring traditions, or did they tend to be imports from the coast who were specifically emigrating west for jobs on the lakes? How did these trends vary over time?

   B. What effects, if any, did short voyages and frequent turnarounds have on Great Lakes crews? Did the development of technological advances, such as faster loading and unloading systems for bulk cargos, have any bearing on the life of the common seaman?

   C. How did Great Lakes seamen perceive the environment in which they were working? Was it considered more desirable, less dangerous or more lucrative than working on the coast or rivers? Did Lake Superior or Isle Royale hold any special significance to these people?

IV. Did the dynamics of social adjustment to the Industrial Age differ on the Great Lakes?

   A. Was it a more intense industrial environment in terms of greater capital investment for high-yield returns, and did technological advances create a more or less stressful milieu for developing lifeways in the region?

   B. Was there a tendency to push limits on lakes navigation in response to heavier capital investment? Was there really a "one-last-voyage syndrome," as identified by

Figure 5. Video documentation was used extensively during the project. This self-contained color unit took the place of tethered black-and-white units used at the beginning of the project. NPS photo by Joe Strykowski.

Murphy (1984), which resulted in a greater frequency of late-season disasters on Lake Superior? Does the shipwreck population at Isle Royale support this contention?

A separate research strategy statement was developed for each phase of the multi-year project before entering the field. These statements of objectives and proposed methodology were discussed in interim reports on the Isle Royale research that were distributed to park managers and to the profession for peer review. The original NPS technical study from which this volume is derived included a lengthy presentation of specific research objectives for each site. This was by necessity repetitious and more a scientific convention than illuminating, so it has been omitted in this volume.

There were also specific questions about vessel construction, architectural elements, etc., that were formulated after analysis of each season's field work that were targeted as research problems for both the archives and the field. It quickly became apparent that there were many questions more effectively answered in the field in some instances and the archives in others.

Figure 6. Diver propulsion vehicles were used to survey the area surrounding the more scattered sites. NPS photo by Joe Strykowski.

Combining the archeologist's method with the historian's resulted in a final product which, it is hoped, adds up to more than the sum of the parts.

Methodology

Logistic considerations significantly influenced the overall research approach. Isle Royale is remote by any standard, has difficult access for heavy equipment and the underwater environment of the sites is cold and usually deep. Water temperatures rarely exceeded 39 degrees Fahrenheit on any of the sites, and air temperatures in June were often below freezing. Visibility was usually quite good, 20 to 50 feet, but low light levels and a high concentration of coarse particulate matter suspended in the water made certain photographic tasks more difficult than might be expected.

The research approach emphasized short, intense field sessions each year (usually lasting about three weeks) that were carefully planned and oriented toward maximum data recovery for every moment in the field. Researchers (usually five or six in number) lived on a 38-foot boat and dived in shifts during a 12-hour day, every day, for the three-week hitch. This proved very cost-effective, but by 1984 the procedure was modified to include a couple of rest days because of possible safety problems developing from diver exhaustion and a growing concern

that residual nitrogen factors were stretching the recommended limits of the U.S. Navy decompression tables after weeks of repetitive diving.

Mapping methodology, in most instances, consisted of laying a small-gauge nylon baseline through major wreckage fields and building a map using the baseline as a backbone. In those cases where limited detail could be rendered due to the size of the site, team archeologists selected features most crucial to a useful interpretation of the remains. These were marked with survey clips made of clothespins and flagging tape. Angles were turned with a large protractor whenever the baseline touched or went over an object. Large pieces of hull, superstructure or machinery were labeled as specific site components and trilaterated from the baseline with measuring tapes after they had been drawn in detail by a mapping team.

The level of detail and accuracy of the maps and other graphic representations of the shipwrecks in this report varies somewhat from site to site. The major wrecks at the Park derive from the late 19th and early 20th centuries, and for some of them partial construction plans were extant. It would obviously not be necessary or desirable to map them to the degree of detail necessary in documenting, for instance, a classical period vessel in the Mediterranean. Other factors that influenced decisions on the level of detail were: extent of scatter material at individual sites; nature of construction (wood or metal); and logistical considerations such as ease of access, depth of water and water temperature. To convey a general idea of the nature

Figure 7. Two remote operated vehicles (ROV) deployed from NPS patrol boat proved effective in studying the *Kamloops* site. ROV photo by Emory Kristof courtesy of National Geographic Society.

of these problems, consider that just the major concentrations of wreckage at Isle Royale, if gathered together, would cover an area more than one million square feet. That is approximately 100 to 1,000 times the site area of most early wooden vessels that are being investigated by our colleagues. On several sites at Isle Royale, baselines of marked string were laid over continuous wreckage for one-third mile. Water depths over the sites ranged from three feet to 270 feet.

Consequently, the following general guidelines were adopted. Wooden wrecks (*Cumberland, Chisholm* and *Monarch*), which incidentally were also the earliest built vessels in this shipwreck population, were mapped to the highest degree of accuracy. In most cases, each individual timber was counted and measured, e.g., the number and size of the limber boards on the section of *Chisholm's* hull bottom depicted in Figure 65 is not an approximation; it is a precise drawing. In other places some license has been taken to sketch or omit detail, e.g., on large sections of metal hull in the case of *Glenlyon* or *Cox*. The pieces are where they should be, but specific details of construction such as fittings, rivets, etc., may be approximated or omitted. Since metal curves and twists as a result of underwater dynamics, its exact replication on paper does not convey enough information to warrant time expenditure past identifying its basic nature, i.e., hull pieces, superstructure, etc. Wood, on the other hand, breaks in discrete units, whether large or small, and it is useful to document in detail where possible. A decision was also made to limit any intensive recording activi-

ties by divers to depths less than 150 feet for reasons of safety and cost efficiency. Remote Operated Vehicles (ROVs) were used in 1985 and 1986 to obtain additional information on the *Algoma* and *Kamloops* wreck sites, which had components well beyond 150 feet in depth.

This was the general philosophy that conditioned the level of detail and accuracy that was strived for on the scattered wreckage fields. In the case of the intact vessels (*America, Congdon, Emperor, Kamloops*), the approach used was that of developing a perspective drawing in association with photography to convey an impressionist view of the site.

The artist's perspective drawings are just that, but they are drawn by illustrators who have spent many years doing precise mapping work underwater, and accuracy has been emphasized in all cases when it conflicted with artistic preference. Drawings of this sort in association with photographs were determined to be the best method for portraying the present condition of a large intact vessel in deep water. It is a dramatic example of a situation in which graphic recording skills still serve a purpose that cannot be effectively duplicated by technology.

The question might be asked: Why not photogrammetry? The answer is that given problems of limited visibility and light penetration and the very high relief of both the topography and the sites themselves, this technique could not be effectively employed, using any technology available to the researchers.

The highest level of technology used in what was, for the most part, a very "low tech" operation was the aforementioned ROVs. An ROV was deployed in 1985 from RV *Seward Johnson* to search in deep water for bow structure of *Algoma*. The research vessel and submersible operators had made a decision not to attempt dives on *Kamloops* or the stern of *Congdon* because of proximity of reefs and fear of entanglement in wreckage. Using two miniaturized units from a 32-foot Park patrol boat in 1986 seemed by far the most effective approach. These units were provided by the National Geographic Society, and their skilled operators were able to penetrate even the engine room of *Kamloops* using two ROVs in a "buddy system."

Shipwrecks vs. Submerged Components of Land Sites

The majority of time and energy spent during this inventory effort was on shipwrecks, rather than underwater components of terrestrial sites, e.g., fish camps, mines, historic landings, etc. This is not due to a value judgment regarding relative significance of the shipwrecks, but for two unrelated reasons. First, the shipwrecks are, by far, receiving the greatest visitor pressure at Isle Royale, and second, shipwrecks are the type of resource that is most effectively dealt with by nautical specialists. Terrestrial archeologists familiar with the local prehistory and history are better qualified to direct work on land-based activity areas with the Submerged Cultural Resources Unit playing a supportive, rather than lead, role. We included a representative sample of land-based sites in the technical version of this report (Lenihan 1987: 475-525), but it was not meant to be as comprehensive as the work done on the shipwrecks. Because the inland waterways of Isle Royale tend to be siltier, and much of the midden material and other cultural manifestations are covered by overburden, investigation of land-based sites demands a more high-impact archeological methodology.

This Volume

This is a study of the submerged cultural resources, i.e., underwater archeological record, of Isle Royale National Park. As such, the "fabric" (submerged archeological sites) has determined the "form" (manner of research and presentation) in this publication. History, in this context, serves in a support role to archeology.

The historical document research for Chapter IV included extensive examination of primary sources. Searches were conducted in the archives of the Institute for Great Lakes Research at Bowling Green University, U.S. National Archives in Washington D.C., Canadian Archives in Ottawa, J. Porter Shaw Library, National Maritime Museum, San Francisco, privately developed collections and at the Canal Park Museum in Duluth.

Chapter III on vessel typology of Lake Superior develops a technological context for understanding the significance and

relevance of the shipwreck component of the submerged archeological resources at Isle Royale. The cross section of vessel types in the Park is used as a springboard for a discussion of processual trends in maritime architecture in the Great Lakes Region. A contemporary backdrop of vessel design and socioeconomic dynamics is interwoven in the chapter to enhance the social scientific perspective from which we have chosen to view the Park's shipwreck population.

Chapter II attempts to move one more step away from the particular toward the general. In this case, the intent has been to identify patterns in the maritime behavior of the region that have relevance to the shipwrecks at Isle Royale. This is not intended to be another history of the Lake Superior region, but a discussion of the broader social processes that in combination comprise the maritime interactive sphere of shipping activity on the Great Lakes.

The management recommendations section in "The Future" section of this chapter deserves the following qualifier. In most cases, according to National Park Service policy, the cultural resources management specialists are expected to make a series of recommendations to the line managers who have responsibility for running the Park and the Region. There has been so much interchange of ideas and cross fertilization between the researchers and management in this particular case that this final statement of "recommendations" is largely an expression of a joint conceptual effort. As always, however, recommendations are to be viewed as suggestions and are not binding on future managers in any sense.

Finally, this report is the product of a labor of love. It is offered to those who manage, those who protect and to those who look and enjoy, by a team of researchers who feel fortunate to have been involved in some small way with the future of this Park.

Retrospective

Our Isle Royale project is over; the technical report marks the last official act of a prototype study of submerged cultural resources in a national park. Although there are exciting new possibilities for further research on submerged archeological sites at Isle Royale and other parks in the Great Lakes area, those happenings will comprise chapters of a different book, probably written by different people. It is incumbent upon us to share some observations from our seven years of part-time involvement with this project, beyond what can be gleaned from the informational and methodological presentations in the body of the report. This section begins with some reflections regarding what worked and didn't work in our experience at Isle

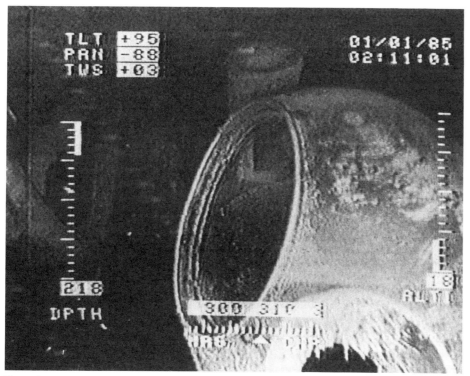

Figure 8. An electronic image of the Sea-rover video display taken from video tape. ROV photo and electronic image by Emory Kristof courtesy of National Geographic Society.

7

Figure 9. RV *Seward Johnson* was available to project investigators for a brief period in 1985 as a part of a NOAA-sponsored data collection project on the Great Lakes. NPS Photo by Joe Strykowski.

Royale, followed by some recommendations and a discussion of further research potential.

We made some right choices and some wrong ones in the conduct of this project. Among the former was the decision to be highly interactive with the Park Superintendent and staff – an important "right choice" that was instrumental in keeping our mistakes at a reasonable level. Isle Royale is not the place to work in a vacuum, regardless of the experience and technology you may have at your disposal. The knowledge gleaned from "locals," i.e., charter captains, sport divers and fishermen, about the whereabouts of sites and tips on when and how to safely examine them, were invaluable.

Our decision to employ a "low tech" documentation system based on string and measuring tapes was partly a function of a modest budget. It proved, however, to be an effective approach in a remote Park where a demystified methodology allowed us to easily recruit off-duty rangers, maintenance personnel and volunteer sport divers to assist us in data gathering. The same low budget that helped us make the decision to "keep it simple" also forced us into short, intense field periods, typically running about three weeks each year for a total field time of 16 weeks. There was some advantage to short field seasons the first two years when we were still developing our strategies; it gave us time to reflect on our Isle Royale work while we were involved in many other field projects, and probably helped

keep us from locking into approaches that were not efficient or cost effective. After the initial phase of the project, however, this proved to be of no advantage. Mobilization and demobilization activities absorbed precious field time; it doesn't take much more effort to mobilize at Isle Royale for two months than it does for two weeks. Also, the pressure to obtain a lot of information in a short time period stressed researchers making it an inviting option to push limits of safety and prudence to get the job done. The lake is not famous for its forgiving nature, and, although we were fortunate to have had no serious accidents, future researchers are encouraged to develop funding parameters that permit longer, easier-going field sessions with ample time for recuperation between dives. It would also be advantageous to have a team that could work full time on the project, rather than three to four people able to devote only one-fourth of their annual work schedule, which was the state of affairs for this study. If we had it to do over again and budget permitted working full time at Isle Royale, we would execute the operation in three to four years: one month in the field the first year, three months the second, and a one month follow-up the third year. Writing would be completed the fourth year.

Other approaches that proved effective included emphasizing the use of diving scientific illustrators in association with videotape as a documentation strategy. Although underwater still photography certainly played an important role in the final report presentation for this project, the prime information generators for the graphics were hard-swimming illustrators backed by analog image acquisition from video. The original video system used in the project was dependent on a hard-line cable to the surface and helmet communication to apprise the diver of what was actually being taped. The camera contained no monitor, so taping was in the blind. Although this approach was immediately anachronized when low-priced, self-contained color systems with underwater monitors became available in 1983, the old unit had already helped greatly in the analysis of many of the shipwreck sites.

Among the things that didn't work so well at Isle Royale was an attempt to obtain a good photographic image of the relationships of the three shipwrecks at Rock of Ages from an aerial perspective. Two days were spent in laying plastic jugs around the perimeter of the sites, with each site color-coded: a bright red for *Cox*, white for *Chisholm*, etc. A seaplane was then hired to circle the lighthouse and reefs while research team members shot rolls of film and ran video cameras through ports in the aircraft. In short, the effort was a complete failure with the only benefit being that the principal investigator learned an expensive lesson about proportional size in aerial imagery. Milk jugs were magnitudes too small for the purpose. It would have been considerably more appropriate to use objects the size of milk cows to accomplish the objective. Future researchers are encouraged to try again, but be advised that the distances and light conditions at Isle Royale compel a project of greater scope than we had envisioned.

At the end of the Isle Royale project, the research team was given access to Remote Operated Vehicle (ROV) technology with which it heretofore had no experience. An ROV is a cable-tethered submersible robot that is operated from a surface vessel. NOAA Sea Grant funding enabled access to RV *Seward Johnson* for two days in 1985 with its ROV and submarine, *Sea Link*. In 1986, the National Geographic Society contributed two miniaturized ROVs and a team of technicians to the Isle Royale project for a week. In the latter case the ROVs were deployed in tandem

from a small (32-foot) Park patrol boat, a contrast to the previous year's work with the 170-foot *Seward Johnson*. The difference in success and cost-effectiveness was remarkable, with the second year's activity being dramatically superior in both areas.

Seward Johnson is an impressive research vessel, but its very size and complexity in configuration made it less useful in near-shore environments. Unfortunately, most shipwrecks don't occur in deep open water, far from dangerous reefs or underwater obstructions. Because of the concerns of the ship

Figure 10. CORD ROV aboard *Seward Johnson* used to search deep areas for additional wreckage near *Algoma*. NPS photo by Joe Strykowski.

captain with reefs and the submarine operators' reluctance to "fly" near underwater entanglements, the limited vessel time had to be applied to our fourth level of priority – a search for additional remains of *Algoma*. The vessel captain and vehicle pilots made professional judgments about the risks involved in the other sites and decided that they were not acceptable. This was partly due to the nature of the specific hardware they had on board, and partly because they felt more information was needed, such as comprehensive side-scan sonar coverage on the sites, before deployment of the submersible. The operation might be judged a failure, but, if so, it was an instructive failure. RV *Seward Johnson* could probably be a useful research tool at Isle Royale with some changes in approach gleaned from the problems experienced in 1985. Underwater archeology cannot just be tagged onto oceanographic ventures without significant communication between the archeologists and shipboard technical personnel in the early planning stages. There must be respect for the different constraints and needs that accrue from historic shipwreck investigations, from project conception through execution. With the right preparation and communication, the use of the manned submersible could provide important information obtainable in no other fashion.

In contrast to the difficulties experienced with *Seward Johnson* was the dramatic success that devolved in 1986 from the use of miniaturized ROVs operated from Park patrol boats. *Kamloops*, which was the first priority for the 1985 investigations, was surveyed in 1986, and even penetrated by the ROV "pilots." Data generated from these remarkable machines helped answer many questions about the site and permitted the development of artists' perspective drawings.

Table 1 – Isle Royale Shipwrecks

Vessel Name	Official Number	Description	Owner/Manager	Place and Date Built	Relation to Isle Royale
Madeline	None Issued	Wooden Schooner	American Fur Company	La Pointe, WI 1839	Lost at Isle Royale in 1839
Siskawit	None Issued	Wooden Schooner	American Fur Company	Probably La Pointe, WI 1839 - 1840	Grounded, 1840 in Siskiwit Bay Recovered in 1841 by *John Jacob Astor*
Lamplighter	U.S. Gov.	Wooden Schooner	U.S. Lighthouse Board	Youngstown, NY 1852	Grounded at Isle Royale, September 1857
George Hand	100998 U.S.	Wrecking Tug	Gilbert & Curry Algonac, MI	Buffalo, NY 1858	Sank at Little Schooner Island, August 1886
Alice Craig	None Issued	Wooden Schooner	Frank Boutin Bayfield, WI	Milan, OH 1858	Grounded on Menagerie Island, October 1884
John Jewett	13414 U.S.	Wooden Schooner	Moses Stone Detroit, MI (prob.)	Vermilion, OH 1866	Grounded in Grace Harbor, October 1898
Cumberland	None Issued	Wooden Steamer	Lake Superior Navigation Co. Toronto, Ont., Canada	Port Robinson, Ont., Canada 1871	Sank on reef near Rock Of Ages, July 1877
Maple Leaf	None Issued	Wooden Schooner	R.D. Pike Bayfield, WI	Bayfield, WI 1872	Grounded, lost masts/cabin off Isle Royale, Sept. 1872
Maggie McRae	None Issued	Wooden Schooner	Capt. J.C. Graham	Dalhousie, Ont., Canada 1872	Reported lost 10 miles off Thunder Cape, May 1888
Golden Eagle	85213 U.S.	Wooden Work Tug	J. Croze Houghton, MI	Sandusky, OH 1872	Grounded on reef between Grace & Washington Harbors, August 1892
Northern Belle	130099 U.S.	Wooden Schooner	James Malone Isle Royale, MI	La Pointe, WI 1877	Sank at Wright Island Winter of 1884-85
Chris Grover	125677 U.S.	Wooden Schooner	M. Daniels Marquette, MI	Lorain, OH 1878	Lost anchor and 600 feet of cable off Passage Island or Hog Island, November 1895
Henry Chisholm	95610 U.S.	Wooden Steamer	M.A. Bradley Line Cleveland, OH	Cleveland, OH 1880	Sank on reef near Rock Of Ages, October 1898
Osceola	155063 U.S.	Wooden Steamer	Ward's Detroit and Lake Superior Line, Detroit, MI	Bay City, MI 1882	Grounded on Mott Island, November 1898
Comrade	34132 U.S.	Wooden Schooner Barge	J.C. Gilchrist Cleveland, OH	Buffalo, NY 1883	Lost between Keweenaw Peninsula and Isle Royale, September 1890
Algoma	85766 Canada	Steel Steamer	Canadian Pacific Railway Montreal, Quebec, Canada	Kelvinhaugh, Scotland 1883	Sank at Mott Island, November 1885
A.B. Taylor	106257 U.S.	Wooden Steamer	Rogers & Bird Saugatuck, MI	Saugatuck, MI 1884	Grounded on Menagerie Island, July 1890
St. Andrew	90694 Canada	Wooden Steam Barge	Playfair & White Canada	St. Catharines, Ont., Canada 1885	Grounded on Passage Island, September 1900
Harlem	95972 U.S.	Steel Steamer	Western Transit Co. Buffalo, NY	Wyandotte, MI 1388	Grounded on Harlem Reef, November 1898
Monarch	96843 Canada	Wooden Steamer	Northern Navigation Co. Ontario, Canada	Sarnia, Ont., Canada 1888	Sank at Blake's Point Palisades, December 1906
George Rogers	86064 U.S.	Wooden Steam Tug	J.A. Moore, Dollar Bay, MI	Toledo, OH 1889	Grounded near Glenlyon Shoal, June 1907
Northern Queen	130436 U.S.	Steel Steamer	Mutual Transit Co. Buffalo, N.Y.	Cleveland 1889	Grounded on reef near Rock Of Ages, September 1913
Sainte Marie (1)	116574 U.S.	Steel Barge	T.L. Durocher Company Detour, MI	Detroit, MI 1893	Grounded at Isle Royale, 1926
Glenlyon	81427 Canada	Steel Steamer	Great Lakes Transportation Co. Midland, Ont,, Canada	West Bay City, MI 1893	Sank on Glenlyon Shoal, November 1924
Centurian	126994 U.S.	Steel Steamer	Cleveland Cliffs Iron Co,	West Bay City, MI 1893	Grounded five miles west of Menagerie Is., Oct. 1895
John B. Trevor	77173 U.S.	Steel Whaleback Steamer	Pittsburgh Steamship Co.	West Superior, WI 1895	Grounded between Grace Harbor and Rainbow Cove

It is hard to imagine that any future research on the deeper sites at Isle Royale would not involve use of miniature ROV technology after the utility and cost effectiveness of those machines were so dramatically demonstrated.

The Future

Isle Royale has fast become a prototype for the management of submerged archeological sites in parks and preserves in the United States. The Fathom Five Provincial Park in Tobermory, Ontario, is the only other administrative entity known that has taken an active, positive approach to the management of a large shipwreck population using a conservation ethic. Some states, such as Michigan, Wisconsin and Florida, are experimenting with an underwater shipwreck preserve concept, and a few other nations, such as Australia, are experimenting with active shipwreck protection, on-site management and interpretation programs.

The National Park Service's first obligation, however, is to protect and preserve; if that mandate cannot be met through an open, positive relationship with any segment of society, it may choose more negative and restrictive approaches.

Land-associated sites were closed in 1986 by Superintendent's orders. This decision was made by Park management because the submerged components of land sites, largely untouched by divers so far, have considerable archeological value and are very vulnerable to attrition from collecting. It was also felt that they presented a much less impressive experience to divers than shipwrecks, and the threats outweighed the potential benefits to the public. If the shipwreck resources suffer significant attrition from the increased accessibility and

Vessel Name	Official Number	Description	Owner/Manager	Place and Date Built	Relation to Isle Royale
Frank Rockefeller	121015 U.S.	Steel Whaleback Steamer	Pittsburgh Steamship Co.	West Superior, WI 1896	Grounded on Rainbow Cove with steel barge *Maida,* November, 1905
City of Bangor	127139 U.S.	Steel Steamer	Lake Transit Co. Bay City, MI	West Bay City, MI 1896	Grounded on Menagerie Is. Reef, December 1915
Maida	92844 U.S.	Steel Schooner Barge	Pittsburgh Steamship Co.	West Superior, WI 1898	Grounded at Rainbow Cove, November 1905
America	107367 U.S.	Steel Steamer	Booth Fisheries Co. Delaware	Wyandotte, MI 1898	Sank near North Gap, June 1928
George M. Cox	150898 U.S.	Steel Steamer	Isle Royale Transportation Co. of Arizona	Toledo, OH 1901	Sank on reef near Rock Of Ages, May 1933
Prindoc	116578 Canada	Steel Steamer	Paterson Steamships Ltd. Fort William, Ont., Canada	West Bay City, MI 1901	Sank off Passage Island, June 1943
Luzon	141783 U.S.	Steel Steamer	Morrow Steamship Co. Cleveland, OH	Chicago, IL 1902	Grounded on Passage Island, October 1923
Bransford	3925 U.S.	Steel Steamer	W.A. & A.H. Hawgood Cleveland, OH	West Bay City, MI 1902	Grounded on Brandsford Reef, November 1909
William T. Roberts	202866 U.S.	Steel Steamer	American Steamship Co. Buffalo, NY	Wyandotte, MI 1906	Grounded near Blake's Point, May 1917
Sir Thomas Shaughnessy	203170 U.S.	Steel Steamer	Jenkins Steamship Co.	Wyandotte, MI 1906	Grounded on Passage Island, November 1909
Chester Congdon	204526 U.S.	Steel Steamer	Continental Steamship Co. Minnesota	South Chicago, IL 1907	Sank on Congdon Shoal, November 1918
Dunelm	123950 Canada	Steel Steamer	Inland Navigation Co. Hamilton, Ont., Canada	Sunderland, England 1907	Grounded on Canoe Rocks, December 1910
Daniel B. Meacham	205349 U.S.	Steel Steamer	Frontier Steamship Co. Tonawanda, NY	Ecorse, MI 1908	Grounded on Passage Island, July 1908
Emperor	126654 Canada	Steel Steamer	Canada Steamship Lines Montreal, Quebec, Canada	Collingwood, Ont., Canada 1910	Sank on Canoe Rocks, June 1947
Stanley	212885 U.S.	Wooden Fish Tug	John E. Johnson Isle Royale, MI	Two Harbors, MN 1914	Sank (probably intentional) near Star Island, Early 1930s
Dagmar	213130 U.S.	Wooden Gas Boat	Brazell Motor Freight Co. Grand Marais, MN	Beaver Bay, MN 1914	Lost 1/2 mile northeast of Chippewa Harbor, June 1935
Peggy Bee	224145 U.S.	Wooden Yacht	Homer W. Bleckley New York, NY	Watervliet, NY 1917	Burned and sank in Washington Harbor, August 1928
Ah-Wa-Nesha	240064 U.S.	Wooden Gas Boat	Holger Johnson & Otto Olsen Isle Royale, MI	West De Pere, WI 1922	Abandoned at Chippewa Harbor, 1955
Kamloops	147682 Canada	Steel Steamer	Canada Steamship Lines Montreal, Quebec, Canada	Haverton Hill, England 1924	Sank near Kamloops Point, December 1927
Fingerling	Unknown	Wooden Cabin Cruiser	Park Visitor	Unknown Circa Late 1940s	Burned and sank off Blake's Point, 1948
Airplane Frame	U.S.	Float Plane	Unknown	Unknown	Sank off Siskiwit Mine, June 1935
PC 782	U.S. Gov.	Steel Steamer	U.S. Naval Reserve Training Vessel	Unknown	Grounded at entrance to Malone Bay, May 1949
Unknown	U.S. Gov.	Wooden Motor Launch	U.S. Coast Guard Passage Island, MI	Unknown	Burned and sank in Passage Island Cove, 1949
Five Finger Tug	Unknown	Wooden Work Tug	Michigan Tag #68 (1920)	Unknown	Located in Five Finger Bay, 1976
Unknown	Unknown	Paint and rust found in fishing nets off north side of Captain Kidd Is. Reported in 1978 by a park commercial fisherman.			

*Compiled by Ken Vrana with assistance from Thom Holden

NOTES: The listing is restricted to vessels with actual or potential remains lying on bottomlands within Lake Superior boundaries of Isle Royale National Park. Mishaps noted as grounded indicate that vessels were later removed from Isle Royale National Park. Name given is based upon vessel listing or contemporary accounts at time of loss or accident. Information was assembled from primary and secondary sources and is not a complete listing of Isle Royale vessel casualties or accidents.

enhanced interpretive programs, then selective or complete closing of dive sites might be in order. Experience has shown that the easiest regulation to enforce on underwater sites is the most comprehensive. It may be difficult to prove a particular artifact came from a specific wreck, but it is easy to prove that someone has been diving in an area closed to that activity under the aegis of the Code of Federal Regulations.

It is very unlikely that such moves would ever have to be taken at Isle Royale given the excellent communication that exists between the diving public and the Park, but it is important that it be understood that restriction would be the only responsible option the Park would have if the situation got out of hand.

The documentation of *Kamloops* from the ROV study in 1986 revealed the problems and benefits associated with the interactive philosophy that typifies Isle Royale management's open relationship with sport divers. The unblinking eye of the video camera panned over several areas where the ship had been vandalized by sport divers. The saddest example was the empty bracket where at one time the port running light of *Kamloops* was intact; it is now apparently a trinket in some diver's home, viewed only by friends, if at all. By contrast the ROVs also sent imagery back to the surface of a chain and lock that fixes the auxiliary steering wheel of *Kamloops* to the ship. The chain had been attached by sport divers, of their own volition at considerable personal risk and expense, to help preserve the integrity and ambience of the extraordinary site.

The inevitable question arising when one has finished an inventory of known sites is: what about the ones that have not been found? It is safe to say that there is much potential for new submerged archeological discoveries at Isle Royale. The more specific one gets on that issue, the more speculative they become.

The historical record clearly indicates that there was a considerable amount of past cultural activity that has not been accounted for in the archeological record, i.e., we have not found a good number of sites that should have left clear residues in the ground or on the lake bottom. The full spectrum of missing historic sites includes entire vessels that have been documented as lost near Isle Royale, as well as sections of the known vessels we have mapped (see Table 1).

Certainly many submerged areas associated with historic fishing, mining and resort activity on land have not yet been located or even looked for. The prehistory of the archipelago is also a book that is yet to be written, and much of the residues of behavioral patterns preceding European contact will eventually be found underwater.

We can anticipate that in future years the remains of several ships will be discovered, either through a systematic survey by the Park Service or through the efforts of sport divers. A listing of potential sites is presented in this chapter, but at the writing of this report they only exist in the realm of the historical record. If and when their existence is confirmed, some of them will be important sites for archeological documentation. Perhaps none of the possibilities is more compelling to the maritime archeologist than finding *Madeline*, or some other vessel tied to the early fur trade era. Mansfield (1899) lists a number of wooden vessels employed by Northwest Fur Company in the area during the later 18th and early 19th centuries. The loss of one or more of these craft in their travel between Fort William and Sault Ste. Marie is possible. American Fur Company papers refer to the loss of *Madeline* at Isle Royale in 1839.

Some other possibilities are particularly provocative because of the significance of the vessels; e.g., the schooner *Comrade*, which vanished in 1890, possibly in the vicinity of Isle Royale. Certainly *Prindoc*, if found, would be of value as an object of study and Park interpretation.

Research results for this report also indicate that significant portions of some of the major shipwrecks documented in this study have not been located in the main wreckage fields. Eventually, someone will find more of the bows of *Monarch* and *Cumberland*. Significant superstructure from a majority of the wrecks at Isle Royale is also still missing. The *Algoma* bow, although still elusive, may not prove to be the spectacular discovery that has long been anticipated. Analysis of the material record and a rereading of the historical record suggests that the bow may not be the dramatic intact two-thirds of the ship as popular lore would have it, but may actually be broken up in an area south and west of the stern wreckage field.

Other possibilities become compelling just because of the comparative ease of confirmation, should a moderate amount of time and effort be expended. The location of *George Hands* is so clearly indicated that the high probability areas could be examined by a research team in one or two days. Enough incidents have occurred in Washington Harbor that it would be well worth the effort to make one side-scan sonar pass through the harbor to Windigo and back out on the other side of the channel. Any historic shipwreck remains of even moderate size would probably be located with this technology, given the size and bottom configuration of the channel.

The reports by Milford Johnson Sr. of torn and rust-stained nets being removed from some obstacle in approximately 200 feet of water off Captain Kidd Island definitely bear follow-up investigation through remote sensing or divers. If there is something one learns from long association with underwater archeological finds, it is not to discount the observations of local fishermen. A torn net is no small concern for a man who makes his living from fishing, and observations about where such happenings occur are seldom based on idle fancy. Routine aerial flyovers by Park staff should also prove revealing, if the possibility of new wreck discoveries is always kept in mind.

The list of "possibles" is extensive, as Table 1 illustrates. The question of how to approach establishing management control over these sites is a dynamic one; the conditioning factors change over time. The options include conducting full scale in-house surveys, partial in-house surveys, contracting out such activities, encouraging discovery by sport divers and, on the other end of the scale, being totally restrictive about further new site discovery activities. The answer is not an easy one and depends largely on the nature of the relationship that exists between the Park and the diving community. The final deciding factor should always be "what is in the best interest of the resource and its long-term enjoyment," with all management decisions predicated on the answer to that question.

Visiting divers should be encouraged to continue enjoying the wrecks in a safe manner, and those who have consistently demonstrated a conservation ethic and commitment to the management philosophy of the Park over the years should be encouraged to continue looking for new sites. Such discovery activity, however, causes certain risks to the resource; inevitably a "found" shipwreck is more subject to impact than one whose location is still a mystery. When something new is found, it should be made clear that the first to be notified is the Park management, and any indications that this trust has been violated should be dealt with firmly. Divers should be encouraged to conduct their searching activities through a Park staff designate of the Superintendent. Although it is sometimes a difficult regulation to enforce, divers should be reminded that engaging in search for antiquities on federal land without a permit is a violation of federal law. Towing remote-sensing instruments behind a boat could reasonably be construed as engaging in such activity. If the searching is being done with good intentions, why not do it openly and under permit? If necessary, it should be noted that 36 CFR, Part 2, Section 2.1 (7) specifically prohibits "possessing or using a mineral or metal detector, magnetometer, side-scan sonar, other metal detecting device or subbottom profiler" in national parks, except during officially authorized activities.

After all these caveats, the final recommendation would be to "go for it" in partnership with the sport diving community. The discovery of new shipwreck sites by the Park, or persons or groups working with the Park, is probably in the best interest of the resource base, because it increases the likelihood that newly discovered sites will be brought under management control before they can be severely vandalized. The key to this approach is to allow the thrill of discovery by well-meaning amateurs who are doing so in a framework permitting the agency to exercise management control and stewardship of a site once it is discovered.

Chapter II

Lake Superior Maritime Tradition, Socioeconomic Context

It is noteworthy that writers and historians are comfortable using the terms "maritime" and "marine" when discussing the Great Lakes. The "of and pertaining to the sea" connotations of those terms seem appropriate. The reason is that most people regard those bodies of water, located hundreds of miles from any ocean, as seas and not lakes. Although due consideration will be given in this study to the differences between ocean and Great Lakes, it is significant that the commonalities in their nature have had the greatest effects on common linguistic usage. A regional periodical popular with many nautical buffs is entitled *Inland Seas*, and a book dealing with the history of the Coast Guard on the Great Lakes is entitled *Guardians of the Eighth Sea* (O'Brien 1976). There are no such marine metaphors evident upon examining the equally rich and technologically developed riverine traditions. Riverboats are not ships, and they are not run by sailors; riverboats are riverboats, and they are operated by rivermen. They have traditionally stopped at river landings, not at ports of call.

To a lesser degree, Long Island Sound and Chesapeake Bay share some of the same attributes associated with large semi-contained bodies of navigable water. Puget Sound is also occasionally referred to as an "Inland Sea," and there are, in fact, some interesting aspects of ship design in that region that parallel vessel architectural adaptations in the lakes.

There is a danger, however, in trying to look at any of these confined maritime spheres (lakes, sounds, or rivers) in a vacuum. None of them were really closed systems, especially after the building of networks of canals in the 19th century. Maritime innovation on the western rivers, for example, did not go long unnoticed by lakes seamen and traders, and Atlantic coast trade had a particularly strong influence on the lakes.

Although the lakes have their own unique maritime heritage, it is clear that the traditions of those sailors that plied the lakes are closely tied to the blue water sailor. The major difference is the size of the respective spheres of maritime interaction. Most sailors on Lake Superior never interact with populations other than those found in a handful of ports in the heartland of the United States of America. Their salt-water brethren have rubbed shoulders with every race and nationality on the planet and engage in journeys of much greater duration.

The collective self image, which is perpetuated in stories and songs of Great Lakes navigation, is one that combines respect and fear of the lakes' moods with an interesting combination of grim determination and fatalism. The sense of community among lakes sailors was reinforced by their comparative ease of maintaining family ties in their smaller interactive spheres, a fact that additionally helped them develop greater networks of community support and empathy in time of conflict.

Some of the earliest inroads of trade unionism were made among the more stable Great Lakes seamen community. The Lakes' Seamen's Union was organized in 1878, although it had antecedents as far back as 1863 (Standard 1979: 25). Associations of owners such as Lakes Carriers' Association and Cleveland Vessel Owners Association became the nemesis of the unions, and the level of bitterness never lessened as the pendulum of success swung between labor and management through the turn of the century. A heavy concentration of capital in fewer hands in the iron and steel industry, subsequent economic depressions and booms and wars all influenced the lot of the Great Lakes seamen in this volatile industrial environment.

As navigational entities, the bodies of water on which lakes seamen work comprise one of the most dangerous shipping environments in the world. The diminutive size of the lakes compared to that of the oceans offers little in the way of comfort to the captains or crews of Great Lakes vessels. With little warning, all five Great Lakes can change their demeanor from flat calm and peaceful to ominous and violent. The shallowest, Lake Erie, is the most susceptible to these volatile shifts in temperament. Lake Superior, the largest and deepest, can generate waves that compare in height to those found in major ocean storms. The smaller wave lengths and periods associated with lakes storms also offer no solace because the stress factor they place on ship hulls is sometimes of a magnitude greater than those inflicted by ocean swells.

An additional curse of the comparatively small size of the Great Lakes' environment is the lack of sea room available for maneuvering, which offers a slim margin of grace for navigational errors. The option of heading out to open sea to ride out a storm is not a viable one, and in the days preceding the development of sophisticated electronic positioning equipment, lack of sea room was a critical issue for lake skippers. These inland water bodies are also subject to pervasive heavy fogs, which cause aggravated difficulties in narrow waterways. Many of the vessels lying at the bottom of the Great Lakes came to grief on quiet water, victims of shoals or collisions with other vessels in thick fog.

In addition, air temperature variations are extreme. Portions of the Upper Lakes straits and waterways have frozen solid, occasionally trapping entire fleets of vessels for the remainder of winter.

It is understandable, therefore, that the impulse of Great Lakes historians is to focus on the violence of the lakes environment, if for no other reason than to ensure that the uninitiated reader will grasp the fact that an inland body of water can hold the awe and menace of an ocean.

A factor of equal importance in identifying the lakes as a major maritime entity is sheer socioeconomic intensity. By the end of the 19th century, the Great Lakes had more tonnage being moved from place to place and more vessels plying each square mile of water area than all the rest of the United States, Atlantic and Pacific seaboards combined. The lake vessels were, at their peak, also the most prosperous ship tonnage in the world. Bulk freighters, for example, loaded and unloaded quicker and moved a ton of cargo a mile for less cost than any other vessels on earth (Ashburn 1925: 81). It should also be noted that these superlatives occurred in a season duration of eight or nine months a year.

Waves of immigrants filled the passenger vessels heading west. Ore from the Missabe and other iron ranges surrounding Duluth comprised some of the largest bulk freight shipments ever moved. Coal destined for the Upper Lakes passed downbound shipments of iron. Grain flourished, faltered and restarted at other points in the Great Lakes region during the 50 years following the Civil War.

This small but environmentally severe and socioeconomically intense maritime environment provided all the ingredients necessary for a high occurrence of shipwrecks. Capital investment in the movement of these vessels was heavy, as was the promise of high profits; factors that encouraged attempts at one more voyage well after seasonal changes would indicate the rational decision to winter in.

Demographic changes during the period of development of lakes navigation reflected the economic dynamics and what were to become the most densely populated cities in the Nation began their almost exponential rate of growth in the 19th century. The remainder of this chapter will be focused on the various socioeconomic processes that influenced the development of shipping on the Great Lakes. It will begin with general trends and narrow to the particulars of Great Lakes maritime activity. Where appropriate, comparisons to western rivers, Atlantic and Pacific trades will be made to establish a meaningful context for understanding the Great Lakes.

One may ask why such a discussion of socioeconomic context is relevant. The collection of ships at Isle Royale was part of a complex cultural system. An understanding of these shipwrecks could only be realized from a consideration of the behavioral patterns and processes that were responsible for their existence, the physical form, cargo and location of their demise. It is clear that the wrecks are not totally random, although their specific loss resulted from an accident. These vessels were parts of the large national economic, political, demographic structure influenced by technological and ecological constraints. This chapter describes the patterned behavior that surrounded and resulted in the collection of shipwrecks at Isle Royale National Park. We see this discussion as a necessary step to the eventual understanding and explanation of the collection of Great Lakes shipwrecks and the cultural processes they represent.

Socioeconomic Processes Affecting Lakes Navigation

The American Revolution ended British mercantilism and unleashed the economic potential of a new nation. The restrictive policies of mercantilism had been designed to increase the wealth of Great Britain by controlling the market economy of the colonies. The newly independent colonies could now enact policies that would further their own interests.

Population and trade, both internal and foreign, grew rapidly, and transportation needs expanded along with them. The interaction of watercraft with railroads, canals and roads combined to form a national transportation system. Watercraft offered the cheapest and, in many cases, the only means of transportation of raw materials, goods and people. The changes in the number of commercial watercraft, and in their form and function, reflected the trends of economic development.

Sectional differences in production and consumption appeared early in the 19th century. The Northeast rapidly industrialized, forming a manufacturing belt centering on New York that ultimately reached the Great Lakes and contained 65 percent of the manufacturing capacity for the country (Pred 1970: 274).

The South developed a dependence on a few staple crops, and the West produced the majority of agricultural products, transported down the Mississippi, for the other regions. The Middle Atlantic and New England states developed financial structure and marketing for foreign trade, as well as the shipping and ports.

The early south-northeast trade was primarily coastal, due to the Appalachian Mountains, a formidable obstacle to the trade between the East Coast and the interior. After penetration of the mountains, first by canals and later by railroads, interregional trade shifted. Goods could go more directly between the East and West. Regional specialization became more entrenched. The rise of East-West trade was implemented by the Great Lakes and the canals connecting the East with the Mississippi River system (North 1961: 105).

The main early port cities were New York, Philadelphia, Boston and Baltimore. After the War of 1812, New York became the principal port and controlled both coastal and European trade. Charleston and New Orleans became the primary southern ports, as a result of the increasing focus on cotton production. Southern cotton was the main export and foreign exchange after 1815 and into the 1830s and 1840s. Later, western grain would supersede cotton in importance, a change reflected in the shift of predominate vessel traffic from the western rivers to the Great Lakes.

During the first quarter of the 19th century, population growth in the U.S. was primarily the result of the fecundity of the inhabitants. Immigration did not become a significant contributor until about 1825, the year that annual total immigrants passed the 10,000 mark. The 20,000 mark was reached in 1828. Regular passenger service was established on Lake Erie in 1830 (Havighurst 1944: 124).

By 1832 there were 60,000 new immigrants, and in the decade of the 1840s, yearly totals sometimes exceeded 100,000, even 200,000, with 369,000 immigrants entering the country in 1850 (U.S. Dept. of Commerce 1960: 57). Before the Civil War, the majority of the immigrants came from the countries of Ireland, Great Britain, Germany and Scandinavia.

The shift in population distribution clearly represents a westward movement. In 1810, 54 percent of the population lived in the Northeast and 13 percent were in the West. By 1860 the relative population in the Northeast was 36.5 percent; the West, 37.8 percent (North 1961: 257).

Many immigrants stayed in the East, but the majority composed the great westward expansion, at first into the contemporary Midwest areas surrounding the Great Lakes. The United States population grew nearly eight-fold before the Civil War. Although laborers comprised the largest single occupational category of immigrants, farmers, skilled workers and merchants together formed the majority (U.S. Dept. of Commerce 1960: 60-61).

The immigrants brought capital and agricultural and industrial skills, as well as an economic and technological orientation, particularly newcomers from Great Britain, which led the world in technology. The skilled and technologically sophisticated immigrant was in large measure responsible for the predisposition of the United States to accept, revise and rapidly transfer new technologies, whether of foreign or national origin. In general, immigrants seeking American opportunities for advancement were highly motivated and economically oriented.

There was sufficient land available for the new population influx. The land area of the country had been nearly doubled by the Louisiana Purchase, which also gave the U.S. control of the mouth of the Mississippi. The Florida territory was added in 1821, providing virtually complete control of the Mississippi. The acquisition of Texas, the Oregon Territory, California and the Gadsden Purchase soon followed. The continental U.S. land acquisition was completed during the 1850s.

The Midwest, particularly around the Great Lakes, was extremely productive under European agricultural practices. New resources and raw materials became available with the opening of each new territory. The demand of the swelling Western populations fueled the industries of the manufacturing and capitalizing East, and strengthened the developing market economy.

Eastern investment capital spread west. Economic growth was predicated on the system of transportation and attracted eastern investments (see Neu 1953). The economic potential of the rich farmlands and mineral deposits of the Midwest could not be fully realized until it was possible to transport the products to market. The canal system, begun with the opening of the Erie in 1825, was necessary for exploitation of agricultural and mineral resources of the new country, along with the growth of vessel transport and the development of the rail system.

The growing economy and the influx of immigrants quickly taxed the obsolete transportation system. The War of 1812, with its naval blockade, prompted the development of inland roads and private turnpikes in the absence of a federal road system. However, the cost of moving materials over roads was very high. Water transportation remained the primary mode of inland travel until the expansion of the railroads and development of the automobile. This period is often referred to as the Canal Age by historians.

Exploration usually followed river systems, and the first settlements and first population centers were invariably near rivers and other bodies of water. Agricultural expansion occurred in areas with access to waterways. This pattern is still reflected today: of the 150 U.S. cities with populations of 100,000 or more, more than 130 are directly served by the inland waterway system.

The 19th century can be characterized by rapid industrial growth and expansion. By the end of the century, annual iron production exceeded 15 million tons (U.S. Dept. of Commerce 1960: 365-6). Prior to the Civil War, the new acquired territory and its settlement gave agriculture the major role in economic development. After the war, industry came to be of greater importance to economic growth. In 1860 more than 60 percent of the workers were engaged in agriculture, but by 1910, it was reduced to 30 percent (Fite and Reese 1965: 310).

The growth of the U.S. economy was not a steady incline, but a series of fluctuations punctuated by booms and economic recessions, aptly termed "panics." The principal panics, those of 1819, 1837 and particularly 1857, 1873 and 1893, affected industrial production and population movements. Lakes navigation, like that of the western rivers, coast and oceans, was altered significantly by each panic, as well as by the general trends of economic growth.

Development of Inland Transportation

The Mississippi River system and Great Lakes became the primary inland routes of commerce. The chain of lakes formed a natural east-west route, and the Mississippi River provided a north-to-south route. Because of the natural barrier of the Appalachians, prior to mid-century agricultural products were shipped down river and transferred to coastal craft for delivery to the busy northeast ports. Agricultural and raw materials moved eastward through the Great Lakes for distribution to the North and East, and south through the Mississippi River system. Manufactured goods moved west and south on these waterways from the populous manufacturing centers of the East.

America led the world in the development of inland steam navigation, a phenomenon largely a result of geographical conditions. Great Britain and Europe, which lacked the extensive inland waterways but had accessible coastlines, lagged behind in the application of steam to inland navigation, although they led in ocean steam. Conversely, Great Britain utilized many more stationary steam engines for motive power in manufacturing. America had the benefit of many flowing streams and rivers appropriate for water-powered machinery.

River Steamboats: Prior to the advent of steam, there was only wind, current and muscle to move the vessels of commerce. Smaller sailing vessels could enter the mouths of the larger rivers and could meet the early post-Revolution transportation needs. As the population moved across the Appalachian Mountains and into the Ohio Valley, western river navigation became more important.

Boats could easily float down the inland rivers, taking advantage of the current, and flatboats were one type specifically designed to do so. The down river advantage was offset by the necessity of relying on muscle power to ascend the great rivers in keel boats.

The need and profit potential for vessels capable of upbound navigation on the western rivers was realized early in the experimental stages of applying steam to ships. Although the early experiments of steam navigation were carried out on the eastern rivers near the more populated cities, they were directed toward developing boats for western river navigation. The experiments of James Rumsey, John Fitch, John Stevens, Oliver Evans and Robert Fulton were focused on western river navigation.

As early as 1785, Rumsey wrote to George Washington regarding the feasibility of upstream western river navigation. Evans recognized the potential of high-pressure steam engines for western rivers, and worked on their refinement. The early steam pioneers attempted to monopolize steam on the western rivers, but in 1817 all monopoly claims to western river navigation were nullified.

Fulton reportedly designed *Clermont* for navigation on the Mississippi (from contemporary newspaper account of the maiden voyage quoted in Hunter 1949: 8). The concept may have originated with his partner and financial supporter, Chancellor Robert Livingston, who had been instrumental in the negotiation of the Louisiana Purchase and had floated down the Mississippi. Fulton had written to Livingston, "Whatever may be the fate of steamboats for the Hudson, everything is completely proved for the Mississippi, and the object is immense" (Ibid.).

Western river steam navigation was initiated in 1811 with the maiden voyage of the 371-ton *New Orleans* from Pittsburgh to New Orleans. In the first year of operation, the owners realized a $20,000 profit on an investment of $40,000 (Fite and Reese 1965: 190). The ascendency of the steamboat was rapid on the western rivers, and by 1830 the steamboat was the dominant mode of transportation, a status that remained unthreatened until the growth of railroads in the late 1850s.

The western river steamboat soon became a unique craft particularly well adapted to the seasonal environment of the rivers. Flat-bottomed, shallow draft and powered by high-pressure steam, it soon lost any resemblance to eastern river steamboats. The critical factors in the design of western river vessels were the necessity for shallow draft, sediment and mineral-loaded feed water, maximum reliability and quick handling, minimum machinery space, low fuel costs and low first-cost because of short average use-life (Bryan 1896: 387-8).

In 1842, total western river steam tonnage was 126,278 tons, a figure that would double by 1846 (Abert 1848: 12). The number of steamboats would increase to 557 in 1845 and 727 in 1855, the latter year representing a tonnage of 173,000 (Hunter 1949: 33).

Unlike the western river vessels, which were equally adapted to both passengers and freight, the eastern river steamboats were primarily passenger vessels, and more closely reflected their heritage from *Clermont*. They retained a deep-draft hull similar to sailing vessels, and the often palatial craft were invariably low-pressure side-wheelers. Because of competition among steamboat lines, the eastern vessels emphasized luxury and speed.

Many eastern steamboats were organized into more capitalized shipping lines that maintained regular schedules of sailing, quite unlike the western river steamboats that were mostly tramps, picking up passengers and cargo wherever possible, and keeping quite irregular schedules, if any at all. Most western river vessels were owned by individuals or small partnerships.

The development of steam navigation on the Great Lakes was not nearly as rapid as on western rivers. The use of sail was much more advantageous on the lakes, a factor that retarded the adoption of steam navigation in the region.

Canals: The completion of the Erie Canal in 1825 was the initiation of the American canal building effort. The construction of the 363-mile Erie Canal from Albany to Buffalo was begun in 1818. The original canal measured 4 feet deep and 28 feet wide at the bottom.

The canal was an immediate economic success. The cost for transporting a ton of freight from Buffalo to Albany dropped from $90 to less than $8, including toll charges. In the first year of operation, $750,000 in tolls were collected (Fite and Reese 1965: 193).

The western terminus of the canal was Buffalo, which was victorious over the village of Black Rock for the honor (Hatcher 1945). Soon other canals were dug in Pennsylvania and through Ohio to link Lake Erie with the Ohio River. Toledo, Cleveland and Detroit became important port cities and grew rapidly as a result of the increased commerce from the canal. Along with the commerce, capital moved west. New York businessmen sent representatives to the western cities, particularly Detroit. The cooperative association between the growing western markets and New York City secured it the status as the primary eastern port in North America.

The Erie Canal shifted the principal routes of the immigrants northward from the western rivers. More than half of the arriving immigrants traveled through the newly completed Erie Canal on their way west (Mansfield: 1: 1899: 183-4). By 1836 there were 3,000 canal boats operating on the Erie Canal in the lucrative immigrant passenger business (Havighurst 1944: 127).

There were 4,027 miles of canals built in the United States by 1840, almost half in New York and Pennsylvania (computed from Tanner 1840: 223-234). Most canals were built in the 1830s, but their total mileage (reached in 1851) was eclipsed by the construction of railroads, which reached 5,132 miles by 1840 (Ibid.).

Railroads: From a historical perspective, the growth of railroads in America was not systematic, but a seemingly haphazard linkage of towns and production centers with waterways. At first, the railroads were welcomed by those with vested interests in shipping, but as the rail system grew, the competitive transportation threat was realized. Rail transportation was not competitive in cost, but had the advantages of speed, reliable schedules, direct routes and, especially, year-round operation. These attributes, coupled with transshipment between lines, specialization of freight and passenger express lines, government subsidies and the formation of large corporations, cut deeply into the canal and river commerce.

Railroad mileage expanded rapidly after 1840. By 1860 there were more than 30,000 miles of tracks operational; that amount tripled by 1880. Ten years later there were more than 200,000 miles of track in operation (U.S. Bureau of the Census 1960: 427).

The midcentury railroads came into direct competition with the western river steamboat. Rail lines extending south from Lake Erie ports shifted passenger and freight from the western river-coastal route. Soon the railroads connected the major riverport cities of the Mississippi and Ohio rivers, and the competition became direct with the mainline steamboat.

The western river steamboats lost in the competition with the railroads, and were only able to temporarily maintain or increase business in the far West and northwest territories. The situation was somewhat different in the East and on the Great Lakes.

In some areas (for example, Long Island Sound), steamboats were able to increase business when they managed to connect with major railroads. Steamboat passenger lines, especially those owned by railroad companies, continued to grow until the advent of private transportation in the form of the automobile. On the lakes, the ability to move bulk freight at a cost far below the railroads has allowed the continued existence of waterborne transportation to the present.

Growth of Great Lakes Navigation

Early lakes navigation can be divided into stages marked by the completion of two important canals: the opening of the Erie Canal in 1825 and the opening of the St. Marys Falls Canal at Sault Ste. Marie in 1855. Both had tremendous impact on Great Lakes navigation and initiated new stages of regional growth.

The Erie Canal opened the western lands for migration, and marked the end of the exploration and fur trade that was characteristic of the earliest period. Populations and development spread west, and followed a similar pattern for each lake. The Sault Ste. Marie Canal gave ready access to the area around Lake Superior and opened the entire Great Lakes system to navigation.

The early period of the eastern lakes was devoted to the fur trade. Trade with the Indians and shipment of supplies to the remote military posts on the frontier became important elements of commerce after the War of 1812.

The opening of the Erie Canal brought large numbers of immigrants and additional commercial trade to support the westward expansion. The new canal had the effect of shifting the main transportation route north from the Ohio River. Detroit and Buffalo became principal ports; Chicago was a developing outpost. In 1830 the articles of shipment to Buffalo were corn, fish, furs, whiskey, lumber and shingles with return cargos of merchandise and passengers. Small cargos of flour, whiskey, beef and merchandise were transported to the far western port of Chicago (Mansfield 1899: 1: 182-3).

Michigan's development did not begin until after the opening of the Erie Canal. By 1836 there were about 3,000 canal boats in operation carrying the growing numbers of immigrants. The Black Hawk War of 1832 ended the Indian threat and brought knowledge of the rich soil of northern Illinois, Indiana and Wisconsin. Speculation fueled the land boom in progress. Chicago became a growing commercial port serving the new territories; its population grew from 150 to 2,000 in 1832. Twenty thousand passed through town the same year on their way into Illinois. In 1835, 255 sailing ships arrived in Chicago; a thousand schooners and 990 steamer arrivals were recorded for Cleveland the next year. Chicago and Toledo were incorporated in 1837; Chicago had a population of 8,000 and Detroit had 10,000 (Hatcher 1944: 207).

The vessels prior to 1816 were all sail craft, locally built on the shores of Ontario and Erie. The number of sailing vessels grew yearly to meet demands of the growing trade. Steamboats had proven reliable on the western rivers and the Hudson, and in both cases the cost of passage and shipping had been reduced. The advantages of steam were realized, and both Canadians and Americans began the construction of steamboats for service on Lake Ontario.

Steam navigation on the lakes was initiated in 1816 by the Canadians, closely followed by the Americans. In 1820, there were only four steamers on the lakes compared with 71 on the western rivers and 52 on the Atlantic. By 1830 there were 296 western river steamboats, 183 eastern river steamers and only 11 lake steamboats in operation (Purdy 1880: 5). In the summer of 1833, those 11 lake steamboats carried 61,000 passengers west (Mansfield 1899: 1: 185,394).

The first two steamboats were built by groups of merchants in partnership. The third vessel, *Walk-In-The-Water*, was built by the newly formed Lake Erie Steamboat Company of Buffalo in 1818 (Hatcher 1944: 178).

The formation of a company with the capital and means for steamboat construction and operation represents the organizational form that steam navigation would take on the lakes. Most sailing vessels, considerably cheaper to build and operate, were owned by single owners or a very few partners. The eastern river steamboats were owned by corporations, and were organized early into transportation lines, supported by the investment of eastern capital. This is in contrast to vessel operation on the western rivers, where ownership patterns resembled the ownership of sail vessel on the lakes – single owners or limited partnerships.

The concentration of capital and the power it represented markedly affected the development of lakes navigation, particularly in obtaining government subsidies for navigation improvement. The American canal-building era resulted directly from corporate interests obtaining government support for continued navigation and harbor improvements, on a scale that would be impossible by any other means. Continued navigation improvements reduced risk and allowed the use of ever larger vessels that could benefit from the economies of scale, reducing transportation costs and boosting profits.

The Canadians were similarly organized in business corporations. They observed that the Erie Canal would draw trade from their St. Lawrence River ports, particularly Montreal, to New York. Before the completion of the Erie Canal, the Welland Canal Company was formed, and construction was begun on the canal around Niagara Falls. The completion of the Welland Canal in 1829 brought about the development of the first vessels specifically designed for the limitations of the Great Lakes: the canallers – sailing ships built to pass through the canal locks.

The first Great Lakes steam vessels were influenced in a more direct way by Eastern steamship developments. The early lake steamers were constructed by Eastern builders, again, the result of capital and expertise being centered in New York. For example, Noah Brown of New York was responsible for the design and construction of *Walk-In-The-Water* (Walker 1902: 315; Hatcher 1944: 178). *Frontenac*, the first steamer on the lakes, was built by two ship carpenters from Long Island (Cuthbertson 1931: 215). A number of the early steamboats for the lakes were built at Sacketts Harbor, New York: *Ontario* 1817, *Sophia* 1818 and *Queen Charlotte* 1818 (Croil 1898: 248-9).

The success of the Erie and Welland Canals and the explosive growth of trade prompted the construction of other canals. By 1848 there were seven major outlets available to the Great Lakes, six of which tapped into Lake Erie (Hatcher 1944: 190). The port cities of Lake Erie became centers of commerce tying the expanding west to the industrial east.

In midcentury the railroads came into importance. Buffalo became a rail center greatly augmenting its position as a prime port. Fourteen freight and 300 passenger trains entered and left the lake port every 24 hours; Buffalo's population grew from 42,000 to 74,000 between 1850 and 1855 (Hatcher 1944: 231). At first, most railroads were not in direct competition with vessels and served as connecting lines for passenger steamers. However, some railroads went into the steamship business to capitalize on the growing demand for passenger vessels. Package freight commerce on the lakes was taken over by the rail companies, which ultimately owned almost all the package freighters (Ericson 1962: 15).

The 1850s represented a high-point in passenger steamboat development on the lakes. The growing demand supported three lines of steamboats between Buffalo and Chicago operating 16 steamboats (side-wheelers) and 20 propellers (Mills 1910: 123,145). The completion of east-west trunk line railroads cut deeply into the passenger trade, and the appearance of screw freighters, which were cheaper to operate and build, cut into the freight business (Mansfield: 1: 190-191).

Later, the railroads, unhampered by the seasonality of the lakes, cut deeper yet into the freight trade and precipitated a general decline in Lakes navigation that was only relieved by the opening of the Sault canal. Railroad tonnage carried was about equal to that carried eastward on the Erie Canal in the late 1850s, but it was much more valuable. The railroads tended to carry the more valuable commerce leaving the heavier and bulkier products for the lake and canal carriers.

An example of the tendency for rail to cut disproportionately into the more valuable cargos is Chicago, which had both railroads and lakers available for transportation. The 1859 Chicago data indicate that corn, wheat and lead moved predominantly by water, whereas hides, livestock and general merchandise moved by rail (Taylor 1951: 167).

The exploration and, soon, the population pushed farther westward. The canal system had opened the whole of the Great Lakes to navigation, except for Lake Superior. The falls in the Saint Marys River blocked vessel access.

Growth of Lake Superior Navigation

Resource extraction was a prime motivating factor in European incursion into the Lake Superior area, as it was into the Great Lakes region in general. The economic development and exploitation of the Lake Superior region lagged behind the other lakes, retarded primarily by the St. Marys Falls at Sault Ste. Marie, which impeded navigation into the lake. There were only two options for operating a vessel on Lake Superior: portage around the falls or construction on the lake.

Earliest commerce revolved around the fur trade. The panic of 1837 brought about a contraction in economic activity that seriously debilitated the fur and fishing trades. The American Fur Company failed in 1842 (Nute 1944: 180), ending the early period of commerce of the region.

The discovery of copper in 1843, 1844 and 1845 generated increased interest in the Lake Superior region. Most navigation on the lake prior to this time, except for six schooners, was conducted in birch-bark canoes, bateaux or Mackinaw boats.

Prior to the start of construction on the locks around the St. Marys River Falls at Sault Ste. Marie, 15 vessels had been laboriously hauled across the overland portage. Their total displacement was 3,000 tons, and apparently all were eventually wrecked (Havighurst 1944: 165).

Although side-wheel steamers began plying the Lower Lakes in 1816 with the launch of *Frontenac*, it was not until 1845 that the first steamer appeared on Lake Superior (Mansfield 1899: 1: 197; Barry 1973: 38). The propeller *Independence*, rigged as a fore-and-aft schooner, was hauled over the portage at Sault Ste. Marie to meet the increasing demand for passenger service resulting from the mineral discoveries. In 1846, the side-wheeler *Julia Palmer* was also brought over the portage, and became the first steamer to ply the North Shore (Croil 1898: 257).

The question of a canal at Sault Ste. Marie was raised even before the time of the copper discoveries. The financial success of the Erie and Welland canals, and the growing canal system in the East, piqued the interest of the commercial firms of the new state of Michigan. The opening of the Sault Canal in 1855 initiated large scale navigation and exploitation of the Lake

Superior region.

As originally proposed in 1837, the lock of the canal would be 100 feet long, 32 feet wide by 10 feet deep (Williams 1907: 118). Much discussion surrounded the ideal size for the system. In April 1855, when the work on the canal and locks was completed, the final measurements were: 100 feet wide at the water surface, 64 feet wide at the bottom, with a depth of 13 feet. The locks were 70 feet wide, 12 feet deep, and 350 feet long (Mansfield 1899: 1: 243; Williams 1907: 133). The canal was deepened in 1870 to 16 feet. In 1881, the sides were straightened and a single lock installed measuring 515 x 80 feet. Further growth in commerce demanded more improvements, and in August 1886 the new canal was opened with 21 feet of depth and a lock 800 feet by 100 feet (Mansfield 1899: 1: 244).

By 1887, it was apparent that the Sault Canal, even with its many improvements, was not sufficient for shipping demands. Vessels often had to wait 12 to 36 hours to pass through. In 1895, the Canadian Sault Ste. Marie Canal, with a lock size of 900 feet by 60 feet and 22 feet deep, was opened. The first vessels through were American (Mansfield 1899: 1: 244). The U.S. canal and lock alterations and introduction of the Canadian canal are indications of the rapid growth of commerce and shipping in the Lake Superior region.

The establishment and improvements of Lake Superior ports also reflected the rapid development of regional commerce. The nature and extent of the trades of each harbor affected the establishment of routes and the characteristics of vessels engaged in those trades in certain areas of the lake. Analysis of data such as these can lead to the understanding of the socioeconomic factors that influence specific wreck depositions over time, leading to the development of a predictive model for shipwreck location (see Hulse 1981).

Pattern of Harbor Establishment and Development: Some of the principal harbors of Lake Superior and their development as noted by Mansfield (1899: 1: 354-364) and others follow. The pattern of development and the increasing scale of growth and decline closely reflect the trends of Lake Superior commerce and demographic shifts. The dates the harbors formed and entered into the transportation network of Lake Superior and the nature and extent of shipping are key factors for the generation of a predictive model of the nature and locations of shipwrecks.

Marquette: Primarily involved with iron ore since the 1840s, the port was developed to transport ore from the Marquette Range, the oldest on Lake Superior. Iron Mountain Railroad was completed from the mines to the harbor in 1856. In the fiscal year ending June 30, 1872, there were 390 arrivals of vessels at the port with a tonnage of 185,000; by 1896 more than 1,032 vessels arrived with a tonnage of 793,092, which generally indicates imported coal. There were 2,292,556 tons of iron ore exported from this port in 1897, with the total shipped consistently above 3 million tons well into the 1940s. Marquette is the third largest U.S. city on Lake Superior (*Skillings Mining Review*, Duluth Aug. 20, 1949).

Ashland: Established 1854, little activity occurred until the 1870s. Increased from 898 arrivals with 1,400,000 tons of car-

go in 1887 to 5,164 arrivals with a cargo tonnage of 2.4 million in 1896. Ashland exported 1.5 million tons of iron ore that year. Very little activity since World War II.

Duluth: A main port of Lake Superior settled in 1854, it became a port of entry in 1871. Prior to completion of the Lake Superior Railroad, the population was 100. Four years after completion of the railroad, the population reached 4,000. The principal exports were grain and iron ore. The first ore docks were completed in 1893. In 1897, the harbor received 885,623 tons (more than half was coal) and shipped out 2.3 million tons of ore, 1 million tons of flour and grain and 454,000 tons of lumber. By the turn of the 20th century, Duluth would rank as one of the major ports of the world in terms of tonnage handled. By 1913 it ranked second only to New York, a position it would hold for decades (Hall 1976: 99). The combined ports of Duluth-Superior are included in the top 10 in the U.S. in terms of tonnage handled.

Superior: Settled in 1853, its first ore docks were completed in 1892. Connected by rail with Duluth in 1896. Had traffic of 8.4 million aggregate tons in 1897.

Two Harbors: One of the largest ore ports on Lake Superior, and the first in Minnesota. Opened in 1864, natural harbor dredged in 1886. Growth from 174 vessels arriving with aggregate tonnage of 295,800 in 1885 to the 1897 total of 2,064 vessels with 6.2 million tons. First steel ore dock on the lakes built in 1909 with a storage capacity of 44,000 tons. Peak ore record was 1953 when more than 21 million tons of ore were shipped. The harbor declined after that period. Three-quarters of a billion tons of ore shipped through this harbor from the Mesabi Range in its 100 years of operation (King 1984: 1-4). Considerable forest products shipped between 1904-1931. Depletion of high grade ore temporarily shut down port in 1963 (U.S. Army Corps of Engineers 1975: 11).

Port Arthur: Most important Canadian port on Lake Superior, and known as the Canadian Lakehead. Terminal for Canadian Pacific Railroad. Exporter of lumber, grain and, later, iron ore. The first grain was shipped in 1883. Combined with Fort William in 1906. The port now contains the largest water shipping grain elevator in the world. Canadian Pacific has one of the largest coal docks in the world. In the early 1970s an average of 3 million tons of cargo handled a month, making it the largest of all Canadian ports (Hatcher and Walter 1963: 154).

Iron ore shipping began at Port Arthur after the discovery of the Steep Rock Mine. Mining operations began in 1942 (Nute 1944: 155-6).

As the ports of Lake Superior developed, they influenced the routes of the various types of vessels carrying certain cargos. The main commerce on Lake Superior was the transportation of passengers, grain, iron ore, coal, package freight and lumber. As each of the trades expanded, larger vessels were produced to accommodate that growth commensurate with physical navigation limitations.

At the turn of the century, there was more freight being carried on the Great Lakes in an eight-month season than all other nations combined using the Suez Canal in 12 months (Curwood 1909: 13). The development of the trades that made up the bulk of Great Lakes freight will be briefly discussed, before presenting a general view of the growth of navigation.

Principal Products in Lake Superior Navigation: Lake Superior experienced a tremendous growth of commerce beginning with the opening of the Sault Canal. One of the most remarkable aspects of overall Great Lakes navigation is the increasing percentage of the total commerce that Lake Superior navigation represented. In 1870, Lake Superior shipping tonnage was about six percent of the total for the Great Lakes; by 1911 it was more than 55 percent (Williamson 1977: 179). The majority of Lake Superior's tonnage is represented by iron ore, always making up two-thirds of the total tonnage, and sometimes 90 percent.

Iron Ore: The first major shipments began in 1856 from Marquette to Ohio (Mansfield 1899: 1: 584). By 1899 iron ore comprised one-third of all the trade on the Great Lakes. By 1911 iron ore shipments comprised more than 50 percent of the commerce on the Great Lakes (Williamson 1977: 175). This tremendous growth of percentage took place as the overall trade on the lakes swelled from 6 million tons in 1870 to more than 80 million in 1911 – a growth of 1,300 percent.

Experiments in producing pig iron in the Superior region were unsuccessful. Companies attempting to manufacture iron failed to produce the expected profits. The rapidly disappearing hardwoods necessary for the production of charcoal iron were a major factor in the failure. Coke, a coal product, became the fuel for iron production, making it cheaper to move the ore to the blast furnaces and manufacturing centers in the East, rather than build furnaces in the iron ore regions and transfer the coke to them (Hatcher 1950: 96-105).

Four major ranges were opened up in the Lake Superior region from 1854 to 1884. The demand for the ore was from the iron and steel mills in the East, and the cheapest transportation was over water. From the opening of the Sault Canal to 1930, more than 150 billion tons of ore were sent down the lakes from the Superior ranges.

The increased volumes resulting from improvements in mining techniques and the refinement of shore facilities around 1880 put mounting pressure on shipping capabilities. These pressures, coupled with the progress of ship design, materials and building techniques, led to the launch of the iron, lake-built *Onoko* in 1882. This vessel incorporated some of the attributes of the wooden *R.J. Hackett,* which had been built in 1869 for the ore trade and dimensioned to the contemporary Sault locks, as well as to the ore docks at Marquette.

The basic characteristics of the lake bulk-freighter were full body (high block-coefficient), high ratio of length to breadth, clear decks with hatches spaced to align with loading docks and deck structures only on the bow and stern. The bulk carrier continued to increase in size as the demand for ore grew, the navigation channels deepened, the locks enlarged and the shore facilities were refined to handle the immense quantities of ore pouring down the lakes from Lake Superior.

Ownership and utilization of the ore carriers is best characterized as that of increasing concentration of capital, particularly involving eastern financiers. Beginning in the 1880s, merg-

ers consolidated interests into large corporate organizations that absorbed smaller firms, or simply put them out of business. The Panic of 1893 helped to eliminate the smaller corporations. Ore, pig iron, coal and limestone transportation and production became interlinked.

Political power was wielded from both a corporate and personal position by company executive officers. Company officials were active in government on a national and state level. Ultimately, the varied interests of Carnegie and Rockefeller, including the fleets of ships used for ore transport, consolidated under U.S. Steel in 1901, which directly controlled more than half of the known iron ore resources in the United States (Hatcher 1950: 181).

The formation of company-owned fleets of freighters, begun by the Rockefeller-owned Bessemer fleet in 1895, altered the social organization aboard the ships. The captain, once master of the ship in every way, became a company employee answerable to managers for all details of operation from strict schedules to fuel consumption. The old tradition of hiring crews for each voyage was replaced with inducements to motivate and maintain a permanent crew. Captains were shuffled from boat to boat, and all the crew was hired by the company (Hoagland 1917: 24-26, 40). The days of owner-operator shipmasters and vagabond crews on the lakes was over in the bulk freighter business in the last decade of the 19th century.

The contribution to the total U.S. production of iron ore from the Great Lakes grew from five percent in 1860 (Mansfield 1899: 1: 566) to almost twice as much as all the other parts of the country combined in less than 15 years (Tunell 1898: 63).

The rapid increases of the iron ore and grain commerce of the Lake Superior region created the need to handle both cargo types quickly. In the early period the cargo was loaded and unloaded by hand with buckets. The advent of grain elevators speeded the process for grain, and special loading docks and unloading equipment did the same for ore.

Ore docks developed unprecedented loading and unloading capabilities in the Great Lakes region. Elevated tramways that took advantage of the cliffs on the south shore of Superior were used for loading ore at Marquette in 1858. The size of the "pocket" docks continued to grow until the Northern Docks at Superior in the 20th century had 1,352 pockets capable of loading 16 of the 600-foot vessels simultaneously.

Prior to the application of steam, all unloading of ore was done by hand, a process that took a week for a cargo of 300 tons. Unloading technology development began with the use of steam winches in 1867. In 1880, the first improvements appeared. A movable tram was put in operation by Brown that allowed the unloader to move along the dock to work above the hatches without moving the ore boat. Self-filling grab buckets soon appeared and design modifications quickly followed until 1899 when the first Hulett unloaders were installed on the Conneaut docks by Carnegie Steel Company. The Hulett unloaders were rigid affairs that significantly reduced the interior hull damage of the earlier cable-operated grab buckets.

The rigid Hulett design became the standard, and they soon began to grow in size, influencing bulk ore carrier hull design.

The first Huletts were steam operated and carried five-ton buckets. These would grow to the contemporary 50-ton unloaders. Soon after the Huletts were adopted the 540-foot, 30-hatch ore boats appeared. These vessels had no interior stanchions or bulkheads, and hatches on 12-foot centers to match the ore dock spouts (Burke 1975: 275). The result was that a vessel of these dimensions could discharge 10,000 tons of ore in 4^1/$_2$ hours, or less. An ore unloading record was established in 1930 when *Wm. G. McConagle* discharged 11,445 gross tons of ore at the Pittsburgh and Conneaut Dock in 2 hours 20 minutes (U.S. Board of Engineers 1930: 30).

Ore loading capabilities of the Lake Superior ports developed similar capabilities as the unloading docks of the Lower Lakes. The lake steamer *D.G. Kerr* on September 7, 1921, loaded 12,508 tons of ore in 16.5 minutes at the Duluth and Iron Range Railroad ore dock at Two Harbors. This was a rate of 758 tons a minute (U.S. Board of Engineers 1930: 29).

Coal Trade: Coal was an upbound cargo imported into the Superior region. The mineral was brought into the major ports by vessels that received grain or iron ore for the downbound journey. Duluth and Superior were primary ports for the regional distribution of coal for the West and Northwest in the late 1890s (Mansfield 1899: 1: 551). The first shipments of coal arrived in Duluth in 1871 (Hutchinson 1914: 282). Most of the coal, approximately 80 percent, was shipped out of Lake Erie ports, with Toledo the major exporter. Coal as the upbound cargo contributed significantly to the early financial success of the large bulk freighter system on the lakes.

By the early 1850s, there was a demand for coal in any of the population centers or ports for use as fuel for homes, industry and steam vessels (*Buffalo Morning Express* March 2, 1852). Wood was the chief fuel in the early period of development for the region. Movement of coal through the Sault Ste. Marie Canal in 1855 was 1414 tons; in 1875 100,000 tons; 1,000,000 in 1886; 10 million in 1898 (Mansfield 1899: 1: 547) to more than 20 million tons by 1911 (Williamson 1977: 178).

Coal, like iron ore, was handled in quantities that soon demanded automation. Bituminous coal is easily broken and must be loaded more carefully than ore. Hulett railroad dumpers appeared in 1892. These and later revisions such as telescoping chutes were used to keep breakage at a minimum.

Prior to 1876 coal was unloaded by horse-operated bucket lifts. A vessel carrying 500 tons or so took about a week to unload. Tramways and, later, clamshells were introduced in the late 1890s, and electric power was introduced in 1901 at the Lakehead. The electric clamshell system could unload a 5,000-ton boat in 10 hours in 1902 (Hutchinson 1914: 297-303). By 1928, the coal unloading record had halved: The *Elbert H. Gray* discharged 9,336 tons of bituminous coal at the Duluth, Missabe and Northern Dock in 6 hours 5 minutes (U.S. Board of Engineers 1930: 30).

Grain: The opening of the Erie Canal made grain transportation practical. The earliest traffic in grain on the Great Lakes was westward. The demand resulted from a rapidly increasing population and a growing foreign export market. Soon after the opening of the Erie Canal, principal grain movement shifted as Western agriculture developed. By 1835 all the grain arriving at Buffalo was from Ohio, and amounted to 112,000 bushels (Mansfield 1899: 1: 526).

After the development of grain cultivation in the new territories, the eastward flow of grain increased to meet the demand from the rapidly growing and industrializing East. The production of wheat began in the Lake Superior region as the grain belt of the country moved toward the northwest (Tunell 1898: 41). After 1848 corn became more important. By 1860 Chicago export of grain totaled about three-fourths of the output of the top seven ports of Europe (Mansfield 1899: 1: 530). By 1871, the 10 states bordering the Great Lakes produced more than half of the grain crop of the U.S. (Andrews 1910: 11).

The principal grain ports were Buffalo, Chicago and Duluth-Superior. In both receipts and shipping, Chicago was far in advance of the others. Duluth-Superior was ranked second in amount shipped, and third in amount received (Andrews 1910: 15).

The initiation of grain commerce occurred on Lake Superior in about 1870. The total shipped eastward from the Lakehead that year was 49,700 bushels (Andrews 1910: 34). Duluth became a grain depot, with its first elevator constructed in 1870, the second in 1872.

The Northern Pacific Railway reached 150 miles west of Duluth, and in 1878 the prairie market began delivering grain for eastward shipment from Duluth-Superior. By 1881, the grain trade of Duluth compared favorably to the long-established market of Chicago, which at the time had a population of a half-million more people (Hall 1976: 67-68).

Grain shipments from the Superior ports reached 124 million bushels by 1905. From 1905 to 1909, shipments through the Sault Canal increased from 176 million to 192 million bushels (Andrews 1910: 35). Two million bushels of grain, if all wheat, would produce about 12 billion one-pound loaves of bread (Curwood 1909: 50).

Canadian grain production grew as a result of westward expansion. After railroad connections were established, Canada shipped its grain through the Duluth-Superior harbor; there was not an important port on the Canadian side until the Canadian railroad connection between Winnipeg and Port Arthur resulted in the creation of a harbor. From 1883 to 1920 Port Arthur and Ft. Williams were the main grain- and flour-shipping cities for the Canadian trade.

Grain commerce through St. Marys Falls Canal at Sault Ste. Marie expanded from 353,777 bushels in 1870 to 88,418,380 bushels in 1898 (Mansfield 1899: 1: 193). By 1911 grain had declined from 25 percent of the total tonnage on the lakes in 1870, to about 10 percent. The value of the shipped grain and flour amounted to 25 to 37 percent of the total value during 1901-1910 (Williamson 1977: 175; Andrews 1910: 35).

Lumber: The lumber trades moved westward in a similar manner to grain production. The exploitable forests of the eastern lakes territory were cleared in the 1870s, and commerce soon became reliant on those of the Superior region. The Duluth area became a mainstay in the 1890s, at the same time Canadian exports were rising.

The Chicago receipts of lumber moved by lake carrier indicate about one billion board feet a year from 1868 to 1897. During this period, rail receipts were rarely half the lake total (Mansfield 1899: 1: 521).

The lumber trade entered a general decline in the 1880s as a result of the depletion of forests. The railroads became more competitive as the exhaustion of desirable timber close to the lake shores and logging streams progressed, and it became necessary to push farther into the interior to reach exploitable stands of timber. In 1891, rail and lake shipments out of Michigan were about equal for the first time (Mansfield 1899: 1: 519). The same general pattern of development continued to move west. Many people involved in the lakes' lumber trade moved to the Pacific Northwest and continued much as they had done in the lakes region.

The unique practice of towing vessels developed in lakes navigation as a result of the lumber trade. Small vessels predominated in the trade because they could navigate further up the rivers than the larger craft. The move to towing barges was influenced by the falling freight rates after the 1873 panic. A Chicago city ordinance of 1875 requiring noncombustible materials for building, a result of the disastrous fire of 1871, further reduced lumber demand and freight rates. Railway competition was also instrumental in reducing freight rates (Gjerset 1928: 88-93).

The falling freight rates made the general competitive disadvantages of sail apparent and heralded the demise of sail on the lakes. Small schooners operating singly were not profitable, but three or four vessels towed by a steamer were. Many older schooners were transformed into barges by cutting down the masts and removing the bowsprit. They were taken into the lumber trade.

These barges were towed by a side-wheel tug, replaced in the later 1870s by a propeller, called a steam barge, which also carried a cargo (see Tuttle 1873). The towed barge system, which came to be known as the "consort system," was developed by John S. Noyes of Buffalo in 1861 (Mansfield 1899: 1: 520) and was common in the bulk and lumber trades on the lakes in the 1870s and 1880s. The practice of multiple barges powered by a single steamer appeared in the coal trade on the Mississippi River about the same time (Hunter 1949: 210). They were called tows, but were actually pushed.

Towing vanished on the lakes when navigation, progressive shipbuilding technology and advanced loading and unloading machinery in the bulk trades made larger vessels more profitable. A large cargo could produce a profit even with low rates, since a larger freighter could be unloaded or loaded and under way while a smaller propeller waited for its consorts to be handled.

The south shore of Superior was logged principally between 1880 and 1900, the north shore in the 1890s, with the last major shipments leaving in 1924. Shipments out of Duluth fell from 174 million board feet in 1894 to 11 million in 1924, when only one mill was operating (Nute 1944: 195, 201). Between the years of 1870 and 1911, the annual percentage of the total commerce moved on the Great Lakes represented by lumber fell from more than 50 percent to three percent (Williamson 1977: 175).

A perspective of the immense quantity of lumber that was removed from the Great Lakes region can be gained from a consideration of the 1.5 billion board feet that was carried by lake ships in the 1909 season. Assuming it takes about 20,000 board feet of lumber to make an eight-room house, the total 1909 cargo could have built 75,000 houses, enough for a city of about 400,000 people, roughly the population of Detroit at that time (Curwood 1909: 48).

Passenger Service and Package Freight: The rapid migration west to the Superior region began soon after the mineral discoveries of 1843 and 1844. The population of Michigan increased from 31,639 to 212,269 between 1830 and 1840, then nearly doubled by 1850. The population growth of Wisconsin paralleled that of Michigan a decade later (Havighurst 1944: 129), and created a keen demand for freight and passenger service.

The introduction of packet line systems in the trans-Atlantic trade was an innovation that affected most American vessel organizations. There had previously been ships that sailed a specific route but followed no set schedule. The operation of ships on definite routes and preset schedules was initiated in the Atlantic trade soon after the War of 1812, closely followed by the Hudson River and Long Island Sound steamboats. The dependable schedules were a boon to shippers and passengers alike (see Albion 1938).

Increasing demand for passage instigated the steady increase in size and numbers of side-wheel passenger steamers. After the initial surge of immigrants, the demand for first-class accommodations grew. The 1840s and 1850s were particularly good for the passenger trade, and Great Lakes passenger traffic in 1845 was about 250,000 (Mansfield 1899: 1: 188-189).

In the 1850s, railroad construction grew competitive with steamers, as railroad companies began to buy vessels and enter into the steamship business. The railroad steamers were palatial, representing a new era in passenger service; some vessels reached 2,000 tons. The era was short-lived, however. The Panic of 1857 and the depression following it curtailed luxury travel, and many of the larger side-wheelers were permanently docked (Havighurst 1944: 232).

The high point of passenger travel of the 1840s and 1850s was not approached again until the 1870s and 1880s. Buffalo was a pioneer in the reintroduction of the short-run passenger vessel, while the Canadians led in the recovery of the long-run trade.

As in the early era, railroad companies were the capital formation under which the luxury steamship prospered. Northern Steamship Company, Canada Steamship Lines and the Canadian Pacific Railway were particularly notable in their introduction of ocean-going type vessels in the long distance runs. The newer vessels were not side-wheelers, but propellers of iron and steel, although there were a few large side-wheelers built after the turn of the century. As the railroad and automobile, and later the airplane, siphoned off passengers from the longer distance passenger service, the trade was reduced to short-run excursions. Lake Erie was the last lake to have significant passenger traffic.

Package freight, a term that may be peculiar to the Great Lakes, is used to differentiate general merchandise from bulk cargos. In the early periods vessels carried both package freight and passengers, and those specializing in either were often owned by the same companies. Later, the passenger trade was secondary to the package freight business.

The primary flow of freight traffic was east-west. The primary eastern ports were Buffalo, Cleveland and Detroit; the western termini were Chicago, Milwaukee and Duluth-Superior. The majority of the freight was eastbound, consisting primarily of agricultural products, particularly flour.

Railroad companies usually dominated the package freight business. The Pennsylvania Railroad led the way by acquiring the control of the Anchor Line, the largest package freight line on the lakes. By World War I, railroads controlled all major lines. The Interstate Commerce Commission forced a reorganization of the package freight lines in 1916, and made the rail companies divest their holdings of Great Lakes vessels. A new company was formed, the Great Lakes Transit Corporation, which controlled 85 percent of the passenger and package freight on the Great Lakes (Ibid. 1960: 9-13).

1934, a depression year, was the first year the package freight lines suffered a deficit. The start of World War II marked the end of the package freight fleet on the Great Lakes (Fletcher 1960: 30-31). The National Park Service vessel *Ranger III* is the last package freighter operating on the lakes.

Basic Trends: There are two basic trends that are apparent in Great Lakes navigation. Although there was a wide range of commodities carried by Great Lakes ships over time, the general tendency was an overall decrease in the number of commodities being shipped by the end of the century. The second general trend was the growth in importance of bulk products.

The ranking of relative importance of bulk products shifted over time. Prior to the 1880s, lumber comprised the largest bulk cargo on the lakes, with grain a close second. By the 1890s, iron ore had assumed primacy over all other bulk products. As iron ore became the dominant cargo, a shift in the northern trade terminus from Lake Michigan to Lake Superior was evident.

Growth of Shipping and Navigation Improvements

At the close of the 18th century there were fewer than 20 sailing vessels on the Great Lakes, with only one on Lake Superior (Mansfield 1899: 1: 132). Throughout the 19th century the vessels grew in number and size commensurate with the rapidly growing transportation requirements of regional commerce. New vessel types were developed to fit specific regional needs. As commerce grew, the demand for improved navigation increased.

Navigation improvements have been critical to the expansion of Great Lakes waterborne commerce. Harbor improvements were necessary at most major ports on the lakes before vessels could approach the docks. Typically, the ports were on rivers that had formed offshore bars at the mouth. It was necessary to dredge a channel through the bars to overcome the costly inconvenience of lightering vessels offshore (Walker 1902: 291).

Dredging and harbor improvements began in Buffalo as early as 1819. Buffalo came to be a major port as a result of the

Erie Canal commerce. As Chicago became a major port, the trade between the two cities increased, until a regular route was established by the 1840s.

The four main obstacles to Great Lakes navigation were: the St. Clair Flats in Lake St. Clair; the Lime Kiln Shoals in the Detroit River; Niagara Falls (Welland Canal); and the St. Marys Falls at the Sault, which have been discussed. Canals were constructed around the falls, and channels were dredged through the flats and shoals. Each, at different times, became a critical factor in lake navigation. The Sault Canal governed the Superior trade, the St. Clair Flats and the Lime Kiln Shoals together restricted the trade between the Upper Lakes and the Lower. These channels were essential to all east-west commerce on the Great Lakes.

Various changes in critical depths as represented by the four principal navigation impediments are listed below. Harbor improvements had to keep up with channel improvements to benefit from the larger ships and cargoes. Other improvements, such as the placement of lighthouses and channel markers, were constructed concurrently to reduce shipping risks.

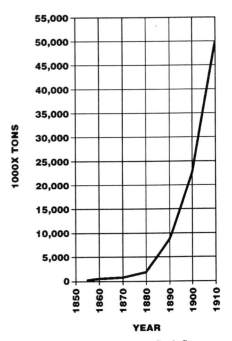

Figure 11. Freight Through the Sault Ste. Marie Canal (from U.S. Engineer Dept. 1930:

Table 2 – Critical Navigation Improvements

1855 – Sault Locks 350 x 70 x 11.5.
1860 – St. Clair Flats 10 ft.
1869 – 10.5 feet over sill at the Sault. 60 ft. width at bottom.
1872 – St. Clair Flats 13 ft.
1881 – Weitzel Lock at Soo. 515 x 80 x 17.
1884 – St. Marys channel deepened to 16 ft.
1892 – Lime Kiln 20 ft.
1895 – Canadian Lock at Sault 900 x 60 x 22.
1896 – Poe Lock at Sault 800 x 100 x 21.
1898 – St. Clair Flats 20 ft.
1903 – St. Marys Canal deepened to 25 ft.
1908 – West Neebish Channel in St. Marys River 300 x 21.
1912 – Livingstone Channel in Detroit River 300 x 22.
1914 – Davis Lock at Sault 1,350 x 80 x 24.5.
1919 – Sabin Lock at Sault 1,350 x 80 x 24.5.
1936 – Livingstone Channel 450 x 26 downbound.

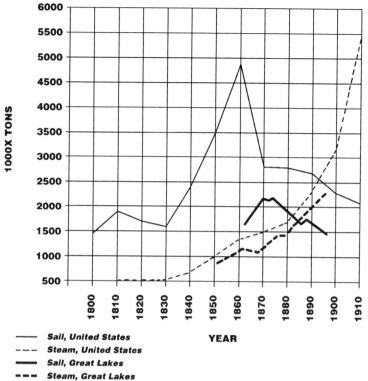

Figure 12. U S. Documented Merchant Vessels, Sail/Steam (U.S. Bureau of the Census).

The dimensions of the locks and the depth of the channel have imposed limits on the size and depth of vessels that could be employed in interlake shipping. The controlling depth for maximum vessel drafts were 12 feet to 1871; 13-16 feet to 1891; 18 feet to 1897; 20-21 feet until 1911, when a 23-foot channel was maintained (Mansfield 1899: 1: 253-4), and 27 feet since 1958.

Major channel and lock dimension changes were directly reflected in shipbuilding and operation practices. Vessel types and sizes came and went as the restrictions changed. Vessel types often represented compromises between the imposed size restrictions and maximum cargo-carrying requirements. As a result of increased carrying capacity and efficiency, transportation costs on the lakes fell from .23 cents per ton mile to .13 cents between 1887 and 1890. Railroad costs were .974 and .941 per ton per mile for the same years (Pankhurst 1893: 256). It was noted in 1907 that a 10 percent increase in freight capacity was gained (with no additional operation cost) with each additional foot of draft (Annual Report of the Chief of Engineers 1907: 846). In 1930, each inch of draft lost below 20 feet represented a loss of 90 to 100 tons of cargo capacity (U.S. Engineer Dept. 1930: 32).

Evidence from the last half of the 19th century indicates that the largest vessels in use could load to deeper drafts than could be accommodated by the contemporary harbor and channel depths (Tunell 1898: 38). For example, the largest vessels of 1876 loaded only to a depth of 15 feet because of the channels and harbor depths, but could safely load to a depth of 17 feet (Laurent 1983: 11). Apparently, vessel designers and builders

anticipated deeper channels and did not just respond to their increases, whereas vessels built to exploit changes in critical lock size appeared only after the locks were constructed.

Technological and operational developments also influenced vessel attributes. For example, the appearance of the steam tug in the 1860s allowed vessels to be towed through the channels and in harbors, particularly through the Detroit River and across the St. Clair Flats. The towing business flourished midcentury at Detroit, when there were more than 50 tugs employed (Mansfield 1899: 1: 503; Hatcher 1945: 144).

The steam tug was at least indirectly responsible for the increase in size of the sailing ships in the 1860s and early 1870s, the peak years of sail on the lakes. In this period, the barks (actually barkentines, a term that was shortened on the lakes to "bark") and schooners dominated the freight trades and reached a length of 200 feet with a displacement of 700 or 800 tons (Barkhausen 1947: 1). The growing numbers of propellers that increased in size to exceed each navigation improvement, and the short-lived consort system put the steam tugs out of business by the end of the century.

One of the best indicators of the intensity of navigation on Lake Superior is the data from the canals at Sault Ste. Marie. Comprehensive data have been collected for both the American and Canadian canals since the initial opening in 1855 and are presented in Figure 11 (computed from U.S. Board of Engineers 1930: 60-61).

The growth of shipbuilding kept pace with the burgeoning demand for lake transportation. In 1908 it was estimated that three-fifths of the total ship tonnage in the U.S. was constructed on the lakes. The graph in Figure 12 depicts a comparison of the yearly tonnage of documented U.S. merchant sail and steam vessels in the country as a whole and on the Great Lakes. The graph shows that lakes vessels were the largest category of merchant vessels documented in the U.S. Also shown is the date that documented steam tonnage superseded sailing tonnage. Steam tonnage superseded sail on the lakes almost a decade earlier than in the rest of the U.S., an indication of the advanced technological development of lakes vessels. The number of steam vessels passing through the Canadian and U.S. locks to Lake Superior exceeded the number of sailing vessels in 1874 (U.S. Board of Engineers 1930: 60), a reflection of the heavy, early capitalization of the Lake Superior trades.

The collection of commercial steam vessels currently known within the waters of Isle Royale comprise a remarkable cross section of the trades and vessel types of Lake Superior navigation as reflected by the socioeconomic context. The archeological analysis and interpretation of the Isle Royale shipwrecks in Chapter V of this report was heavily influenced by the context as discussed above. This brief study has reinforced the necessity of interpreting and understanding shipwrecks from a regional perspective within a cultural context, rather than as discrete, disparate elements.

Chapter III

Major Vessel Types on Lake Superior: Sail to Steam

The first vessels constructed on the Great Lakes were built and rigged with the environmental peculiarities and sailing conditions of Great Lakes navigation in mind, and such has been the case with thousands of vessels that followed. Shallow water, combined with twisting channels and limited maneuvering room, imposed special considerations on vessel designers and builders. The builders and designers of Lakes vessels have been forced to experiment, adapt, refine and develop particular answers to the problems posed by the unique environment of the Inland Seas.

Griffon, one of the first ships to be built on the Great Lakes, was constructed in 1679 and modeled on the lines of a Dutch galiot. The galiot was capable of carrying large cargoes in a beamy shallow-draft hull, which was useful for the shallow open-sea conditions found in the Netherlands and surrounding North Sea. *Griffon*'s hull, about 70 feet long, probably carried a high stern. The vessel, sometimes referred to as a "barque," probably carried three masts typical of the ship-rig of that period, with two masts square-rigged and the mizzen lateen-rigged (Barry 1973: 15).

The first decked-vessel built on Lake Superior was the 25-ton ship built by the Frenchman Sieur de la Ronde, who is considered to be the first practical miner on Lake Superior (Nute 1944: 161-162). This little craft was built at Sault Ste. Marie in 1735 to remove copper from the mines of the Superior region. This enterprise can be considered the forerunner to the tremendous extractive industry that would cause the generation of a huge fleet of ships of Lake Superior to carry the ores.

In 1755, there were four French ships on Lake Ontario. War between France and Great Britain prompted the construction of British vessels. A shipyard was established at Oswego on Lake Ontario. The first British vessel, a schooner named *Oswego,* was built, soon followed by the sloop-rigged *Ontario.* Both ships were about 43 feet in length and measured about 100 tons (Barry 1973: 17).

By 1762, when the British had two vessels on Lake Erie, a schooner and a sloop, they had already reached the conclusion that fore-and-aft rigged vessels were the most suitable for all classes of naval and commercial vessels on the Lakes (Cuth-

bertson 1931: 227). Most ships built and used were fore-and-aft rigged and were operated by the British Provincial Marine; there would be no privately owned commercial vessels on the Great Lakes for another 20 years.

The first commercial vessel built on the Great Lakes was constructed in 1785 by the large Montreal trading concern, the North West Company. The company sent a group of men to the head of Sault Ste. Marie to build a vessel. The 75-ton sloop *Otter* was the result. The same company soon constructed another ship, also a sloop, in Detroit (Barry 1973: 24).

In 1810, the trade on Lake Ontario exceeded that of the four Upper Lakes. There were many vessels employed in the Indian and fur trade, in supplying military posts and Western settlements, and providing fish, lumber and salt for the Pittsburgh, Pennsylvania, market. This growing Lakes trade produced a demand for new ships to be built (Mansfield 1899: 1: 128). The first regular commercial transport line on the American side of the Great Lakes was formed in 1806 to portage and forward freight around Niagara Falls.

Although the U.S. government built a 100-ton brig in 1802 *(Adams),* it primarily purchased and built schooners or sloops. The Provincial government of Canada built the 86-ton brig *Caledonia* in 1807 and an armed brig, *Queen Charlotte,* in 1809. The 97-ton brig *Lady Prevost* was built in 1810.

The War of 1812 provided impetus for the design and construction of sailing vessels on the Lakes. Competition between Britain and the U.S. in the Lakes region prompted a vigorous shipbuilding program by both sides (Barry 1973: 33). During the winter of 1812-13 the American government decided that a fleet of at least six ships was needed for naval operations on Lake Erie. These ships were to be constructed near Erie in a virtual wilderness. Captain Dobbins, the officer who had been put in charge of the project, brought in a naval architect and a master builder from New York (Mansfield 1899: 1: 155). The vessels that resulted included two 20-gun brigs, three gunboats and a "clipper" schooner which was apparently the first of its type on the Great Lakes.

The principal fighting ships of the war were square riggers. The main reason for the military preference of the square rig over the fore-and-aft rig was that the square rig was simply more difficult to put out of commission during sea battles. The more numerous square sails offered smaller targets to the enemy's cannon, and when a shot did strike true, it did less damage to the square sail's rigging than to the fore-and-aft. During the exchange of broadsides, the fore-and-aft sails set parallel to the keel offered large, vulnerable targets compared to the square sails, which were set at right angles to the centerline. The military advantage becomes a liability when considering the square rig for merchant service. The square rig vessel required large crews to handle the many sails, a serious concern to merchants seeking the lowest cost when transporting cargoes.

Some sailing characteristics of the square rig, however, were desirable in commercial transport. Square rigs sail fast before the wind. The prevailing westerly winds of the Lakes allowed for fast downbound passages for these ships. The geographic constraints of the Lakes require frequent course changes, especially in the rivers and narrow channels. Fore-and-aft rigs allow quicker course changes with only a fraction of the crew required for effecting the same maneuver on a square rigged vessel. It was probably realized early that combination rigs were the most desirable for commercial uses on the Great Lakes, because they contained advantages of both rigs.

Many of the vessels that survived the naval battles of the War of 1812 were bought or salvaged for use in commercial transportation (Mansfield 1899: 1: 172). Agreements entered into by both the British and American governments in 1817 stipulating that only one warship of not more than 100 tons and armed with one 18-pounder gun would be allowed on the Lakes contributed to the availability of the naval vessels. An act passed in 1824 required that all public vessels be sold (Mansfield 1899: 1: 181).

Many lessons were learned during the War of 1812. It was noted that a two-decked frigate could carry more guns than a comparable ship in salt water service. The Lakes craft did not have to carry fresh water or provisions for a long voyage as did the ocean going warship. British Lakes vessels were also more narrow of beam and had less displacement than comparable ocean ships, making them faster and more able to beat to windward – two desirable qualities for Lakes vessels (Barry 1973: 35). One of the most important lessons was that the larger ships sailed well, despite their shallow draft. In fact, the vessels used during the war were the shallowest draft square-riggers in the history of naval architecture (Cuthbertson 1931: 229).

Barkentines and brigantines became popular on the Lakes with their combination of square and fore-and-aft sails, deriving some of the benefits of both arrangements. Often these vessels were simply (and inaccurately) called "barks" or sometimes "barques" or "brigs" in historical accounts of the Lakes.

The word "brig" originally was an abbreviation for "brigantine." The origins of this rig are to be found in the Mediterranean where it referred to a small lateen-rigged vessel meant for rowing. In Northern Europe during the 16th century, the rig developed into the familiar two-masted rig with square sails on the foremast and a gaff-sail with a boom on the main mast. Ocean sailors would probably consider the Lakes brigs "hermaphrodite

brigs," technically a combination of the brig and the schooner. Lakes brigs carried staysails and jibs on their foremasts in addition to the square sails and staysails on the mainmast with the gaff-top spanker. On the Lakes the brigantines ranged in size from 80 or 90 tons to 500 tons (Cuthbertson 1931: 230).

The barkentine is a more modern development in sailing rigs. The bark rig, which preceded the barkentine, is a three-masted vessel with square sails on the foremast and mainmast and fore-and-aft sails on the mizzen. This can be considered the ship rig of the 16th century brought up to date. In somewhat the same way the barkentine rig, with square sails only on the foremast and gaff sails on the other masts, can be considered the modern revival of the 16th century caravel rig with its square-rigged foremast and lateen-rigged main- and mizzen-masts (Anderson and Anderson 1963: 192-193). Apparently, there were very few true barks ever operating on the Lakes.

Basically, the barkentine is a brigantine with additional fore-and-aft rigged masts. The sails carried on the foremasts of both these rigs were: square foresail, topsail, topgallantsail and one royal, with rarely a small skysail (Cuthbertson 1931: 231-232). There are some records of studding sails. Fore-and-aft canvas consisted of a staysail and two jibs set forward on the bowsprit and jibboom, fore-and-aft sails set aft and two, or sometimes three, staysails set between the fore- and mainmasts. After 1820, nearly all vessels lowered their gaffs when furling sails instead of taking them up to the gaff by hand (brailing). The custom of brailing was, however, still evident on some steam vessels much later, such as *Algoma*, which wrecked at Isle Royale in 1885.

Some writers have asserted that the barkentine rig was a Lakes innovation. This is a doubtful contention and difficult to substantiate. It is clear, however, that there were few appearances of either the barkentine or brigantine rig on salt water until after 1835, some years after they appeared on the Great Lakes (Cuthbertson 1931: 231).

Merchants and sailors determined very quickly the most profitable rigs for navigation of the Great Lakes. Although there were some variations, primarily in small craft, the sailing vessels of the Lakes are notable for their similarity. All were combination rigs designed for quick voyages carrying heavy cargoes in favorable winds (characteristics of square rigs) and maneuverability with only small crews necessary to change sails, coupled with the ability to sail close to windward to make quick passages upbound (characteristics of fore-and-aft rigs). The rig of choice on the Lakes early became the schooner, at first with topsails and later, when competition with steamers made minimum operating costs important for survival, without. Because of the numerical superiority of schooners and their role in Great Lakes navigation, they will be considered separately.

Schooner Development

Schooner development can be reasonably traced to old northern European two-mast shallop traditions. There may have been two separate sources of development: one for schooners with square topsails on the foremast, and another for those without (Greenhill 1980: 19). Schooners with square topsails may have developed from small square rig vessels that continued to add ever larger fore-and-aft sails as technological developments progressed until they became the main part of the sail area. The other line of development may have been from the two-masted shallops carrying only sprit sails, gaff sails or triangular sails. The sprit sail apparently grew larger first, becoming quite large in Classical times, and from it developed the standing gaff with brailing sail. The brailing sail is taken up or let out from the yard from which it is suspended on square-rigged vessels or the mast in fore-and-aft rigs. From this rig the lowering gaff developed. The origin of the gaff sail is obscure, but it was common in northern Europe in the 1600s (Greenhill 1980: 18-19).

The gaff schooner without topsails began to appear in illustrations in the early 1600s and was probably in existence in the late 1500s (Greenhill 1980: 19). Both types of schooner, with and without topsails, appeared in Colonial America in the early 1700s. There were generally seven types of vessels classified in Colonial records: ships, sloops, pinks, brigantines, shallops, ketches and barks. Schooners were listed for the first time around 1717 (Chapelle 1935: 11). During this period, vessels were classed more by the hull than by the particular rig carried. For example, "bark" was used generically, much like "ship" is today.

The first schooner appeared on the Great Lakes in 1804 and the rig was the most seen on the Lakes until the end of the days of sail. The 25-ton *Surprise* was built at Buffalo that year and was soon followed by *Mary*, built at Erie. The 45-ton *Zephyr*, one of the first ships launched at Cleveland, was hauled down the ways in 1808 by oxen and was of the size found to be the best suited to the Lakes trade during the first decades of the 19th century (Hatcher 1945: 138).

The 132-ton schooner *Michigan* was the largest American merchant vessel on the Lakes in 1817. The ship was built by a shipwright from the East and was rigged as a double-topsail schooner, "resembling in most particulars the down-easters that ply upon the Atlantic coast" (Walker 1902: 293). This vessel represents one of the major lines of influence in the development of Great Lakes schooners – that of the Atlantic coastal trade in the east. As stated above, the first "clipper" schooner on the Lakes was built for naval service on Lake Erie in the winter of 1812-13, also by an eastern builder. It is clear that eastern builders and their designs were present at an early date in the Lakes area. This line of development led to the sharp-model schooner on the Lakes. There can be little question as to the flow of information from the East. Before 1820 not only shipwrights, but most of the commanders and seamen were from the seaboard (Walker 1902: 296).

The "clipper"-model hull, with its fine lines and great speed, was a development of southern builders that grew out of the demands of the Atlantic smuggling trade of the first half of the 18th century. It is not possible to establish the exact date for the beginning of the evolution that produced the well known "Baltimore Clipper," but it was probably around 1730 (Chapelle 1935: 31). In these early days, the schooner rig demonstrated its superiority over the sloop rig. The schooner was very weatherly and could be handled by a smaller crew. It was also

learned that the schooner rig could be used in a longer and narrower hull than a sloop. This was an advantage for the design of hulls, because it became known during this period that when two vessels had the same capacity or displacement, the one with the narrower hull would be the faster (Chapelle 1935: 32).

Large American schooners developed a remarkable degree of sharpness before the War of 1812 and the fore-topsail schooner rig was very popular in the first half the 19th century for ocean vessels (Chapelle 1935: 234). The addition of the square topsails on the fore, and sometimes on both masts, gave excellent speed when running before the wind. This characteristic was desired by Lakes mariners when taking advantage of the prevailing westerly winds of the Lakes on their downbound travels.

The second line of influence for Lakes schooner development can be found in the establishment of packet lines in the East soon after 1800. It was in the packet trade where vessels began to carry freight for hire rather than only the cargo of the owner. Regularly scheduled departures were set up between certain ports. The first vessels employed in this innovative trade were large sloops capable of carrying cargo and passengers. Leeboards were in use as early as 1812 on the Hudson River where shallow draft hulls were necessary, and centerboards were common by 1825 at the latest (Chapelle 1967: 164). In the areas where the distance between ports was not great, schooners and brigs were employed. The requirements for vessels in the packet trade were speed, capacity, seaworthiness and the ability to sail on schedule year-round with any available cargo. To meet these requirements, sturdy vessels were designed on a rather full model with flat floors for maximum capacity (*Ibid:* 271). The results of this influence on the Lakes schooners were in the full hull-models that were to become the common carrier of the Great Lakes.

The available depth in the rivers and harbors has imposed limitations on the practical draft of Great Lakes vessels to the present day. The early vessels were often abominable sailors. The flat-bottomed vessels in operation before 1820 were characterized by a contemporary captain as "dull sailors, some of them could hardly claw offshore under canvas" (Walker 1902: 291). This was a particular disadvantage because ships had to be lightered of cargo and passengers by small craft due to the shallow conditions of most harbors, and an onshore breeze could result in disaster. Structural features were incorporated into these early vessels to overcome the limitations of extremely shallow draft. Before the adoption of Dutch leeboards, slip keels, drop keels or centerboards, it was almost impossible to design shoal-draft vessels that could take advantage of the schooner rig and sail close to windward.

Red Jacket, a 53-ton schooner, was apparently one of the first on the Lakes to be fitted with leeboards, although they had been successfully used earlier in the east. One leeboard would be in the water at a time to aid in sailing by preventing leeway, much the same way as the keel of a deep-hulled sailing ship. The board could be raised in shallow water (Walker 1902: 301). Leeboards never became popular devices on the Lakes, although they were occasionally used. One reason for their unpopularity may have been that the leeboards were easily damaged by the Lakes waves.

The centerboard was the method of choice to meet the limitations of shallow draft and the poor sailing qualities of flat-bottomed hulls. The centerboard protruded through the bottom of the hull within a watertight case to prevent leeway. The centerboard could be raised or lowered from inside the hull.

The invention of the centerboard is usually attributed to a British naval officer, Capt. Shank. Like many "inventions," it is more accurately an adaptation. The sliding keel as originally proposed by Shank was a board about three-quarters of the length of the keel that was lowered by tackles through a case. He later tried three smaller separate boards that proved easier to handle and took up less room in the hold. There was a 65-foot cutter built to his specifications in 1790 in Plymouth, England, and a few other vessels were also built with drop keels. They did not prove satisfactory due to the tendency of the cases to leak. Shank found it difficult to convince the Admiralty that his idea was practical, and the idea was dropped by the British (Chapelle 1935: 169).

The interest in centerboards shifted to the United States. In 1810, there were a large number of leeboards in use in the Hudson River, but a less cumbersome arrangement was sought. A number of patents were granted for types of centerboards. The centerboard differed from the drop or sliding keels by being attached on the forward edge by a pivot, with the lifting tackle on the after end of the board. After the War of 1812, a number of large sloops were built with centerboards, and they were used in schooners on the Chesapeake Bay by 1821, and perhaps in the Great Lakes by 1828, though this early date may be doubtful (*Ibid.* 1935: 169, 268.) Slip or sliding keels may have been in use on the Lakes before 1820. Capt. Augustus Walker, a contemporary, recorded in his observations that vessels varied between 18 and 65 tons burden, and for the most part were built with slip keeps between 1817 and 1820 (Walker 1902: 300). Centerboards were to become the rule for Great Lakes sailing ships and were placed in brigs and barks as well as schooners.

Two man-made canals affected early 19th century Lakes schooner development. The opening of the Erie Canal from the Hudson River to Lake Erie in 1825 created a rapidly expanding market for the transportation of passengers and cargo (for a more detailed discussion, see Chapter II). Prior to its opening, most sail craft were put out of commission for two months or more during the summer due to the lack of upbound freight (Walker 1902: 304). The Welland Canal, constructed at the Niagara Falls portage, was opened by the Canadians in 1829 and allowed trade between Lake Ontario and the Upper Lakes. Four of the five Lakes were then opened to trade. The locks of the Welland Canal could accommodate a vessel no larger than 100 feet long, 26 1/2 feet of beam, and a draft of 11 feet (Barry 1973: 123). Any merchant who wished to trade directly with the ports of Lake Ontario had to use vessels that could pass through the canal locks. The limitations of the locks produced a vessel unique to the Great Lakes – the "canaller."

In the 1840s, canallers that were built as large as possible to take optimum advantage of the economies of scale in the growing demand for transportation and intended for Lake Ontario

trade, became noticeably similar in hull shape. Typical characteristics were a plumb bow, relatively narrow beam for the vessel length and flat sides as far fore and aft as possible to allow for the largest cargo capacity (Barry 1973: 124). The hull form was described as "heavy, stubby and square Hollander-type" (Hatcher 1944: 210). The stern was square with little overhang aft. The canallers also had their moveable bowsprits tilted upward almost to vertical when clearing the locks. As their size grew beyond 100 feet in length, it may be assumed that some sort of longitudinal reinforcing was used. The canaller was the first distinctly Lakes vessel type, a product of the environmental and economic conditions of the Lakes and developed from revised technology specially adapted from the eastern shipbuilders.

Development of Structural Support Systems

Intense competition in the eastern packet trades fueled the design of larger ships on the Lakes. These ships were required to carry heavy cargoes, often in bulk, and sail well in any weather to meet their schedules. There is a structural problem, however, when wooden ships that are required to carry heavy loads are lengthened. The ends of the hull tend to droop and cause the keel to arch. This condition, known as hogging, compresses the bottom planks and puts the deck planks in tension, weakening and changing the hull form enough to open up serious leaks. This problem especially plagues vessels with narrow beams and fine bows and sterns due to the relative decrease in buoyancy in these areas when compared to the midsection.

The French were probably the first to attempt the prevention of hogging by the addition of longitudinal members and stanchions set on the keelson. In 1746, they built a vessel with diagonally planked ceiling (Chapelle 1967: 207, 269). The British studied the problem in the latter part of the 18th century, and again after the War of 1812. A series of reforms in vessel construction was carried out by Sir Robert Seppings. These reforms became known as the "Seppings System" and included the addition of internal diagonal bracing and filling in the spaces between the floor frames in the ships of the Admiralty (Lavery 1984: 43). During the British investigations into the problem it was discovered that the more flat sided ships tended not to hog because the hull planks provided additional longitudinal support, a condition that may have benefited the early canallers.

Hogging frames and trusses of wood were used in the eastern river steamboats as early as 1820, and by 1837 experiments were being made with diagonal wood planking placed inside the frames with no additional ceiling in order to save weight. Diagonal iron strapping was begun by the British who first placed iron straps across the inside of the frames and partially covered them by ceiling planks (Chapelle 1967: 270).

Other methods to increase longitudinal strength were tried. Improved scarphs, edge fastened hull and ceiling planks and the caulking of the ceiling planks all met with some success.

Developments in Form and Technology

Between 1817 and 1820 sail vessels grew in number, but not in size. These vessels varied from 18 to 65 tons burden and most contained a slip keel (Walker 1902: 300). The shallow draft hull had a lot of deadrise and during this period rarely exceeded five feet; that was the depth of water on the St. Clair Flats in the Detroit River. The 53-ton *Red Jacket* was built in 1820 and was the first merchant vessel on the Lakes with bulwarks; all previous vessels were built with rails and stanchions and were wet sailors. Solid bulwarks were necessary because *Red Jacket* had little freeboard when loaded (Walker 1902: 295, 301-302).

The typical sail arrangement for schooners was with one or two square sails on the foremast and gaff topsail on the main. The square sails would be placed above the crosstrees. Another arrangement was to hang a large square sail from a yard placed at the hounds (just below the crosstrees). This sail hung down almost to the deck and was called a runner (Cuthbertson 1931: 233).

After 1820, most vessels furled their sails by lowering the gaff rather than by brailing. The loosely woven flax sailcloth began to be replaced by the tighter and more uniform loom-woven cotton-duck cloth. This hard and durable sailcloth was developed in Massachusetts and became standard after the War of 1812 (Chapelle 1967: 211).

There were many technical developments in addition to those of sails. In 1823, the first chains were employed as anchor cables. They were introduced on the schooners *Michigan, Red Jacket* and *Erie* (Walker 1902: 302). Between the years 1820 and 1845 many new innovations appeared. Rod rigging and turnbuckles came into general use in the 1820s and 1830s. Geared capstans and windlasses, iron-strapped blocks, geared steering, hold ventilators, geared winches, new mast and spar ironwork, improved marine stoves and water closets appeared during this period (Chapelle 1967: 279).

The demand for transportation on the Lakes was limited before the completion of the Erie Canal. There was little advantage to larger vessels before 1825-1830. An 1810 96-ton schooner *Charles and Ann* built in Oswego attracted much attention because of its large size (Mansfield 1899: 129). The economic pressures for the increase of navigation continued into the mid-20th century. Ever larger vessels would be required to meet the huge demand that was initiated with the opening of the Erie Canal.

By 1846, the registered U.S. Lake tonnage had reached 106,836 tons. This was a remarkable growth from the 56,252 tons registered in 1841. The number of mariners also increased accordingly from 3,750 in 1841 to 6,972 in 1846. There were 59 barks and brigs with an average tonnage of 230. The number of schooners in the same year was 319 with an average tonnage of 152. Sloops and scows averaged 46 tons (compiled from Abert 1848: 8,24). The growth of tonnage of both sail and steam vessels on the Lakes and in the U.S. is depicted in Figure 12 in Chapter II.

Steam Vessels

In 1840 there were more than 100 side-wheel steamers operating on the Lakes, most of them built within eight years of that date. (There are no records of experimentation with stern-wheels on the Lakes.) About 40 of them served as ferries or ran short, local routes out of the larger ports, while the remainder, mostly the larger boats, ran from Buffalo to Upper Lakes ports or from Niagara and Toronto to Lower Lakes destinations. Most of the boats ran independently, although "combinations" and "opposition lines" resulted in some cooperative scheduling by various owners and tended to stabilize rates (Mansfield 1899: 1: 185ff). A decade later, several lines dominated the steamboat business and managed most of the steamers then in service. Immigration had begun its boom with the opening of the Erie Canal in 1825, and by 1840 it brought tens of thousands of settlers to Buffalo each year, seeking passage to the American West. The total population of cities bordering the Upper Lakes was said to have quadrupled in the eight years previous to 1840 (Mansfield 1899: 1: 634) as a result of that influx. The Lakes steamers ranged from about 85 feet (150 tons) to nearly 185 feet (800 tons). The steamers *Illinois* (1837) and *Great Western* (1838) were the largest and finest of the steamboat fleet. ("Steamboat" on the Lakes invariably meant side-wheelers.)

While steamboats demonstrated many advantages over their sailing contemporaries, they could not navigate between the Upper Lakes and the Lower because of the bottleneck effect of the Welland Canal. Any steamer that was large enough to battle the elements and capacious enough to make a profit in the competition for cargoes was much too large for the 100-foot locks (Hatcher 1945: 121). Even after the canal was enlarged in 1845, it would only accommodate vessels 145 feet long and 26 feet wide. As a result of this impediment, all of the freight bound for Oswego, Toronto or Montreal was necessarily carried in schooners. It was in this setting that several Lake Ontario vessel owners began to experiment in 1840 and 1841 with a brand new steamboat technology that might enable them to compete more effectively with Buffalo for the trade of the West. They built the first "steam schooners," adopting the efficient new machinery recently developed by Swedish inventor John Ericsson (Barry 1973: 52) with screw propellers. The first screw-powered commercial craft in the United States was the 63-foot tow boat *Robert F. Stockton,* built in England in 1838 and sailed across the Atlantic in 1839 to serve on the Delaware and Raritan Canal (Baker and Tryckare 1965: 42). Although a small screw steamer called *Ericson* (Registry of Merchant Shipping, Montreal District, Book 175: 102) was built at Brockville, Canada, in 1840, the 138-ton *Vandalia* is usually credited with being the Lakes' first "propeller," as that class came to be known. It was built at Oswego, New York, in 1841, and was the first such craft in the Lakes above Niagara. Three other "propellers" were built that year in Canada, and two more on each side of Lake Ontario in 1842.

Contemporary newspaper accounts describe *Vandalia* as a sloop, and several other of the first propellers as "steam schooners." It is clear that they were all built as sailing craft, with boilers, engines and screw-propellers introduced after their completion, sometimes at ports quite distant from the shipyards where they were constructed (*Cobourg Star* May 4, 1842). It appears that the Ericsson wheels were intended to be the primary means of propulsion even in the first of these vessels, rather than an alternative to sail power or for use as auxiliaries. In the case of *Stockton,* the ship was sailed across the ocean without its propellers, and then fitted out to operate under steam only after arriving in the sheltered waters of the American canals. Despite the owners' evident confidence in the new technology, all of the early propellers carried sail rig, and indeed most of them were capable of sailing faster than the five to eight miles an hour they ran under steam (Finn 1979: 100), though at no predictable or consistent rate, because of their dependence on wind conditions.

Vandalia and its contemporaries on the Great Lakes were all built to carry passengers and freight, while the pioneer screw-powered craft built in England were, almost without exception, towing steamers (Baker 1965: 41ff). *Vandalia* was designed to trade through the Welland Ship Canal and to divert some of the lucrative Lake Michigan trade from Buffalo to Lake Ontario ports (Finn 1976: 96). It demonstrated that propellers could pass easily through the narrow locks, while side-wheelers could not. Thus the advent of the propellers was a turning point in the economic history of Lake Ontario and St. Lawrence River ports. The propellers helped diminish the Buffalo trade monopoly. When the St. Lawrence Canals were completed all the way to tidewater in 1847 and 1848, propellers could run all the way from Chicago to Montreal. Schooners could navigate the same route, of course, but they had to be towed upstream at great expense.

When the first propellers were built, the maritime industry of the Lakes was guardedly optimistic. The ships' owners and investors, on the other hand, expressed boundless confidence. The *Kingston Gazette & Chronicle* said of the propeller *London* in June 1842, "these vessels fitted with the Ericsson propellers...will form a new era in the history of navigation." The *Oswego Palladium* (Dec. 1, 1841) said of *Vandalia,* "We are firmly persuaded that this enterprise marks an epoch in the progress of the Western trade!" In fact, the propellers seem to have performed admirably, and the whole industry was quick to acknowledge their advantages over both sailing craft and side-wheel steamers.

The sailing craft of the Lakes fleet were all functionally general-cargo carriers. Whether they were sloops, schooners, brigs or barkentines, all carried whatever commodities were offered for trade. Their cargoes included passengers, livestock, bulk and package cargoes, or even such specialized payloads as small buildings, locomotives and rolling stock. Few of the ships were adapted for specific cargoes, although that would change to some small degree in the last days of the Age of Sail, when every effort would be made to compete for cargoes with the mushrooming numbers of steam freighters.

When side-wheelers were introduced to the commercial trades, they functioned largely as cargo carriers, although their particular suitability as passenger conveyances soon became obvious. Fast, comfortable and dependable transportation were prerequisites for the passenger trade, and it was also desirable for livestock and the more valuable package cargoes such as perishable foods, liquors, furniture, mail and precious metals like copper and silver ore. For this reason, side-wheel steamers

tended to carry certain cargoes more than others. With the exception of passengers, it was not so much because they were designed to accommodate those cargoes, but simply because they could move them expeditiously. The cargo spaces were generic, just as they were in schooners of the time. The advantages offered by a steamboat operator was fast, efficient and predictable delivery, but it was at considerable cost, because steamers were much more expensive to build and to operate than sailing ships.

Steamers usually cost several times as much as sailing ships, both in initial investment and operation. Propulsion machinery, in particular, was expensive. The steamer *Cleveland,* for instance, was built in 1837 for $22,500, but its machinery cost another $50,000 (*Detroit Daily Advertiser* Sept. 21, 1840). Because the engines and boilers were so costly, they were often used in more than one ship before they were discarded as scrap, sometimes serving in three or more different hulls before they were worn out and useless. A classic example was the engine of the steamer *Canada,* built in 1846, which was used afterward in the side-wheelers *Caspian* (1851), *E.K. Collins* (1853) and *North West* (1867). The engine was finally junked in 1876 after surviving several wrecks and fires (Heyl 1969: 106). Steamers also required cordwood for fuel, usually consuming two or three cords per hour at the cost of $80 to $125 per day (Mills 1910: 130). They employed larger crews than schooners did, as well. A large steamer required up to 40 in the crew, while the largest Great Lakes sailing craft, even with square rig, carried only 12. Because of the difference in resulting freight rates, steamers came to dominate the passenger trades and to carry selected cargoes, but other less valuable commodities were transported in the more numerous sailing craft, and predictably they took two or three times as long to reach their destinations, albeit at more modest costs.

Screw steamers or "propellers" served exactly the same purposes as did side-wheelers. They were built with the same general configuration as their paddle wheel predecessors, most frequently being double-deckers with main and spar deck and a passenger cabin on top. They carried their cargo between decks and in the hold beneath the main deck. Their 'tween-decks cargo space was served by a series of freight openings or gangways in the side of the ship, usually several to each side. The freight was carried in packages such as barrels, boxes, bags or bales, and it was referred to as "package freight." It was loaded by gangs of longshoremen using hand-trucks or dollies, brought aboard through the gangways and either stowed on deck or lowered into the hold through deck hatches, using overhead tackles or winches. "Bulk freight" like coal or grain was simply poured into the holds and removed by buckets. Loading was a very labor-intensive process, often involving dozens of dock workers under the supervision of the ship's officers. The process was similar in both side-wheelers and propellers.

Propellers were soon found to be very economical ships. They were much cheaper to build and outfit than side-wheelers. Their machinery was simpler and far less expensive. They also proved to be more economical to operate. They burned about one-fourth the fuel of steamboats (Mills 1910: 130), and required about half the crew. Moreover, a propeller could carry far more freight than a side-wheeler of comparable tonnage, because its machinery was so much more compact. The engines and boilers in a side-wheel steamer had to be located nearly amidships, where they often occupied a major portion of the hull. Propeller engines and boilers were placed far in the stern where they displaced little cargo and occupied much less space (Mills 1910: 129). All of these factors made it possible for propellers to offer freight rates somewhere between those of sailing craft and side-wheelers, and this meant that propellers could compete for much of the less valuable cargo that had previously been carried economically only in sailing ships. Not long after their introduction, propellers began to gather contracts for larger and larger proportions of the flour, grain and provisions shipped down the Lakes.

The number of propellers on the Lakes grew rapidly as the vessels demonstrated their strengths as efficient, economical carriers. Several companies organized around 1850 to carry freight in connection with the Erie Canal or with the various railroads running to the eastern end of the Lakes from the coast. Among the new firms were the American, Lake, Western and Northern Transportation companies, the New York and Erie Railroad Line and others. Each of these companies built fleets of screw steamers. Between 1840 and 1849, 81 propellers were built at Lakes shipyards; during the next 10 years 133 more were added; and during the 1860s another 88 were built, not including screw tugs (Labadie 1981). The journalists in 1841 and 1842 had correctly predicted that propellers would revolutionize the carrying trades.

Screw towboats or "tugs" appeared on the Lakes shortly after the first propellers. In fact, the first screw steamer in the nation was built for towing and not for cargo at all, and it is not surprising that the type was readily adopted on the Inland Seas as well. The first screw steamer on the Lakes known to have been built for towing was the 111-ton *Clifton,* built at Dexter, New York, in 1847.

Several suspiciously small screw steamers were registered at St. Lawrence River ports in 1843 and 1844, and since side-wheel tugs were known to be employed in the same district, there was a demonstrated need for towing craft. Buffalo newspapers indicate that several side-wheelers were in use as towboats on the Niagara River and the Erie Canal by the mid-'40s, too. There can be little doubt that there was a tremendous demand for towing vessels, and literally hundreds of them were built during the next decades. At least two screw tugs were built before 1850, more than a hundred during the '50s, and nearly 400 in the '60s (Labadie 1981). They were the first diversions from the passenger and freight style of screw steamer on the Lakes. In later years, other types of tugs were also introduced for specialized uses. When the trade in lumber grew after the Civil War, log rafts were often floated long distances to lumber mills; rafting or "outside" tugs were developed at that time. Unlike the common "inside" (harbor) tugs, the raft tugs were large double-deckers with very powerful engines. Their bows were enclosed or "housed-in" in order to operate safely on the open Lakes. Some of these rugged craft measured

160 feet in length, although 120 feet was average. "Inside" tugs were usually 60 to 80 feet long.

Within a few years of the introduction of the propellers, the first all-freight screw steamer was built. It was the 250-ton *Sampson,* built in 1843, a 135-foot craft with the capacity for 300 tons of cargo. It carried package freight or livestock and was the forerunner of the "package freighters." Package freighters were screw steamers with double decks and gangways just like propellers, but without passenger cabins on the spar decks. Because there was so little difference between the two types, many ships were changed from package boats to propellers or vice versa by the addition or removal of cabins. Changes of this nature were common during the days of wooden ships, when cabins could be added or dismantled at modest cost as changes in the market required, or deterioration of the ship dictated. This was most common during the 1860s and 1870s. As the tide of immigration and settlement slowed in the region, the proportion of passenger-carrying propellers dwindled and more of the propeller-type vessels were simply built without cabins. During the 1840s there were 79 propellers built and only two package freighters. In the '60s there were 72 propellers and 16 package freighters. In the '70s there were 56 propellers and 31 package-boats built. After 1880, few passenger and freight propellers were built, although more package freighters were added until after the turn of the century. The propellers were largely supplanted by cruise ships and excursion boats.

Screw steamers in general, including package freighters, propellers and later variants, tended to grow in size much like sailing craft. All were influenced by the same factors. The largest ships would carry their cargo at the cheapest rates, but their growth was limited by canal systems, shallow connecting channels and shipbuilding technology, all of which improved as time passed. *Vandalia* and its running mates were less than 100 feet long, having been built for the first Welland Canal. After 1845, virtually no propellers were built less than 140 feet in length, because the Welland had been enlarged and improved with 150-foot locks. Most of the propellers built during and after the 1850s were not required to pass through the Welland at all, and so many of them were built larger than 150 feet. Despite the canals, the average size of new propellers grew from 141 feet (337 tons) in 1845 to 182 feet (641 tons) in 1862, and to 220 feet (1,300 tons) in 1877 (Labadie 1981). Because the Welland system was not enlarged again until 1884, it can be inferred that this progression reflects the fact that most of the latter day propellers and package freighters were "Upper Lakes" craft that operated above Lake Ontario; i.e. from Buffalo to Lake Michigan or Lake Superior ports. Relatively few ran through the Welland to ports further east. When the locks were enlarged in 1884, the typical 220-footers could navigate all the way through the St. Lawrence River to Montreal and the seaboard.

Wooden screw steamers, like side-wheelers, required extraordinary means of strengthening their hulls as their dimensions grew beyond 150 feet; when their lengths surpassed that figure it was necessary to add to the hull structure some form of a truss to provide longitudinal strength and rigidity. The technology was borrowed from the side-wheelers of the Hudson River, and arches, trusses or hogging chains were built into the fabric of the propellers. The most common form of strengthening propellers became the "Bishop arch" or crown arch, a simple curved arch extending from the deadwood at the stern to a point high over the rail amidships and then back down to the deadwood at the bow (for an example see Figure 14, Chapter IV). The chord or arch was supported by a series of parallel, vertical stanchions that were tied into the vertical frames of the ships on each side. These powerful structural elements towered over the cabins in many propellers and package boats, and they were the hallmark of Lakes craft for many years. Such structures were not necessary in ocean vessels because of their deeper, more rigid hulls. The few wooden propellers which were built on the Lakes after 1880 often employed internal arches of iron in their construction, so they were able to eliminate the distinctive external arches, and many earlier propellers that were fitted with arches eventually had them cut down or truncated by using iron or steel straps along the sheer strake or rail to replace the arch. An example of various types of structural support systems see the discussion of *Cumberland*, *Chisholm* and *Monarch* in Chapter V.

With the Civil War years came the beginning of a shift in the commerce of the Great Lakes. Railroads had penetrated into the West, cutting into the lucrative package-freight business. There were still enormous quantities of foodstuffs and manufactured goods to be transported by ships, but less and less was the profitable package cargo, and more and more each decade was bulk material such as salt, grain, coal or lumber, all of which generated smaller profits for vessel operators. The Civil War years were "flush times." They marked the slow, steady recovery from the terrible effects of the 1857 Panic, but they went far beyond recovery to a real boom like that of the late 1840s. Immigrants and pensioned-off Union veterans swarmed into Minnesota and the Dakotas and began tilling the rich Red River Valley soil. Immense quantities of grain began to flow from the West across the Lakes and into the East. Enormous markets for building materials were generated by Reconstruction in the South. Coal was delivered to Lake Michigan and Lake Superior docks for distribution by rail to a great Western hinterland. Demands for lumber could scarcely be met despite prodigious output from the Saginaw Valley in Michigan, and hundreds of Lakes craft turned to that trade. For several seasons, not enough ships could be found to meet the demand. The *Detroit Free Press* (March 31, 1864) observed, "The class of vessels most earnestly sought are those best adapted for the lumber trade. Nearly all our spare vessels in this locality have been disposed of, and...a dozen more would meet with ready sale."

Because of the weakening traffic in package goods, many propellers and package freighters were idle, and so they turned to the bulky unremunerative lumber cargoes, but their profits were small because few of the ships were really suited for that commodity.

One prominent vessel owner found a practical solution for the scarcity of lumber carriers. He purchased two of the great passenger side-wheelers which had been retired at the time of the 1857 Panic a few years earlier. Several of the craft were idle and rotting in Buffalo and Cleveland, and they were offered for sale at a fraction of their original value. He dismantled them and made barges of them, employing powerful tugs to tow the mammoth barges to the Saginaw River to load pine lumber. Each of the craft was found to have enormous capacity, up to five times that of contemporary propellers. By towing two or more of the barges, the operator found a cheap means to move the bulky cargo to market, and make the lumber trade profitable for the first time (Mansfield 1899: 1: 414). This was the start of what was known as the "consort system," which revolutionized the carriage of bulk cargo on the Lakes. The system was employed in all of the bulk trades until the turn of the century, and it resulted in sharp decreases in shipping costs not only for lumber, but for every other bulk commodity as well.

Between 1861 and 1870, dozens of superannuated passenger craft were made into lumber barges, and other ships were built from the keel up as barges. In addition, a new class of steamers appeared. These new vessels were screw steamers with schooner-built wooden hulls. They were built without enclosed freight decks, but rather were single-decked with small, compact cabins at the stern. This pattern was said to have been introduced in 1848 in a little screw steamer called *Petrel*, which was built to haul lumber (*Detroit Free Press* May 13, 1873), but there was too little demand for lumber then, and the ship was not profitable. "Steambarges" were introduced again in 1865 with the construction of the 115-foot *Trader* in Marine City on the St. Clair River, and they were an immediate success this time, partly because of the newly adopted consort system. The *Detroit Free Press* (June 26, 1866) commented: "A new arrangement is being inaugurated for the transportation of lumber, consisting of the use of propellers especially adapted for the purpose. They have no upper works forward of the engine room, which gives space for additional cargo. Several are now running."

These efficient little ships were designed to tow barges, but also to carry lumber themselves. Every effort was made to maximize the capacity for lumber, and because the vessels were patterned after their consort barges, they were known as "steambarges."

A handful of small side-wheel-powered lumber steamers was built in the mid-'60s to carry cordwood and lumber in shallow rivers tributary to the Lakes. At least 15 or 20 were built around Toledo and Sandusky, or at Detroit, Port Huron or Saginaw. It was not until the first screw-powered steambarges were constructed, however, that lumber steamers were really adapted to towing barges and to operating on the exposed waters of the open Lakes. These vessels moved very slowly when towing a string of loaded barges, often no more than five or six miles an hour, and they were susceptible to heavy weather damage. Side-wheel steambarges, as a result, proved impractical except for the sheltered waters of rivers and bays.

The typical steambarge measured 145 feet in length and carried about 350,000 feet of lumber, although ships of that class ranged from 80 or 90 feet to fully 200, and some hauled more than a million board feet. All steambarges were single-decked craft like their schooner forebears. Most had raised poopdecks. The earliest steambarges had their pilothouses aft, but after

1880 most carried them on a raised forecastle with a well-deck between bow and stern. Most steambarges were fitted with a tall mast near the bow where they usually spread a single gaff-rigged sail and a jib. The larger boats built after 1880 often had two or even three masts, and because they carried working sails, most had centerboards (another link to their schooner-rigged cousins). A prominent structural feature of the early steam-barges was the hogging arch, that same bridge-like truss used in larger Lakes propellers that towered high above the rails at either side. Because the steambarges were smaller vessels with a lower silhouette, the arches appeared larger than they did on the passenger and freight propellers, looking all out of proportion to the small steamers. Some builders substituted hogging-chains or iron rods with a single Sampson-post near the after end, but it was not until internal bracing was perfected around 1880 that the steambarges could dispense with some sort of very visible external reinforcing. In the older steambarges the arches so complicated the loading of lumber that dock gangs were paid a premium to load them.

Steambarges, some of which were called "lumber hookers" or "rabbits," carried their lumber cargoes in the hold and stacked high on deck. Some carried square timber or logs as well as "deals" (cut lumber), shingles, cedar posts or railroad ties. The cargo was usually piled on deck to heights of 12 or 14 feet, and the consort barges carried similar loads. Most tows consisted of three or four barges, but some of the more powerful steambarges were known to tow up to eight or nine at a time. *Antelope,* a former passenger and freight propeller, regularly towed eight loaded barges extending more than a mile from the steamer to the last of its consorts (Mansfield 1899: 1: 517). Like most of its contemporaries, *Antelope* traded from Saginaw Valley ports all the way to Buffalo and Tonawanda, New York. The huge lumber cargoes were all loaded and unloaded entirely by hand.

The consort system and the steambarges caught on very quickly. Forty-five were built before 1870, and a number of passenger and freight propellers were also converted for the same use when their cabins were removed and their spar decks cut down to accommodate lumber. More than 20 were rebuilt in this way by 1870, and dozens more were made lumber steamers in the next decade. Nearly 600 steambarges are esti-mated to have been built during the 30 years between 1870 and 1900 (Labadie 1982). The lumber business moved to the Pacif-ic Coast around 1905, and the use of steambarges on the Lakes declined sharply after that. Some were employed carrying salt, coal, sand, iron ore and some lumber for a few years more.

The practicality of the consort system was not strictly limited to the lumber trade. Some of the first steambarges were occa-sionally used to haul grain and ore cargoes when the rates were right. The little steamers and their barges were not entirely suited for these cargoes, but what they lacked in capacity they made up for in efficiency. They ordinarily had too little capacity below deck and were usually fitted with rather small deck hatches. Iron ore and grain had to be kept dry during transportation, and so had to be carried below deck where the cargo could be entirely enclosed and protected from the elements. Both ore and grain

were loaded by the gravity system, and in vessels with small hatches it was necessary to do a great deal of costly trimming of the cargo, redistributing it in the hold so that the ship rode on an even keel. Small hatches also made unloading difficult.

Capt. Elihu M. Peck of Cleveland devised a ship in 1869 that would meet all of the demands of the ore and grain trades. It was to be double-decked, with plenty of space below decks for dry bulk cargo, fitted with wide hatches evenly spaced to match the 24-foot spacing of the loading chutes at Marquette's ore docks. It would have the capacity for 1,200 tons of ore and be provided with engines powerful enough to tow one or two barges as large as the steamer. The result was the 210-foot bulk freighter *R.J. Hackett* (True 1956: 3). Bulk freighters had their pilothouses far forward to improve visibility, and their machin-ery, like that of steambarges, was placed in the stern. They usu-ally had three or four tall masts with sails to steady them and help power them. This practice of carrying sails was abandoned around 1890 because of improvements in steam engines, and the construction of bridges in many of the Lake Erie harbors made tall spars impractical.

Bulk freighters were profitable because they carried large quantities of bulk commodities economically. For this reason, few bulk freighters measured less than 200 feet in length, even when the type was first introduced. They were only competi-tive if they were large, and so they have always been built as large as technology and sailing conditions would allow. The construction of these long, narrow shoal-draft steamers was characterized by very heavy longitudinal framing. Huge oak keelsons, parallel to the ships' centerline keels, were laid on top of the floor timbers, which were the lower portion of the transverse frames in the ships' bottoms. These keelsons, termed side or floor keelsons, usually measured from 12 to 18 inches square and ran the length of the bottoms of the vessels, spaced at intervals of about three feet. No other Lakes vessel type used these long, heavy members (True 1956: 30). In addition to the rugged keelsons, the wooden bulk freighters were reinforced with iron straps that criss-crossed the frames every four feet, and a heavy band of 3/4-inch iron ran the length of the ship just under the rail as well (see discussion of *Chisholm* in Chapter V for an example of this reinforcing system). Little of this strengthening would have been required in a deeper ocean-going hull, but Lakes channels have always kept hull depth to a minimum. Ocean ships of the same era seldom required extraordinary reinforcing because their hulls were much deeper in proportion to their lengths.

From the time *R.J. Hackett* was christened in 1869 until shipbuilding was suspended in the 1873 Panic, 47 bulk freight-ers were constructed averaging a little more than 1,000 gross tons. *V.H. Ketchum,* built in 1874, was 1,661 gross tons and the largest in the fleet. When vessel construction resumed again in 1880, still larger bulk freighters were launched: 170 of them were built during the 1880s alone, and almost without excep-tion, each had at least one consort barge built to run with it, usually of similar tonnage and dimension. The typical bulk freighter built in 1890 was 2,200 gross tons and averaged 260 feet in length. The growth in vessel size was made possible in this case not so much because of shipbuilding technique as improvements in connecting channels such as the St. Marys River, the St. Clair Flats and the Detroit River. Greater depths made it possible to build longer, larger ships.

The next significant event in the evolution of the bulk freighters was the introduction of iron and steel to shipbuilding. Iron ships had been built in Scotland and England since before 1800 (Morrison 1945: 2). Several iron vessels were built in the United Kingdom during the 1850s and 1860s for Canadian owners on the St. Lawrence River and Lake Ontario. The iron steamers *Abert* and *Michigan* were built for the American government on the Lakes in 1843, and the 200-foot iron propeller *Merchant* was built at Buffalo in 1862, the first commercial craft of iron built entirely on the Great Lakes. After the Civil War, some iron-hulled blockade runners, for example *Southern Belle* (*Rothesay Castle*) and *Chicora,* both side-wheelers of more than 200-feet in length, were brought into the Lakes. During the 1870s, several propellers and package freighters of iron were built at Buffalo, and all were highly successful craft, most with long, profitable careers (Barry 1973: 110).

The first bulk freighter built of iron was the "monster" steamer *Onoko*, a 287-foot giant, almost 30 feet longer than the largest wooden craft then afloat. It was built by the Globe Iron Works at Cleveland, and was a sensation. It had double bottoms with water-ballast tanks, and was designed to carry 3,000 tons of ore on a 14-foot draft. It was said that *Onoko* made money when few other craft in the industry could generate profits, averaging from $25,000 to $40,000 annually *(Detroit Free Press* Nov. 23, 1898). For nearly 10 years, *Onoko* carried the biggest cargoes on the Lakes.

The principal advantage in the use of metals for shipbuilding is their very high ratio of strength to weight. A 200-foot wooden ship required an oaken hull more than 18 inches thick, while a similar craft of iron had shell-plating no more than 1/2 inch thick and roughly one-tenth as heavy. Iron ships drew so little water that they had to carry ballast to keep their propellers below the surface when they were without cargo. Double bottoms and water ballast systems were developed to satisfy that need and to provide for safety in case the outer shell was punctured. Indications are that water ballast systems were developed on English colliers. Iron and later, steel ships had much greater longitudinal strength than their wooden counterparts, and that made it possible to build larger hulls. Although iron and steel shipbuilding plants required specialized equipment, it was also cheaper to build hulls of metal than of wood, and repairs were far simpler. Some shipbuilders persisted in the use of wood until the turn of the century. The famous Davidson and Wheeler yards at West Bay City, Michigan, built several wooden bulk freighters more than 300 feet long before they finally succumbed to progress and abandoned wood in 1902.

Several iron freighters were built in the 1880s, but steel was introduced in 1886 with the construction of the steamer *Spokane,* and it was almost universally adopted thereafter. Steel proved stronger and more flexible than iron, although not as resistant to oxidation. Some of the iron ships built on the Lakes were still in service a century after their construction. The fa-

mous gunboat USS *Michigan* lasted for 104 years, and then was broken up for scrap, the hull still in sound shape.

Between 1869 and 1902 when the last were built, the largest wooden bulk freighters went from 210 to 310 feet. Steel freighters grew much more quickly, from the 287-foot *Onoko* in 1882 to the 400-foot *Victory* in 1894, the 500-foot *John W. Gates* in 1900 and to 600-footers by 1906 (True 1956: 27). In steel freighters, the growth in size was not simply a process of enlarging the component parts of the ship, but resulted from several improvements in technology and changes in the arrangement of the vessels' framing. The earliest iron and steel ships had transverse frames patterned after wooden ships, but spaced at wider intervals. The arrangement of longitudinal keelsons was also similar to wooden bulk freighters in that the latter members were laid on top of the crosswise frames in the ships' bottoms (True 1956: 31). Later steel hulls had combinations of transverse and longitudinal framing, and the standard after about 1920 has become a system of longitudinal framing on the deck and bottom, with transverse framing on the sides and ballast tanks extending well up the sides. This system, with its particular emphasis on longitudinal strength, has made possible recent construction of 800- and 1,000-foot superfreighters.

The consort system was largely abandoned after 1900, because the ships grew too large to tow barges safely, and they could carry sufficient cargo to dispense with the added capacity of a barge. The last barges still in service were not used after 1950. The consort system lasted for almost 100 years.

While bulk freighters became more numerous in the 1880s and 1890s, several other vessel types dwindled in numbers and eventually disappeared. Sailing craft were entirely displaced by steamers, except in the lumber trade where they found a niche in later years as tow barges, with their tophampers cut away and their graceful bowsprits cut short. There were 1,699 sailing craft on the Lakes in 1870 (Mansfield 1899: 1: 439). After that date, sail craft began a slow decline, and relatively few were built to sustain their numbers after 1880 (see Figure 12 Chapter II). In 1900, there were still 1,068 left (*Blue Book of American Shipping* 1900), many in the form of unrigged consort barges, and still others that had been idle for years. The last full-rigged schooner ended its career in 1933 with the burning of the 60-year-old *Lyman M. Davis* in Toronto Harbor. The last schooner-barges were laid up and abandoned at the time of the Great Depression.

Steambarges lasted only as long as the lumber trade on the Lakes. When the forests had been stripped away in Michigan, Wisconsin and Minnesota and the supply of lumber was gone, the industry moved to Washington and Oregon. Some of the lumber steamers also went to the West Coast to serve the industry there, but most were simply abandoned and dismantled. Their design was too specialized and their capacity too limited to make them suitable for any use but the lumber trade. By 1930 only a handful of steambarges remained, carrying coal or sand and gravel, or converted for dredging. Virtually none survived the Depression years except as moldering curiosities in a score of ship boneyards.

The development of side-wheel steamers was largely

stemmed by the rapid ascendancy of screw steamers in the various Lakes trades, and although they remained popular in the passenger business for many decades, there would never again be the great numbers of side-wheelers built that there were in the 1830s and 1840s. Side-wheelers reached their zenith with the construction of the 300-foot "palace steamers" between 1848 and 1856. Twenty-two of the elegant craft were built, but their heyday was short-lived because of the 1853 Panic. Side-wheelers made something of a comeback following the Civil War, after which time the greatest concentrations of their numbers centered on Lake Erie and Lake Michigan, where the Detroit and Cleveland Steam Navigation Company, the Goodrich and Graham and Morton fleets employed many of their finest examples. A few paddle wheel giants were constructed on the Lakes after 1900, including the largest side-wheelers ever built: *Seeandbee* in 1913 was 485 feet long, and the twin steamers *Greater Detroit* and *Greater Buffalo* in 1924 were 520-footers. The latter vessels were the last of their type. At the time they entered service, only 37 other side-wheelers were still left (*International Shipmasters Association Directory* 1925: 170-181). After 1950, none were still in use.

Passenger and freight propellers, like their package-freight stepdaughters, were most successful when they were coupled with the railroad systems stretching to the East and West from the Lakes states. After 1880, relatively few large propellers were built, and those were principally for local routes rather than the system-wide Buffalo-to-Chicago or Buffalo-to-Duluth services typical in earlier days. Some of the new propellers constructed after 1890 were exclusively passenger craft, with diminished freight capacity or no cargo space at all. A large proportion of the last propellers were "day boats," excursion steamers with neither overnight accommodations nor cargo space. Excursion vessels and ferries are very old types, and in the end, they outlasted all of the other passenger vessel types. A dozen passenger propellers survived the opening of America's highway networks in the 1930s, but the last of them succumbed to the economic pressures and regulatory requirements to lay up in the mid-'60s. The Georgian Bay Line steamer *South American* was the last active representative of its type. She retired at the end of the 1967 season. Many consider the NPS vessel *Ranger III,* which regularly runs between Houghton and Isle Royale, the last package freighter on the Lakes.

Package freighters numbered 116 in 1890, which was probably their peak; much package cargo was also carried in passenger and freight propellers, of course. The tonnage of package freight carried in Lakes craft, however, was reduced as the nation's railroads were extended, and the number of package boats and propellers shrunk in direct proportion. In 1900 there were 90 package freighters (*Inland Lloyds Vessel Register* 1890). In 1915, anti-trust legislation forced the disposal of most of the package freighters by the railroads, which were their operators; many of them never saw service on the Lakes again. Most of those which were left in service were requisitioned for coastal service during World War II, so that virtually no U.S. package freighters remained on the Lakes after 1940. A couple of Canadian fleets ran package boats until 1980 in specialty trades such as rolled newsprint or barreled chemicals. Finally, in 1982, Canada Steamship Lines announced that it would discontinue service with its last five package freighters (*Log Chips* 10 #18). It was the end of a colorful era. At this writing, only the bulk freighters have survived in service on the Lakes. The only representatives of the many vessels that once plied the Great Lakes are the shipwrecks that lie beneath their surfaces.

Table 3 – Comparison of Ten Steam Vessel Wrecks: Isle Royale National Park

Vessel/Dates	Point of Origin	Destination	Cargo	Propulsion/ Construction	Wreck Location
Cumberland (1871-1877)	Prince Arthur's Landing, Port Arthur, Ontario	Duluth, Minnesota	Passengers	Side-Wheeler/Wood	SW end Rock of Ages Reef
Chisholm (1880-1898)	Duluth, Minnesota	Buffalo, New York	Barley	Single Screw/Wood	SW end Rock of Ages Reef
Algoma (1883-1885)	Owen Sound, Ontario	Port Arthur, Ontario	Passengers	Single Screw/Steel	South Side Greenstone Island
Monarch (1890-1906)	Port Arthur, Ontario	Sarnia, Ontario	Grain, canned salmon, flour	Single Screw/Wood	NE tip Pallisades
Glenlyon (1893-1924)	Ft. William, Ontario	Pt. Colborne, Ontario	Wheat	Single Screw/Steel	South Side Menagerie Island
America (1898-1928)	Duluth, Minnesota	North Shore Route Fort William	Package freight and passengers	Single Screw/Steel	SE end North Gap
Cox (1901-1933)	Houghton, Michigan	Ft.William, Ontario	Passengers	Single Screw/Steel	SE end Rock of Ages
Congdon (1907-1918)	Ft. William, Ontario	Pt. McNicholl, Ontario	Wheat	Single Screw/Steel	NE end Congdon Shoal
Emperor (1910-1947)	Port Arthur, Ontario	Ashtabula, Ohio	Iron ore	Single Screw/Steel	NE end Canoe Rocks
Kamloops (1924-1927)	Sault Ste. Marie, Ontario	Port Arthur, Ontario	Package freight	Single Screw/Steel	North side Kamloops Pt.

Chapter IV

Shipwrecks of
Isle Royale:
The Historical Record

This chapter is a presentation of the results of a search of primary archival and secondary sources into the background history of the shipwrecks of Isle Royale. The site locations have become common knowledge to the diving public, and they are the focus of the Park's submerged cultural resources management activities.

Ten total vessel losses, in addition to the *Dunelm* stranding incident, have all left material residues in the archeological record that are discussed in detail in Chapter V of this report. Following are the contemporary notions of what transpired before and after the wreck event, a historical backdrop intended to complement the archeological investigations. The order of presentation is chronological according to year of construction.

History written for archeological purposes is somewhat different than normally encountered in popular periodicals or historical monographs. The attempt here is to use the historical record as one of several major links in an evidence chain that leads to an understanding of why certain material residues appear as they do in the archeological record. The most appropriate analogy would be to a medical examiner at a crime scene. That person may ask questions of witnesses or read their depositions, but always with the end in mind of understanding why there is a body on the living room floor.

The authors of this section were instructed to seek facts relevant to the birth (construction), life (operational history) and death (wreck event) of the victims (shipwrecks) at Isle Royale. The degree to which this could be done through direct quotes from the contemporary accounts was encouraged. Although no particular effort is made to be entertaining, much in the way of new information on the ships is included that might help establish vessel significance, historical context or eventually be of use for park interpreters. The "post-mortem," or archeological record section of the report, benefits much from this sort of approach, but the reader should be prepared for what may be viewed as a comparatively dry approach, rather than an attempt at telling a lively historical tale.

The amount of text devoted to each wreck is widely variable. This is somewhat a function of the disparity in what is available in the archives, but also reflects a conscious decision-making process. Ships that bare a special relationship to Isle Royale, such as *America*, or ships whose wreck events left many questions to be answered, such as *Kamloops*, are discussed in greater detail than others. In addition, aspects of a wreck event or its aftermath that had implications for the general socioeconomic processes of the region are also stressed.

Cumberland: History

Construction

The side-wheeler *Cumberland* was built in 1871 at Port Robinson, Ontario, by Melanchthon Simpson for Charles Perry and Co. It was launched Wednesday August 9, 1871 (*Detroit Telegram* Aug. 15, 1871). The vessel was named for Fred W. Cumberland, general manager of the Northern Railway, parent company of the Toronto and Lake Superior Navigation Company, which had the ship designed and built to run the Duluth and Collingwood or Owen Sound route.

The railroad men who formed the navigation company were pioneers in the Lake Superior trade prior to the construction of the railroads in the area. The towns of Collingwood, and later Owen Sound and Midland, were the main points of rail connection between train and Lake boat. The Lake Superior ports were all served by Lakes vessels at the time of formation of the new navigation company. *Cumberland*, along with *Algoma* (previously named *City of Toronto* and *Racine*) were the core of the new enterprise, which incorporated connections between the railroad and steamship line. Later, *Chicora* would join the line (Williams 1909: 43-47).

Cumberland was a typical example of the Great Lakes sidewheel steamers built from the late 1840s through the 1880s. The first of the 200-foot steamers appeared on the Lakes in the early 1840s, and by the next decade had assumed the classic configuration as represented by *Cumberland* and the dozens of other steamers produced for the passenger and package trade on the Lakes.

Figure 13. Side-wheel steamer *Cumberland*, built for the elegant passenger and package trade. The lack of visible hull support structures is evident in this photograph. U.S. Army Corps of Engineers Canal Park Marine Museum Collection.

Ships of *Cumberland*'s type had overhanging guards the full length of the hull and freight space on the main deck. Usually, there were one or two cabin decks above the main deck. The number and size of accommodations are, as other details of construction, uncertain for *Cumberland*. A steamer of comparable size would likely have about 60 cabins, plus parlors. The ladies' cabin would normally be aft, steerage and crew accommodations below (Labadie personal communication).

The ship was powered by a vertical "walking-beam" engine with one boiler and a single stack. No description of the boiler has been located in the historical material reviewed. The engines for the new ship had been in service before. Originally the 44-inch diameter engine, with a 132-inch (11-foot) stroke, was placed aboard *Cataract* (*Detroit Free Press* May 11, 1871). U.S. *Cataract* became the Canadian steamer *Columbia* before it was broken up and the engine transferred to *Cumberland*. Information contained in the Lytle-Holdcamper List (Mitchell and Hall 1975: 31) states that *Cataract* was 577 gross tons, built in Ogdensburg, New York, in 1846 and sold foreign (Canadian) in 1867. The list also erroneously indicates that *Cataract* was a screw steamer.

Cumberland was reported to be 208 feet on the keel and 214 feet overall with a beam of 28 feet, 43 feet 8 inches overall. The draft was 10 feet 6 inches, and it was 229 tons burden, 750 tons gross measurement. The engine was rated at 400 horsepower (*Detroit Free Press* Oct. 1, 1871). The ship had a round

fantail stern, and its cabins were warmed by steam. The steamer had paddle wheels 30 feet in diameter (*Ibid.* Oct. 4, 1871).

Operational History

The *Collingwood Bulletin* (May 9, 1872) reported that:

the splendid new steamer *Cumberland* will leave on her first trip to Fort William next Friday. She has been fitted up in the most elegant style, and under the command of Captain Orr will meet the highest expectations of the travelling public.

Cumberland's first full season of navigation was 1872, a year that initiated a series of incidents that were to afflict the steamer throughout its relatively short history of operation. *Cumberland* carried about 600 passengers and a heavy load of freight, horses and cattle on its first 1872 trip (*Toronto Mail* May 11, 1872; *Meaford Monitor* May 16, 1872).

Cumberland provided assistance to the steamer *Manitoba* in July. The two steamers had been built at the same time in Port Robinson for competing owners (*Detroit Free Press* March 21, 1871). *Manitoba* had run aground on Michipicoten Island in heavy fog. The ship had been in that position for nearly 24 hours when it was spotted by the crew of *Cumberland*. It took nearly 30 hours more before the grounded steamer was again afloat (*Meaford Monitor* July 25, 1872).

September 1872 was a stormy month, and some vessels were

lost. The schooner *Maple Leaf* was swamped near Isle Royale and eventually capsized in rough weather. The captain and crew were able to abandon ship and were taken to Silver Islet. During the wreck, the captain reported he had sighted *Cumberland*, but it was not able to render assistance due to the heavy seas (*Meaford Monitor* Oct. 17, 1872).

In November 1872, *Cumberland* was frozen in the ice in Bear Lake in the St. Marys River. Captain Orr, the chief engineer and four of the crew arrived on foot in Collingwood on December 27. Several days after them, 18 of the crew arrived after making the 20-day trek down the north shore of Georgian Bay. According to their reports, they suffered terrible weather and privation on their journey; all were frostbitten. Captain Orr had left *Cumberland* in the charge of the first mate, with the steward, stewardess and two waiters left on board (*Toronto Mail* Dec. 27, 28, 1872; *Marquette Daily Mining Journal* January 4, 1873). There were also 50 passengers aboard (*Toronto Mail* Dec. 11, 1872).

The details of how *Cumberland* was extracted from the ice or how those remaining onboard were rescued have not been located. This suggests it apparently wintered in the ice. It is known *Cumberland* was the first boat of the 1873 season to arrive in Collingwood, although there was still much ice present (*Meaford Monitor* May 8, 1873). The 1873 season was apparently without serious incident.

In early November 1874, nearly on the anniversary of being frozen in the ice, *Cumberland* was caught in a storm between Sault Ste. Marie and Prince Arthur's Landing (renamed Port Arthur in 1884) and very nearly wrecked. *Cumberland* may have been near Passage Island when it was caught (*Meaford Monitor* Nov. 10, 1874).

The caulking came out of the hold planks in several places and the ship began leaking badly. To keep from sinking, either 75 (*Duluth Minnesotian* Nov. 7, 1874) or 150 (*Ashland Press* Nov. 14, 1874) head of cattle and some freight were thrown overboard. It was reported that $3,000 worth of cattle, sheep and hogs belonging to Brown Bros. and all the deck cargo were dumped overboard (*Meaford Monitor* Nov. 10, 1874). *Cumberland* arrived at Prince Arthur's Landing, with six feet of water in the hold, and promptly sank (*Duluth Minnesotian* Nov. 7, 1874; *Ashland Press* Nov. 14, 1874).

The November 1875 newspapers reported that *Cumberland* was ashore and scuttled. The vessel was again caught in a late season storm and went ashore three miles from Silver Islet at Lee or Tee Harbour in a blinding snowstorm, with gale-force winds from the east (*The Daily Globe* Nov. 3, 1875; *Cleveland Herald* Nov. 5, 1875). There was little damage, and the steamer, with passengers and freight intact, arrived in Thunder Bay November 4 after being pulled free by tugs (*Cleveland Herald* Nov. 8, 1875; *The Daily Globe* Nov. 5, 1875). The freight carried by *Cumberland* included "copper ore, fish and 14 span of horses and about 100 passengers" (*Chicago Inter Ocean* Nov. 8, 1875).

On Sept. 15, 1876, *Cumberland* ran aground at Owen Sound. While trying to get the vessel off by using a line wrapped on the shaft of the wheel, Capt. Orr was injured. The line snapped and broke both of the captain's legs. Captain Parsons took the command for the trip (*Duluth Minnesotian* Sept. 23, 1876).

Some of the marine notes of the *Duluth Minnesotian* of 1876 give insight into the nature of the cargo and passengers carried by *Cumberland* this season.

June 27, 1876: Arrived Duluth with 231 Mennonite emigrants and 10 other passengers.

June 27: Cleared Duluth, cargo for Collingwood: 4 boxes of personal effects, 1 mower, 22 boxes of merchandise.

July 10: Arrived Duluth. Cargo: 25 passengers, 17 packages household goods.

July 10: Cleared Duluth Light.

Aug. 7: Arrived Duluth. Cargo: 2 cabin passengers, 400 Icelandic emigrants and baggage, 2 cases furniture, all in transit to Manitoba.

Aug. 7: Cleared Duluth. Cargo: 1 case hardware, 1 bale robes.

Wreck Event

Cumberland was delayed for three days while en route to Prince Arthur's Landing. The vessel had been grounded on a bar in Nipigon Harbour (*Thunder Bay Sentinel* July 26, 1877), arriving in Prince Arthur's on Tuesday (July 24). The ship probably cleared port the same day, as was its practice.

Cumberland started taking on water, and its passengers were transferred to an upbound American boat she met. Later, on the 25th, *Cumberland* struck Rock of Ages reef (*Thunder Bay Sentinel* July 26, 1877). The day was mild

Figure 14. Side-wheel steamer *Western World*, a larger vessel than *Cumberland*, built in 1854, shows a typical arched truss hull-support system to give longitudinal strength to the hull. U.S. Army Corps of Engineers Canal Park Marine Museum Collection.

when *Cumberland* struck. The weather was dry and clear, with a light southwest to south-southwest breeze blowing (*Menagerie Isle Light Station Log* July 23, 24, 1877).

Cumberland struck the reef going at a speed sufficient to push its bow solidly aground. It was reported that all the forward half of the vessel was on the reef. Several tugs and steamers unsuccessfully attempted to pull it off. It was also reported that had *Cumberland* run 100 feet to either side, it would have missed the reef (*Duluth Minnesotian* Aug. 4, 1877). The steamers *Quebec* and *Francis Smith* worked on the stranded ship. These steamers parted all their lines in the unsuccessful attempt to remove the side-wheeler. *Cumberland* was reported in bad shape, "lying 18 inches out amidships" (*Chicago Inter Ocean* July 30, 1877). Some of the freight was loaded onto *Francis Smith,* a ship owned by the same line (*Chicago Inter Ocean* Aug. 1, 1877).

Jennie Oliver was another vessel on hand to render aid along with insurance tugs from Prince Arthur's (*Thunder Bay Sentinel* Aug. 2, 1877). Wrecking tugs and apparatus were sent for from as far away as Detroit (*Duluth Minnesotian Herald* Aug. 4, 1877). The propellers *Asia* and *City of Owen Sound* may have also tried to pull *Cumberland* off the reef (*Chicago Inter Ocean* Aug. 1, 1877).

The newspapers ran frequent reports on the progress of the attempts to save *Cumberland*, and it was clear from the stories that the people of both Duluth and Prince Arthur's hoped she would be saved. The *Duluth Tribune* (Aug. 3, 1877), for instance, printed the comments: "We hope the fears entertained that she will go down before she reaches Collingwood will not be realized, for she is a trim, staunch and fast-sailing craft, and would be greatly missed from our commerce."

A telegram sent on August 4 gave the condition of *Cumberland* (*Chicago Inter Ocean* Aug. 8, 1877):

Got to steamer *Cumberland* this morning; find her shear planks broken, hull twisted, mast and a great part of upper works carried away. The captain of the tug will try to pull her off today if he can get her pumped out. They are afraid she will be a total loss if more bad weather sets in. Tug arrived 12 hours too late. Storm on Wednesday did all the damage.

Unfortunately the worst fears were realized. The wreck was abandoned August 12 (*Chicago Inter Ocean* Aug. 13, 1877). By August 18, it was rapidly going to pieces and had broken entirely in two (*The Marquette Mining Journal* Aug. 18, 1877). The same newspaper reported it a total loss by August 25. The owners were already negotiating for the purchase of the Union Steamboat Company vessel *Atlantic* as a replacement. The loss of *Cumberland* was put at $50,000. It had been insured for $34,000 (*Duluth Minnesotian Herald* Aug. 11, 1877).

Soon after the wreck, a rumor circulated in Canada that the master of the vessel (Capt. Parsons) had been relying on the charts of Lake Superior produced by the United States, and that the reef *Cumberland* struck was not marked. The rumor reached H.M. Adams, Captain of Engineers, who wrote a letter to the *Detroit Daily News* in response (*Portage Lake Mining Gazette* Aug. 16, 1877). Enclosed with the letter was a copy of the U.S. chart that indicated six feet of depth and a rock bottom at the point *Cumberland* hit the reef. It was the Canadian charts that were at fault.

Cumberland remained visible until the end of August. The steamer *Francis Smith,* downbound from Duluth, reported that the wreck was in the same position as when it was abandoned (*Toronto Globe* Aug. 31, 1877).

Cumberland was entirely submerged by early September. The *Duluth Minnesotian* (Sept. 8, 1877) reported that, "She is now quietly laying on the bed of Lake Superior. Some wreckers went to look for her lately, but could not find her."

Speculations as to the cause of the accidents must rely on the scant information appearing in contemporary newspapers, because records of any official inquiries have not been located. The captain of *Cumberland* may have taken a short cut in an attempt to make up the time lost while aground at Nipigon Bay. The captain of the steamer *St. Paul* reported that *Cumberland*'s captain had hailed and transferred the passengers aboard his vessel because he did not want to be delayed by proceeding further on to Duluth. "After the transfer of passengers, the *Cumberland* started on her return, and taking a short cut ran hard on to the southwest part of Isle Royale" (*Chicago Inter Ocean* Aug. 1, 1877).

Another possibility was raised – *Cumberland* may have been allowed to break up because of the insurance.

The *Cumberland* was insured for $35,000 or $40,000, and it is generally understood that although she was a fine boat, she is well sold, considering the depressed condition of the vessel interests. Whether this fact had anything to do with the "circumlocution office" way the affair was managed of course cannot be told, but people knowing the circumstances will talk, and such is the burden of the conclusions drawn (*Cleveland Herald* Aug. 25, 1877).

Apparently, some felt that the vessel could have been saved if those involved had dispatched wrecking tugs to the site earlier. A professional insurance agent had waited until he reached Collingwood to send out a hawser, rather than dispatch the wrecking tugs. The delay was fatal to *Cumberland*, because of the storm that broke it up (*Chicago Inter Ocean* ran the above under the title "How Not To Do It," Aug. 24, 1877. The original appeared in the *Cheboygan Tribune*.)

Salvage

There was some salvage done on *Cumberland*. The initial efforts were completed prior to September 1877. The following announcement of the sale of materials from the wreck appeared September 1, 1877 (*Toronto Globe*):

Salvage Auction Sale of Effects
Saved from the Wreck of the Steamer *Cumberland*
on View Today at 56 Yonge Street
The subscribers have received instructions to sell on behalf of the underwriter by public auction, at the warehouse, No. 56 Yonge St., the whole of the effects saved from the

wreck of the Steamer *Cumberland*, consisting of two metal lifeboats, two wooden yawl boats, two anchors and cable chains, about two tons Manila rope, blocks, tackle, capstans, 130 life preservers, zinc pails, wheel and wheel stand, wire rope and rigging in large quantities, deck pumps, hoisting machinery, steam gauges, engine gong, pony engine, steam heater, tools, etc., also the whole of the furniture saved, which is in excellent condition, consisting of 100 cane seat dining chairs and stools, 125 spring and mixed mattresses, 100 sponge and feather pillows, card and extension dining tables, gilt mirrors, 20 pieces velvet carpet, a large number of crimson and gold armchairs, sofas and settees, superb rosewood Pianoforte and many more articles, as well as the hull, engines and boilers of the steamer as she now lies off Isle Royale Island.

The sale took place September 5 and realized about $3,000 (*Toronto Globe* Sept. 6, 1877). The sale notice is a good indication of the extent of salvage that occurred on the vessel. Most of the material, except the machinery, was salvaged to some extent.

There is, as yet, no record of hull or machinery salvage after the unsuccessful attempt by wreckers to locate the vessel in September 1877. Apparently, the machinery and boilers were not salvaged. There are, however, reports of additional wreckage attributed to *Cumberland* being washed ashore on Isle Royale; the westernmost portion of Isle Royale has become locally known as Cumberland Point. Another point of land just inside Grace Harbor has also become locally known as "Inner Cumberland Point," another site of wreckage. There may also be some portions of the old Grace Harbor Lumber Company dock, located in the vicinity of *Cumberland*. Bow wreckage was found and photographically documented by members of SCRU in 1984. Patrick Labadie and Monty Florentz returned in 1985 to map the area (see Chapter V, Figure 60).

Cumberland wreckage was reported in 1909 to be distributed along the entire south shore (Adams 1909: 49), but that wreckage most likely belongs to *Chisholm*, lost in 1898. Arthur Veierthaler of Madison, Wisconsin, reported ribs (frames) and planking in the waters off Cumberland Point in the mid-1960s (personal communication to Holden).

Henry Chisholm: History

Construction

Henry Chisholm was built in Cleveland by the firm Thomas Quayle's Sons, under the direction of master carpenter John Drackett (ship documents). The new bulk freighter, the largest steambarge on the Lakes, slipped down the ways August 28, 1880 (*Chicago Inter Ocean* Aug. 30, 1880).

The builder was an old, established firm well known for the high quality vessels they produced. The ship building company was founded by Thomas Quayle, whom some acknowledged as the father of Cleveland shipbuilders (Mansfield 1899: 1: 427).

Quayle was born in England, came to the United States at the age of 16 in 1827 and began work as a shipbuilder apprentice. After his apprenticeship was completed, he started business in partnership with James Cody. The partnership lasted three years during which it built barks, brigs and schooners that were considered large craft for the time.

Soon after the partnership with Cody was dissolved, Quayle formed a partnership with Luther Moses, the new firm called Moses and Quayle under which the first Quayle steamers were built. The next partnership was with John Mart. It lasted 20 years, and together they constructed a large number of sailing vessels and steamers, reputed to be some of the finest on the Lakes. In one year, 13 vessels were built, including the bark *William T. Graves* (1867), then the largest carrier on the Lakes (Mansfield 1899: 2: 692).

After John Martin's death in 1873, Quayle took his sons into the business and formed Thomas Quayle and Sons. During this company's operations it again produced the largest fresh-water vessel of its time, *Commodore,* built in 1875 and of 2,082 gross tons (Mansfield 1879: 2: 692).

Thomas Quayle retired in 1879 (Mansfield 1899: 2: 692), and upon the entry of a third son his firm became Thomas Quayle's Sons. The sons of Thomas Quayle reaffirmed the company's reputation for building large, staunch Great Lakes vessels; when *Henry Chisholm* was launched it was the largest bulk freighter on the Lakes (Mansfield 1899: 1: 735).

Henry Chisholm's Master Carpenter John Drackett, who was an English emigrant to Cleveland in 1851, had built many Lakes vessels. During most of his career he worked under contract for well-known Lakes shipbuilders on both sailing craft and steamers. In 1874 Drackett moved to Detroit and in 1876 was employed for four years by Alva Bradley during which time he built *Henry Chisholm*. In 1881 he moved to Toledo and built *David Dows,* the only five-masted schooner on the Lakes (Mansfield 1899: 2: 686). *Chisholm*'s construction reflected the expertise of this master carpenter and was generally recognized as one of the finest steambarges on the Lakes. Captain George Stone was the superintendent of construction.

Henry Chisholm was built for Alva Bradley and launched on August 1880. The ship received its first inspection on September 16. It was painted the Bradley colors with a green hull and red stack. The vessel originally carried three masts. *Chisholm* was given U.S. Registry number 95610.

Chisholm was built as a wooden bulk freighter with a single screw. These vessels were commonly termed "steambarges." It was powered by a fore-and-aft compound steam engine, which produced 1,707 horsepower, fed by twin boilers. The compound engine, built by the Globe Iron Works of Cleveland, was reportedly of the "Randolph and Elder pattern, cylinders 30 x 56 inches, four feet stroke" (*Chicago Inter Ocean* Sept. 23, 1880). The speed of the loaded ship was about nine knots.

Chisholm, considered a "leviathan" at the time of construction, was 270 feet of overall length and registered length of $256^5/_{10}$ feet, $39^3/_{10}$ feet in breadth and $20^3/_{10}$ feet in depth. The capacity under the tonnage deck was $1692^{27}/_{100}$ and the capacity of enclosures on the upper deck (poop) was $83^{10}/_{100}$ for a total of $1775^{37}/_{100}$ gross tons. Deductions allowed by the Act of August 5, 1882, totaled $443^{19}/_{100}$ for a total net tonnage of $1332^{18}/_{100}$. Permanent enrollment was dated at Cleveland, Ohio, September 18, 1880.

Chisholm was built just as shipbuilding was approaching the maximum sizes possible with wood as the principal material. Quayle's company had been experimenting with the construction of the largest of wooden hulls, and their experience was incorporated into *Chisholm*. Iron, a recently introduced competitor, and later steel, would supersede wood for the construction of large hulls. The latter were more expensive when *Chisholm* was launched, which may account for the owners' decision to build their hull with traditional materials. *Chisholm* cost $125,000. This may be compared with *Lehigh,* an iron vessel of the dimensions of 240 x 35 x 17 which cost $140,000 (*Chicago Inter Ocean* Sept. 23, 1880).

Chisholm was a powerful towing vessel and was built with the intention of pulling one, and sometimes more, barges, as was the typical practice of the time. The barges were generally older schooners converted for towing, although some schooner barges were constructed specifically for the purpose.

The building of *Henry Chisholm* was a matter of much interest and the contemporary press carried details of its construction:

The *Henry Chisholm*, the largest steambarge ever built in Cleveland, was launched yesterday in the presence of 2,000 people....Fully 800,090 feet of lumber were consumed in her construction.... (*Chicago Inter Ocean* Aug. 30, 1880).

Her strength is all that can be got with wood and iron. She has 150 tons of iron in her construction besides the engines and boilers. She has a wide, heavy band of iron running from bow to stern, her whole length, at the head of the frames, from which double diagonal heavy iron straps run down the sides and under the turn of the bilge, and fasten to the long frames under the bottom and bolt through the bands when they cross and outside of the frames under the planking. This is called iron strapping, and it entitles her to a rating of A1* for 10 years to A1½ for three years more, and A2 for three years more, making 16 years before she classes below A2. She is expected to carry 2,000 gross tons of iron ore from Escanaba and also tow as many vessels as can get tow lines to hold them; 75,000 bushels of wheat, or 80,000 bushels of corn to Buffalo....She came out of Cleveland without having tried her engines, and ran eight and a half miles an hour to Detroit with everything new and rough...She is all right in every way. She steers well in rough weather, doesn't bend, or work, or give, or

Figure 15. Artist's rendition of *Henry Chisholm*, the largest steambarge built at Cleveland at the time of launch. (Painting by Huntington) Great Lakes Historical Society.

Figure 16. Construction yard photograph during the building of a contemporary steambarge similar to *Henry Chisholm*. U.S. Army Corps of Engineers Canal Park Marine Museum Collection.

creak, or leak. She is as strong as though she was all in one piece, and has power to steam almost any gale of wind....

The iron beams under the boilers, and the iron house over and around the boiler, with the iron coal bunkers, are sure protection against fire. Her outfit includes all the new improvements and tried inventions of the steamboats of to-day. Her cabins and rooms are large, and are heated with steam, and she is well furnished. Without the least exaggeration it may be said that the *Henry Chisholm* is the peer of any craft afloat on salt water or fresh (*Chicago Inter Ocean* Sept. 24, 1880).

Operational History

During *Henry Chisholm*'s operational life it was involved in many accidents, some minor, some serious, which was not unusual for bulk freighters of the period. The high number of accidents was often a reflection of the operation of vessels built to the maximum dimensions of practical navigation. The long series of incidents began the day the ship was launched. Soon after the launch a sailor fell through the open hatchway and was severely injured (*Chicago Inter Ocean* Aug. 30, 1880).

Even the maiden voyage was not without incident. The new vessel ran aground twice. The first cargo *Chisholm* carried was 1,800 tons of coal (*Cleveland Herald* Sept. 9, 27, 1880). The ship grounded in the west draw of the Chicago Avenue Bridge, blocking it overnight. The ship was wedged between the banks of the narrow channel. Six Union Tug Line tugs were unable to budge the freighter until 250 tons of coal were removed (*Ibid.* 27, 1880).

Chisholm was freed only to run aground again in the Ogden Canal "within a stone's throw" of the North Side Gas Company's dock (*Cleveland Herald* Sept. 28, 1880). Lightering operations were again carried out and the vessel finally made it to the dock. The reason for the grounding was a strong south wind that unexpectedly reduced the water in the Ogden Canal to 12 feet; *Chisholm* was drawing more than 13 feet (*Ibid.* Sept. 29, 1880).

During the maiden voyage the steam chest of *Chisholm*'s engines needed adjustment. This was done in Detroit. During the adjustments many people visited the new steambarge (*Cleveland Herald* Sept. 22, 1880).

The operational history of *Henry Chisholm* gives insight to the bulk freighter trade as it was carried out on the Great Lakes in the 1880s and '90s. This was a period of rapid change in navigation on the Lakes, and it is informative to briefly present some of the highlights of *Chisholm*'s history in this context.
- *Chisholm* chartered to carry corn at $4\frac{1}{2}$ cents a bushel from Chicago to Buffalo (*Cleveland Herald* Oct. 2, 1880).
- While carrying 79,600 bushels, *Chisholm* drew but 14 feet $4\frac{1}{2}$ inches (*Ibid.* Oct. 6, 1880).
- *Chisholm* again ran aground, this time at the head of Bois Blanc Island on the Canadian side of the Detroit River. The vessel had to be lightered of 8,000 bushels of corn to get free (*Ibid.* Oct. 8, 9, 1880).
- *Chisholm*, near the end of its first trip, had to again lighter 4,500 bushels of grain before being able to enter Buffalo Harbor (*Cleveland Herald* Oct. 14, 1880).
- 1,700 tons of coal were carried in November 1880 (*Cleveland Herald* Nov. 22, 23, 1880).
- *Henry Chisholm* recovered the anchors of *Negaunee* November 1880 (*Ibid.* Nov. 25, 1880). The steam barge wintered in Cleveland (*Ibid.* Dec. 4, 1880).

At the opening of the 1881 season, *Chisholm* ran aground at the head of Lime Kiln Crossing. "The accident was caused by the valve motion cutting the steam off and rendering the vessel helpless" (*Cleveland Herald* May 9, 1881).

The operational history of *Chisholm* continues on in much the same manner. *Chisholm* was primarily involved in the coal, iron ore and grain trades. *Chisholm* frequently set records for carrying capacity on the Lakes.

In May 1881 *Chisholm* carried 1,800 tons of iron ore from Escanaba. "This is the largest load any vessel has yet brought down" (*Cleveland Herald* May 24, 1881). The load brought down was actually 1,911 tons (*Ibid.* May 30, 1881). *Chisholm* made the run from Cleveland to Escanaba in 62 hours with the schooner *Negaunee* in tow. The ship had made the round trip with the record load of ore in six days (*Ibid.* June 7, 1881). In June *Chisholm* brought down 2,061 tons of ore, "the largest load ever carried in fresh water" (*Ibid.* June 22, 1881).

With the appearance of the iron *Onoko*, the records of *Chisholm* and the other wooden ships were forever surpassed. The new iron vessel could carry 115,000-120,000 bushels of wheat to the 82,000 bushels of corn of *Chisholm* (*Ibid.* April 28, 1882).

Chisholm would, however, still claim records of local note, and these seem to reflect a competition between vessels of large size. In May 1882, the freighter brought down 2,100 tons of ore from Escanaba, the biggest load to date (*Ibid.* May 13, 1882). This record did not last until the end of the month when *City of Rome,* another Quayle ship, but a bit larger, brought down 2,180 tons of ore (*Ibid.* May 30, 1882). In June *Chisholm* loaded 2,184 tons of ore at Escanaba, reclaiming its record (*Ibid.* June 2, 1882).

"*Chisholm* brought in the largest cargo of ore of the season into Milwaukee July 5, 1884. It was 2,163 tons" (*Cleveland Herald* July 6, 1884).

Chisholm frequently towed schooners. For example, it had the schooners *Thomas Quayle, J.C. Harrison* and *Godfrey* in tow on a trip (*Cleveland Herald* Sept. 29, 1881). The schooners did not always accompany the steam barge for the entire trip, rather they were often picked up and delivered to different ports. In April 1882, *Chisholm* left Cleveland with the schooners *Thomas Quayle* and *J.F. Card* in tow. *S.J. Tilden* was picked up at Black River. *Card* was left off at St. Clair while the others proceeded to Milwaukee with their loads of coal (*Ibid.* April 19, 1882). In 1885 *Chisholm* started the season with three schooners in tow loaded with coal; all four vessels had different destinations (*Ibid.* May 10, 1885).

An idea of the carrying capacity of steambarges and their tows is gained from August 1883 when *Chisholm* had *City of Cleveland, Ahira Cobb* and *Scotia* in tow. *City of Cleveland* alone was loaded with 2,500 tons of ore (*Ibid.* Aug. 16, 1883).

Vessels unfortunate enough to come too close to *Henry Chisholm* did not fare well. The canal boat *Tom Wood* was struck by *Chisholm* and sank. There was no damage to *Chisholm* (*Cleveland Herald* June 8, 1881). The tug *Ida M. Sims* had its whistle carried away during a close encounter with the huge steambarge (*Ibid.* Aug 15, 1881).

Chisholm and its tow *Ahira Cobb* both hit *North Cape*, a schooner downbound with a load of grain, in fog and nearly sank it. The stricken schooner was towed to Cleveland by *Chisholm* (*Cleveland Herald* June 25; July 3, 1884).

The only alteration noted in the first year of *Chisholm*'s operation was the change of steering gear from wire to chain

(*Cleveland Herald* June 11, 1881). In 1882 *Chisholm* ran aground in the river at Chicago and broke its wheel. It took five tugs and a locomotive to pull the ship through the Harrison Street Bridge (*Ibid.* Nov 4, 1882). Repairs include a bent key connecting the piston with the crosshead in 1884 (*Ibid.* Aug 24, 1884). The stern bearings were repaired in 1886 (*Detroit Free Press* July 2, 1886).

In 1883 *Chisholm* towed the Bradley-owned barges *Ahira Cobb* and *City of Cleveland.* It was then rated A1* in the *Inland Lloyd's Vessel Register* (1890).

In 1883 *Chisholm* ran aground at the Willow Street bridge in Cleveland and had to lighter some ore to get off. The vessel was damaged and entered the Globe dry dock for repairs (*Cleveland Herald* Oct. 13, 16, 1883).

Chisholm had been recaulked in 1890 and received a Lloyd's rating of A2 with a value of $75,000. The rating and value were both raised in 1896 when the ship was reboilered with two new Scotch boilers.

Wreck Event

The last voyage of *Henry Chisholm* began in Duluth on Sunday, October 16, 1898. *Chisholm* was loaded with 92,000 bushels of barley. The ship was downbound for Buffalo with the 220-foot schooner *John Martin* in tow, carrying 1.2 million board feet of lumber. Captain P.H. Smith was master of *Henry Chisholm* and the captain of *John Martin* was James Lawless, second master of *Chisholm*. Both vessels were majority owned by M.A. Bradley of Cleveland (*Wisconsin State Journal* Oct. 21, 1898).

A gale arose and the weather was heavy by the time the two vessels neared Copper Harbor on the Keweenaw Point. *Martin,* with fore and main sails set, cast off the tow line about 5:30 p.m. Monday (Oct. 17) and was soon lost to view. There was a heavy southeast wind, and *Chisholm*'s captain headed up the Lake across the wind (*Ft. William Daily Journal* Oct. 21, 1898). *Chisholm* cruised about until Tuesday morning in an effort to locate the missing schooner (*Superior Evening Telegram* Oct. 21, 1898).

Chisholm headed for the Apostle Island group and refueled at Ashland. The search for *John Martin* was resumed at 11 a.m. Tuesday. The search route ran to the north shore with a call at Grand Marais, and from there to search the Isle Royale area (*Ft. William Daily Journal* Oct. 21, 1898).

The wreck occurred on Thursday, October 20 at either 5 a.m. (*The Daily Journal* Oct. 21, 1898) or at 8 a.m. while the ship was trying to enter Washington Harbor (*Wisconsin State Journal* Oct. 21, 1898). *Chisholm* was doing about nine knots, full speed, when it struck the Rock of Ages reef. The ship carried a crew of 16 (*Duluth Evening Herald* Oct. 21, 1898).

Soon after striking the reef, Capt. Smith and First Mate Whitsman (or Whitman), who had been consulting in the ship's cabin, rushed to the deck and saw many fragments of heavy oak hull planking floating in the water. The captain decided there was no hope of pulling it off and launched the 18-foot lifeboat or yawl boat (*Detroit Free Press* Oct. 22, 1898) under the command of the first mate. Along with Whitsman in the lifeboat were Second Mate Gilbert Wide (Wilde), Wheelsmen James Agger and Angus MacDonald, and Seaman Harry G. Carrow. These men set out rowing for Victoria Harbor 14.5 miles away. They arrived there about 11 a.m. and were picked up by the steamer *Dixon* (*Ft. William Daily Journal* Oct. 21, 1898).

Dixon (probably *Hiram R. Dixon*, a 329 gross-ton propeller built in 1883 at Mystic, Connecticut) arrived in Duluth with the shipwrecked crew aboard (*Wisconsin State Journal* Oct. 21, 1898). This same account said the crew had gone to Isle Royale before Whitsman was dispatched to report the vessel's loss. *Chisholm* was reported rapidly breaking up and feared a total loss. A wrecking expedition sent by the Inman Tug Line had been dispatched.

Soon after the lifeboat under command of the first mate left *Chisholm*, the captain and remainder of the crew rowed the four miles to Washington Harbor. The vessel was reported in 12 feet of water at the bow and 40 feet at the stern, listing four feet (*Ft. William Daily Journal* Oct. 21, 1898).

John Martin, although feared water logged and lost (lumber had been spotted on the south shore), survived the ordeal in good shape. The steamer *Neshoto,* a 2,255-gross-ton propeller commissioned that year and built at *Chisholm*'s home port of Cleveland, arrived in Duluth on October 21 with a reported sighting of the missing *John Martin* off Eagle Harbor. *Martin* was sailing east. *Martin* was reported at Sault Ste. Marie the evening of the 21st under tow of the Canada-Atlantic liner *Roman. Roman* was a 2,348-gross-ton package freighter built in 1891 in Cleveland. It was reported that *Roman* picked up *Martin* off Copper Harbor, near where it was originally separated from *Henry Chisholm* (*Detroit Free Press* Oct. 22, 1898; *Duluth Evening Herald* Oct. 22, 1898).

Salvage

Soon after the steamer *Dixon* arrived in Duluth with the shipwrecked sailors and news of *Henry Chisholm*'s stranding, Capt. Byron B. Inman sent a wrecking crew to the site.

Inman was the most prominent tug owner of Duluth. He had at one time under his command 22 vessels of all types engaged principally in towing and wrecking. He had built a reputation of note many years before for towing the largest tow on record through the Detroit River: seven vessels with an aggregate tonnage of 4,323 (Mansfield 1899: 2: 44-46).

Capt. W.H. Singer of the Singer Tug Company, a rival of Inman, arrived at the wreck site on Friday, October 21 aboard the tug *Zenith* from Duluth. Singer returned to Duluth on Tuesday, October 25 with a message of dire prospects for *Chisholm*'s being freed (*Marquette Daily Mining Journal* Oct. 23, 1898). Other reports were more optimistic. In Cleveland, M.A. Bradley received a dispatch from Duluth that the steamer *McGregor* had reached the wreck and reported that it was "out two feet forward, but is in good shape and the weather is favorable" (*Detroit Free Press* Oct. 23 1898).

Apparently, Inman abandoned operations on October 24. He sent a telegram to owner M.A. Bradley stating that two steam water pumps had been unable to lower the water in *Chisholm*'s hold an inch. He predicted the steamer would go completely to

pieces in six hours should there be any bad weather (*Detroit Free Press* Oct. 25, 1898).

The bad weather did appear. On October 24, a northwest gale arose blowing 27 miles an hour. It blew that night, and heavy snow squalls began on the 25th (*Detroit Free Press* Oct. 26, 1898). The newspaper reported all vessels were held in port due to this storm. *Chisholm* was mentioned: "...is believed she went to pieces in last night's gale" (*Detroit Free Press* Oct. 27, 1898).

In November, salvor James Reid visited the site aboard tug *Protector.* He reported the ship had gone to pieces, but "the machinery can be saved" (*Detroit Free Press* Nov. 11, 1898).

The people around Lake Superior have a long memory for shipwrecks. It was noted that *Chisholm* was "wrecked at the same spot as the handsome Canadian passenger steamer *Cumberland* was broken in two a few years (21 years) ago. The *Cumberland* was commanded by Capt. Parsons, now mate of the *Manitou*" (*Marquette Daily Mining Journal* Oct. 27, 1898).

If the storm of October 25 and 26 did not break up *Chisholm*, the next one surely did. Another storm struck Saturday and Sunday, October 29 and 30. It exceeded the fury of the earlier storm. The wind blew 34 miles an hour and whipped up a great sea. It was estimated that the velocity was nearer 50 miles an hour on the Lake.

No salvage reports have been located for the time Inman and Singer spent on the site in October 1898. In August 1901, salvage efforts resumed on the wreck of *Chisholm*. Captain England, aboard the 198-gross-ton steambarge *H.A. Root,* arrived in Duluth August 1 with one of the scotch boilers recovered from *Henry Chisholm.* The *Joseph C. Suit,* a 152-gross-ton steambarge, had been salvaging the site. Both boilers were recovered and towed to Washington Harbor.

The value of the boilers was estimated to be $3,500, since they had only been in use for two years when *Chisholm* wrecked. The 1901 price for a new Scotch boiler was between $6,000 and $7,000. The engine was reported to have rolled down off the reef in more than 100 feet of water (*Duluth News Tribune* Aug. 2, 1901). No records of other visits to the site are known until rediscovery of the site by sport divers in the 1960s.

Algoma: History

Construction

Algoma was one of the first steel-hulled vessels on the Great Lakes (*Scanner* 1976: 6 from *The British Whig* Oct. 18, 1883). Like many of the early iron and steel vessels of the Lakes, it was built in British shipyards. Britain led the world in the development of iron and steel shipbuilding, and Great Lakes owners were frequent customers. Fleet orders from the Lakes were not uncommon, particularly from Canada, for vessels constructed on the Clyde. Kelvinhaugh was a leading producer of iron and steel vessels, and some Scottish companies (particularly in the 1920s) specialized in the manufacture of Lakers (Walker 1984: 58; Carvel 1950: 46).

The one problem faced by the foreign shipbuilders and Great Lakes owners was that the vessels had to pass through the canal system from the ocean to the Lakes. A vessel that was built small enough to pass was too small to benefit from the eco-

Figure 17. Canadian Pacific Railway passenger vessel *Algoma*, one of the first steel-hulled vessels on the Great Lakes. U.S. Army Corps of Engineers Canal Park Marine Museum Collection.

nomies of scale enjoyed by larger vessels constructed on the Lakes. The solution was to design vessels to pass through the St. Lawrence Canals in pieces, to be reassembled once in the Lakes. This was accomplished in two ways: by either producing the vessels in sections and transporting to the Lakes on other ships (Carvel 1950: 46), or designing the vessels to sail under their own power to the Lakes and then be severed in two and bulkheaded for the passage through the canals.

Algoma was built by Aitken and Mansel of Glasgow, Scotland, for Canadian Pacific Railway (CPR). The ship, with its two sisters *Alberta* and *Athabaska* (the later spelling was *Athabasca*), were the first steamers to be purchased by the new line and were used in the Owen Sound-Port Arthur run that connected the railway across Lake Huron and Lake Superior. The three vessels were similarly built, with steel hulls of 263.5 feet in length, 38.2 feet in beam and 23.3 feet in depth (*Scanner* 1974: 8), giving a gross tonnage of about 1,750 as originally built. The completed vessels would be able to accommodate about 240 first-class passengers and 600 steerage passengers.

The first of the sisters to be launched was *Athabaska* on July 3, 1883. The Scottish press carried the story (*Scanner* 1974: 6-8 from *Glasgow Herald* July 4, 1883):

Yesterday about noon, Messrs. Aitken and Mansel launched from their shipbuilding yard at Whiteinch the steel screw-steamer *Athabaska,* the vessel being the first of three presently building to the order of the Canadian Pacif-

ic Railway Co....Miss Govan of 2 Athole Place, Glasgow, performed the usual ceremony of naming the vessel....As the completion of these vessels will not be carried out until they reach the Lakes, it is estimated that their actual tonnage will be about 2,400 when a contemplated extensive range of houses built in the American system has been erected on the upper deck.

The contract for these vessels was placed in the hands of Mr. David Rowan, engineer, Elliot Street, and they will be fitted by him with compound direct-acting screw engines, capable of working to about 1,700 indicated horses, the cylinders being 35 in. and 70 by 4 feet stroke, supplied with steam by two steel boilers with a working pressure of 125 lb. per square inch. To obtain strength as well as lightness of draught the hulls are constructed of Siemens-Martin steel supplied by the Steel Company of Scotland, and the bulkheads are arranged to allow the vessels being divided into two parts to permit their passage through the limited dimensions of the locks of the Welland and other canals leading to the level of the Upper Lakes.

Alberta was launched July 12, 1883, and *Algoma* on July 31. Miss Shaw of Glasgow performed the ceremony of naming the latter vessel (*Glasgow Herald* July 13, Aug. 1, 1883, in *Scanner* 1974: 7).

Athabaska was the first to sail for Montreal, leaving on August 24. The boilers were found to be leaking and the vessel returned to port on August 29. The repaired ship sailed from Glasgow three days later with a load of coal. *Alberta* and *Algoma* followed on September 25, also loaded with coal (*Glasgow Herald* Sept. 27, 1883). The two sisters arrived 13 days later in Montreal, making better time than the trouble-plagued *Athabaska* (*Glasgow Herald* Oct. 12, 1883).

The arrival of the new Clyde steamers generated much interest, and the *Cleveland Herald* (Nov. 30, 1883) carried a description of *Athabaska* that is informative of the procedures and details of the sister ships:

Buffalo, Nov. 27. The *Athabaska*...has arrived in this port. She came in two sections, which will be joined into a complete hull at the lower dry-dock of the Union Ship-yard. The arrival of a Clyde-built boat has naturally occasioned considerable interest in marine circles. The *Athabaska* is one of five steamships that will form a line from Algoma Mills, Georgian Bay, to Port Arthur, Lake Superior, a distance of 350 miles....The *Athabaska* is of steel throughout and measures eight feet between decks. She is quite sharp forward, and has a clean cut stern though having barely half the overhang of the average Lake steamer. The hull is divided into seven compartments. Her carrying capacity is about 2,000 tons. The steamer is provided with no less than 12 engines, including two for working the rudder. One of the most remarkable of her appliances is what is called a repeating telegraph. By means of this the pilot gives the signals to the engineer, who receives them on a dial in the engine room, and sends them back to the pilot on the bridge. The latter can thus tell whether his orders have been understood. Another indicator on the bridge shows the direction of the rudder at all times.

The *Athabaska* left Glasgow about September 1st for Montreal, with a cargo of soft coal and pig iron....She arrived at that port after a tedious trip of 21 days, her air pumps giving out fully eight times on the trip. It was necessary to cut the hull in two in order to take it through the shallow canals of the lower St. Lawrence. As she was built with this object in view, the work was readily accomplished. The sections were placed on pontoons to go through the canals. Arriving at the foot of Lake Ontario the pontoons were removed, and the parts rested on their own bottoms. Two more ships are now in the Welland Canal, and are expected daily.

Buffalo, Nov. 29. The tugs *Williams* and *Alpha* this morning brought in the two sections of the Clyde-built steamer *Alberta* from Port Colborne. They were placed in the Union ship-yard's upper dock. The *Alberta* is the duplicate of the *Athabaska*.

The two sections of *Algoma* were brought to the docks the next day, but the job of towing the sections of the three sisters was difficult because of bad weather. The newspapers commended Maytham's tugs for succeeding (*Cleveland Herald* Dec. 1, 1883). There had been some problems encountered while towing.

The CPR ships were not the first vessels too long to pass through the Beauharnois and Cornwall canals to be cut in two at Montreal. Some iron gunboats had previously been cut apart, as had the passenger steamer *Rothesay Castle,* a former block-ade runner. One of the earliest vessels to be severed in Montreal for canal passage was *Campana* (*Scanner* 1976: 7 from *The British Whig* Oct. 18, 1883). The cutting and transportation for these earlier vessels was long and difficult. However, the CPR vessels were constructed to ease the operation:

...the vessel[s] having been constructed with the knowledge of the required operation. In consequence, the sheets of iron [steel] were made to fit and to end at the place where she was cut, and iron bulkheads five feet apart erected on each side of the connection. Accordingly, all that was necessary was to knock off the heads of the rivets at the joint and float the two pieces to their destination (*Scanner* 1976: 7 from *The British Whig* Oct. 18, 1883).

The task of joining the sections of the new steamers was not

as easy as first surmised. Reassembling *Athabasca* (for the first time appearing with a "C") took about a week – "a delicate job to get the rivet holes exactly in place" (*Cleveland Herald* Dec. 2, 1883). It was an expensive operation to move the steamers from Port Colborne to Buffalo, where they would winter. It cost more than $18,000 to move the vessels (*Thunder Bay Sentinel* Dec. 1, 1883).

The cabins may have been fabricated in Montreal (*Cleveland Herald* Dec. 5, 1883). There has been some uncertainty as to whether they were installed in Port Colborne or Buffalo. The *Sarnia Observer* May 16, 1884, reported that the cabins were installed at Port Colborne. However, it was probably Buffalo where the cabins were added while the ship was wintering. The configuration of the cabins was a long structure of wood on the upper deck. There was a lengthy gallery with staterooms flanking the sides. Accommodations were superior to those found on earlier steamers. There was no dining salon, so tables were set in the old-fashioned manner in the main lounge between the rows of staterooms. The galley had a clerestory deckhead that protruded above the boat deck to form an observation deck (*Scanner* 1974: 8 from *Glasgow Herald* Oct. 12, 1883). The cabinwork was done through the winter of 1883-84; the ship was ready to begin its Lake career in early spring.

When the vessels appeared in Lakes service each ship was painted black with a narrow white stripe below the deck level. Cabins were painted white and the funnel was black with a wide red band, also carrying a very narrow white band (*Scanner* 1974: 9).

Newspapers reported many details of *Algoma*. One of the most extensive descriptions was printed shortly after *Algoma* made its first run to Port Arthur (*Thunder Bay Sentinel* May 16, 1884):

The model is admirable, not a hollow line about the bows, and without the tendency to sit down by the stern so noticeable in many of the old style. The graceful adaptability for space, even to the eye unlearned in the science of ship building. The hulls are built of steel plates of varying thickness....The Plimsoll mark, white circle with a black band through it, is a novelty on the Lakes, but every sailor knows that it points out the line beyond which no vessel shall be loaded, thus preventing overloading. The Plimsoll marks on the CPR vessels will allow them to load to 15 feet of water on which they could carry 2,000 tons dead weight of freight, but as a rule they will only be loaded to 13 feet. The hold is divided into compartments by six watertight steel bulkheads.

The motive power is supplied by compound engines driving a screw 13 feet 6 inches in diameter and having a pitch of 21 feet....The boilers, two in number, are each 12 feet 3 inches long and are made of Seimens-Martin steel, $^{15}/_{16}$ inch thick and tested to a cold water pressure of 210 psi. The furnaces are of the latest improvements, being built of corrugated iron. The screws are not cast all in one piece, but the blades are bolted to the center-piece so that an injury to one piece does not necessitate the renewal of the whole screw. She carries two steel masts, with such a spread of fore and aft canvas as to be quite easily handled in case of a breakdown of the steam power. Besides the main engine she has auxiliary donkey and hoisting engines, steam pumps and siphons. The anchors, windlasses and capstans are handled by steam and all freight is taken in or out by a hoisting engine on the main deck running the four hatches.

The equipment is in keeping with the superior hull and motive power. She is steered by steam, and large as she is her course could be directed by a child. There is no top heavy texas [deck] as is usually seen on Lake boats, but instead there is a spacious bridge above the wheelhouse and extending the whole beam of the vessel. In the wheel house a small wheel, not three feet in diameter, stands before a regulated compass. Under the feet of the wheelsman is a small but exceedingly beautiful steam engine, controlling the wire cables, which serve as tiller chains. On the bridge is another similar wheel facing one of Sir William Thompson's patent compasses....The Thompson compass is the result of the highest scientific research in navigation, and a product of human knowledge as [is] the great steel ship itself. The steering apparatus is not completed by the two wheels we have mentioned. There is another aft, to be used in case of accident to the others. It is a large hand wheel, on the shaft of which are right and left hand screws, with a binnacle compass in front of it.

...She carries six large life boats and about 600 life preservers, with a liberal allowance of life buoys about the decks. Of chain and steel wire cables and patent anchors handled by steam there is also a good supply. She was built and equipped according to the English Board of Trade regulations.

Large as the *Algoma* is she is without an oil lamp. She is lighted throughout by the Canadian Edison Electric Light Company, of Hamilton, in a style never before seen on the Lakes. She has a 6½ by 8 Armington and Sime engine of 330 revolutions, driving an Edison Dynamo, supplying 110 lights of 16 candle power each, and having all the regular attachments and details as used by the Edison Company in steamships. The lamps can be controlled by the engineer of the dynamo, or each single lamp can be turned on or off by a key attached to its socket....A novel and useful feature of lighting is an electric lamp with a long, flexible conductor. It can be taken from the boat and carried up dark decks or can be used in the examination of the screw, rudder or any submerged part of the hull....Matches are not used on board, not even for lighting pipes or cigars, electric cigar lighters being provided for that purpose. The CPR boats are the first on the Lakes to be lighted by any system of electric appliances.

Her passenger accommodation is of the highest class. Single berths are provided for 180 first class passengers, and steerage bunks for 200, with room to increase steerage

accommodations for 1,000 persons. The steerage is on the main deck and is roomy and well lighted. All the bunks are single, and the steerage is supplied with hot and cold water. Closets are numerous, and the steerage passengers are well provided for in every way. The furniture of the main saloon is first class and accords with the general equipment of the vessel. Bath rooms and smoking rooms are provided; and the steward's room is on the upper deck instead of on the main deck. The engineer's, porter's, purser's and express messenger's quarters are on the main deck, which is well lighted by deadlights. The crew have a very comfortable forecastle.

The protection against fire is the most ample that human ingenuity can devise. In the first place the vessel itself is of steel, and the hull, of course, cannot burn. The main and upper decks are of steel, though they have an extra flooring of wood. Only the cabins or the cargo can burn. The cabins, and in fact all parts of the boat, are furnished with cold water pipes, for fire purposes, the water being supplied by a donkey engine. The hold being divided by fireproof bulkheads, fire cannot spread beyond the compartment in which it may originate, and there it can be controlled, by the steam pipes in each hold, through which steam can be blown to extinguish it. The cooks quarters and the oil room are encased in steel, and a steel casing is about the boilers and runs clear to the crown deck. The engine works, which is seen in the main saloon, is encased in teak.

Some additional details are provided by the descriptions of the new sisters from the *Sarnia Observer* (May 16, 1884), which appeared soon after their introduction:

Her hull is divided into watertight compartments by six steel bulkheads...There is no communication whatever between these compartments, so that in a collision there will be no doors to shut to prevent the water running from one to another. The main and promenade decks are of steel....The main saloon is nearly as large as a side-wheel steamer but it is made so at the expense of the staterooms which are somewhat small and cramped.

The kitchen and oil room are encased in steel. The fire protection of the steamer is arranged somewhat after the manner of the Holly system and there is at all times a pressure of 50 p.s.i. on all the hydrants and the hose is at all times screwed on ready for use.

The boilers are built of steel plate one inch in thickness and each one has 220 three and one-half inch tubes.... She has in all 14 engines on board, used for hoisting anchors and freight, working steam pumps, steering and everything else that requires power. Her steam steering gear, which is the most perfect made, can be worked in the pilothouse or on the bridge, and she has an auxiliary wheel aft to be used in case of accident to the steam gear....She has two steel masts rigged with fore-and-aft canvas. These masts, together with her short thick smokestack, rake aft in a style that gives a decidedly business-like appearance to the ship. She carries six yawl boats, each of which is provided with a compass, sailing gear, water bucket, etc., and each is arranged so that when it is lowered and the proper number of people in it, it will unhook itself from the ropes by which it is lowered. Besides the boats, she carries a large number of life preservers and rafts.

There have been published reports that *Algoma* carried the first Plimsoll mark on the Great Lakes, an assertion that appears unsupportable (e.g. one of the earliest, and the probable source for later authors, is Young 1957: 90). The first of the three sister ships on the Lakes was not *Algoma*, but *Athabasca*. If all three ships carried the mark, and they were the first on the Lakes, the originating honor would go to *Athabasca*.

The lengthy contemporary descriptions above are the only two that were located mentioning the Plimsoll mark. One refers to its appearance as a "novelty on the Lakes," but recognized by any sailor (*Thunder Bay Sentinel* May 16, 1884). The other reference only states: "she (*Alberta* as representing all three) carries the Plimsoll loading mark" (*Scanner* 1976: 10 from *The Sarnia Observer* May 16, 1884). The CPR sisters may have been some of the first to carry the familiar circle and line of the Plimsoll mark, but if they were *the* first, it was apparently not noted in the press reports of the time. It would be surprising if the three ships indeed had carried the first Lake Plimsoll marks and the press failed to highlight that fact, especially since the newspapers made much of the other remarkable attributes of the vessels, such as all steel construction, employing an engine telegraph, Thompson compass and electric lights, etc.

There can be little doubt that some of the first electric lights on the Lakes were on these vessels. The first ship to carry electric lights anywhere in the world was the Fall River Line passenger liner *Pilgrim,* built in 1882. *Pilgrim* plied Long Island Sound with lights installed by Thomas Edison (Johnston 1983: 44). There is little possibility of another Lakes vessel having been fitted with this innovation before *Algoma* and its sisters. (*Garland,* built in 1880, had electric lights, but these were probably a retrofit.) Further historical research will undoubtedly produce more detail on the construction details of the remarkable CPR vessels and perhaps clarify which attributes of Lake craft originally appeared on these ships. Until then, the influence of *Algoma* and its sisters remains only partially documented.

Operational History

Algoma, completed in March (*Thunder Bay Sentinel* March 14, 1884), was ready to begin operations in May 1884. The ports of call on the first voyage were to be Cleveland, Detroit, Windsor and Sarnia, with a public

gathering planned for the arrival at Owen Sound. Before its departure from Port Colborne, some concern was expressed that the new CPR ships had such a deep draft that, even when light, they would be able to enter few of the Lake harbors (*Cleveland Herald* May 2, 1884). The ships drew a little more than seven feet when light and could carry 1,000 tons on 12 feet of draft (*Cleveland Herald* May 24, 1884).

On May 16, *Algoma* was the first of the new steamers to arrive at the Lakehead port. The ship had left Owen Sound at 3 a.m. on Sunday and arrived at the Sault River that evening and made Sault Ste. Marie by 9:30 p.m. Along the way ice was encountered. An indication of the speed capability of the new ship was demonstrated when *Algoma* overtook the steamer *Nyack,* quickly passing it, and in a run of 17 miles gained four miles on the older vessel. *Algoma* had 250 tons of pig iron aboard and 16 carloads of baggage (*Thunder Bay Sentinel* May 16, 1884).

Eight hundred to 1,000 people were waiting on the wharves when *Algoma* pulled into the Marks' Dock at 8:30 a.m.

The appearance of the vessel as she neared the dock was striking. Every available piece of bunting was spread to the wind, and she rode in as stately as any ocean steamer ever entered harbour. The scene which presented itself upon the main deck can only be likened to the appearance of an ocean emigrant ship upon her arrival at an American seaport. More than a thousand steerage passengers were crowding round the gangways ready to land as soon as an opportunity offered.

Of the general excellence of the boat herself too much cannot be said in her favour. She is certainly the finest boat that has ever sailed upon these great inland seas, and her superiority over all other Lake craft in every particular is at once apparent. She has a crew of 35 all told, Captain

Figure 18. *Algoma* at the dock with schooners. U.S. Army Corps of Engineers Canal Park Marine Museum Collection.

Moore commands her, and her first and second mates are M.S. Hastings and R. McLeod, respectively. George Petti-grew is the chief engineer and his assistant is A. McDer-mid. R. McKenzie is purser, and G. Taylor is steward (*Thunder Bay Sentinel* May 16, 1884. See also *Owen Sound Advertiser* Nov. 12, 1885).

The CPR steamers demonstrated their success "for the pur-pose for which they were intended" by entering all the harbors; they also demonstrated their success in fast runs and quick deliveries (*Cleveland Herald* May 24, 1884). Goods ordered from Toronto were delivered to Thunder Bay in record time. They had traveled nearly 700 miles, most of which was over water aboard *Algoma*. During this run, *Algoma* set the record for the fastest run between Owen Sound and Port Arthur. The distance was 545 statute miles and the run was made in 39 hours 42 minutes. The run across Lake Superior was made in the extraordinary time of 20 hours. Passengers aboard this run made the journey from Toronto to Port Arthur, a distance of 670 miles of which 545 was over water, in the "unprecedented short time of 47 hours" (*Thunder Bay Sentinel* May 23, 1884).

All fellow mariners were not happy with the fast new CPR ships. The masters of the sisters, seeking to enhance the reputa-tion of their new vessels, pushed the limits for speed as they made their passages.

There is a good deal of complaint among vessel men about the speed at which the Canadian Pacific steamers are rushed through the Sault Ste. Marie River. It is said they never slow up even when passing vessels where the chan-nel is bad, and the wonder is that more accidents have not happened through vessels sheering or being crowded ashore (*Cleveland Herald* July 22, 1884).

The accident feared by the vessel men occurred between *Alberta* and the wooden steamer *Osborn* 3½ miles off White-fish Point near the mouth of St. Marys River on July 27, 1884. The two ships, neither of which reduced speed, collided in heavy fog. *J.M. Osborn,* with two barges – *George W. Davis* and *Thomas Gawn* – in tow, sank with a loss of three lives (Mansfield 1899: 1: 742; *Scanner* 1974: 9). The collision caused $12,000 in damage to the bow of *Alberta* (*Duluth Tri-bune* Aug. 8, 1884).

Local people were outraged by the disaster. The *Meaford Monitor* (Aug. 1, 1884) wrote, "Any boat which comes against one of the CPR steel steamers stands a poor chance....The *Alberta* received some damage to one of its plates in the bow, but it did not prevent proceeding on its trip as if nothing had happened. There is a screw loose somewhere in the manage-ment of these steamers, and the railroad company had best find out where it is before their boats are all smashed to pieces" (*Duluth Tribune* Aug. 8, 1884).

Algoma was involved in an accident in August, apparently through no fault of the crew. The steamer *Sovereign* collided with *Algoma* while the steel ship was lying at the Government dock. *Sovereign,* under command of the first mate, reportedly struck the starboard side of *Algoma*. The stem of *Sovereign* was carried away from the collision, and *Algoma* had one of its

plates stove in near the main guard (*Thunder Bay Sentinel* Aug. 7, 1884).

The remainder of the season was uneventful for the CPR sisters.

Wreck Event

As the 1885 season drew to a close, it was clear it would be a poor one for Lake transportation. Severe competition, low rates and smallpox were listed as the principal causes of the worst season on the Lakes in years. Several lines of steamers were laid up during the season. The only company to report a decid-ed improvement was the Canadian Pacific Company, owners of the three new steel sisters *Athabasca, Alberta* and *Algoma* (*Cleveland Leader* Oct. 18, 1885). The season was not over for the successful company, however. Before the 1885 season closed, CPR would suffer the worst human life disaster in Lake Superior history.

Algoma left Owen Sound for Port Arthur Thursday, Oct. 5, 1885, loaded with cargo and the fewest passengers it had ever carried. There were seven cabin and six steerage passengers (or five cabin and six steerage, *Owen Sound Times* Nov. 12) aboard; the cargo consisted of 134 tons of general merchandise and 297 tons of railway supplies (*Duluth Tribune* (Weekly) Nov. 13; *New York Times* Nov. 11, 1885). The light passenger list could be attributed to the lateness of the season and to the general decline of passenger traffic as a result of the opening of the "all rail" route around Lake Superior (*Owen Sound Adver-tiser* Nov. 12, 1885) earlier in 1885.

According to Capt. Moore, *Algoma* passed through the Sault Ste. Marie canal on Friday, Nov. 6 about noon. The steel steamer ran into a heavy gale and blinding snow storm at the halfway point of crossing Lake Superior. The storm increased in intensity until it quickly reached hurricane proportions. The storm of Friday night and Saturday morning was "beyond a doubt one of the greatest hurricanes that have occurred during the last five years. The dreadful storms of 1881-2-3, which did so much damage, were exceeded in violence by the terrible tempest of the 6th and 7th, in the opinion of many old seamen" (*Port Arthur Sentinel* Nov. 13, 1885).

The storm-racked ship was rolling so severely that the first mate ordered the sails set to steady it. Under sail and steam combined, *Algoma* made 15 miles an hour or better, but was drifting to leeward off the set course. A lookout was posted about 3 a.m. to sight the Passage Island light. The steamer maintained its speed until about 4 a.m. when the captain ordered the sails down and a change of course. The engines were stopped while the sails were lowered and the new course set. At 4:40 a.m., less than five minutes after the engine tele-graph bells sounded to go ahead, there was a crash (*Port Arthur Herald* Nov. 14, 1885). *Algoma* was aground on Isle Royale.

An early newspaper report recounted the wreck event (*Port Arthur Herald* Nov. 14, 1885):

A tremor shook the steamer from stem to stern, and a mo-ment afterwards she parted, just forward of the engine [ac-tually, just forward of the boilers-LM], while the waves rushed in at the vents and over the forward decks. Panic immediately ensued, and all was chaos and confusion. Passengers, who were calmly reposing in their berths...were rudely awakened by the grinding of the hull on the rocks and the roar of the storm. There was no time, however, to consider the situation. The water poured in through the broken timbers and over the deck, putting out the fires, which soon had the effect of stopping the engines and shutting off the electric light. All was darkness, storm and snow. Daylight was just breaking, but did not afford sufficient light to enable the crew to see where they were.... The steamer had shifted around after striking and was resting with her stern upon the rocks, while the forward cabin and the bow of the boat were fast crumbling to pieces so furious was she being beaten upon the reef. The purser, second mate and steward, who were all forward, made an attempt to reach the after part of the vessel, which was now the only place of safety. In doing so they were struck by a large wave, carried overboard and disappeared beneath the surface.

Some fishermen sighted them and went to their rescue. After taking in the dreadful situation the fishermen went out and intercepted the *Athabaska* which was then coming up the Lake.

The first news of the disaster arrived late on Nov. 9th in Port Arthur with the survivors aboard *Athabasca*. (It would be two decades before wireless appeared on the Lakes.) The first reports of the wreck were in the press the next day. The early reports indicated about eight passengers and 25 crew were lost (*Wisconsin State Journal* Nov. 10, 1885). Other accounts reported various numbers for those lost in the wreck (e.g., *Cleveland Leader* Nov. 10, 1885, reported 37 lost; *Wisconsin State Journal* Nov. 11, reported 47 drowned, and in another article of the same issue stated: "Other officials freely say that fully 100 have gone down with the vessel"). The lack of company records accounts for the confusion regarding the number aboard – the only passenger list was apparently aboard the lost vessel.

As is usual in the aftermath of a shipwreck, much speculation was generated to account for the disaster. The *Wisconsin State Journal* (Nov. 11, 1885) stated that the official dispatches "intimated" that *Algoma* was making for shelter in Rock Harbor when the wreck occurred.

A lengthy article titled "The Captain's Statement" appeared in some of the regional newspapers. The statement, evidently fabricated by someone other than the captain, describes panic aboard the vessel during the storm. The captain had unsuccessfully attempted to quiet the fears of those on board. The wreck of *Algoma*, according to this account, occurred as the captain was seeking refuge in Rock Harbor (*Owen Sound Advertiser* Nov. 12, 1885. This account also appeared in the Nov. 11, 1885, issue of *New York Times*).

This report, which had circulated as an Associated Press dispatch, was discounted by the captain and others. Captain Moore, still suffering from injuries received during the wreck, said the statement was wholly untrue, and must have been simply manufactured by the reporter (*Port Arthur Weekly Sentinel*

Nov. 20, 1885). The same newspaper labeled the report "shameful."

An accurate statement of the captain was printed in the newspaper (*Owen Sound Times* Nov. 19, 1885):

The steel steamer *Algoma* cleared from Owen Sound at 4:20 p.m., Thursday, the 5th inst, bound for Port Arthur, having on board a general cargo of merchandise of about 400 tons. We had a good run to Sault Ste. Marie, which port we cleared at 1 o'clock on the afternoon of Friday (6th) and passed Whitefish Point at 3:50 the same day. It was blowing a strong breeze from the east and northwest. The wind was increasing. We made sail at Whitefish Point at 7 p.m. The weather was the same, but the wind was slightly increased, with occasional squalls attended with rain. At midnight the wind had increased to a moderate gale with frequent squalls, accompanied with rain and sleet and a sea getting up. At 4 a.m. [7th] the wind shifted northeast with violent snow squalls and a heavy sea running, when we checked down and commenced taking in sail. At 4:30 a.m. all sail was in except the fore trisail [probably fore staysail, cf. notarized statement of Capt. Moore *Duluth Tribune* Nov. 13, 1885 ed.], which was partly in, and we put the wheel hard to starboard, and the ship was coming around to head out on the Lake again on account of the snow. After leaving Whitefish Point, our proper course was northwest by west, but the wind being from the northwest, we steered northwest by west quarter west until 10 p.m. to allow for leeway, when the course was changed to northwest until 4 a.m. We then steered west by south for the purpose of taking sail in. While the ship was coming around as mentioned above she struck aft about 4:20 and continued to forge ahead, driven in by the heavy sea. About 4:40 she settled, the seas making a clean breach over her all the time and smashing the ship up. A blinding snow storm continued. On account of the seas that were running and the surf, it was impossible to make any effort to save the ship or cargo, and about 6 a.m. she parted at the fore side of the boiler, and the freight got washed out and some of it was driven ashore.

There were 14 survivors (*New York Times* Nov. 13, 1885), two passengers and 12 crew including Capt. Moore. Forty-five or 47 persons were lost. This shipwreck claimed more lives than any other in Lake Superior history.

One widely circulated account had all the survivors coming ashore in a single lifeboat (*New York Times* Nov. 10, 1885). This is not an accurate account of the wreck events, and led to the press raising the question as to why there were but two passengers saved with the 12 crew. The later appearance of accurate statements of survivors cleared the insinuations (*Port Arthur Herald* Nov. 21, 1885).

The accounts of the survivors add much detail to the events of the wreck. Mr. William R. McCarter, a journalist and one of the two surviving passengers gave the following account (*Owen Sound Times* Nov. 19, 1885):

After leaving White Fish Point the wind increased, but the vessel was a staunch one and no fears were entertained, as she stood the storm splendidly. About 9 o'clock on Friday evening, I was on deck, and although there was a heavy wind, the steamer was making splendid progress. The passengers all went to bed, and about 20 minutes to five I felt a slight shock, which alarmed me, and I jumped up. I found a general alarm, and several deck hands rushing aft excitedly. I followed them and asked what was wrong, but they did not seem to know. One of them said, "This is a terrible affair, but I hope it will come out all right." As soon as the hull became fast on the rocks, the force of the waves dashing in fury against it soon broke up the saloon, and it was swept away. I think the women and children never got outside, but were probably drowned or disabled by the waves rushing in, and were carried off with the cabin when it was swept away. The sea was terrible, the waves rushing in great mountains over the deck, and every few minutes the despairing shriek of some poor fellow would be heard as he was carried off and lost. One thing followed another with such rapidity that there was not time to do anything with the boats, and they were swept off with the cabin. The electric lights went out, and it was intensely dark, so that I could only see what went on immediately around me. A great many jumped overboard, and tried to get to shore with life preservers, but only three of them succeeded, the others being dashed against the rocks. The men from below had crowded up on the upper deck, near the stern, although some had rushed forward and were lost. Amidst the terrible excitement and confusion, Capt. Moore was brave and cool.

At great risk to himself he seized a rope, and ran it along as a life line, telling us to hold on to that, and had it not been for it, more of us would have shared the fate of those who were lost. The forward part of the saloon had all gone, but a little piece was standing near the stern, and we were under the projecting roof outside of that. Timbers were crashing in every direction, and we were afraid that the protecting roof would fall on us. The Captain went aft to get a post to prop it up, and as he was coming back, there was crash, and I heard him cry out, "I'm done for – what will become of these poor people?" But he stuck to the post and dragged it along, wounded as he was, though it did not prove of much service after all. When the captain was struck, another man called out, "I'm crushed, I'm gone!" Though I could not see him, those who were next to him said he was carried off by the next wave. Twice when the waves had carried me off my feet and I was nearly gone, Capt. Moore, who was next to me, caught me and helped me up again, saying, "I will save you, old man, if I can." Two of the men had got down by the fender and were holding on there. I asked them how they were doing, when they said it was terribly cold there, I did not attempt to go. One of them gave up and was lost soon after. When it became daylight, we could see the rocks towering up in front of us, close at hand, but with the terrible sea it was

impossible to get to shore. We managed afterward to get down to the lower deck, where we all lay, cold and wet, listening to the terrible storm raging, and not knowing but we might share the fate of the poor follows who had already gone. We spent the whole of Saturday night in that position. On Sunday morning the storm had abated, and we descried a fishing tug, which we hoped would see us, but it went away. Near noon, when the sea had calmed, the three who had escaped to shore took a line from us – it was only about 40 or 50 feet – and pulled us to shore on a raft. The captain was sent first, with a man to hold him, as he was unable to stand, from his injuries. The land proved to be Green Stone Island, a small rocky islet off Isle Royale. Shortly after, some fishermen saw us, and took us to their shanty, where we spent Sunday night. On Monday they intercepted the *Athabaska,* which took us to Port Arthur.

Joseph Hastings, the first mate, gave the following description of the wreck (*Owen Sound Advertiser* Nov. 19, 1885):

"Nothing of any account occurred during the voyage to Sault Ste. Marie, the *Algoma* passed Whitefish Point about 1 o'clock on the afternoon of Friday. The wind was at that time blowing a stiff breeze from the east and northeast. At Whitefish Point sail was made, and the steamer proceeded on her way under a full head of steam. The wind kept increasing in violence, and was accompanied with snow and sleet. At 4 o'clock Saturday morning the wind shifted to the northeast and a violent snow storm raged. The sea was running mountains high, and the boat was tossed about like a cork. Fifteen minutes past 4 o'clock the order was given to take in all sail and put the wheel hard a starboard, to bring the ship about and head out on the Lake again, on account of the snow and darkness. While the ship was coming about she struck Greenstone Point, on Isle Royale about 50 miles from Port Arthur and one mile from Passage Island Lighthouse, which has been abandoned since the first of the month. After striking the first time the boat forged ahead, being driven by the wind. A second shock occurred shortly after the first. The vessel struck the reef violently, and she immediately began to break up.

"Most of the passengers and a number of the crew were in bed at the time, but were awakened by the shock, and the scene that followed beggars description. Water poured in through the broken vessel and over the bulwarks, putting out the fires in the furnace, and extinguishing the electric lights. Screams of women and children were heard above the fury of the storm. The crew hurried hither and thither, doing what they could in the darkness to render assistance; but their efforts were of little avail, for in 20 minutes after the vessel struck the entire forward part of the boat was carried away, together with her cargo of human freight. Several clung to the rigging and lifeline the captain had stretched along the decks, but were soon swept away and swallowed up by the angry waves. The stern of the boat was steadily pushed along the rock, and those who were not too much exhausted with fatigue and benumbed by the cold, crept to the after steerage and sought its shelter. Less than an hour after striking all was over, and but 15 out of over 60 were saved."

When the shock was felt he ran down to the purser's room. He then pushed forward amid the stifling steam and aroused the steward and other employees as well as the steerage passengers. Finding the escaping steam almost suffocating, he again rushed up to the cabin, aroused all the passengers whom he had not awakened on the way down and conducted them to the forward end. A lady passenger and her sister were wildly crying in a saloon clothed in only a thin nightdress. The mate urged quiet and obeying orders. While he was advancing forward with one of the lady's hands in his and holding the little girl with his other hand a great wave dashed through the cabin, caught the woman and child and swept them out into the Lake. Some of the men lost their reason completely, and rushed into the stormy depths. About 17 persons followed the men and climbed into the rigging. The terrible sea swept the boat and the masts were washed clean under the waves. Every time they came up there were two or three forms missing. Once the mast made a dip with 10 men, and when it came up right again only two persons were seen on it. The next swept all the brave strugglers away. One man fought nobly for his life. He was washed off the boat and clung to some rope. Slowly, inch by inch he struggled along the ropes, hand over hand, back to the vessel. Every few seconds a wave would hurl him around like a feather, dash him up, and then bury him under a mountain of icy cold water, but he struggled on until just a few feet from the boat, when his strength gave out and he passed away with a wild, wailing appeal for aid. Many of the passengers could be seen on their knees, loudly calling for mercy and succor. The waves spared none. They dashed in and around each shrinking form and bore away as their prey with each returning visit dozens of human beings.

John McLean was one of the two waiters who survived the wreck. His account appeared with the others (*Owen Sound Advertiser* Nov. 19, 1885):

McLean felt the shock when the boat struck and jumped out of bed. He saw the engine had stopped, and the electric lights were out, while the boat was full of steam. He ran up the hurricane deck and saw the captain blowing off steam, which he continued until all was exhausted. "The captain told us there was no great danger and the safest place was down on the lower decks. We started to run there, when the waves carried away the hurricane deck, and we grasped the rigging. The captain passed us a life line along, and we hung on to it for over eight hours, believing that every minute would be our last. It was dark and freezing cold, with a terrible sea. There were two ladies and three little girls that I noticed. They were swept away with the cabins. We could hear the ladies and girls calling piteously, but no one could help them. After a while their voices ceased, and

we all knew they were out in the Lake. The cabin went to pieces in 10 minutes after the boat struck, and only the stern part of the boat was left when we came away. All our clothing was lost. We all owe our lives to the exertions made by the captain. If it had not been for his coolness and prompt action we could not have gone through the first night. I have been on the Lakes for five rough seasons, but this is the roughest I ever saw."

Particulars of the wreck can be gleaned from many sources. Most reports indicate there were two shocks. The initial one, according to the captain, was near the stern (captain's account above). The boat moved forward and struck a second time. "A second shock occurred shortly after the first. The vessel then struck the reef violently at the fore side of the boiler, and she immediately commenced to break up" (*Cleveland Leader* Nov. 11, 1885).

The hull was immediately opened and water poured through the fractured plates. The wooden deck houses were quickly washed overboard, and the forward portion of the hull apparently broke up very shortly after. (Other accounts indicate the bow went to pieces an hour and a half after striking.) "The water poured in through the broken vessel and over the bulwarks, putting out the fires in the furnaces and extinguishing the electric lights....In less than 20 minutes the entire forward part of the boat was carried away" (*Cleveland Leader* Nov. 11, 1885).

A letter from Joseph Buckley Hastings, First Officer of *Algoma,* to Miss MacKenzie, sister of Alec MacKenzie, Purser, lost when the ship sank, gives some details of the ship's shifting position as it broke up (Michigan Technological University Archives Collection; Isle Royale National Park Underwater Cultural Resources File):

It being at this time so pitchy dark one could not recognize another standing three yards away and it was snowing hard at the time. This part of the cabin where Alec was standing [near the kitchen smoke stack stays] was washed away very quickly as the ship had swung around from the time I left the deck until I returned, in all not five minutes. Those of us who were saved had left the forward end and gone aft as the stern had by this time swung inshore and was now sheltered by the bow which on my going below was the sheltered end, the bow now acting as a breakwater for the after end, but she stood for but a short time the heavy seas completely breaking and sweeping over her and each sea washing away portions of the forward end till she was completely demolished forward of the engines and all the cabins gone fore and aft.

First Mate Hastings returned to the wreck site at the earliest opportunity and led the first extensive search of the area. Hastings had arrived at Port Arthur, frostbitten and bruised, with the other survivors aboard *Athabasca* on Monday, Nov. 9. The next morning he left aboard *Siskiwit* with the search party bound for the wreck site.

They searched 20 miles of coast line. The only articles they found were two passenger trunks and three bags of mail. There had been four bags of mail on the boat. One of the mail bags had been found buried five feet deep in the sand. There was little wreckage reported near the boat; most was found four miles down the shore (*Port Arthur Daily News* Nov. 16, 1885; *Port Arthur Sentinel* Nov. 20, 1885).

Officers of the company visited the site to check the progress of the search operations. H.M. Kersey, chief clerk of the CPR lines, chartered *Butcher Boy* with two captains aboard. Kersey ascertained the search had been thoroughly performed and considered it useless to keep the men out any longer. He instructed four Norwegian fishermen to continue the investigation whenever possible and to bury any bodies they found on the island for identification in the spring.

The company officers and search party returned to Port Arthur with the *Siskiwit* and scow, reporting little of value found. They planned to leave for the east aboard *Athabasca* on the 17th. (*Port Arthur Sentinel* Nov. 20, 1885).

The tug *Hattie Vinton,* with about 15 citizens aboard, started out for the wreck site on November 10. The weather was marginal for the crossing, and the captain decided to lay up in the lee of Green Island overnight. The sight of the wreck was described in detail (*Port Arthur Herald* Nov. 14, 1885):

The whole of the after portion of the vessel, from the engine cylinders, with the exception of the upper cabin work, lies about 40 feet from shore, listed well over to the port side; and a more dismal looking sight could hardly be imagined. In consequence of quite a heavy swell breaking over the wreck, no attempt was made to board the remains of the once staunch craft, but the whole party at once proceeded to search the shore for the corpses of the unfortunate people who were drowned. The first body was found by Mr. Harry Micholson about 75 yards southwest of the wreck, well up on shore, among the debris. A large piece of the upper cabin partially covered the body, which proved to be the corpse of poor Hanson, the wheelsman, who was at his post at the time the vessel struck....About three hours after the above discovery, one of the surviving waiters, who was with the party, noticed a body lying amongst a lot of wreckage, wedged in the crevice of a rock about 40 yards from the stern of the boat....No other bodies were found, although the search was continued all day.

Hattie Vinton returned to Port Arthur with its grim cargo. The bodies were crushed and battered. The searchers reported that the bodies had been robbed. Hanson was known to have had a gold watch and $12.00 in his pockets. When he was found his pockets were turned inside out. Several fishing boats had been spotted loaded with carpets and other goods near the wreck site, and fishermen were suspected of robbing the bodies. The bodies were placed aboard *Athabasca* bound for Owen Sound (*Port Arthur Sentinel* Nov. 20, 1885; *Cleveland Leader* Nov. 14, 1885).

A party of fishermen returned to Hancock Nov. 23, from the north shore of Lake Superior after visiting the *Algoma* wreck site. They had picked up four floating bodies from the shore of Rock Harbor. The fishermen reported more than 300 tons of freight strewn on the shore. "Portions of the pilothouse cabin wheel, and a number of life preservers were picked up....The steamer can be plainly seen on the sandy bottom of Rock Harbor" (*Cleveland Leader* Nov. 24, 1885).

An indication of the force of the storm that sank *Algoma* can be obtained from some of the accounts of scattered wreckage. "The piano belonging to the wrecked steamer *Algoma* was washed high and dry upon the rocks of Isle Royale, some 15 feet above the water's edge" (*Port Arthur Herald* and *Lake Superior Mining Journal* Nov. 14, 1885).

The wreckage was badly broken up and widely scattered. The only intact items were "one barrel of brandy, one of beer, a box of axe handles, candles, etc., lying along the beach. No doubt a large quantity will be found some five or six miles up along the beach and among the islands, where it is expected" (*Port Arthur Daily Herald* Nov. 14, 1885). "There was not a piece of wood left longer than a foot in length. Every piece of furniture was broken in small portions" (*Port Arthur Sentinel* Nov. 20, 1885). The Menagerie Islet Lighthouse Station Journal reported sighting material from *Algoma* on November 9, 1885. A uniform coat was picked up at the edge of the water 17 miles from the wreck. The coat had 14 first class tickets in the pocket.

There were other grim indications of the force of the storm. Pieces of bodies were found along with the battered wreckage. "Portions of other bodies were found, showing that the waves were tremendous having dashed them to pieces against the rocks, breaking bones and crushing bodies like egg shells (*Portage Lake Mining Gazette* Nov. 26, 1885).

The hull of *Algoma* was reported all "washed away," but the after part, up to the main mast. "The rest of the boat is completely flattened out, the iron sides being laid out even with the shores. The wreck is piled all along the coast for two miles" (*Port Arthur Sentinel* Nov. 20, 1885).

A remarkable correspondence from the archives of the Canadian Pacific Railway Company indicates that the company investigated the circumstances of the wreck of *Algoma*. A letter, dated Nov. 24, 1885, from Henry Beatty, Manager of Lake Traffic, and W.C. Van Horne, Vice President, contains the results of the company's investigation (Corporate archives, Canadian Pacific, Montreal; Portions of this correspondence appeared in Lavelle 1974: 234):

Dear Sir:
I returned from Owen Sound last night where I have been for some time taking the evidence of the survivors of the *Algoma*, for the purpose of ascertaining the cause of the loss of that ship.

The Steamer left Sault Ste. Marie at 1 p.m. on Friday, Sixth of Nov., and passed Whitefish Point about four, wind blowing a strong breeze from E.N.E. After passing Whitefish Point, they made sail and steered N.W. by W.$\frac{1}{4}$ W, her proper course being N.W. by W. $\frac{1}{2}$ W, but the wind being from the northward they allowed one quarter of a point for leeway.

At 7 p.m. the wind slightly increased with occasional rain. At 10 p.m. wind increased to moderate gale with rain and sleet, the course was changed to N.W. by W. At 4 a.m. Saturday, the wind shifted N.E. with violent snow squalls and blowing a gale.

The engines were then slowed down and shortly after, the ship's course was changed to W. by S. for the purpose of taking in sail and running back into the Lake. She immediately after struck a reef, aft, she continued to forge ahead, being driven in among the rocks by the heavy sea.

At 5 o'clock she settled down forward and her stern swung on shore, the sea making a clear break over her all the time from when she first struck.

Owing to the gale of wind, the heavy sea running and the surf, nothing could be done to save either ship or cargo. At 6 o'clock, she parted forward of the boilers.

Before the ship was turned to run back into the Lake, the Captain, First Officer and Chief Engineer, consulted, and all were of the opinion that they were 15 miles off Isle Royale, but as a matter of fact they were much farther up the Lake. The only one of the engineer's crew saved, a fireman, says they were running under easy steam all that night, for the purpose of saving fuel, and on account of the wind, but notwithstanding this the ship must have been going very much faster than they calculated, carried along by the wind, which was far stronger than they had any conception of, owing to its being nearly after them.

The distance from Whitefish Point to where she turned is about 190 miles so that the ship was going nearly 16 miles per hour.

I have carefully looked for the cause of this deplorable accident. I learned that the captain did not leave the bridge the whole night except for five minutes at midnight. The first officer was also on the bridge from midnight. Both Engineers were on watch, every precaution seems to have been used and everything done that was necessary except putting out their log. This was not done, for the reason, which they give, that they had the ship's time so accurate, that they could, in ordinary weather tell from the revolutions of the wheel, exactly where they were. They also claim that there is always a strong current in the Lake during the continuance of a stiff breeze, and therefore the log would be of no use, but would rather tend to deceive.

I may say that logs are not used on the Lakes, I do not think any Steamers but ours are furnished with them. Lake Captains depend on their compasses, revolutions of the wheels and landmarks to guide them.

The cause of the accident was, in my opinion, entirely due to the wind being much stronger than they thought, and the ship was therefore going along much faster than they calculated. When they supposed that they were 15 miles from Isle Royale, they were actually running up along it, and in turning the ship to run back into the Lake, the stern struck a reef running out from Green Stone Island.

The ship was exactly on her course before she turned, and had the Captain been reckless enough to have gone on,

there is no doubt he would have passed Passage Island all right, but this, of course, he did not know at the time, and to avoid one danger, he runs straight into a greater, the effect of which was the loss of our fine ship and a number of valuable lives.

Capt. Moore is badly injured, and the chances are about even whether he will recover. I have therefore been unable to get his testimony.

Yours truly,
Henry Beatty,
Manager Lake Traffic

An official inquiry was held regarding the loss of *Algoma*. A tribunal was appointed by the Canadian government consisting of Lt. A.R. Gordon, R.N. and Capt. Thomas Harbottle of Toronto (*Cleveland Leader* Nov. 17, 1885; *Owen Sound Advertiser* Nov. 26, 1885). The men were instructed to "inquire into the cause of the wreck and place blame where it belongs."

Principal concerns of the inquiry focused on the actions of the managers of the company as well as the captain and crew.

It is hoped they will spare no pains in placing blame, if any exists, where it belongs. If it is found that the managers of the line compelled their captains to navigate the boats without regard to wind or weather, the fact should be made known to the public. If passenger boats are run without regard for those who ride on them, the public is entitled to know it….It is not improbable that a considerable share of the blame will be found to rest with the managers of the connecting line of the Canadian Pacific. From the very first an undue pressure has been brought to bear by the management on the masters sailing these vessels, as evidenced by the frequent disasters from the *Alberta* in the summer of 1884. A prominent vessel man who had been interviewed recently in Buffalo says, "I was up at Owen Sound last summer and saw those three great steamers coming and going just on the minute, and all the while making such high speed, and I was astonished. I went on board of the *Athabaska,* and I believe one of the others, and I asked some of the officers how they could make such time. Were they not obliged to run fast in thick weather to do it? They replied that their orders were to make their time anyhow. I told them their iron hulls were ill-suited for going on the rocks. They have succeeded in about running the smaller Canadian craft off Lake Superior, and that is how they have done it. Now, with the *Algoma* gone, and so many passengers with her, their success is not anything to be proud of" (*Cleveland Leader* Nov. 22, 1885; cf. *Owen Sound Advertiser* Nov. 26, 1885).

Other sources also focused some of the blame for the wreck on the management of the company and their push for quick voyages and tight schedules. An example of this sentiment appeared soon after the wreck:

…Over all this terrible affair hangs the appalling fact that the result was largely due to carelessness or blind obedience to orders, the captain saying his orders were to "Push Through" and he did push on to death, carrying, while the storm was at its height, a full spread of canvas. At the time of the wreck the boat was 40 miles farther along than the captain had supposed her to be, showing that from the time of starting she had sailed over 16 miles an hour. It is barely possible that the captain shall ever sail a vessel again, and therefore the law may not reach him, but in the meantime what punishment should be meted to a company that gives such orders and with the expectation that they will be implicitly obeyed? (*Portage Lake Mining Gazette* Nov. 26, 1885).

The Canadian Pacific Railway Company, like most other companies that have lost vessels, was quick to rally to the support of their captain.

No man could stand higher in the opinion of the company than Captain Moore does. If the company was having another boat built tomorrow, costing $500,000, no one would be offered the command in preference to Captain Moore, who is known and trusted as one of the ablest, most discrete and careful masters on the Lakes. There is no doubt that all who survived the wreck owe their lives to the Captain, and had he not been stricken down by the fall of the cabin many more lives would have been saved. He never attempted to make Rock Harbor, and did not want shelter as so stated. The boats do not fear any sea when there is plenty of room. He did not sight Isle Royale and was turning out for the open Lake when the reef was struck (*Cleveland Leader* Nov. 22, 1885; cf. *Port Arthur Sentinel* Nov. 20, 1885).

The Commissioners of the official inquiry made a partial report of their findings on Nov. 28. They had not been able to interview Capt. Moore, who was still suffering from his injuries. Moore was reported dying from shock and exposure (*Duluth Tribune* Nov. 27, 1885). Moore did eventually recover from his injuries, including multiple rib fractures (*Cleveland Leader* Nov. 29, 1885).

The partial report, released to the government, indicated that:

the reports as given in the newspapers are correct in all important points with one exception. This is a correction of the statement that the *Algoma* was making for the harbor when she struck the rocks, as it is now shown that she was putting around and heading for the Lake when it was found she was nearer to the fatal rocks than was anticipated by the officers. It remains, therefore, for the court to decide who, if any one, was responsible for the vessel being out of her course and in that dangerous locality the time of the wreck. It is said the evidence shows also that after the vessel struck, the crew behaved like heroes, and all hands had a terrible experience" (*Cleveland Leader* Nov. 29, 1885).

The Commissioners traveled to Owen Sound to interview the injured captain. The final decision of the inquiry came in January 1886. Captain Moore and Chief Officer Hastings were censured. Captain Moore was found negligent, and his certificate was cancelled for a year. First Officer Hastings' certificate was suspended for six months (*Duluth Daily Tribune* Jan. 16, 1886). The Minister of Marine approved the sentences, but shortened the suspension of the captain to nine months "owing to previous good record" (*Portage Lake Mining Gazette* Feb. 4, 1886).

The loss of *Algoma* also prompted discussion as to the merits of iron and steel vessels for Lake transportation. "The general opinion is that they are unsafe unless built with a double bottom and water tight compartments. The CPR vessels have neither" (*Duluth Tribune* Nov. 27, 1885). *Algoma* had multiple water tight compartments, but not a double bottom. The loss also prompted a re-evaluation of the remaining sister ships. "Outside of passenger accommodations the vessels of the line are now said to be inferior to many others on the Lakes" (*Ibid.*).

Salvage

The CPR company contracted to recover the machinery of *Algoma* in early June 1886 after sending an agent to various wrecking companies (*Port Arthur Sentinel* June 11, 1886). They agreed to pay $6,500 for delivery of the machinery to Owen Sound. An effort was also directed to the recovery of the railroad iron on the wreck (*Duluth Tribune* June 18, 1886). Detroit and Port Huron parties were awarded the contract "to blast the hull of the Canadian Pacific Railway steamer *Algoma*." Fred L. Merryman (or Merriman), of Port Huron, was placed in charge of the expedition (*Ibid.* Aug. 2, 1886).

Henry Beatty announced that a contract had been let to the Moffat Tug and Wrecking Company of Detroit, with L.B. Montgomery assisting the operations. (The company also appears as "Moffat Tug and Canada Wrecking Co." in *Port Arthur Sentinel* June 11, 1886, and may actually represent two companies working together.) CPR had taken over the wreck from the insurers after a settlement had been reached. The company was particularly interested in recovering the engines and machinery for eventual reuse because they had no counterpart in the country except for those in *Algoma*'s sister ships (*Owen Sound Advertiser* June 10, 1886).

The tug *George Hand* and schooner *L.L. Lamb* were engaged in recovery operations by early July (*Detroit Free Press* July 7, 1886). The operations were expected to be completed within a month (*Detroit Free Press* July 21, 1886).

Commercial salvage companies were not the only ones engaged in the salvage of materials from the *Algoma* wreck site. Sport fishing parties were visiting the wreck, as well as prehistoric sites, to gather artifacts and relics (*Duluth Daily Tribune* July 20, 1886).

One of the "darkest mysteries known to the Lakes" developed in connection with the salvage of *Algoma*. The commercial wreckers made a careful search for more victims of the disaster. There were only

…one or two bodies found pinned in the timbers and frame-work of the vessel. The theory for this mysterious disappearance is that the bodies were despoiled by the islanders and then sunk in the Lake. This theory is strengthened by the finding of mutilated clothes and articles of value in their cabins. Such is the explanation advanced by the wreckers as the reason why the bodies have never been recovered (*Detroit Free Press* Aug. 2, 1886).

The revenue cutter *Andrew Johnson* left Milwaukee August 3 to investigate the wreckers' allegations. Captain Baker of *Andy Johnson* reported his findings four days later. As to the alleged robbery of bodies from the wrecked steamer *Algoma*, he "... found no truth in it. Only a few bodies were found and they were shipped to Canada. The railway company that owned the steamer has had guards on the island continuously since the wreck" (*Detroit Free Press* Aug. 8, 1886).

Indignant responses to the allegations came quickly:

Of course the story about fishermen plundering the bodies off the wrecked steamer *Algoma* is all pure bosh, and no one, who ever knew anything about the habits of the fishermen of Lake Superior, ever believed for a moment. The report was a cruel slander upon as honest and industrious a class of men as exist in the northwest, and very probably was started expressly to gull some innocent. If it was, the bait took (*Duluth Daily Tribune* Aug. 8, 1886; see also *Portage Lake Mining Gazette* Aug. 19, 1886).

The contracting wreckers suffered more than the indignation of the fishermen and press. The tug *George Hand* was reported wrecked and subsequently abandoned on the rocks at Rock Harbor. The tug was lying on its side and filled with water (*Detroit Free Press* Aug. 12, 1886). The uninsured tug was reported to have gone to pieces in a storm, the crew barely escaping with their lives (*Detroit Free Press* Aug. 26, 1886). Mr. Montgomery, who was in charge of the operations, was brought to Port Arthur aboard the tug *Katie Marks* from Passage Island. He reported *George Hand* broke in two on a reef near Passage Island. Montgomery chartered the tug *Beebe* and left for Passage Island to pick up the crew (*Port Arthur Sentinel* August 20, 1886). The boiler and engine may have been salvaged. They were reported raised and put aboard *L.L. Lamb* (*Port Arthur Sentinel* Sept. 3, 1886).

The newspaper accounts of the location of the wreck of *George Hand* as Passage Island or Rock Harbor are evidently in error. The journal of the Menagerie Islet Lighthouse Station for the date of loss records the following:

August 10 – We discovered a tug on the Schooner Island reef almost a wreck. I found her to be the *Geo. Hand* of Alconac Mich. The tug that was wrecking the steamer *Algoma* at Rock Harbor. Full particulars of how she got on there are not known yet. We have had very thick smoky weather here lately. She is laying in about four feet of water on her starboard side and about five hundred yards from the Little Schooner Island Rocks. She is listed a starboard full of water. She is surrounded with very shole water. The foggy weather prevented us from seeing the main shore.

August 11 – Wrecking party are at work raising the machinery of tug *Geo. Hand*.

The machinery that had been salvaged from *Algoma* was not lost. The schooner *L.L. Lamb* arrived in Owen Sound August 26 with the salvaged engines aboard. The boilers had been recovered, but stored at Isle Royale. *Lamb* brought machinery to both Owen Sound and Port Huron (*Detroit Free Press* Aug. 27, 1886). The engine and other machinery estimated to be "some hundreds of tons weight" were displayed on a number of platform cars at Owen Sound (*Meaford Monitor* Sept. 10, 1886).

There were 13 engines from *Algoma* reported on board when *L.L. Lamb* arrived at Owen Sound (*Port Arthur Sentinel* Sept. 3, 1886; *Daily Mining Journal* Sept. 13, 1886). This is an important clue to the nature of the deposition of the wreck. Some historians and divers believe the *Algoma* bow to be "lost" in deep water. One source for this belief is probably Dana Thomas Bowen's (1952: 127) account of the *Algoma* wreck that implies the bow sank in deep water.

The missing bow has been considered somewhat of a mystery and divers have periodically searched the area in hopes of finding an intact section of *Algoma*. Rather than breaking off and sinking as intact structure, the probability is that the bow was broken up during the wreck event and sank as fractured hull elements. The references to deep water in the historical accounts are probably only in relation to the water at the stern. The stern of *Algoma* had hit and lodged on the reef; the bow was still afloat, free to work with the wave action.

The evidence indicates clearly that the bow was accessible to the 1886 salvagers. Detailed descriptions of *Algoma* published soon after its appearance on the Lakes state that there were a total of 12 auxiliary engines aboard (see above *Algoma* Construction; *Cleveland Herald* Nov. 30, 1883). A total of 13 engines aboard *L.L. Lamb* indicates all engines aboard *Algoma*, including the main engine were recovered. In order to have salvaged all the engines from the wreck, the salvagers had to have worked on the bow portion of the vessel. It could not have been "lost," and it was not likely to have been in very deep water. This may account for the fact that no anchors or cables have been located. If the wreckers were able to recover the bow windlass and capstans (all having steam engines to operate them), they most likely recovered the anchors and cables. Additional research into the records of the salvage companies and other sources may clarify some of these points. A complete mapping operation of the material record of *Algoma* will certainly augment our knowledge of this important historic site.

The salvaged engine from *Algoma* was installed in *Manitoba* in 1889. The new passenger steamer was launched that year and had a safe 60-year career on the Lakes. The vessel was only retired after the enactment of stringent new safety regulations prompted by the disastrous burning of *Noronic* in 1949 (Landon 1970: 313-315).

A later salvage effort stated that the *Algoma* wreckage as seen in 1903 remained much as it had been in 1886. Captain Ryan aboard *Joseph C. Suit* salvaged portions of the wreck in that year, apparently the second commercial salvage effort. A newspaper account records Ryan's comments as: "Her bow is resting above water on shore, but the stern is sunk about 30 feet below the level of the Lake" (*Duluth Evening Herald* May 22, 1903). Evidently, "bow" and "stern" were reversed in the newspaper account. If that is the case, the recognizable bow sections were located in shallow water some 19 years after the wreck.

Ryan carried out fairly extensive salvage operations. The operation employed a diver and a steam crane. "About 80 tons of iron plates, fish plates and railroad iron have been recovered. Dynamite was used to break the wreckage into pieces that could be easily handled by the crew." It was reported that this was the second trip of *Suit* (*Duluth Evening Herald* May 22, 1903).

Apparently, there have been other commercial salvage efforts on *Algoma*. A silver-plated crown jug from the wreck was exhibited in 1906. A Great Lakes Dredging Company diver had given the artifact to L.G. Andrews, who was displaying it in Port Arthur (*Port Arthur Daily News* Dec. 6, 1906).

In more recent times, *Algoma* has been the site of scuba diving activity. Many portable artifacts have been removed from the wreckage, but the site still proves an interesting dive, particularly when searching for new wreckage. The site has not been thoroughly surveyed and mapped. There are many discoveries to be made on this widely scattered shipwreck, both for divers and for those interested in Lakes' vessel architecture.

Dives conducted by Patrick Labadie with SCRU personnel in 1985 have produced indications that portions of the bow of *Algoma* lie to the west. Other divers have reported sightings to Labadie that may be other bow-related structures, such as the gaff from the forward mast and the ship's galley stack reported by Scott McWilliam. Videotapes made during 1986 also show a bulkhead that is believed to be from the bow. There is much exploration and documentation to be done on this site.

Epilogue

To better understand the contemporary perception of the nature of the *Algoma* disaster, it may be instructive to consider the following song. It was written by Thomas Hughes, a resident of Port Arthur, Ontario and printed in Toronto in 1885.

THE WRECK OF THE *ALGOMA*

On the sev'nth day of November
Our Dominion look'd with pride
On a steam boat which spread her
Reputation far and wide,
The world's two mighty oceans
Were join'd by iron band,
And the great work so accomplish'd
Was the pride of our fair land.

But no one thought that ere the dawn
Of that glad triumphant day,
A sad and fearful accident
Would take that joy away.
The noble ship *Algoma*
With some sixty souls set sail,
And only fifteen of them all
Were left to tell the tale.

CHORUS:

Hear the cry of us poor sinners
Cast upon the friendless wave,
And protect us we implore Thee,

Thou alone hast power to save.

On the shore of Isle Royale that morn,
The vessel struck upon the shoals,
And 'mid tempest, storm and blinding snow
Sank forty-five poor souls.
The captain of the gallant ship
With courage few would dare,
Oft risked his life to save the lives
Of those placed in his care.

Full thirty hours they lay exposed
To the fierce relentless wave,
Uniting in their prayers to Him
Who only now can save.
On Sunday morn, that morn on which
Christ burst the bonds of death,
He heard the prayers poured forth to Him
With supplicating breath.

Their wounded helpless captain now
They fasten on a slender raft,
And with what feeble strength remains
They leave the ill-fated craft,
And reaching shore on bended knees
They joined in praise to One
Who saved them: but for those who're lost
Whispered "Thy will be done."

Monarch: History

Construction

Monarch was built in 1890 by John Dyble, formerly of Parry and Dyble. The combined firm had, in 1882-83, built *United Empire, Monarch*'s running mate. The new ship was built for the Northwest Transportation Company of Sarnia, Ontario, on the southern tip of Lake Huron and launched June 27, 1890 (*Chicago Inter Ocean* June 27, 1890). The company, owned by the two Beatty brothers, was known as the "Beatty Line." James H. and John Beatty had built the Northwest Transportation Co. from a partnership they formed in 1865, which became the Lake Superior Line in 1870.

The demand for their transportation services on the Upper Lakes grew, and the two brothers incorporated their enterprise in 1882 to form the Northwest Transportation Co. This firm continued to grow into the largest company transporting package freight and passengers under the Canadian flag on the Upper Lakes. It was locally called the "Blackline."

In early 1899, the Beattys merged with the Great Northern Transit Company of Collingwood. The latter company, known as the White Line, operated steamers on Georgian Bay and the North Channel. This merger formed the Northern Navigation Company and evolved into the Northern Navigation Co. Ltd., which dominated Upper Lakes transportation of freight and passengers for many years. This company was, in 1915, to become a part of the Canada Steamship Lines Ltd., which still carries the original Beatty Line funnel design, red with a white band and black top, maintained throughout the series of mergers.

United Empire, Monarch's running mate, formerly known as "Old Betsy," was an arch-trussed wooden propeller, 252 feet 8 inches by 36 feet 15 inches with a gross tonnage of 1,961 and a registered tonnage of 1,296. The ship originally carried a sail on the foremast. This ship had a fore-and-aft compound engine of 1,000 horsepower. This vessel was rebuilt at Collingwood in 1904 and renamed *Saronic* in 1905.

United Empire was a well-appointed vessel sometimes referred to as the "Queen Vessel of the Inland Seas" (*Thunder Bay Sentinel,* Port Arthur, Dec. 1, 1883). Captain Edward Robertson and his crew of 50 became known for their competency and courteous attention to passengers.

A perspective on *Monarch*'s passenger and freight capabilities may be gained from comparison with those of *United Empire. United Empire* carried 200 cabin passengers and at least another 200 (some sources give 400) in steerage, and it made the Sarnia-Port Arthur run on the average of 60 hours. In a single season, *United Empire* carried more than 5,000 passengers and 40,400 tons of freight during 16 trips, netting the owners some $40,000 (*Thunder Bay Sentinel,* Port Arthur, Dec. 1, 1883; *Chicago Tribune* May 21, 1883).

Continued demands prompted the company to construct another vessel for the Port Arthur-Duluth-Sarnia run. This new vessel was to become the flagship of the Beatty Line and bear the appropriate name of *Monarch.* Edward Robertson was made captain of the new steamer, which was considered a "high but entirely deserved compliment to Capt. Robertson" (*Duluth Evening Herald* Oct. 22, 1890).

Monarch was built in Sarnia, Ontario, on the St. Clair River for a cost between $150,000 and $200,000 (*Chicago Inter Ocean* June 27, 1890; *Duluth Evening Herald* June 28, 1890). The vessel was built for extended season service on Lake Superior and was strongly reinforced with iron. The hull was of white oak. The vessel was 259.0 feet long overall with a beam of 34.8 feet and 14.8 feet depth, with a waterline length of 245 feet. The registered tonnage was 2,017 gross tons and 1,372 net. The hull was originally painted white to the main deck rail; the cabins were also white.

The engine of *Monarch* was a three cylinder, triple-expansion, inverted, vertical steam engine, which some sources say was built at the Phoenix Iron Works of Port Huron, Michigan. Other sources, such as the *Duluth Evening Herald* of Oct. 22, 1890, state the engines were built by Kerr Brothers of Walkerville, Ontario. The cylinders of the engine were 21 inches, 33

inches and 54 inches in diameter with a common 42-inch stroke. The engine, with a 900 horsepower rating at 80 revolutions per minute, was capable of making the 26-mile run from Thunder Cape to Passage Island in a normal running time of 2 hours 20 minutes. The ship averaged 32 hours to Sault Ste. Marie. Some sources say the engines developed 2,000 horsepower (e.g. *Chicago Inter Ocean* June 27, 1890), although this is unlikely.

The engine required 160 pounds of steam from the two Scotch marine boilers. These boilers were 11 feet 4 inches long and 16

Figure 19. Passenger/package freight vessel *Monarch*. An early photograph of the ship before alterations. The iron hull support arch is visible above the gangways. U.S. Army Corps of Engineers Canal Park Marine Museum Collection.

feet in diameter, and were built by the Lake Erie Boiler Works of Buffalo, New York, and installed there in July 1890 (*Chicago Inter Ocean* June 27, 1890).

Apparently, *Monarch* was the last vessel to be constructed at Sarnia for 54 years until the MAC-Craft Corporation used its shipyards during the second World War. When the company's first vessel went down the ways, there were none present who remembered the last launching in Sarnia (Young 1957: 107).

Monarch was appointed with luxury fittings and was unsurpassed for elegance of furnishings until the company built the 321-foot steel steamer *Huronic* in 1902. *Monarch*'s cabins were finished in white enamel trimmed with gold moldings and carefully crafted; they

…had a fair rake and that meant that all the window sashes were cut out of square to follow the lines of the cabins. Every sash had to be made separately for its place and paired off, port and starboard, a nice piece of work which W.H. Pitfield carried out the whole length of the cabin (*London, Ontario, Free Press* Dec. 1, 1956).

One of the best descriptions of *Monarch* appeared in the *Duluth Evening Herald* (Oct. 22, 1890):

A Beautiful Ship: The magnificent New Monarch of the Beatty Line. Far the Finest Running to Duluth, Destined to be the Popular Passenger Ship of the Upper Lakes....

On her first trip, which was enjoyed by about 30 passengers, she made an average speed of 13 miles an hour. She was built, however, for a speed of 14 miles an hour and that rate can easily be attained....This will make her the fastest passenger boat running into Duluth harbor.

The smoking room and washroom for the gentleman as well as the offices for the captain and purser are on the main deck.

The cabin is finished in white and gold, and will be lighted by electricity. There are 62 staterooms and a bathroom. Doors between each alternate stateroom can be thrown open....Each stateroom has a double lower and single upper berth for nearly 200 passengers.

In the center of the cabin is the pantry and steam tables, the kitchen being on the main deck below. Forward of the pantry is the dining room, there being 12 tables with room for 10 people at each. The ice box is a model one and is large enough to hold several tons....There are five separate holds, the hoisting machinery being operated by pony engines....

The stack of the *Monarch* is a trifle smaller than that of the *Empire,* and is a little further astern. The low steel sustaining arch visible amidships on the upper deck of the *Empire* is in the *Monarch* clear out of the way below decks thus entirely obliterating one objectionable feature.

The new ship was special in every way. The ship's menus made the news; it carried the most famous names on its passenger list. The decor, orchestras and salons were noted in the social columns (Doner 1958: 121).

On the first trip the boat was loaded to capacity, and the working of the new vessel in a heavy sea wedged the stateroom doors shut. When the vessel returned to Sarnia, this was corrected (*London, Ontario, Free Press* Dec. 1, 1956). The original appearance of *Monarch* was completely white; later, its hull was painted black. The pilothouse was later raised, and the Texas deck lengthened some 30 feet. Examinations of photographs taken before and after the alteration reveal that there were also port holes installed in the aft crew quarters.

Operational History

The normal route for *Monarch* and running mate *United Empire* was from Sarnia, Ontario, on Lake Huron, through Sault Ste. Marie to Fort William in Thunder Bay, Ontario, and to Duluth, Minnesota. Passengers and package freight were carried both ways. The ship had a relatively uneventful career, except for these few known incidents.

In the first incident, the vessel ran its bow aground at the river's mouth at Port Arthur in August 1892. *Monarch* was released after its cargo was lightered (*Detroit Free Press* Aug. 8, 1892).

A second incident, which took place on Thanksgiving Day 1896, was considerably more exciting. *Monarch* was downbound from Port Arthur to Duluth with cargo and passengers aboard; there was some speculation in Duluth as to whether Capt. Robertson would leave Port Arthur because there was a storm approaching. The storm became a gale and continued to build in force until it became one of the worst in the recent memory of those reporting the event.

Capt. Robertson and crew left Port Arthur at 1:30 a.m. expecting a wind shift from easterly to westerly. Instead of a shift came sleet, snow and gale force winds that whipped waves up to a height level with the ship's rail. Several times the sea came over the stern of the vessel, which sometimes occurs when Lakes ships run before a gale. The full force of the gale struck when *Monarch* was about 70 miles out of Port Arthur. The weather was too fierce to turn back.

By 4 p.m. it was already getting dark as the ship passed Two Harbors. The captain had trouble picking up the range lights to align the vessel with the Duluth Ship Canal and came close enough to the south shore to hear the breakers. When the ship was not more than 1,000 feet from the piers, the wheel was put hard to port. *Monarch* responded to the helm splendidly for a vessel laboring in such a heavy sea. The captain finally made out the ranges and struck for the entrance under a full head of steam.

Figure 20. *Monarch* after alterations that included the addition of cabins aft of the pilothouse. The vessel had this configuration when lost. U.S. Army Corps of Engineers Canal Park Marine Museum Collection.

A large wave threw *Monarch* against the south pier, damaging the hull slightly. The heavy current threw the ship toward the north pier, but because Capt. Robertson had ordered full steam, the ship avoided a serious collision and sped safely through the narrow waterway. The spectators who had gone to the piers to see the huge breakers were witness to the additional performance of masterful seamanship that Thanksgiving night (*Duluth Tribune* Nov. 27, 1896; *Duluth Evening Herald*, Nov. 27, 1896).

Monarch was involved in minor collision with the steamer *Mahoning* October 4, 1898. *Monarch* was lying at the outer end of the St. Paul and Duluth slip, and *Mahoning* was entering the channel. Apparently, there was a problem with *Mahoning's* steering, and it collided with *Monarch*, causing some damage to its stern hull planks (*Duluth Evening Herald* Oct. 4, 1898).

Figure 21. Bow of *Monarch* on the rocks at Isle Royale after the wreck. This photo may have been taken the following spring. U.S. Army Corps of Engineers Canal Park Marine Museum Collection.

One incident in *Monarch's* career has only been documented in the biography of salvor Tom Reid (Doner 1958: 121-2). *Monarch*, in later years, was overhauled in the shipyard and thereafter ran package freight. The year the ship was refitted it froze in the ice in mid-November near Sailors Encampment on St. Joseph's Island at the Soo. The tugs *Reid, Sarnian* and eventually *Protector* were sent to the rescue. *Monarch* was reportedly freed at a cost of $20,000.

The 1903 season ended with reduced business for the company. It was reported that *Monarch* would only make the trip between Duluth and Sarnia once every 10 days (*Duluth Evening Herald* Oct. 10, 1903).

Wreck Event

The final voyage of *Monarch* would have been its last trip of the 1906 season. It was not unusual for a Great Lakes vessel of this period to be lost on the last trip of the season. November and December are busy months on the Lakes as vessel operators attempt to make as many trips as possible before the close of the season. Freight rates are at the highest of the year, and pressure is great to make one more passage.

According to the *Marine Protest, Monarch* had run into heavy weather on the upbound trip from Sarnia. The vessel suffered some water damage to the cargo in the Number 3 and Number 4 holds (*Marine Protest: Monarch* 12-11-06, Canadian Archives).

On Thursday, December 6, 1906, *Monarch* was loaded at Port Arthur with a cargo listed as "grain and general merchandise" (*Marine Protest: Monarch*). The *Toronto Daily Star* Dec. 10, 1906 and the *Toronto World* Dec. 11, 1906, both list the cargo as "35,000 bushels [which would be about 1,050 tons weight] No. 1 Northern wheat; one car oats for Thessalon; one car oats for

Gore Bay, four cars for the Soo; one car of flour for George Gardner, Sarnia; one car of salmon for Montreal; one car of salmon for London; 200 tons of flour for the GTR, Sarnia." (A car of grain was equal to 350 bushels.) Unfortunately, little mention has been made of any additional "general merchandise." The ship was downbound through the Soo Locks to Sarnia.

At 5:25 in the afternoon, with loading completed, *Monarch* departed its berth and started out into Thunder Bay, arriving at Thunder Cape at 6:48 p.m. Here the course was changed to a heading toward Passage Light, off the northeast tip of Isle Royale. The *Marine Protest* (December 11, 1906) states that the wind was from the northwest, with snow, fog and a heavy sea running; the temperature was below zero degrees Fahrenheit. The normal running time for *Monarch* from Thunder Cape to Passage Light would have been 2 hours 20 minutes. Near the end of the normal running time the second mate went aft to check the log, only to find it frozen and registering 10 of the 26 miles between the Cape and Passage Light. Passage Light had been glimpsed twice during the voyage. At the normal time, the captain set the course for Whitefish Point (recorded in the *Protest* as southeast by east $\frac{1}{4}$ east, or about 120 degrees). Six minutes later the captain adjusted the course "to allow for leeway," to east by $\frac{3}{4}$ south, or about 110 degrees. The wind was blowing fresh from the north-northwest. The time must have been about 8:54 p.m. About 9:30 p.m., *Monarch* ran into the solid rock wall known as the The Palisades, about 900 yards west of Blake Point, the northeastern tip of Isle Royale.

The exact cause of the wreck is not readily apparent. Popular explanations for the vessel being off course seem rather weak when subjected to scrutiny. For example, the loss has been attributed to the compass being out of order, possibly from the cold (*Fort William Daily Times Journal* Dec. 11, 1906; *Toron-*

to World Dec. 12, 1906; Wolff 1979: 88). This seems unlikely on two counts: 1) it would certainly have been an advantage to report such a malfunction during the *Marine Protest,* but it was not reported; 2) *Monarch* carried steam radiators for heat, many were located by the Park Service dive team on the site, and the pilothouse was surely heated. The taffrail log, however, was reported frozen so that their distance out was not known. Coupled with snow, fog, wind and heavy seas, it was sufficient to put the *Monarch* hard up on Isle Royale.

Wolff (1979: 88) reports that the pilothouse crew mistook the Blake Point Light for Passage Light and they were steering "some 70 degrees" off course. While the varying reports do mention that in a couple of instances during the voyage the Passage Light was visible, there could have been no confusion as to which light it was. Blake Point Light was not installed until 1917, 11 years after *Monarch* had wrecked. (See examples of criticism of U.S. Government after the wreck from the Canadian press for not marking *both* sides of the Channel, Barry 1980: 18).

Wolff does not mention how he computed the course variance of 70 degrees. The difference between the route of *Monarch* from a point clearing the north of Thunder Bay by Thunder Cape Light on the current downbound route to the site of the wreck is a course variation of about 6½ degrees. At the latter course, the vessel would have hit the Palisade Cliff at an angle of somewhat greater than 103 degrees true. The course recorded for *Monarch* was east by south ¾ south, or about 110 degrees. An examination of the five side-scan sonar passes of the wreck site done by the Submerged Cultural Resources Unit in 1980 show the bearing of *Monarch's* structural remains to be about 110 degrees true. Although those data coincide with the course as stated in the *Marine Protest,* the position of the remains may not precisely represent the final course heading of *Monarch.*

The weather was extreme during *Monarch's* last voyage. Two Booth Line steamers, *America,* a later casualty at Isle Royale, and *Easton,* were held up in Duluth due to weather conditions (*Port Arthur Daily News* Dec. 6, 1906). The same newspaper reported the lowest temperature reading of the season on December 7; the reading was 22 degrees below zero Fahrenheit. Charles Thomas Davis, the lighthouse keeper at Copper Harbor Ranges, recorded in the log for December 5, 1906, a fresh east wind and snowstorm, with a northeast gale that evening. The log entry for December 6 was: "north wind, gale, cold and heavy snowstorms, freezing very hard today."

The intense cold of this storm caused the formation of six to nine inches of ice in Lake Superior, which trapped 20 vessels. The Lake Carriers Association organized an ice breaking expedition that left Sault St. Marie on December 11 to free the trapped vessels (*Fort William Daily Times Journal* Dec. 10, 1906).

Damage to vessels resulting from this December 6 storm was not limited to Lake Superior. Three vessels, one steamer and two schooners, were damaged on Lake Huron (U.S. Department of Agriculture 1907: 10). The 1906 shipping season closed abruptly because of the storm; it was reopened only briefly by tug ice-breaking operations.

During the season 229 vessels were damaged and 53 were lost to weather causes. The financial loss for the season was put at $2,043,850. The greatest loss to heavy weather conditions was in the month of December and amounted to $471,750. The wreck of *Monarch,* a loss of $100,000 for the vessel and $60,000 for the cargo, was the largest single loss of the 1906 season (Henry and Conger 1907: 5-6). The single largest cargo loss from the *Monarch* disaster was probably sustained by Parish and Lindsay of Winnipeg, who had 35,000 bushels of wheat on board (*Duluth News Tribune* Dec. 11, 1906).

Monarch hit the rock face of Isle Royale Thursday, December 6 a little after 9 p.m., on the coldest day of the year; a heavy snow had been falling, driven by gale force winds. Visibility had been reduced to less than 50 feet, a distance little further than the bow from the bridge. Captain Robertson had gone outside and "with his face to the full brunt of the storm [he] endeavored to regain his course" when the "vessel veered to the right and there was a scraping, grinding sound, and then a crash; the *Monarch* had struck" (*Fort William Daily Times Journal* Dec. 11, 1906).

Capt. Robertson reported (*Port Arthur Daily News* Dec. 11, 1906) that he caught a glimpse of Passage Light twice before the ship struck, but could not hear the fog whistle. He also said to the newspaper reporters that he assumed his compass must have been at fault. The ship had been proceeding at the "usual speed" when it struck, and immediately the order for full speed astern was signalled to the engine room. The engineer (Samuel Beatty), realizing the ship was on the rocks, disobeyed the order and kept the engines in gear and moving forward to hold the damaged ship on the rocks. A great hole was torn in the bow (*Port Arthur Daily News* Dec. 11, 1906).

Plight of the Survivors: Soon after the impact the passengers and crew rushed up on deck, but the brief confusion was soon put in order (*Port Arthur Daily News* Dec. 11, 1906). The electric lights went out leaving the ship in darkness. Quickly, a lifeboat was lowered and manned by fireman Walter Houghton and three sailors: Edwin Brealin, Jacob Smith and Robert Berry. The boat was evidently lowered on the starboard side, the side closest to the rocks, but floating wreckage and the force of the waves prevented the men from rowing to the closest rock, a scant 25 feet away (*Fort William Daily Times Journal* Dec. 11, 1906).

Shipwrecks often prompt acts of courage; indeed, many people have survived only through heroic acts, their own or those of others. The wreck of *Monarch* produced a hero, James (Jack) D. McCallum. McCallum, a deck hand and brother of the second mate, was working off his passage down the Lakes. It was he who, after the failure of the landing attempt, managed to get a line to shore. Accounts vary as to what actually took place. Some say he tied a rope around his waist and used a ladder to get ashore (*Port Arthur Daily News* Dec. 11, 1906), or was swung pendulum-like until he managed to cling to the rocks and was passed a ladder (*Fort William Daily Times Journal* Dec. 11, 1906); others say that he gained a foothold on sacks of grain and mattresses thrown over the bow (Particulars of Service rendered in Saving Life, rendered by John D. McCallum to passengers and crew, S.S. *Monarch*).

However McCallum did it, he managed to get up the bank to

the shore apparently with the aid of a ladder and secured a line. One account said the rope broke and a tow line was thrown to him and he secured it to a tree (*Fort William Daily Times Journal* Dec. 11, 1906). Using this line, the passengers and crew were able to leave the ship and make their way up the rocks. There may have been a boat used to aid the crossing. One passenger (R.M. Lockhead) in his account stated that he fell off the line and hit the gunwale of the boat that had been used to pass the lifeline to the shore (*Port Arthur Daily News* Dec. 11, 1906).

When about half of the ship's company was safe on the rocks, *Monarch*'s stern began to sink (*Port Arthur Daily News* Dec. 11, 1906). This shift of the wreck apparently caused some confusion among those remaining on the vessel. In the confusion, the only fatality occurred. Joseph Jacques (reported elsewhere as James Jacques, e.g., *Port Arthur Daily News* Dec. 11, 1906), an 18-year-old watchman aboard *Monarch*, drowned (*Fort William Daily Times Journal* Dec. 18, 1906). Jacques, whose family lived in Point Edward, had been working at the Grand Trunk elevator all summer and had only quit two weeks before, deciding to take his ill-fated trip on *Monarch*. His mother, Mrs. A. Jacques, had begged him not to go, but young Jacques shipped as a watchman aboard the vessel on the upbound trip. His mother was in shock for some time after hearing the news of her son's death (*Fort William Daily Times Journal* Dec. 18, 1906).

There are some slight discrepancies regarding this single *Monarch* fatality. In the *Fort William Daily Times Journal* (Dec. 18, 1906), it was reported that Jacques was asleep in his bunk when the boat foundered and sank. Accounts that appeared immediately after the wreck state that in the confusion that occurred when the stem section broke off and sank, that Jacques by mistake seized a fender rope rather than the shore line and fell into the Lake. His cry could be heard by those on deck, but no assistance could be rendered (*Port Arthur Daily News* Dec. 11, 1906). Other accounts state that Jacques had been subject to temporary blindness (*Fort William Daily Times Journal* Dec. 11, 1906). No trace of Jacques was ever recovered. In this latter article, it is reported that Jacques was trying to lower himself into the rowboat and had slid down what he thought was a fender rope, but was actually a short line that reached only halfway down the vessel.

The exhausted survivors huddled together in the bitter cold. The rocky shoreline was covered with ice. At least one passenger had fallen into the water during the crossing, and his clothes had become frozen solid. W.H. Lockhead was spared serious frostbite by a fire that was started with the few dry matches found among the other passengers (*Duluth News Tribune* Dec. 11, 1906; *Port Arthur Daily News* Dec. 11, 1906). Along with the fire, a crude windbreak was constructed of branches. The only blanket was given to the one woman aboard, the stewardess: Rachel McCormick. Before morning, a second fire was started on high ground to attract the attention of the lighthouse keeper on Passage Island, or of passing vessels (*Fort William Daily Times Journal* Dec. 11, 1906). Later, a tent was constructed of sails recovered from the wreck (*Port Arthur Daily News* Dec. 11, 1906).

On Friday, food was obtained from the wreck. Either that morning (*Port Arthur Daily News* Dec. 11, 1906) or in the evening (*Fort William Daily Times Journal* Dec. 11, 1906), a case of salmon was found on shore, or a bag of flour and a box of salmon washed ashore. A sailor was lowered by rope to retrieve them (*Fort William Daily Times Journal* Dec. 11, 1906). Sometime Friday the wreck was boarded and a quantity of damaged bacon, bread and pie was secured and served. These meager supplies did not last long. The remainder of the time the survivors ate salmon and flour. The flour was made into flapjacks by Rachel McCormick and cooked in the ashes. The flapjacks "resembled a piece of frozen asphalt block" blackened, no doubt, by the ashes in which they were cooked. The survivors had divided into three camps on Friday. Each camp maintained a fire for warmth, and together they chopped wood for the beacon fires on the point (*Port Arthur Daily News* Dec. 11, 1906).

The beacon fires were kept burning all day Saturday (December 8) in an effort to attract the attention of the Passage Island lighthouse keeper. Saturday passed without a response. Although the keeper had seen the light of the fire during the night, heavy seas prevented an attempt to reach the island. Sunday the waves subsided enough to allow Lightkeeper Shaw (*Port Arthur Daily News* Dec. 10, 1906) to row the four-mile distance to the wreck site. Waves were still heavy enough to prevent Shaw from landing the rowboat, but he was able to take off one person, purser Reginald Beaumont. Beaumont waded and swam out to the boat (*Duluth News Tribune* Dec. 11, 1906; *Fort William Daily Times Journal* Dec. 11, 1906). That evening Beaumont and Shaw signalled the steamer *Edmonton* downbound with a load of grain. Beaumont was picked up and *Edmonton* immediately headed back to Port Arthur after finding that she could not get near the wreck (*Port Arthur Daily News* Dec. 10, 1906).

Edmonton arrived in Port Arthur Sunday about 2 a.m. bearing the news of the wrecking of *Monarch*. Immediately, Agent Bell of the Northern Navigation Company began to organize the rescue of the survivors. By 6 a.m. the owners, crew and masters of the tugs *James Whalen* and *Laura Grace* had been roused and dispatched to the wreck site (*Port Arthur Daily News* Dec. 10, 1906).

The rescue party aboard *James Whalen* and *Laura Grace* was led by Capt. Campbell of *Monarch*'s running mate *Saronic* (earlier *United Empire*), which had just arrived in Port Arthur. Several of *Saronic*'s boats were taken on the rescue trip to aid in removing the survivors from Isle Royale. Doctors McCougall and E. McEwen were taken to provide medical aid to the survivors feared to be in bad shape after their ordeal. The relief party left at 6 a.m. on what was expected to be a six- or eight-hour round trip (*Port Arthur Daily News* Dec. 10, 1906).

Meanwhile on Isle Royale, a party of four men set out from the main camp on Monday (10th) soon after purser Beaumont left with the lightkeeper. Firemen Walter Houghton and three sailors, Styles Fisher, John McPherson and Edwin Brealin, walked 12 miles to Tobin Harbor on the opposite side of the island (*Fort William Daily Times Journal* Dec. 11, 1906). It is informative to trace the probable route of the party with distances reported in the contemporary press and the geography of the island to establish possible terrestrial site locations. Historic fish camps are still on Isle Royale and are like the one to which this party went (probably the site now known as Mattson Fishery). The four men probably came across the central ridge of Isle Royale from The Palisades (near the present-day Merritt Lane Campground) down along the shore to a position across Tobin Harbor from Scoville Point, the location of the Matson Fishery, a distance of about two miles, or 2³/₁₀ miles from the wreck. The men had no choice but to walk around Tobin Harbor to reach the fish camp, another 8.5 miles, or a little more than 10 miles total, unless they were able to cross on the ice that was probably in the mouth of Tobin Creek. They located several fishermen's huts, all deserted. Fortunately, provisions had been left by the fishermen, and the four spent the night. They secured more supplies and started back across the frozen trail Tuesday (11th) morning, arriving a few minutes before the rescue tugs arriving from Port Arthur were spotted by the survivors (*Fort William Daily Times Journal* Dec. 11, 1906).

Whalen and *Grace* approached the wreck, but could not launch their boats for the pickup. The tugs signalled and went around to the south side of the point into Tobin Harbor. The survivors had to walk across the island, the second such trip of the day for the four-man party that had just returned. The survivors were taken aboard the rescue tugs, their injuries attended.

In the report given by Capt. Robertson (*Port Arthur Daily News* Dec. 11, 1906), he says the survivors had to walk a distance of eight miles. The route they took from the wreck site over to Tobin Harbor to be picked up by the rescue tugs is not recorded. The distance straight across the tip of the island to a point near present-day Merritt Lane Campground and opposite Merritt Island is about 1,500 feet. If the tugs could not pick them up at this point, it is hard to conceive of a reason for traveling down shore another 7³/₄ miles. This would have placed them beyond Tobin Harbor, but they could have come across to Rock Harbor to be picked up at a point near Rabbit Island. The only explanation for going to Rock Harbor was if ice or wave conditions prevented the tugs from approaching the island. However, this is unlikely on both counts, because *James Whalen* was an ice-breaking tug and most probably could have landed virtually anywhere. The four-man party apparently walked around Tobin Harbor to the fish camp, something they would not have done if they could have crossed the ice. The southeast shore of the island should have been in the lee of the diminishing storm. The most probable explanation is that the survivors' walk to reach the tugs was nowhere near eight miles, but it seemed that it was because of the extreme conditions.

The survivors were in good condition, considering their plight. Mr. Farquar had evidently come through the worst. He had frostbite and perhaps pneumonia and was in a seriously exhausted state (*Port Arthur Daily News* Dec. 11, 1906).

The tugs made their way back to Port Arthur and arrived about 8 p.m. (Monday, 10th). Both Mr. Farquar and Capt. Robertson were made comfortable on board the steamer *Huronic,* the newer vessel of Northern Navigation Co. Mr. Farquar was transferred to St. Joseph Hospital for treatment, and Capt. Robertson went to the Algoma Hotel (*Fort William Daily Times Journal* Dec. 11, 1906).

At the Algoma Hotel, a beaten and exhausted Capt. Robertson gave reporter Sarah Stafford an account of the disaster (*Port Arthur Daily News* Dec. 11, 1906). It was not a formal interview, the captain simply talked while eating his dinner.

> We were near Isle Royale about half past nine at night. I was standing on the bridge, when I heard a ripping sound and a part of the upper cabins were torn away....It was found we were on a rock, and that the stern was slowly sinking....I had a number of farmers on board, and they made just as good a scramble for their lives as the rest of us. We

Figure 22. Bow of *Monarch*, offshore view. This photograph was reversed when published in the contemporary press. This view is correct. U.S. Army Corps of Engineers Canal Park Marine Museum Collection.

had only one women on board, the stewardess, and she was a good one. She went down that rope 30 feet, hand over hand, into the boat, and the way she stirred up that flour with a stick and made us pancakes was a caution!

We had nothing to eat for six hours, and not being able to get water over that high bluff, we had to melt snow for a while. After a time the men went back to the ship and yanked out something to eat.

The *Monarch*'s bow stands up 10 feet above the water on the rock.

I lost all my clothes and shoes but I got an old belt I have had for many years, and I was glad to get it.

We made a tent out of some sails, and I had to watch the fire, or some fellow would put it out with his feet, covered with snow, as he lay sleeping.

We had canned salmon, but after a few mouthfuls we did not want to eat.

We had to walk eight miles before we could get to the tugs. The way that woman walked through the woods with the best of them! I was on my face half the time.

The old ship stands there up against the side of the rock. You might pass her by a hundred times and not see her. Everything is covered with snow and ice.

Apparently, the survivors were taken on the steamer *Huronic* to Sarnia. The passage was courtesy of the Northern Navigation Co. The arrival was heralded by the citizens, replete with brass band. The following report appeared in the *Port Arthur Daily News* (Dec. 19, 1906):

Sarnia, December 18th…Pandemonium broke loose when the steamer *Huronic* arrived on Sunday night with the survivors of the wrecked steamer *Monarch* on board. It appeared as if the entire town came down to the wharf to welcome the shipwrecked crew. A brass band added to the din of whistles, and seldom has such a demonstration occurred on thc Great Lakes.

Every man was a hero, but it remained for the woman, Miss Rachel McCormick, one of the crew, to carry off the real honors.

The Northern Navigation Co. responded quickly. The following statement appeared in the *Port Arthur Daily News* on December 12, the day after the rescue:

No compensation will be offered by the Northern Navigation Company to passengers who lost their effects on the wrecked steamer *Monarch*. That is one of the risks taken by passengers, and they have no case for damages against the company.

Company representatives also pointed out that the passengers had been given transportation on *Huronic*, but, even this was more than it was required to do, as the loss of the steamer terminated their contract with the passengers.

The captain and crew of *Monarch* were exonerated for their actions involving the wreck, although some rumors to the con-

trary had been circulated (*Port Arthur Daily News* December 12, 1906). A special address of esteem and sympathy was presented, along with a purse of gold, to Capt. Robertson on the evening of December 12. The ceremony took place at the Algoma Hotel in Port Arthur, and many prominent citizens of both Port Arthur and Fort William were in attendance, including the mayor, members of the Council and Board of Trade of Port Arthur.

In addition to the captain, Jack McCallum received recognition. On July 6, 1907, it was reported that he had been presented with a Royale Humane Society medal at a special session of the Board of Trade for his gallantry the previous season (*Superior Evening Telegram* July 6, 1907).

Salvage

Commercial operations were not undertaken on the wreck for two years. The Northern Navigation Co. did invite bids for salvage of the wreck (*Canadian Railway and Marine World* Nov. 1907: 855). Apparently none were submitted.

Plans to remove the machinery were expressed in 1907. A description of the site was published six months after the wreck (*Detroit News* June 9, 1907):

The wreck of the *Monarch* bow presents a most interesting sight, while the stern is buried deep in water. Where it was wrecked the shore can easily be reached by a Lake boat, the drop being so rapid. Portions of the machinery are exposed, the timbers and planks covering it having been torn away by the severe storms which occurred since the wreck.

Huge timbers 12 inches through and bolted by long steel bands were broken like so many matches. Pieces of wreckage can be seen along the Lake shore….Masses of iron twisted into all conceivable shapes show how the wind must have buffeted the ship from the time that it went on the rocks.

The time of the separation of the large stern section from the bow is uncertain. The newspaper account above indicates the stern may have been attached as late as 1907. At least one newspaper account that reported the wreck events stated that the stern broke before all the survivors were removed from the wreck. All contemporary photographs of the wreck of *Monarch* located so far show the only the bow section on the rocks. These photographs may have been taken the next year.

Monarch's machinery was salvaged in 1908 by Reid Wrecking Company under the direction of Capt. Thomas Reid. The salvage operations began in late August or in September 1908. The Reid Wrecking Company apparently purchased the salvage rights to *Monarch* from the underwriters in late August (*Port Arthur Daily News* September 9, 1908) and work was in progress soon after (*Ibid.*, September 17, 1908). It was reported that the salvage of *Monarch* was complete after 25 days of work.

Capt. Reid was quoted in a newspaper article (*Port Arthur Daily News* September 26, 1908):

We took in everything of value out of the wreck…having found conditions such that we were able to make a very complete job of it. We have the boilers, engines, dynamos, chains windlasses, etc., loaded onto the barge *Kelderhowe* (this is certainly the *Kelderhouse,* see *Port Arthur Daily News* Oct. 6, 1908) ready to be taken to Sarnia, and we will likely leave for our trip down the Lake tomorrow.

In the same article, it was reported that *Monarch*:

...stood with her nose shoved upon the rocks of Isle Royale and her bow and forward cabins out of the water to withstand the onslaught of the waves, but now that has been broken away by the salvage crew, the engines and all moveable material of worth taken away and the remnants of the hull and the last cargo loaded into it left to be scattered by the waves or swallowed up by the waters of Superior...of the cargo Capt. Reid says he saw little. The flour was still in the hold, also an amount of canned goods.... The hull was practically all broken up and all that remains in place now is the bottom, underwater.

The crew of *Salvor* reported *Monarch*'s engines were set about half speed (*Duluth News Tribune* Oct. 1, 1908): "When the *Monarch* struck she must have been running alright as her engines indicated that she was open to about half speed." This may, however, not have been the speed the vessel was running when it struck. The *Port Arthur Daily News* (Dec. 11, 1906) reported that Capt. Robertson called for "full speed astern" immediately after running aground, but Chief Engineer Samuel Beatty, realizing the extent of hull damage, kept the engines ahead to hold the steamer against the rocks. The decision probably saved those on board; the engine telegraph was probably found in the position left by the engineer when he abandoned his post.

The final disposition of *Monarch*'s machinery is currently uncertain. It is known that one of the salvage barges, *Bennington,* sank soon after the completion of the salvage of *Monarch* while en route to the Soo Locks, somewhere in the vicinity of Whitefish Point. The *Port Arthur Daily News* (Oct. 6, 1908) reports the overturning of the scow owned by Reid, and the loss of two lives. The barge was reportedly loaded with derricks and other machinery and in tow of the schooner *Kelderhouse* with the tug *Salvor* in close proximity. Beeson's *Marine Directory* (1909: 131) reports the loss of the Reid Wrecking Company schooner *Bennington,* 250 gross tons, due to foundering. *Kelderhouse* was probably *John Kelderhouse,* a 500-gross-ton vessel built in 1857 (Mansfield 1899: 1: 844).

The newspaper report quoted earlier (*Port Arthur Daily News* Sept. 26, 1908) stated the machinery was placed aboard *Kelderhouse.* There is some speculation that it was in fact aboard the schooner *Bennington* when it was lost while en route to the Soo.

It may have been the case that some of *Monarch*'s machinery was lost. It is known that the triple-expansion engine itself was not lost when the salvage vessel sank. The engine was not placed aboard another vessel, as was a frequent Great Lakes practice. *Monarch*'s engine was taken to Reid's Port Huron salvage yard where it sat until 1913, when it was finally broken up for scrap. "It was necessary to use dynamite to break up the

machinery, and for several days the town echoed to the rumbles of the explosions" (*Detroit Free Press* Dec. 4, 1913).

Research into the activities of the Reid Wrecking Company in their salvage efforts would contribute to the understanding of wooden wreck formation processes in the Great Lakes. It would be quite helpful to know what impact the salvage activities of Reid Wrecking Company had on the site. Many questions were raised when the distribution of the structural elements of the vessel was examined; e.g., are their current positions the result of natural impacts such as wave activity and ice shelving and reflect the process of normal wreck formation (the breakup of the hull on points of weakness, such as along the bilge) or is it the result of breaking apart the stern with tugs to ease removal of machinery?

More recent salvage activity of sport divers visiting the wreck has removed some of the material Reid missed. The capstan was brought up in the 1960s and is now on display at Isle Royale National Park. Other artifacts from *Monarch* have been recovered and returned to the Park, such as the ship's wheel, lamps, china and some pieces of tea service.

Glenlyon: History

Construction

Glenlyon was built as *William H. Gratwick* in 1893 at West Bay City, Michigan, by F.W. Wheeler & Company. The original U.S. registry number was 81427. Prior to 1893, Wheeler-built vessels carried engines built by one of two Detroit engine companies, S.F. Hodge & Company or the Frontier Iron Works. Wheeler later expanded its operations to include engine construction, and its own new engine works were put in operation in the latter part of 1892. The foreman of the new Wheeler facility was William Willis, formerly of the Hodge Company. Willis supervised the placement of the first Wheeler-built engine in hull 93. *William H. Gratwick* had the distinction of carrying their first engine (Wright 1969: 124). The triple-expansion engine had cylinder diameters of 20, 32 and 54 inches on a 42-inch stroke, with an indicated horsepower of 1200. The original cylindrical Scotch boilers, 12 feet x 13 feet, were built by the Wickes Brothers Boiler Works of Saginaw, Michigan.

Gratwick was built to serve as a package freighter for John Mitchell & Company of Cleveland. The hull was of steel with a length of 328 feet, a beam of 42.5 feet and a depth of 20.5 feet. Gross tonnage of the vessel was 2,818.27 and the net was 2,202.90. In the builder's certification of March 13, 1893, *Gratwick* was described as a screw steamer with two decks, three masts, plain head and round stern. *Gratwick* was launched Saturday afternoon, February 4, 1893 (*Port Huron Times* Feb. 6, 1893).

This was the fourth vessel to carry the name *William H. Gratwick.* Others were a steam tug built in 1882 in Buffalo; the 475-ton (1880) propeller later renamed *John C. Pringle;* and a

1,687-ton wooden vessel built in West Bay City in 1887. All three earlier vessels were in commission at the same time that *Glenlyon* was constructed (Mansfield 1899: 1: 832). The fourth vessel was the first *Gratwick* to be made of steel. When constructed, the steel *Gratwick* was notable because of its large size (*Lake Carriers' Association* 1924: 118-119).

The first owner of *William H. Gratwick* was the Mitchell Steamship Company of Cleveland (*Doc. of Enrollment* April 15, 1893, Huron, Ohio). The president of the company was Capt. John Mitchell, a prominent businessman, who was born in Canada in 1850.

Apparently, the Mitchell Steamship Company was a personal entrepreneurial concern for Mitchell, who was also a member of the board of directors of the Hopkins Steamship Company when *Gratwick* was built. F.W. Wheeler, whose company built the boat, was vice president of the same company. In 1894 Mitchell became vice president of the newly formed Gratwick Steamship Company. In 1895, Capt. Mitchell was made secretary and general manager of the Etna Steamship Company of which William H. Gratwick was president (Mansfield 1899: 2: 435).

Operational History

A change of ownership is recorded for *Gratwick* in 1899. In October, the documents list the new owner as the Drake-Maythem Steamship Company of Mentor, Ohio (*Duluth News Tribune* Sept. 16, 1899; *Doc. of Enrollment* Oct. 16, 1899,

Cleveland). This company retained ownership until 1902 when the ship was sold to the United States Transportation Company of Syracuse, New York (*Doc. of Enrollment* Oct. 14, 1902, Oswego).

Gratwick was sold again in 1907 when the Prindville Transportation Company of Michigan City, Indiana, became the owner (*Doc. of Enrollment* Nov. 29, 1907, Chicago). While owned by the Michigan City firm, *Gratwick* was chartered by the Graham and Morton Transportation Company of St. Joseph, Michigan. The G&M Line operated ships in the fruit and passenger service from Lower Michigan ports to Chicago, but ran to Lake Superior ports for a few seasons (*Detroit Marine Historian* 1951, Vol. 4, No. 10: 3). If *Gratwick* carried the G&M colors at this time, she had a dark green hull and a black stack during this period.

The vessel was reboiled while under Prindville ownership in 1908. The Wickes-built boilers were replaced with 13 feet 9 inches x 11 feet 6 inches Scotch boilers built by the American Shipbuilding Company of Cleveland.

The Chicago and Duluth Transportation Company of Michigan City purchased *Gratwick* in 1910 (*Doc. of Enrollment* April 8, 1910, Chicago). While owned by this company, *Gratwick* was noted for receiving the first load of iron ore taken from the Cuyuna Iron Range in Minnesota. In May 1911, *Gratwick* loaded 4,000 tons of ore at the Soo Line's newly constructed St. Louis Ore Dock on St. Louis Bay in Superior, Wis-

Figure 23. Later view of package freighter *Glenlyon*. Note freight elevators and gangway hatch cranes. U.S. Army Corps of Engineers Canal Park Marine Museum Collection.

Figure 24. Stern of *Glenlyon*. Both this and the view in Figure 23 are of the configuration of the ship when lost. U.S. Army Corps of Engineers Canal Park Marine Museum Collection.

consin, and headed east (*Duluth Tribune* May 22, 1911). It is not clear, however, that this is the same *Gratwick* associated with Isle Royale.

In August 1911, the company changed *Gratwick*'s name to *Minnekahta* (*Doc. of Enrollment* Aug. 23, 1911, Chicago). Apparently, the company converted both *Minnekahta* and *Minnetonka*, ex-*Alva*, into passenger/package boats (*Lake Carrier's Association* 1924: 119).

A "Coasting and Foreign Trade" document was issued in Chicago for the vessel in February 1913. *Minnekahta* was sold to the Lake Michigan Steamship Company of Gary, Indiana, in September 1913 (*Doc. of Enrollment* Sept. 23, 1913). This company owned *Minnekahta* for less than a year before reselling it. The ship's documents were surrendered in April 1914 when she was "sold foreign" to the Great Lakes Transportation Company Ltd. of Midland, Ontario, who returned the ship to the grain and coal trades. *Minnekahta* received Canadian registry number 126,660.

Four years later, the ship was overhauled at the Midland Shipbuilding Company and renamed *Glenlyon*. Among the alterations were a steel deck house with accommodations for the master and mate added forward, another steel deck house built aft and some minor repairs made to the hull (*Canadian Railway*

and Marine World 1918: 126). At this time the ship had a light blue-gray hull, white cabins and a rose-red stack with a black top (Williams 1956: 255). At the time, *Glenlyon* was one of a dozen vessels owned by this company, all the names of which began with "Glen" (e.g. *Glenfinnan; Glenledie*).

Glenlyon had a rather unusual operational history. During the course of its serviceable life, the ship participated in the package freight trade, the passenger/package freight trade and the bulk grain trade in two countries. Few ships were involved in all the major trades of the Great Lakes.

Glenlyon was slightly damaged in an incident that occurred in August 1920. While entering Sarnia, *Glenlyon* was diverted from its course by the schooner *Hattie Hutt* and a sand sucker working at the port. *Glenlyon* lost steerage and struck the Grand Trunk Railway freight sheds causing $5,000 worth of damage (*Canadian Railway and Marine World* 1920: 463).

Wreck Event

The last navigation season for *Glenlyon* was 1924. On the last trip, the boat left Ft. William, Ontario, on Thursday, October 30 downbound to Port Colborne (*Port Arthur News Chronicle* Nov. 1, 1924) with a cargo of 145,000 bushels of wheat (*Port Arthur News Chronicle* Nov. 3, 1924. The *Superior*

68

Evening Telegram Nov. 1, 1924, reported 245,000 bushels; the *Port Arthur News Chronicle* Nov. 4, 1924, reported 318,000 bushels). The last three or four weeks of the season were very stormy and foggy with gales and snowstorms. Ships in many ports were delayed while seeking shelter from winds and seas (*Canadian Railway and Marine World* 1925: 642). *Glenlyon* was one of the vessels delayed. The boat cleared Ft. William Thursday night only to remain at anchor in the shelter of the Welcome Islands all of Friday, October 31 (*Superior Evening Telegram* Nov. 4, 1924) while a northeast gale raged (*Port Arthur News Chronicle* Nov. 1, 1924). The captain was William Taylor. It was his first season as master of *Glenlyon*. The chief engineer was Edward Hurl (*Great Lakes Redbook* 1924: 72).

The weather lessened somewhat by Friday afternoon, and Capt. Taylor resumed the voyage. The weather worsened and the wind shifted to the north, then to the southwest, soon reaching a heavy gale (*Port Arthur News Chronicle* Nov. 1, 1924). Shortly after clearing Passage Island, the course was altered to run down the south shore of Isle Royale to Siskiwit Bay to seek shelter from the storm (*Canadian Railway and Marine World* 1924: 642). The storm of Friday night and Saturday would be labeled by mariners as one of the worst encountered in years. "Whitefish Light, which stands up some 60 feet out of the water, was deluged by the breaking waves, running mountains high" (*Port Arthur News Chronicle* Nov. 3, 1924). John Collins, wireless operator off *G.J. Grammer*, a vessel crossing Lake Superior Friday and Saturday, made the following comments:

Rough, I should say it was rough. The waves in Lake Superior on Friday last were mountains high. We had to ballast the boat with water to keep her on some sort of even keel. After a short lull Friday afternoon the wind at midnight reached the hurricane velocity of nearly 60 miles per hour. It came from the southeast to southwest. Our boat was tossing about like a cockle shell. Many of the crew had never been through such an experience before. I never want to go through it again (*Port Arthur News Chronicle* Nov. 4, 1924).

At about 1 a.m. on November 1 (*Houghton Mining* Gazette Nov. 2, 1924), *Glenlyon* reached the entrance of Siskiwit Bay. While entering, the vessel ran hard aground on a submerged reef off Menagerie Island.

The first reports of the disaster were received by wireless in time to be carried in the November 1, 1924, edition of the *Port Arthur News Chronicle*. The account of the wreck that follows is taken from that source, except where otherwise noted.

Siskiwit Bay was a known sanctuary from gales for ships in the area, and the entrance channel was not considered dangerous. The crew expected nothing out of the ordinary. "The off watch were asleep in their berths when the grinding, crumbling, grating of ship's keel awakened them" (page 1). Roger Paige, *Glenlyon*'s wireless operator, was on watch at his key and immediately sent a distress message giving the ship's position. The message was received aboard running mates *Glensannox* and *Glenlinnie,* who rushed to their stricken mate's aid (reported as *Glensannox* and *Glenfinnie* in *Detroit Free Press*

Nov. 2, 1924). The vessels stood off in the lee of Isle Royale throughout the early hours of the morning.

As soon as *Glenlyon* struck the submerged reef, all crew members were ordered to their watch stations and the pumps were manned. The pumps were later abandoned, and the captain scuttled the ship to secure it to the reef (*Canadian Railway and Marine World* Dec. 1924). (It is interesting to note that the captain scuttled the vessel to secure it but did not drop the anchors – they were found still shipped during the site investigations of 1982-84.) During the night *Glenlyon* communicated with the government wireless station at Port Arthur. John Bell, agent for the Great Lakes Transportation Company, was notified, and he dispatched the salvage tug *Strathmore* to the scene at 6 that morning. Agent Bell and *Strathmore* were familiar with shipwrecks at Isle Royale – they were both involved in the events of the wreck of *Monarch* in 1906.

Shortly after the wreck, two men set out in one of the ship's open lifeboats (referred to as a yawl in some reports). Mate John McLaughlin (reported as Daniel Mclaughlin, *Daily Mining Gazette* Nov. 4, 1924, and as Donald in *Superior Evening Telegram* Nov. 3, 1924) and Watchman (or wheelsman as reported in *Detroit Free Press* Nov. 2, 1924) Wilfred Roy were soon missing and were presumed lost in the first reports to reach Port Arthur. A search for the two men was begun.

It is not known why these two men left the ship. The reasons for their departure has been the subject of some speculation. One source (Wolff 1979: 127) stated they launched the lifeboat to seek help. This is unlikely when one considers that the vessel had been in wireless communication with Port Arthur and a lifeboat would be quite unmanageable in the heavy seas, especially with only two men aboard. Another account asserted that the two crew members launched the boat in a panic against the direct orders of the captain and were blown across the Lake to the Apostle Islands (Stonehouse 1974: 9). Neither statement is supportable as far as we can determine. In his next edition the latter author said the two men lowered the lifeboat in the confusion of stranding (Stonehouse 1977: 51). Stonehouse may have confused the account of three sailors from *Glenlochie,* who were drowned when their lifeboat was crushed against the side of their vessel after it was grounded in Lake Ontario. These men launched the lifeboat against their captain's orders (*Detroit Free Press* Nov. 18, 1924). It seems most likely that the two men from *Glenlyon* were sent overboard to carry out a damage inspection and were accidentally swept away. No historical accounts have been located that shed any light on this event of the wreck.

The U.S. Coast Guard was notified of *Glenlyon*'s stranding. The Portage Lake Ship Canal crew under the command of Capt. C.A. Tucker and the Eagle Harbor crew commanded by Anthony Glaza responded. The Canal crew left for the site Saturday morning about 11:30 only to return to port at midnight due to the heavy weather. This crew was unable to make the 45 miles to the site in the face of "one of the most severe storms in the history of the Lakes. Marine men estimated that the wind attained a velocity of between 50 and 60 miles an hour" (*Daily Mining Gazette* Nov. 4, 1924). Eight-foot waves were washing over the breakwater when the Coast Guard vessel entered the Lake (*Daily Mining Gazette* Nov. 4, 1924).

The Eagle Harbor crew aboard the cutter *Cook* left Sault Ste. Marie about 10:45 a.m. The Lakes Division Office of the Coast Guard had received the message of the stranding from Lt. Commander R.B. Hammes of the U.S. Navy, who had transmitted the message by the steamer *James E. Ferris,* which had intercepted the original distress signal (*Detroit Free Press* Nov. 2, 1924). At 11:45 a.m. the gaskets on the manifold of *Cook*'s engine had to be replaced. Repairs were completed by 4 p.m. The cutter locked through and proceeded up the St. Marys River in a fresh west-southwesterly breeze that was shifting to the north. At 6:15 p.m. the flywheel on the main engine loosened due to a defective key. By this time the wind had hauled to the northwest at gale force, and there was a heavy sea running. The captain turned his vessel back and anchored to make repairs.

In the incident report that was filed Capt. Glaza stated that it would add greatly if their vessel was equipped with a wireless (this information taken from U.S. Coast Guard report from Commander of *Cook* to Commander, Lakes Division, November 3, 1924). Apparently, *Cook* did reach Isle Royale late on the evening of November 2 (*Daily Mining Gazette* Nov. 4, 1924).

At 10:30 a.m. Saturday the steam tug *James Whalen* and barges *Empire* and *Green River* were dispatched to the site. By noon they had not reached the Welcome Islands because of the heavy weather that impeded the progress of the tug and its two tows. The Great Lakes Transportation Company indicated that it would also send the barge *Strathbuoy* to the wreck as soon as tug *Strathmore* returned. The plan was to pump out and refloat *Glenlyon* after she had been lightered of its cargo. The grain was to be removed by *Empire,* which was equipped with two clams, and then loaded onto *Green River.*

Strathmore reached the wreck site about 1 p.m. Saturday. By 2 p.m. Agent Bell reported that he had received radio communication from Capt. Brown of *Glennlinnie.* Brown was able to pull alongside *Glenlyon,* remove the crew and transfer them to *Glennsannox.* It was also reported that the weather had subsided and *Glenlyon* was in no immediate danger of breaking up.

At midnight the Canal Coast Guard crew arrived at Siskiwit Bay. A light was spotted on shore and the crew investigated. They found McLaughlin and Roy, the two men who had disappeared in a lifeboat. They had been washed ashore further up in Siskiwit Bay (*Daily Mining Gazette* Nov. 4, 1924). An earlier account said the men were picked up on the open Lake (*Port Arthur News Chronicle* Nov. 3, 1924). It is assumed the November 4 report is the accurate account. The two men were transferred to *Glennsannox* with the rest of the shipwrecked crew. *Glennsannox* soon left the site and headed east (*Port Arthur News Chronicle* Nov. 3, 1924).

Salvage

The first reports received from the wreck were encouraging. The *Port Arthur News Chronicle* of November 1 reported "that any immediate danger of the ship breaking up had passed." Later the same newspaper (Nov. 3, 1924) was able to report that "unless a disastrous southeast gale sets in the *Glenlyon* is

in no immediate danger. Although storm signals are now up for a westerly blow, such a gale will have little effect on the wrecked steamer owing to her protected position."

Lightering operations were under way by the barges *Green River* and *Empire.* They were interrupted for a time by an east wind. They had only managed to lighter 10,000 bushels before having to cease operations because of weather (*Canadian Railway and Marine World* Dec. 1924: 642). Agent Bell told the press of the company's plans to bring *Glenlyon* to Port Arthur for dry-docking to make repairs if the lightering efforts were successful (*Port Arthur News Chronicle* Nov. 3, 1924).

A report on the vessel's condition on the 3rd was radioed by Capt. Taylor: "On the starboard side her decks have been pushed up some 20 inches. Actual damage to her hull has not been determined" (*Ibid.*). The November 4 edition of the same newspaper said the steam tug *Butterfield* had been visiting the wreck site and was expected back at Port Arthur that afternoon.

By November 4 reports being received from the wreck were sounding more serious. "The *Glenlyon*," a report said, "is in bad condition. Its hull is broken and its engine room is taking water. It is believed the ship will be a total wreck" (*Daily Mining Gazette* Nov. 4, 1924).

Lightering operations were resumed whenever weather allowed, but the entire fleet of the Dominion Towing and Salvage returned to Port Arthur November 13. Heavy southeast gales had plagued the operation, and they were only able to lighter 75,000 bushels of the cargo. The wheat was transferred to the Richardson's Elevator. The salvors reported that *Glenlyon* had broken in two and settled on the shoal. It was thought that the insurance company would call for tenders for the wrecking of the steamer since all efforts to remove the boat had been unsuccessful (*Port Arthur News Chronicle* Nov. 13, 1924).

The Great Lakes Transportation Company called in the well-known Reid Wrecking Company to ascertain whether it was possible to raise the wreck (*Canadian Railway and Marine World* Dec. 1924). Captain Reid visited the site to assess the possibility of saving *Glenlyon.*

The reports on *Glenlyon* that were made public later in November dispelled any remaining hope for refloating the wreck.

The freighter *Glenlyon*...will probably be abandoned as a total loss by the underwriters. This statement was made jointly by John Smith, General Manager of the Port Arthur Shipbuilding Company, and Captain Thomas Reid, of the Reid Wrecking Company of Port Huron, following a trip to the scene of the wreck early this morning. Disagreement between the tendering wrecking companies and the underwriters is given (as the reason) for abandonment.

It is believed the underwriters were willing to award a contract to the Reid Wrecking Company, but the delay of two weeks has altered the position of the vessel, and the company is not ready to undertake the hazardous task at this season of the year. Mr. Smith, who with Captain Reid returned from the wreck at 3 this afternoon, told the *News Chronicle* that the *Glenlyon* appeared to have settled considerably since last week. The vessel has also twisted and the stanchions are forcing the deck plates. The crack, however, had not widened any further, although the aft section has been working. The *Glenlyon* is in a more difficult position for refloating than at any time since she went on the shoals.

The question of refloating appears to be now up to a decision from the wrecking company, and indications late this afternoon were to the effect that the Company was not over anxious to tackle the job (*Port Arthur News Chronicle* Nov. 20, 1924).

The Reid Company did not tackle the salvage job. On November 21 the announcement was made that the wrecking companies had abandoned *Glenlyon* as impossible to refloat. The vessel had settled another 18 inches and swung to port. The tank tops were also gone (*Port Arthur News Chronicle* Nov. 21, 1924). The Port Arthur Shipbuilding Co. was disappointed by the news. It was expected that repair of *Glenlyon* would provide work for a large force of men.

The wreck remained on the shoal through the winter. In mid-December wreckage was reported washing up on the northwest coast of the Keweenaw Peninsula, and the Eagle Harbor Coast Guard responded. A thorough investigation was carried out, but no wreck was located. Captain Glaza said he believed the wreckage came from *Glenlyon*. He went on to suggest that the vessel had been broken up in a northeast storm the week before and wreckage had been driven ashore by a nor'wester (*Marquette Daily Mining Journal* Dec. 16, 1924).

An April 30, 1924, report said *Glenlyon* had completely disappeared over the winter (*Canadian Railway and Marine World* June 1925).

America: History

The passenger/package freight vessel *America* was more closely tied to the people of Isle Royale than any of the other ships that remain in its waters. *America* was tied also to those who lived along the Lake Superior north shore between Duluth-Superior and Thunder Bay. Few Lakes vessels are recalled with more genuine affection than the popular *America*. The popularity of this vessel was renewed with the advent of scuba diving; *America* is by far the most dived shipwreck at Isle Royale National Park.

Construction

America was Hull Number 127 for Detroit Dry Dock Company (Edward N. Middleton notes, Canal Park Marine Museum Collection, Duluth). Events surrounding the launch of the *America*'s hull on Saturday, April 2, 1898, were carried by the *Detroit Free Press* (May 22, 1898):

> Yesterday afternoon at 3:26 o'clock the steel passenger steamer *America* was launched at the Wyandotte yards of the Detroit Dry Dock Co. There were about 400 people

present….At exactly 3:17 the first click of the hammers was heard and in just nine minutes the axmen had cut the ropes that held the big beams in place and the boat slid gracefully off the ways….She was christened *America* by Mrs. E.C. Dunbar, wife of one of the owners.

The new boat, which was intended for the Lake Michigan service between Michigan City and Chicago, was built on the same general lines as the *City Of Erie,* though much smaller (*Detroit Free Press* April 3, 1898).

Less than a month later, after the new ship was completed at the Detroit Dry Dock (about June 10) and began the daily run between Chicago and Michigan City (*Detroit Free Press* May 22, 1898), Chicago marine men were expressing their satisfaction with *America* and remarking on its speed of 15 to 17 miles an hour.

America's first document of enrollment was a temporary one issued on June 13, 1898, in Detroit. This document listed E.C. Dunbar of Michigan City as three-fourths owner and M.B. McMillan of Detroit as one-fourth owner. The master of record is Capt. M.F. Morgan. A master must be assigned at the time of ship enrollment. In many cases this master, as shown on the documents, is not actually the captain of the vessel, but rather a representative of the company or individual who owns the vessel. In this instance, Capt. M.F. Morgan was also the captain. The document shows that *America* was built by Detroit Dry Dock Company in 1898 at Wyandotte, Michigan. United States registry number 107367 was given to *America*, which was classed as a steel hull screw steamer. This document states the steamer had one deck, no masts, plain head and round stern, with registered dimensions of 164.6 feet in length, 31.0 feet in breadth and 11.0 feet in depth. The gross tonnage was calculated to be 486.37 tons, consisting of 309.79 tons capacity under the tonnage deck and 176.58 tons capacity of enclosures on the upper deck. *America*'s net tonnage was 283.40 tons, allowing for deductions of 28.90 tons for crew quarters, 28.90 tons for master's cabin, 18.43 tons for anchor gear and 155.64 tons for propelling power (Temporary Certificate of Enrollment, No. 69, Port of Detroit, issued June 13, 1898; *Detroit Free Press* May 22, 1898).

The 1899 edition of *Great Lakes Register* (p. 7), issued in conjunction with *Bureau Veritas,* gives similar information to that shown on *America*'s first two documents, with some additions and differences noted: Michigan City, Michigan, was shown as *America*'s home port. The construction materials were given as "Oak and Steel," meaning steel hull and oak superstructure. In this register *America*'s dimensions differed from the official documents with a length of 154.0 feet rather than 164.6 feet, a breadth of 27.0 feet rather than 31.0 feet and depth of 13.0 feet rather than 11.0 feet. It is not clear why this discrepancy occurs other than, perhaps, differences in the rules of measurement used by Bureau Veritas and the U.S. Government. *America* was also shown as having three decks in *Great Lakes Register* rather than one as shown on the documents.

America's engine and boilers were listed as built in 1898 by Dry Dock Engine Works of Detroit. It is a triple-expansion engine with cylinder diameters of 15, 24 and 38 inches and a stroke of 24 inches. The engine produced 700 indicated horsepower at 160 RPM. Steam for the engine came from two Scotch boilers, 10.0 feet in diameter and 10 feet 2 inches long. The boilers had four furnaces with grate surface of 48 square feet and heating surface of 2,242 square feet; working pressure was 125 psi.

Figure 25. Passenger and package freighter *America*. 1905 view at the Duluth Docks. As-built-configuration prior to alterations. U.S. Army Corps of Engineers Canal Park Marine Museum Collection.

The hull of *America* was lengthened in 1911 at the shipyard in West Superior, Wisconsin. When work was complete, *America* was 18 feet longer with 12 added staterooms for 50 additional passengers. The freight capacity was also increased by about 100 tons. The beam of 31 feet and depth of 11 feet remained unchanged. However, the new length was 182.6 feet and registered tonnages increased to 937 gross and 593 net tons (Doc. of Enrollment Sept. 9, 1911). The speed remained unchanged, but handling and appearance were reported improved with the addition of the 18-foot section.

Master of *America* was listed as E.C. Smith with Louis P. Hogstad of Duluth as the owner's representative. The approximate number of crew required was listed for the first time as 20 persons (Permanent Certificate of Enrollment, No. 79, Port of Duluth, issued June 9, 1911). By the time of its sinking, *America* would be required to carry 30 crew members.

Both the hull (HIR) and boiler inspection report (BIR) books for the *America*'s 1921 and 1928 inspections are in the collections of the U.S. Army Corps of Engineers' Canal Park Marine Museum in Duluth. These inspection reports add much to what is known of details of machinery, equipment, as well as the Lakes passenger/package practices during the period. A comparison between the two inspections gives an indication of the revisions made to the vessel in the last years of operation.

In 1921 *America* was classed by the American Bureau of

Shipping, and it was noted that the hull had been rebuilt in 1911 (1921 HIR: 2-3). The number of staterooms was listed as 51 with 43 "available for passengers only." Of the total, there were 40 double and 46 with single berths. The number of first-cabin passengers allowed was set at 94 persons under the "100 percent clause" and 228 persons under the "50 percent clause."

The square footage of deck space for passengers was 2,666 square feet on the Saloon Deck, 1,420 on the boat and Texas deck and 418 on the Texas alone (*Ibid*: 8-9).

The number of persons allowed in the steward's and other departments not connected with navigation was set at 12 (1921 HIR: 12-13). This was reduced in 1928 to eight with five required at all times (1928 HIR: 12-13). In a handwritten note regarding operation of *America* under Class (A) rules, it was added, "When navigated more than three miles off shore during the interval between May 15th and September 15th, 322 passengers are allowed, a total of 352 persons including crew" (1921: 12-13). These figures were reduced without comment in the 1928 season to 277 and 307, respectively (1928: 12-13). The report gave the ship's hatches as "2 cargo hatches between decks" (HIR 1921: 14-15).

The 1928 hull inspection, conducted while *America* was berthed at the Booth Dock in Duluth, Minnesota, shows that she was previously inspected on April 21, 1927. For the 1928 season, the last brief operational year, accommodations were for 42 staterooms providing 37 double berths and 51 single berths for a total of 88. The number of first-cabin passengers allowed was set at 94 under the "100 percent clause," but increased to 277 persons under the "50 percent clause." When *America* was not laden with freight, the main deck had 2,657 square feet of space for passengers, the cabin deck had 3,739 and the boat deck 1,174 for a total of 7,570 square feet (1928 HIR: 8-9).

Minimum crew requirements were specified as one licensed master and pilot, one licensed first-class pilot, five able seamen, three seamen, 11 certificated lifeboat men, one licensed chief engineer, one licensed first assistant engineer, three oilers, three firemen and four watchmen. An added note stated, "Of the watchmen specified, two are main or deck watchmen included in the deck department and two are cabin watchmen or deck patrol and included in the stewards department" (*Ibid*: 10-11). In all, the number of officers and crew allowed was 30 and the total number of passengers allowed was 94. Thus, the total number of persons allowed to be carried under Class (A) rules equaled 124. An additional handwritten note referring to Class (A) stated, "When running more than three miles off shore during the interval between May 15 and Sept. 15, both dates inclusive, 277 passengers are allowed making a total of 307 persons including crew" (1928 BIR: 13). One additional note was penciled adjacent to the latter saying simply "14 less than last year," but without further explanation.

The inspectors described *America*'s hull as having three decks: main deck, cabin deck and boat deck. It had two cargo hatches and three fuel hatches on the main deck with wood covers for the cargo and metal for fuel. All hatch coamings and covers were said to be in "good" condition. The steel hull was ¼-inch thick with four water-tight cross bulkheads. The type of construction was described as "on angles and channel stiffeners, plate lapped and riveted to frames and deck beams." There were five "sluice gates" located at bulkheads in the hull for movement of bilge water (1928 HIR: 14-15). Listed as in "good" condition were the bulkheads, floor plates and frames in the forward and after holds as well as under the engines, along with the hull and frames in the bunkers, hull abaft transom and "all other accessible parts of hull." It was further noted that the main decking had been repaired since the vessel was last inspected. Additionally, the vessel had permanent stairways from the main to upper decks both forward and aft, and suitable ladders were to be found on each side of the ship for escape to lifeboats with at least two avenues of escape provided passengers from the ship's interior (1928 HIR: 16-17).

Pilothouse equipment was also inspected, and it was recorded that *America* had hand or manual steering gear with wire tiller ropes and no steering engine. All were tested and found in good working condition. The auxiliary or emergency steering gear was also found in good order and efficient for the task using tackle on the tiller aft. Pilot house communication with the engine room was through "wire whistle pulls" and "electric signal speaking tube," presumably meaning an intercom system. *America* had one compass, which was located in the pilot house, in good condition. No record of when it was last swung was located.

The "electric signal" between pilot house and engine room was not noted in the 1921 inspection as it was in 1928, probably reflecting a modification during the intervening years. The 1921 survey listed "bell pulls" as a means of communicating with the engine room, which was not listed in 1928. This equipment may have been removed or simply omitted in the 1928 inspection.

Regarding ground tackle, Inspector Sullivan noted that *America* had two anchors of 2,100 and 1,900 pounds, each fitted with 60 fathoms of 1¹⁵/₁₆-inch chain. The anchor windlass was

steam powered and provided with a devil's claw to hold the anchor chain (1928 HIR 18-19).

Among the miscellaneous equipment carried aboard *America* and noted by Sullivan in his inspection were a hand lead and line for determining depths, a message case and two 10-gallon tanks of storm oil with proper distribution equipment carried in the windlass room (1928 HIR: 42-43).

Lifesaving apparatus was included in the inspection reports. The description within the 1928 HIR is of the same equipment that was deployed during the wreck events. *America* carried five metallic non-motor lifeboats, all built in 1898, with a combined capacity of 93 persons or 936 cu. feet. There were also six life rafts carried aboard *America*. All were of wood frame with metal cylinders. Total capacity of the six rafts was 83 persons (1928 HIR: 36-39).

America carried cork life preservers: 307 for adults, 39 for children and 12 for lifeboats. Sixteen were condemned during inspection in April 1928, perhaps explaining why the number of passengers allowed was reduced by 14 as noted above. The ship also carried two ordinary ring life buoys and two "luminous ring life buoys" (1928 HIR: 40-41).

Apparently, inspectors observed lifeboat drills as this note, which was appended to the 1921 inspection, indicates:

Tested out life boats loaded to full capacity and lowered to water and then lifted clear; boats in good condition. Ordered rail constructed where No. 6 life boat was formerly carried.

The boiler inspections give specific detail on the machinery.

Figure 26. *America* showing the appearance of the ship after the 1911 alterations that added 18 feet of length to the hull. U.S. Army Corps of Engineers Canal Park Marine Museum Collection.

All engine data were the same in 1928 as listed in 1921; however, the cover of the 1921 inspection book noted *America*'s boilers had been "rebuilt" in 1914 while later it stated clearly "Repaired 1914" (1921 BIR cover; 10-11). All boiler data were the same in other respects. The boiler was hydrostatically tested to 249 psi with allowable operating pressure set at 166 psi (1921 BIR: 12-13). New fusible plugs, with a heat number of 20, were installed in the boilers on April 19, 1921, by Marine Iron and Ship Building Works of Duluth, Minnesota. A double-acting hand fire pump was located on the forward port side and another on the after main deck. Both were tested and in good condition (1921 BIR: 30-31). There was no notation made as to the number and kind of fire extinguishers carried in the boiler spaces, if any (1921 BIR: 34-35).

The boiler inspector noted in his record book that the engineering department required one licensed chief engineer, one licensed first assistant engineer, three oilers and three firemen. Thus a total of eight persons were required to properly staff this department (1928 BIR: 2-6).

The boiler report recorded that *America* was powered by a triple-expansion condensing steam engine of an estimated 450 horsepower with cylinder diameters of 15, 24 and 38 inches and stroke of two feet (1928 BIR: 8-9).

The boiler inspection showed two Scotch boilers built in 1898 at Detroit, Michigan by Detroit Dry Dock & Engineering Works. The boilers were each 10¹/₆ feet long and 120 inches in diameter. They were made of rolled sheet steel of 0.875 inches thickness and having a tensile strength of 60,000 psi. The boiler sheets were made by Lukens Iron & Steel Works Co. of Pittsburgh, Pennsylvania. Boiler draft was noted as forced rather than natural. Boiler plate was last drilled for inspection on April 22, 1922, and found to be 0.875 inches thick (1928 BIR: 12-13).

The boilers were of lap joint construction and triple riveted. Rivet holes were drilled, not punched, to diameter of 1⁷/₁₆ inch. Rivet pitch on lap joints was 4¹/₂ x 3¹/₂ inches. The boilers were given hydrostatic testing to 249 psi with allowable steam pressure of 166 psi. Each boiler had four circular furnaces in three sections. Furnace grates were ⁷/₁₆-inch thick measuring 48 x 36 inches and totaling 4,800 square inches. Adamson flues were used. They were 7 feet 9 inches in length and 36 inches in diameter with a thickness of ⁷/₁₆ inches. Each boiler had 188 tubes, each 7 feet 3 inches in length with a 2¹/₂-inch diameter and thickness of 0.109 inches. There were both steam and water connections between the two boilers. One main and one cross steam pipe were installed and last inspected for thickness on April 23, 1926 (1928 BIR: 13-19).

Two spring-loaded safety valves were installed on the boilers and tested by the inspector. The valves were manufactured by Scott Valve Manufacturing Company of Detroit, Michigan. They were set to blow off at 166 psi. The valves were located at a distance of three feet from the boilers. A set of steam gauges were located in the engine and boiler rooms: two in the engine room and two in the boiler room. All steam gauges were in "OK" condition and compared favorably with test gauges. Fusible plugs of heat number 28 and manufactured by Marine Iron & Shipbuilding Co. of Duluth, Minnesota, were installed during the inspection (1928 BIR: 24-25).

Also attached to the boiler was one bilge pump of four-inch diameter and eight-inch stroke. Four other syphonous bilge pumps of four inches diameter and six-inch stroke were also installed. One additional pump of the same size, but designated for fire, was also connected to the boilers.

America had two lamp lockers or oil rooms, both metal lined. One was located in the engine room beneath the dynamo and the other in the fore peak. Location of the sprinkler system that was noted in the HIR was delineated in the BIR as being on the main deck and the crew's dining room and in the kitchen or galley area. It was fed by a ³/₄-inch water line (1928 BIR: 30-31). The boiler inspection also showed *America* to have two electric lighting systems and no refrigeration unit. Both the engine room and the fire or stokehold had two avenues of escape in case of emergency.

Appended to the inspection report was a list of the number of square feet of deck area for passengers on the following decks:

Deck No. 1 (Main Deck)	2,657	
		when not freight laden
Deck No. 2 (Saloon Deck)		3,739
Deck No. 3 (Boat Deck)		1,174
		Total: 7,570

Figure 27. Birth of *America*. On April 2, 1898, *America* was launched at the Wyandotte yards of Detroit Dry Dock Co. U.S. Army Corps of Engineers Canal Park Marine Museum Collection.

74

Operational History

Little historical documentation has been located for the first two seasons of *America*'s operation, other than the ship was periodically chartered for special cruises and to augment the vessels of other lines. One of the early charters was to the International Navigation Co. of New York to run between Buffalo and Niagara Falls (*Benton Harbor Daily Palladium* March 12, 1901; *Holland City News* March 15, 1901).

America's involvement with Isle Royale began in March 1902 when the Booth Steamship Line purchased the new ship. Booth put *America* on "the Duluth Port Arthur and Isle Royale route" (*Canadian Railway and Marine World* March 1902: 109). Before heading up the Lakes, the ship was altered at Grand Haven where the cabin capacity was "materially increased" (*Duluth News Tribune* March 18, 1902). The new Booth Line steamer, due to arrive in Duluth April 15, was rated "one of the finest and fastest freight and passenger boats available" (*Ibid.* April 5, 1902).

America was not in service long before being seriously damaged in a collision with the south pier at the Duluth Ship Canal. "Her bow is bent double and stove in from about three feet below the water line to the main deck" and the plates were torn allowing the forward compartment to flood. The accident was attributed to "a good rate of speed" and a crew unacquainted with the current in the canal. The ship was dry-docked for repairs (*Duluth News Tribune* May 5, 1902).

The competition must have been stiff in the excursion trade between Duluth and Two Harbors. The excursions were heavily advertised and races between competing vessels were not unknown. The Canadian steamer *Huronic* lost a race down the shore with *America* (*Duluth Evening Herald* May 29, 1903; June 26, 1903).

At the end of the 1903 season, the Isle Royale lightkeepers were returned to the mainland aboard *America*, as they frequently were in the years that followed (*Ibid.* Nov. 26, 1903). *America* often had the distinction of being the first passenger out and the last to end the navigation season (e.g. *Duluth Evening Herald* April 20, 1914; *Duluth News Tribune* April 24, 1918).

In July 1904 the steamer *Holmes'* anchor destroyed five staterooms along the boat deck of *America* (*Duluth News Tribune* July 19, 1904). *Holmes* was not equipped with anchor pockets. The cabin repair was done by carpenters who worked while *America* proceeded on its regular trips (*Ibid.* July 22, 1904).

In November 1905 *America* was bound from Two Harbors to Duluth during one of the most severe storms ever to hit Lake Superior. The devastating storm of November 27-29, which became known as the "*Mataafa* Storm," was responsible for 30 casualties on the Lake, the largest from a single storm in Lake Superior history. Casualties from this one storm account for one percent of all recorded casualties on Lake Superior (T.R. Holden collection, Lake Superior shipwreck notes). The crew of *America* saw *Mataafa*, the shipwreck for which the storm was named, during the storm (*Duluth News Tribune* July 23, 1944).

For most of *America*'s career it served as a prime communication and transportation link between the Lake Superior north shore settlements and between the mainland and Isle Royale.

Passengers and freight were connected to the main economic outlet of the port of Duluth, and this trade was the commercial mainstay of *America*'s operation. In the early period of *America*'s operation, the north shore roads were poor (e.g. *Duluth Evening Herald* April 22, 1907). *America* was also a principal summer mail carrier alternating with a stage line that carried during the winter (*Duluth Evening Herald* April 30, 1913). Over the course of the last two decades of *America*'s operation, land transportation along the north shore improved markedly, cutting sharply into the steamer's prime role in communications and transportation. A road was completed around Lake Superior in 1921 (*Duluth News Tribune* May 1, 1921). During the later years *America* expanded operations in the excursion trade, although it never left the north shore-Isle Royale run.

In the 1908 season *America* served as much more than a communication and transportation link for the smaller ports. Early in September forest fires threatened many areas. "Grand Marais is in great danger of being burned and no avenue of escape – forest fires raging within a mile of town and fate of the place is in doubt" (*Duluth Evening Herald* Sept. 8, 1908). It was not only Grand Marais, but a large portion of the north shore with fires at Knife River and at Split Rock, at Chicago Bay (Hovland) and Grand Portage just east of the Susie Islands. "Everywhere on the north shore the flames are slowly crawling through the forests, eating up miles of timber lands and making life a terror for the scattered settlers" (*Ibid.* September 10, 1908). Fires were also seen on Isle Royale (*Port Arthur Daily News* Sept. 12, 1908).

The threatened settlers who had escaped the fires congregated on the shore line. Household goods and belongings were piled on the docks. There was little hope of escape except by water. *America* picked up many of those escaping the flames. The governor of Minnesota sent *America* to Beaver Bay to rescue 300 villagers threatened with destruction by the flames (*Duluth News Tribune* Sept. 12, 1908). The steamer was the only source of news of the fate of the shore towns (*Duluth Evening Herald* Scpt. 12, 1908). The forest fires were not extinguished until September 29 (*Ibid.* Sept. 29, 1908).

While *America* was rescuing villagers from the forest fires, its owner A. Booth and Co. failed and was placed in receivership (*New York Times* Sept. 11, 1908). The fishermen who depended on the company and their vessels for their livelihood were alarmed (*Duluth Evening Herald* Sept. 12, 1908), but the company managed to keep its vessels operating (*Ibid.* Sept. 21, 1908).

In 1909 the old company was dissolved and a new enterprise named Booth Fisheries Company of Delaware was formed that took over the operations (*Duluth Evening Herald* June 3, 1909). *America* had not been affected and was continuing on schedule. A month later Fourth of July was celebrated at Isle Royale (*Ibid.* July 10, 1908). The managing agent of *America* was changed in 1914 to the United States & Dominion Transportation Co., a company formed by the Booth Fisheries Co. (*Duluth Evening Herald* April 22, 1914). Ownership of the vessel was unchanged.

"The steamer *America* ran aground at Burlington Point on the north shore about 6 o'clock this morning. She released herself after about an hour, arriving in port about 11 o'clock. Her forefoot was slightly damaged" (*Duluth Evening Herald* July 9, 1909). "...her bow post and several plates are badly broken and twisted. She will be in dry dock several days" (*Duluth News Tribune* July 19, 1909). "It was found necessary to put in a new stem and replace about 40 feet of her keel. Twelve new plates are being put in which were bent or broken in the accident and seven frames" (*Ibid.* July 14, 1909).

In 1910 *America* had wireless installed (*Duluth Evening Herald* August 1, 1910).

The start of *America*'s 1911 season was delayed while the hull lengthening was completed (*Duluth News Tribune* May 9, 1911). Eighteen feet of length and 12 cabins had been added. The steamer could carry 100 tons more freight as a result of the new alterations. It was announced that the steamer would make three trips a week between Duluth and Port Arthur, and Isle Royale.

One of the popular Isle Royale resorts that *America* frequented was Schofield's Lodge on Belle Isle. It was a popular excursion, and the resort catered to vacation clientele (*Duluth Evening Herald* June 17, 1912).

The sinking of *Titanic,* the largest vessel afloat, in the Atlantic in April led to the documentation of *America*'s passenger, crew and lifesaving capacities that might not have otherwise been recorded. *Titanic,* with more than 2,000 passengers aboard, carried only lifeboat capacity for 1,178, and as a consequence an estimated 1,500 people lost their lives. The disaster prompted newspaper investigation into Great Lakes practice, of which *America* was used as an example:

"Passenger boats on the Great Lakes do not pretend to carry boats and rafts to accommodate all the passengers on board in case of an accident," said a marine man this morning. After the investigation now going on as the result of the *Titanic* disaster, they will probably be forced to either cut down the number of passengers or increase the number of boats and rafts.

But few passenger boats are inspected at the port of Duluth. Only the boats of the Booth line, excursion steamers and ferry boats, are inspected at this end of the Lakes.

The steamer *America*, for an instance, is allowed to carry 450 passengers, but has room for but 108 people in the life boats and on the rafts. She complies with the law in every respect.

The law states that she be required to have 1,080 cu. feet of carry capacity. This she is doing, but...this gives room to but about 108 people.

The *America* carries a crew of 25. She is allowed 450 passengers. There are life preservers to the number of 478 on the boat, one for each one aboard and three over. She has five life boats and two rafts, making up the amount of cubic carrying space required by law.

The law regarding the carrying of life boats and rafts is claimed to be lax. All the boats live up to the law, but...the law is not stringent enough in insisting that sufficient boats and rafts be carried (*Duluth Evening Herald* April 20, 1912).

America was severely damaged when it ran aground a mile northeast of Two Harbors, Minnesota, in early May 1914. It was positioned about 100 feet from *General O.M. Poe*. Five years earlier the two ships had been aground together in virtually the same spot (*Duluth News Tribune* May 6, 1914). *America* was positioned broadside to the waves and was punctured below the boilers (*Ibid.* May 7, 1914). The stranded vessel was lightered and freed on the night of May 7. Necessary repairs were described as "nine plates will be removed and straightened... and about five feet of her keel will be relaid. The hull was quite badly damaged beneath her engines" (*Ibid.* May 12, 1914).

The reinspection of *America* in 1921 by the Steamboat Inspection Service resulted in the issuance of a "Certificate Amending Certificate of Inspection By Changing Character of Vessel, Route, Equipment, Etc." The vessel would now operate under Class B rules that limited it to navigation of not more than three miles off shore. It was allowed to carry 146 passengers or a total of 176 including crew (Certificate dated September 19, 1921, issued at Duluth, copy in Canal Park Marine Museum Collection).

In 1925, the steamer *Bruce* took over *America*'s operation on the south shore. *America* would make three trips weekly to Isle Royale and Port Arthur (*Duluth News Tribune* April 25, 1925). Later that year, *America* ran aground at Scott's Point, near Grand Marais, and damaged the rudder shoe and stern bearing (*Duluth News Tribune* May 30, 31, 1925).

A collision between *America* and *Huronic* occurred in 1926. The vessels were maneuvering in dense fog near the entrance to the Kaministiquia River. Captain Smith was at the wheel of *America* when he saw *Huronic* loom up out of the fog. He quickly turned the wheel and his ship received a glancing blow and slight damage rather than the full brunt of the impact of the other larger steamer (*Port Arthur News Chronicle* Sept. 13, 1926; *Duluth News Tribune* Sept. 14, 1926).

In mid-summer of 1927 *America* was involved in a bizarre series of events at Thunder Bay Harbour. On Thursday, July 21, 1927, *America* was headed toward the Booth dock in Port Arthur when a mix-up in the engine room caused it to ram the tug *Violet G* berthed at the Booth dock, shearing off 15 feet of the tug's stern and tearing away some 20 feet of the dock. There were three crewmen aboard the *Violet G* at the time; they escaped uninjured. Moments later, *America* was aground on the rocks at the head of the dock, requiring assistance to be released. Then it collided with, and nearly capsized, the tug *Con Lynch* that had just freed it. During all this, a lighthouse keeper's gas launch was also slightly damaged. *America* was reported to be carrying "passengers and a cargo of fruit and package freight" at the time (*Detroit Free Press* July 23, 1927).

During the last winter of its operation, *America* steamed to Port Arthur during a severe December storm:

The steamer *America* arrived in port this afternoon from Duluth. She was completely ice-coated. Aboard was a cargo of salt for the Booth Fisheries Canadian company. The vessel is taking back salted herring" (*Port Arthur News Chronicle* Dec. 3, 1927).

76

This would have put *America* on its return voyage to Duluth in the same storm that halted *Kamloops, Quedoc, Winnipeg* and other vessels on their upbound journeys from the Sault toward the Canadian Lakehead.

Wreck Event

America's 1928 season began as many before it. There were no signs at all that this would be *America*'s final season. *America* last steamed out of the Duluth Ship Canal on Wednesday, June 6, 1928, headed up the north shore and expected to touch at all the usual ports of call. From Grand Marais it headed toward Isle Royale to drop off a number of passengers in the darkness of early morning so they would not have to wait out the trip to Port Arthur and around the northeast tip of the island, before landing at their Washington Harbor destinations the following day (*Duluth News Tribune* June 7, 1928; *Superior Evening Telegram* June 7, 1928; Holden interview with Capt. Stanley Sivertson, Duluth, Minn., in 1973 and with James R. Marshall, Pike Lake, Minn., in Oct. 1974, 1986).

The *Great Lakes Red Book* for 1928 listed *America*'s officers as Capt. Edward C. Smith and Chief Engineer Frank McMillan. Edward C. Smith is also listed as master of *America* in a special certificate related to *America*'s carrying of petroleum (Steamboat Inspection Service, Dept. of Commerce. "Certificate Relative to Carrying Refined Petroleum On Routes Where There Is No Other Practicable Mode Of Transporting It," issued on April 21, 1928, at Duluth, Minn.).

Soon after clearing the dock in Washington Harbor, Capt. Smith turned command of *America* over to First Mate John Wick, with Fred Nelson at the wheel, and retired to his cabin behind the bridge. Five minutes later *America* thudded over a reef, bumping four times and tearing a small hole through its single bottom below the engine room on the starboard side. Mate John Wick was a new mate on *America*, having served previously as mate under Capt. Gus Ege on *Jack* of the Minnesota Atlantic Transit Co., popularly known as the "Poker Fleet." Wick quit MATCo because Capt. Ege would not recommend him for his own ship in the fleet (Ken Hafner interview with Capt. Duncan Schubert at Sault Ste. Marie, Mich., ca. 1977, copy in Holden Collection).

At first it seemed as though *America*'s pumps could handle the inrushing water, but Chief Engineer Frank McMillan quickly reassessed the situation – *America* was going to sink. Meanwhile Capt. Smith returned to the bridge where he found Mate Wick ringing the ship's bell to alert all aboard of the disaster. Moments later Capt. Smith yelled, "Beach her! Beach her!" (Holden interviews with Marshall 1974, 1986).

Capt. Smith remembered a small gravel beach nearby in the North Gap of Washington Harbor. It would be a good place to try to nose *America* ashore before she foundered in deep water. He ordered Fred Nelson to swing the wheel to point *America* directly toward the beach. Then another thud and *America* ground to a halt about 30 yards short of the beach that probably would have assured its imminent salvage, subsequent repair and return to service.

Below deck in the engine room, Engineer McMillan ordered

his crew to relieve boiler pressure and grease down everything in sight so *America*'s power plant could be made readily functional when salvage work was completed. Water already had snuffed fireman Hans Fjorne's boiler fires (Holden interviews with Marshall 1974, 1986).

The loss of the steamer *America* was covered in newspapers and journals ranging from the American and Canadian Lakehead port cities to Chicago and New York (*Lake Carriers' Association, 1928 Annual Report* 51-52; *Canadian Railway and Marine World* ca. July 1928). First news of the wreck was carried over the wireless station affiliated with Singer's Resort on Washington Island and sent to Duluth (*Port Arthur News Chronicle* June 7, 8, 1928).

In an "extra" for the *Calumet News* of Calumet, Michigan, was an Associated Press wire story headlined "Steamer Sinks Near Isle Royale; All Hands Are Safe," the same story carried by the *New York Times* (*Calumet News* June 7, 1928). This same wire service article also appeared in the *Superior Evening Telegram* (June 7, 1928).

America was carrying 31 crew and 16 passengers at the time of the accident (*Duluth News Tribune* June 9, 1928):

> In all 10 passengers and at least 30 officers and crewmen were aboard when *America* slipped away from the Singer Hotel dock at Washington Island. Captain Smith officially reported 31 crewmen aboard at the time of the accident. It is possible Louis P. Hogstad, Manager of United States & Dominion Transportation Company, was aboard at the time of the accident and considered by Capt. Smith as a member of the crew (Record of Casualties to Vessels, U.S. Treasury Department, p. 17, bound journal, copy in Canal Park Marine Museum collection).

First reports at the Canadian Lakehead said *America* sank at 4:30 a.m., local time, on June 7th after striking a "reef that split the hull." Word was first received in Port Arthur from Booth Fisheries by S.H. Knauss of the Fitzsimmons Fruit Co. that had a consignment of fruit that was lost in the wreck. In describing the vessel's normal occupation, the newspaper stated that *America* engaged in:

> ...carrying fresh fruit and vegetables from produce housed in Duluth to the Head of the Lakes, and on the East-bound trips called at various fishing stations around Isle Royale. A large number of wealthy Americans, with Summer homes at Isle Royale, used the steamer at Week-ends (*Port Arthur News Chronicle* June 7, 1928).

A Chicago newspaper reported:

> Duluth, Minn., June 7 – An old well-known passenger steamer, the *America*, was lying on the bottom of Lake Superior tonight under 17 fathoms of water....Reports of the sinking and rescue were still vague here early this evening. The only report so far came from the ship's purser, who said that the vessel struck a reef near Washington Harbor on Isle Royale at 3 a.m. and that the ship sank an hour and a half later.

The steamer *Winyah* was sent to take the rescued persons off the island. When the *America* left here yesterday morning she carried 20 passengers in addition to her crew of 30 (*Chicago Herald and Examiner* June 8, 1928).

Winyah was en route from Duluth up the north shore and off Schroeder when its crew was notified to proceed to Washington Island to pick up *America*'s survivors (*Duluth News Tribune* June 8, 1928). *Winyah* was in the fish and freight trade on the north shore and owned by H. Christiansen and Sons of Duluth (*Superior Evening Telegraph* June 8, 1928).

An amusing note pertaining to the importance of a fresh strawberry, at least as viewed by the editors of the Fort William newspaper, was headlined:

Fruit Supply For Lakehead Lost in Wreck

Sinking of the steamer *America* off Isle Royale created a shortage of strawberries and fresh vegetables in Fort William and Port Arthur today. The Fitzsimmons Fruit company had 10 tons of vegetables and fresh fruit on the boat.

These products would have been here for distribution today had the boat not gone down. However, it is reported that two trucks left Duluth at 5 o'clock this morning with a

Figure 28. Demise of *America*. *America* aground in North Gap of Washington Harbor circa June 7, 1928. U.S. Army Corps of Engineers Canal Park Marine Museum Collection.

fresh supply (*Fort William Daily Times Journal* June 8, 11, 1928).

More details of the wreck emerged in the press the day after the event:

In the most orderly manner, without any confusion whatsoever, 15 passengers and 30 members of the crew of the steamer *America*...launched five boats and made for shore early Thursday morning...according to the account of a member of the crew, Fred Nelson, wheelsman, who arrived here last night (*Duluth News Tribune* June 8, 1928).

Wheelsman Fred Nelson gave a detailed report of the events:

"We were out in Washington Harbor about a half mile from the dock when the ship struck the reef....This caused a loud noise which awakened most of the crew and passengers. Those who were not up when the crash occurred came on deck when the ships bells started ringing. Members of the crew went to cabin doors telling passengers and crew of the danger. The boat started sinking slowly. All five of the ship's life boats were launched. Members of the crew were assigned to take charge of these boats and everyone was taken off. Captain Edward C. Smith left on the last boat just before the entire ship was practically under water. There was no confusion while the life boats were being lowered. Everyone behaved wonderfully and the six women aboard, mostly members of the crew, were not a bit excited over the crash as all saw there was no danger. All of the five life boats reached Washington Harbor, a half mile from where the *America* hit the reef, without any trouble" (*Duluth News Tribune* June 8, 1928).

Booth officials reported that John Wick, the first mate, was in charge of *America* at the time of the disaster, having relieved Capt. Smith just five minutes before the crash. These same officials were cautious about providing other particulars of the incident, pending their discussion with Capt. Smith in Grand Marais the night of June 8th (*Duluth News Tribune* June 8, 1928).

On the same day the Fort William press proclaimed the shortage of fruit in their city, it also carried the following based upon a passenger's recounting of the event:

Heroism on the part of Capt. Edward C. Smith and coolness on the part of crew and passengers stand out sharply in the accounts given of the sinking of the steamer *America*....

The veteran captain, with all the love a real tar feels for his craft, stayed with the boat until she was ready to sink to the depths of the Lake (*Fort William Daily Times Journal* June 8, 1928).

Passenger H.S. Cottier said after arriving in Port Arthur:

"There is nothing to be seen of the old *America* now except the top of the mainmast and part of the pilothouse sticking up out of the water....

"I left Duluth along with 14 or 15 other passengers for Port Arthur on Wednesday night....We had an uneventful trip, and put in to Washington Harbor to let off two passengers for Isle Royale.

"I understand that Captain Smith does not care to put in to Washington Harbor on the trip out of Duluth, but prefers to do so only on the return trip from Port Arthur. However, this time, in the middle of the night, he put in to Washington Harbor, and put his passengers off all right. Then we started out for open water again. It had not yet broken day, and we struck a reef just outside the harbor.

"I was in bed and we got a fearful jar, and it woke me and everybody else up. I don't think anyone was hurt. We all dressed, and there were lots of boats to take us ashore. The ship began to settle and all we had to do was to get into the boats....There was no panic whatever, and it was not until an hour later, when it was just breaking day, that the good ship sank almost out of sight in the waters of Lake Superior. It must have been shortly before four o'clock this morning, I should judge....

"Captain Smith stayed on his ship until to do so any longer was at the risk of his life. He saw everybody else ashore, sent all his crew away, and stayed on board himself, and alone until the ship was ready to sink. Then he, too, with evident reluctance, for he loved his ship, was put ashore himself.

"Captain Smith sent the purser ashore with the first news of the disaster, and through the private telephone wire he got the news into Duluth. The purser was taken to the mainland, and proceeded back to Duluth, as did the captain later....

"We are all thankful...to be alive and well today. I have lost some clothes and a few personal belongings. There were two men aboard who were going to Nipigon to fish the Nipigon river. They were on their way up from Detroit and they had a truck in the hold of the boat in which were their fishing tackle, rods, lines and flies, and $500 in cash. They lost it all and did not continue on, but have returned to Duluth, and are now on their way to Detroit.

"...The discipline was perfect....There was complete order; there was no need for the cry 'women and children first' because we had plenty of time. There was no real danger, and the passengers were given the first and every possible consideration" (*Fort William Daily Times Journal* June 8, 1928).

Identity of the two men from Detroit who had the truck with their fishing gear has never been clarified because no one among the passengers listed was identified as having come from Detroit (*Duluth News Tribune* June 9, 1928). An account years later reported the truck as simply being shipped to the Canadian Lakehead for some plasterers (*Duluth News Tribune* Oct. 17, 1967).

In a second account by Mr. Cottier, he said:

"The first we realized that there was anything amiss was when the *America* struck and was shaken from stern to stem. Hurried examinations were made by Mate Wick, and just a minute or so later we were aroused and told to make ready to get into life boats. We were told the boat was sinking. The boats were lowered and, without confusion, we got into them. We were taken to Washington Harbor, where Mr. Singer, proprietor of the resort there, made us comfortable. Captain Smith sent one of the crew to the

wireless station and a message was sent to Duluth" (*Port Arthur News Chronicle* June 8, 1928).

Passengers expressed satisfaction with the way officers of *America* dealt with the disaster, as the following indicates:

"I can tell you very little more than what has already appeared in the press....It was a most unusual experience, I can tell you that, and there was no loss of life. I was particularly struck with the conduct of Captain E. C. Smith, and the crew, and with the dispatch at which they went about the task of getting all people safely away from the sinking vessel" (*Port Arthur News Chronicle* June 9, 1928).

Capt. D. T. Sullivan of the Steamboat Inspection Service announced in Duluth that an investigation into *America*'s sinking would be conducted by his office (*Houghton Daily Mining Gazette* June 6, 1928). Curiously, the Houghton newspaper failed to carry any further news on *America* sinking through the end of June.

Capt. Edward C. Smith filed an official "Record of Casualties to Vessels" report on June 12, 1928, after returning to Duluth (Record of Casualties to Vessels, U.S. Treasury Department, 17, bound journal, copy in Holden Collection). It appears that this volume is what could be termed "a blotter book," that is, a handwritten facsimile of the original, single-page report which was forwarded to higher authorities by the receiving officer. This copy was kept in the receiving office. A synopsis of Capt. Smith's answers is given. The wreck occurred on June 7, 1928, at 2:47 a.m. The ship had sailed from Duluth June 6 and was bound for Port Arthur with 10 passengers and 31 crew. The estimated value of the vessel was $100,000; the 55-ton cargo of miscellaneous merchandise was valued at $10,000. The amount of insurance on the hull was $60,000; disbursements was $40,000. The cargo was uninsured. The cause of the wreck was "hit reef" and the vessel was stranded and beached about 400 feet from where it hit.

The official investigative hearing held by Capt. Sullivan opened in Duluth on June 11 and concluded on June 12, 1928. Nine members of *America*'s crew including the captain and chief engineer testified at the hearing, which was closed to the public. Records of testimony were forwarded to the Marquette office of the Steamboat Inspection Service where a determination of negligence or inattention to duty was to be made (*Duluth News Tribune* June 13, 1928; *Fort William Daily Times Journal* June 13, 1928; *Port Arthur News Chronicle* June 15, 1928).

While it has been believed that Mate Wick was censured for careless navigation (Pomeroy, Dick. "Shallow, Cold, Watery Grave Still Holds Steamer *America*," *Superior Evening Telegram* Oct. 25, 1983; Holden "Above and Below: Steamer *America*," *The Nor'easter,* Vol. 3, No. 4, July-August 1978: 2), records in the National Archives are to the contrary, apparently exonerating all parties:

Summary records there [National Archives] indicate that the hearing on the *America*'s sinking on June 7, 1928, was held in Marquette, Michigan, with the case being dismissed. The actual transcript of the hearing is not available (Correspondence, Bruce C. Harding, Chief, Archives Branch, Federal Archives and Records Center, Chicago, Ill., to Holden Dec. 2, 1974).

The *Fort William Daily Times Journal* carried the most fitting eulogy for the *America* to appear in any of the Lake Superior port city newspapers:

The unfortunate loss of the steamer *America* has, for a time at least, removed from the run between Fort William and Duluth, a boat that has served the public at the head of the Lakes in good stead for more than a quarter of a century.

While connection with Duluth has been maintained by the passenger boats of the Canada Steamship Line, originally of the Northern Navigation Company, it was the *America* which did the local, routine work along the north shore, poking her nose into every little harbor on the coast line and keeping communication between the mainland and Isle Royale uninterrupted. While the *Hamonic* was sailing majestically from point to point, the *America* was serving all the places en route. She was like the local train which unloads its freight at every unimportant siding, past which the stately express train glides as if it never existed....

So accustomed had she become to the run that it seems almost strange that she could not find her way alone through any passage along the north shore or Isle Royale....The work done by the *America* will have to be continued by some other boat, but it will be hoped by all who have made use of the *America* and enjoyed her picturesque trips, that she will be raised and sail the same route again (*Fort William Daily Times Journal* June 9, 1928).

Salvage

Following the accident, there was an almost immediate expression of hope for salvaging *America*. In Port Arthur it was reported:

...The owners of the *America* are preparing to send out a wrecking outfit from Duluth. If possible the vessel will be raised and taken to the Superior shipyard for repairs and reconditioning. In the meantime efforts are being made to get another steamer, as in addition to the freight the company handles between these two ports, a large number of fishermen were accustomed to send in their catches to the Duluth market by the *America* twice a week (*Port Arthur News Chronicle* June 11, 1928).

In a brief editorial in the *Fort William Daily Times Journal,* it was noted that if the spars and pilot house were still visible, it should be possible to salvage *America* (*Fort William Daily Times Journal* June 9, 1928).

Other press reports indicated little optimism concerning salvage as being expressed by Booth Fisheries and the United States & Dominion Transportation Co.

Hopes of salvaging the vessel have been practically abandoned by the United States & Dominion Transportation

Company....The ship is to be replaced by a new vessel (*Detroit Free Press* June 10, 1928).

As the official investigation concluded, it was announced that bids were being sought by *America*'s underwriters for salvage of the vessel (*Fort William Daily Times Journal* June 13, 1928), but aspirations for complete salvage were mixed:

The underwriters interested in the loss of the steamer *America* of the Booth Line have been seeking bids for the boat just as she lies, on the rocks at Isle Royale. It is said that she probably is damaged beyond chance of profit by releasing her and causing her to be repaired. So, in any event, the boat may not bring more than somebody can see profit in recovering the machinery and junking the steel plates, etc. blankets, pillows, and other articles that have floated out of the stranded boat (*Skillings' Mining Review* July 14, 1928).

Four parties were requested to submit salvage bids: Barnett and Record of Duluth with a bid of $35,000; Reid Towing & Salvage Company of Sarnia and Port Huron bidding $65,000; Merritt Chapman & Scott bidding $30,000 to $40,000; and Capt. Cornelius O. Flynn whose bid was about $30,000, but definitely less than Merritt Chapman & Scott. Reid Towing's bid was excessive because he did not have his salvage floating plant on Lake Superior at the time. In fact his bid was not even received until October 1928, affecting low bidder Flynn's ability to begin salvage that year. Consequently, when Flynn did acquire salvage rights from the court in 1929, he had not only a salvage job on the vessel, but also an extensive refurbishing job due to ice and weather damage, as well as vandalism, before *America* could see service again. The onset of the Great Depression also adversely affected Flynn's salvage plans (*Skillings' Mining Review* July 14, 1928; Holden interview with Marshall 1986).

Capt. Cornelius O. Flynn of Duluth is believed to have been the first diver on the wreck of *America*, apparently as owner's representative. He determined there was a single hole in *America*'s hull on the starboard side. Captain Flynn hoped he could raise *America* and place it back in service along the south shore, running between Houghton-Hancock and Isle Royale, perhaps across to Port Arthur and Fort William (*Ibid*).

Unauthorized salvage work on *America* began almost before its boilers cooled as area fisherman found the vessel a new source of prosperity:

It is said that some of the fishermen's boys around the western end of Isle Royale have displayed unbelievable skill at locating and floating pails of candy and crates of fruit, using an iron hook on a long pole, and operating from a small boat. There was $4,000 worth of fresh fruit on the *America* when she went down (*Skillings' Mining Review* July 14, 1928).

Isle Royale's resort operators could not long be without passenger service and survive financially. Arrangements for alternative service to the island were announced by Booth representative Hogstad on June 22, 1928.

Boat service between Duluth and Isle Royale...will be resumed today by an arrangement with the Northern Navigation Company...to operate a passenger steamer from Duluth to Port Arthur and Fort William. From Port Arthur and Fort William a smaller steamer will be used for transporting the passengers to Isle Royale (*Duluth News Tribune* June 24, 1928).

America's document of enrollment issued in March 1927 was surrendered at Duluth on September 6, 1928, carrying the notation that it had last been renewed on March 22, 1928, and that the reason for surrender was "Vessel struck reef and sunk in Lake Superior at North Gap, Isle Royale, Michigan, on June 7, 1928, 48 persons on board, No lives lost" (reverse of Permanent Certificate of Enrollment, No. 89, Port of Duluth, issued March 22, 1927). This document showed no indication of any preferred mortgage on *America*, that is, it was apparently owned outright by Booth Fisheries Company of Delaware.

Booth's own aspirations for salvaging *America* seemed to have been rejected outright by August 21, 1928 (*Duluth News Tribune* Aug. 23, 1928).

Underwriters settled with Booth Fisheries for *America*'s hull, but apparently not for the cargo or the belongings of crewmen or passengers. Confusion and hard feelings resulted all around since Booth Fisheries had been paid for their loss, but those of the passengers and crew who lost personal property and those to whom cargo had been consigned were not subsequently paid by Booth interests (Holden interviews with Marshall 1974, 1986).

Some felt, and still feel, *America* was scuttled for the insurance since the north shore highway had cut drastically into Booth's passenger and freight business. *America*'s loss effectively put an end to Booth's Duluth operations although they apparently ran the *Hollis M*, possibly in 1928, but at least part of 1929 and perhaps longer (Holden interviews with Sivertson 1973 and Marshall 1974, 1986).

The settlement dispute found its way into court. Captain Flynn went to court as well to propose a settlement that would satisfy all parties. He proposed to purchase *America* and its salvage rights from the court by paying a nominal court fee and settling any outstanding claims against Booth or the vessel. Ultimately, Flynn was successful in his bid. It was announced on September 12, 1929, more than a year after the wreck, that Capt. Flynn had obtained ownership of *America* (*Canadian Railway and Marine World* Oct. 1929: 665; *Duluth News Tribune* Sept. 12, 1929). Marshall reports the actual date of transfer of ownership as July 29, 1929 (Holden interview with Marshall 1986).

When sunk, *America* was still protruding above the water, technically a stranding rather than a foundering, since the wheelhouse and forward deck were left above the surface. Ice damaged this portion over the winter of 1928-29, shearing off those cabins. The following winter, 1929-30, *America* was further ice damaged, but more importantly, was buoyed up sufficiently by the ice to be released from the rock pinnacle atop which she rested. By spring of 1930, *America* had slipped totally beneath the surface to 85 feet at the stern and four feet at the bow while listing over on the port side.

Capt. Flynn visited the wreck a couple of times in the next few years and devised ways of raising *America*, but was never able to secure the necessary capital for the venture as the Great Depression descended on the Twin Ports and the nation. Flynn and/or his son Paul visited the wreck in 1930, 1932, 1933 and 1935 (Holden interview with Marshall 1986).

Capt. Flynn never did get the chance to make a real attempt to raise *America*. He died in 1936 at the age of 81 having served the port of Duluth for more than half a century. In that time he had been master of the *Ella G. Stone*, James J. Hill's yacht *Wacoutak*, Thomas F. Cole's yacht *Elvina* and *R.G. Stewart* among others. He had also worked various salvage jobs including that on the *Noque Bay* in the Apostle Islands (*Duluth News Tribune* April 3, 1936; *Duluth Evening Herald* April 3, 1936; Mansfield 1899: 2: 483-84).

Capt. Flynn's plan for raising *America* did not die with him. His son, Paul J. Flynn, also a hard-hat salvage diver, purchased salvage rights to *America* from his father before he died. Paul Flynn purchased the salvage rights with his business partner, Alexander J. McDonnell. These two men also visited *America* several times. But they, too, were unable to fund a real salvage attempt through their inability to raise the necessary capital and interference from World War II. Still, Flynn and McDonnell held documents showing their claim to the *America*'s salvage rights from 1935 until 1965 (Holden interviews with Marshall 1974, 1986).

In June 1943 what is believed to be one of the earliest (there were no anniversary columns on the loss in the *Duluth Evening Herald* or *Duluth News Tribune* on June 6, 7, 1929, or 1939) in a long list of articles recounting *America*'s loss was published in a Duluth newspaper under the title "SS *America* Ends 15th Year at Bottom of Lake Superior." While the article recounted the event briefly, it added an aspect of the wreck brought on by the advent of World War II and attempted to bring the history of salvage efforts up to date.

> During the last 15 years, there has been no effort to raise her [*America*], although when she first went down there were reports this would be done. The hull has entirely disappeared, the cabin the last to drop from view.
>
> Not long ago the War Production board compiled a list of ships resting in Lake Superior which might be salvaged for the scrap iron and cargoes they contain. [*America* was listed for salvage.]

Interest in the salvage of *America* lay dormant through World War II and into the 1950s, although the ship was not forgotten. Transference of Cousteau and Gagnon's military aqualung of 1943 into a post-war recreational outlet brought *America* back into the press; the wreck was being visited by sport divers in the summer of 1956:

> Duluth's intrepid skin divers, aptly named the Frigid Frogs, next week-end will take to the deeps of Isle Royale to look over the sunken passenger steamer *America*....
>
> They won't have much trouble finding the *America*. Any Isle Royale fisherman can point out the reef where she ripped out her bottom. On a calm day, one can see the bow

a few feet below the surface, and it's a spooky sight, too.

If it's salvage they're after, the Frogs won't find much of that either. A couple of generations of fishermen, without today's complicated skin diving equipment, have seen to that (Herbert J. Coleman, "Frigid Frogs to Tour Ship Sunk Near Isle Royale" *Duluth News Tribune* July 8, 1956).

A 24-year-old hard-hat salvage diver, Jack Coghlan of Port Arthur, visited *America* in 1957, calling the dive his "most fascinating experience." Coghlan reported entering the vessel through the "dining compartment" as he described the experience to a Duluth reporter:

"It's sort of eerie," he said last week. "You can still see dishes on the sideboards, and the tables are piled high on one end of the room."

From there, Coghlan swam down a flight of stairs through a hallway and looked into a passenger's compartment. Silt obscured his vision, since he was working with an underwater light.

More rewarding was his entry into the purser's office, which he accomplished by breaking in the door. Rummaging in an old desk, he felt a mass of paper, thought he was wealthy, and found that the 'banknotes' were old snapshots.

Oddly enough, the pictures were legible and Coghlan has had them copied by a photographer. They included a number of scenes of what appears to be the Chicago waterfront....

Coghlan said the ship's hull is ringed with debris which has torn or fallen loose. Still in the hold is an ancient Model T Ford which he said seems in good condition. Coghlan took the car's horn as a souvenir.

Another souvenir was a bottle of meat sauce he found in the dining room. He said it was "sort of ripe" (Herbert J. Coleman, *Duluth News Tribune* April 28, 1957).

Coghlan and the Frigid Frogs' early descents on *America* renewed talk of possible salvage of *America*, although it would be four more years before that interest was coherently voiced and four additional years before the first actual attempt at salvage was undertaken.

Serious talk about raising *America* did not come until 1961 when James R. (Jim) Marshall, Pike Lake, Minnesota, took an interest based largely upon reports of the condition of *America* from various divers, including members of the Frigid Frogs. He personally did not dive on the wreck until September 1965. Marshall rekindled the interest that had been brewing for three decades. In the next four years the S.S. *America* Salvage Company Inc. was formed by Marshall and a Duluth attorney, Patrick D. O'Brien. Salvage rights were purchased from Paul J. Flynn. The firm acquired the cabin cruiser *Skipper Sam* and modified it for salvage and logistics work. A salvage plan was worked out and permission to salvage was secured from the National Park Service. A cadre of local divers was assembled to assist in the project. Many of the divers were in the Canadian Air Force but stationed at Duluth and had been trained in diving by Marshall through his recreational outfitting business (Hold-

en interview with Marshall 1986; Special Use Permit 6-65, Isle Royale National Park, issued to Marshall, Chippewa Outfitters, Duluth, Minnesota, for the period of Sept. 21, 1965, to Dec. 1, 1965, to conduct salvage operations on S.S. *America*, in Windigo Ranger Station files; *Duluth News Tribune* Sept. 24, 1965).

Appended to the Special Use Permit issued for salvage work on *America* were notes indicating that Isle Royale National Park officials had contacted both the Coast Guard and U.S. Army Corps of Engineers in Duluth regarding the vessel. The Coast Guard commented that they had no jurisdiction as long as the wreck and salvage work were properly marked to comply with current rules of the road. The Corps of Engineers said they had no interest in the operation. Neither agency had comment regarding requiring a performance bond for the salvage work (Special Use Permit, 6-65, *Ibid*).

The salvage corporation's primary interest was to raise *America* and return it to the Duluth waterfront where it could be restored over a five-year period, and thus transformed into a tourist attraction of historic interest, as well as a unique dining or hostel facility. This is an idea which has now come into vogue on the Great Lakes. Marshall said in 1965 of his thoughts about salvaging *America* in 1961:

"Talk was about as far as it went [in 1961]...until early this year [1965] when it became apparent that raising the steamer and returning her to Duluth would bring recognition to the city and provide an attraction that people throughout the nation would enjoy visiting" (*Duluth News Tribune* Sept. 15, 1965).

A *Houghton Daily Mining Gazette* columnist agreed that *America* would be a good tourist attraction saying:

"It is likely that the *America* revived might become an important tourist curiosity in the Zenith City [Duluth] region. Duluth has no such other ventures and the reclaiming from Davy Jones Locker the remains of the *City of Hancock* type ship might not be a bad idea" (*Houghton Daily Mining Gazette* Sept. 25, 1965).

However, clarification of the National Park Service's position on ownership of the wrecks and its role in preservation and conservation of shipwrecks located within its jurisdictional boundaries was ultimately the most tangible and lasting result of the salvage attempt, outside of the physical damage done to the wreck itself.

A salvage method was proposed. The plan was worked out by "salvage master" Chuck McClernan. The method consisted of first sealing up the steel hull's major openings. About 50 such openings were identified in preliminary examination of the vessel, including five cargo hatches, smokestack opening, a stairway, the dumbwaiter in the galley, the grocery chute, three coal bunkers and the skylight above the engine room as well as 34 other "minor" openings such as portholes, plus the original hole in the hull. This plan was reviewed and found sound by Marine Iron & Shipbuilding Co. of Duluth and individuals from Fraser-Nelson Shipyard in Superior (*Duluth News Tribune* Sept. 15, 1965; Holden interview with Marshall 1986).

When preliminary work was done, the salvagers would be able to proceed in raising the vessel by removing an estimated 159,000 gallons or about 1,821 tons of water from the vessel using an air lift. The 10-inch airlift was inserted into the hull through the galley stove flue. Air could be forced at 600 cu. feet per minute through the pipe into the vessel. Salvagers expected to force nearly a quarter million gallons of water out of the hull per hour (*Duluth News Tribune* Sept. 15, 1965).

When part of the hull reached the surface, the salvors planned to switch over to two four-inch pumps, which could handle about 160,000 gallons per hour. Once afloat, the *Skipper Sam* would tow *America* into the same gravel-bottomed bay that Capt. Smith was headed for the morning of the wreck. There they could check over the hull and make any further repairs necessary. From Isle Royale *America* was to be towed back to Duluth, possibly escorted by the Coast Guard cutter *Woodrush* (*Duluth News Tribune* Sept. 15, 1965; *Duluth News Tribune* Sept. 24, 1965; Holden interviews with Marshall 1974, 1986).

America Salvage Inc. was not operating in a vacuum without public and political support. Duluth Mayor George D. Johnson and Seaway Port Authority Director Robert T. Smith, both enthusiastic about the project, granted permission to moor *America* at Duluth's port terminal over the winter. Also lending support to the salvage project were the Northeastern Minnesota Development Association, Minnesota Arrowhead Association, U.S. Rep. John A. Blatnik and citizens of Duluth and Superior, many of whom clearly recalled their own trips on the steamer (Holden interviews with Marshall 1974, 1986; *Duluth News Tribune* Sept. 15, 1965).

Once *America* was returned to the Duluth waterfront, plans called for refitting the ship over a five-year period at a cost of about $200,000. The ship's galley, passenger dining salon, engine room and many cabins were relatively undamaged. The engines were believed to be operational with minimal restoration work, and there was still coal in the bunkers (*Duluth News Tribune* April 6, 1966; Holden interviews with Marshall 1974, 1986).

Actual work on sealing up the vessel in preparation for refloating began in September 1965 with the salvagers based at Grace Island, Isle Royale, only a half mile from the wreck site. The entire project, from hull survey to fabrication and installation of all patches and refloating, was expected to take three to four weeks. Work through the first two stages progressed on time or ahead of schedule. Salvors hoped to refloat the vessel by October 20 and have *America* in Duluth-Superior Harbor in November (*Duluth News Tribune* Sept. 24, 1965).

The 1965 salvage report by James Marshall, President of *America* Salvage Inc., to the Park gives considerable insight into the diving operations on the wreck (Letter from James Marshall to Superintendent Carlock Johnson, Dec. 3, 1965, on file Isle Royale National Park). The divers discovered about 200 fathoms of chain remaining in the chain locker and removed. The nine main deck openings were sealed with wooden hatches of 2x6-inch boards.

A great deal of the damaged superstructure was removed....

A large portion of the damaged second deck was removed opening the area over the engine...and the area around the opening in the deck has been shored....The remains of the ship's funnel, weighing some seven tons, were severed from the boilers with a cutting torch, and with the assistance of the cruiser, drifted over the side. This exposed the steel room over the engine and boilers. The galley appears undisturbed....Bad weather set in during September and early October. Finally, the salvors decided to delay refloating *America* until the following spring. They stored their equipment at Grace Island over the winter of 1965-66 under special permit (Holden, interviews with Marshall 1974. 1986; *Duluth News Tribune* Oct. 25, 1965; *Duluth Evening Herald* Oct. 25, 1965).

Despite the weather, members of the salvage group took a reporter down to explore the wreck. His descriptions are informative of the state of preservation of the wreck in the mid-1960s:

I observed that the ship is resting on a rock shoal at a severe angle, the bow being 19 inches below the surface and the stern in 85 feet of water.

As we worked our way slowly toward the bow, it was evident that the upper superstructure – which consists of the ship's two topside decks and pilot house – had been severely damaged, for debris was strewn in wild disarray throughout the steamer's forward section....

[Mike] Pinkstaff showed me where the hull was torn, which caused the *America* to sink. It consisted of a three-foot horse-shoe-shaped dent with a four and six-inch tear on each side....

Pinkstaff and I looked at the ship's big propeller and rudder – which is turned hard left the same way she was the night she sank – and then entered a hatch leading to the ship's dining area.

We started working our way forward by ascending an elaborate carpeted stairway – the carpet is still intact – leading to a large ballroom.

In the ballroom was a large upright grand piano...sitting upside-down and slightly damaged as a result of the sinking.

Forward of the ballroom I saw the *America*'s smokestack, and a little forward of that is a Model T Ford truck resting on the deck. The truck, which was being shipped to a plasterer in Fort William, Canada, is still assembled except for the hood and radiator, which have been taken by skin divers.

My last venture during the dive was a look at the engine room and engines. It's difficult to believe...but the *America*'s engines are as new-looking and shiny as the day they were bought. There isn't even marine growth on them (*Duluth News Tribune* Oct. 17, 1965).

America Salvage Inc. applied for an additional salvage permit by letter to Isle Royale Superintendent C.E. Johnson on April 7, 1966, to complete the salvage. Salvors planned to complete their task by June 12, 1966 (Correspondence, *Ameri*-

ca Salvage Inc. to Supt. C.E. Johnson dated April 1, 1966, and April 7, 1966, Windigo Ranger Station files, Isle Royale National Park; *Duluth News Tribune* April 10, 1966). A salvage permit was issued.

Inspection of the vessel in the spring revealed only the expected; many of the patches would have to be re-secured. However, bad news came on May 11 when divemaster Chuck McClernan reported "their worst fears had been realized," raising *America* was "all but impossible." McClernan and M.W. Gamblin discovered a new hole in the side of *America* apparently caused by dynamite placed by "an unknown party" to stop salvage of the vessel (Memorandum from Windigo District Ranger Jon B. Abrams to Superintendent, Isle Royale dated May 16, 1966, Windigo Ranger Station files).

Discovery of the reportedly sabotaged area marked the beginning of the end of salvage efforts. In August 1966, the U.S. Justice Department indicated they had informed the Federal Bureau of Investigation of the reported "bombing" of *America* and supposed they would send a demolitions experts to assess the situation. A Justice Department attorney, Harold D. Beaton, contacted *America* Salvage Inc. for permission to survey *America* without being held liable for any damage such survey might cause. Permission was granted by *America* Salvage Inc. on August 12, 1966 (Correspondence from U.S. Attorney Harold D. Beaton to James R. Marshall Aug. 9, 1966; correspondence from Marshall, *America* Salvage Inc. to Harold D. Beaton, U.S. Attorney in Grand Rapids, Michigan, Aug. 12, 1966, on file Windigo Ranger Station). No information has been available from the Justice Department or FBI concerning the extent or findings of any investigation.

Marshall reported, too, that the damage went beyond the new hole in the hull. He said the explosion caused the ship to "jump" and as it re-settled, the rudder was swung hard over and that there was tearing in the hull along the shaft tube that would prevent use of *America*'s own engine for propulsion on the return to Duluth (Holden interview with Marshall 1986).

The Submerged Cultural Resources Unit was unable to locate the "bomb hole" in the hull. The bomb incident apparently provided a convenient closing to the salvage attempt. The salvage operation provided the impetus for legal and administrative clarification of NPS policy regarding the submerged cultural resources of Isle Royale.

Recreational diving grew in the wake of the commercial salvage operations and attendant media coverage. In 1974 a sport diver, who was also an amateur historian and certified scuba instructor, wrote of his impressions and experiences on *America* presenting a comparison to the experience Coghlan had on the wreck in 1957. This also serves as an example of the beginnings of observations by sport divers on *America* and other shipwrecks at Isle Royale and the region as a benchmark in the changing attitudes of sport divers toward the objects upon which a majority of their recreational interests were focused:

Many divers have dove on the *America* because she is easy to get to, in rather shallow water, and safe from storms....

The condition of the wreck is very good with ice damage

extending to the boiler room. From the boiler room to the bow the ice has taken away the wood superstructure. The bow lies at the edge of a slope which goes down to the North Gap Channel....

There is much to see on this old wreck, one just does not know where to start exploring. Going down the deck starting from the bow you pass a big deck winch [sic] used once for pulling in the many feet of anchor chain. Just past that there is a hatch and down a ladder you can get to where the crew once slept. There is another point of interest in the bow and this is an air pocket created by the exhaust air of divers. You can go up inside this air pocket and talk to your buddy, but do not breath the air. There is always enough light to see your way out of the wreck but for close inspection a light and lifeline are needed.

Coming out of the hatch and going back down the deck you come to another hatch. This hatch was the coal bunker. There is hardly anything in it because the ship is lying at such a great angle that the coal has run into the boiler room. The hatch to the coal bunker is nearby.

At the edge of the coal bunker is where the wreckage starts. This is caused by a build up of ice which sometimes can go down to a depth of more than 30 feet. The pilothouse is no longer there and many of the cabins are destroyed. The wreckage consists of a lot of wood and pipes.

The main deck starts to take its shape again near the engine room. This is as far down as the ice could go, so from that point on there is very little damage.

Swimming over the top of the ship, the engine room is exposed to view. She had a three-cylinder engine. In the front of the engine and on top of the boiler room there is the remains of a Model A truck that was being shipped to Port Arthur. Divers through the years have taken many things off the truck like the tires and engine parts.

On deck two and in the rear of the engine room there is a hatchway that goes into a companionway. This companionway goes out to the side of the ship and then toward the stern. From the companionway, access can be made into the dining area.

Going through the companionway and to the dining area, you come to a pretty big room which was the dining room. All the tables and chairs that were once in the room are lying in the very rear of the room. Because of the great angle [at which] the ship is lying all the tables and chairs just slid to the rear of the room.

From the dining area you can leave the ship by going out through a cargo door. Following the side of the ship down you come to a small deck on the very stern. There is a hatchway on this deck which goes to deck one. Right inside the hatchway there is a piano, in bad shape. On the after deck there is a hatch going down to deck two. It is a little small for a diver to get through but it can be done.

Letting yourself off the stern and sinking to the bottom you have a most awesome and impressive sight as you look up at the huge size of the stern. All of the decks are intact....

The depth is 80 feet and all around the ship there is wreckage. The rudder and prop are still visible, with the rudder turned hard a starboard. The rudder seems to keep the ship from sliding further into the channel (Engman 1976: 1-5).

Although *America* was lost without loss of life, there has been one death aboard the vessel, a diving accident. In August 1976 20-year-old Donald G. Lienhardt of New Auburn, Wisconsin, apparently became disoriented while low on air and exploring *America*'s interior in a small storage area just aft of the galley. The door is wedged partly open. His brother and another friend had not noticed their partner's absence when they left the galley, nor were they immediately concerned when they surfaced without him. All had entered the wreck while low on air. The divers' air reserves were too low to conduct an effective search and rescue effort. Other sport divers in the area began the search while alerting other dive boats in the area of the problem. Lienhardt's body was recovered an hour and a half later (*Houghton Daily Mining Gazette* Aug. 23, 1976).

The room in which the fatality took place became popularly known to the diving community as the "forbidden room," and consequently became an attractive nuisance. Many divers pushed the limits of their abilities to visit the "forbidden room." In consultation with NPS managers, a decision was made to remove the partially open door. The door was removed with a large pry bar by lifting the door off its hinges.

George M. Cox: History

Construction

The steel passenger screw-steamer *George M. Cox* was named *Puritan* by the Craig Shipbuilding Co. of Toledo, Ohio, in 1901. U.S. Registry No. 150898 (June 7, 1901) listed the owner of the vessel as the Craig Shipbuilding Co., and gave the dimensions: 233 feet long, 40.5 feet wide and 21.9 feet deep. The ship had no masts, two decks, a plain head and round stern. The tonnage capacity under deck was 1169.08; the capacity between decks above the tonnage deck was 378.53 tons, yielding a gross tonnage of 1547.61. A deduction of 495.04 tons was allowed, giving a net tonnage of 1052.

The ship was designed for the overnight passenger service. The first owners, the Holland and Chicago Transportation Co., intended to name the vessel *Ottawa*. Before hull 82 was completed, the Holland and Chicago Co. was bought by the Graham and Morton Transportation Co. The new owners named the vessel *Puritan* and launched the ship on the afternoon of May 1, 1901 (*Detroit Free Press* May 2, 1901).

The Craig Shipbuilding Co. owned *Puritan* from June 7 to June 28, 1901. Graham and Morton Transportation Co. retained ownership until December 27, 1902, when ownership was transferred to J.H. Graham of St. Joseph, Michigan.

A detailed description of *Puritan* was published shortly after the launching in *Marine Engineering* (1901: 458-460). It is one of the best and most complete reports located for any Isle Royale shipwrecks.

She was built throughout to meet the requirements of the Bureau Veritas Classification Society, with extra heavy scantlings, thus making her one of the strongest vessels of her class afloat. The following are a few of her principal scantlings:

The center vertical keel is 48 inches deep by 17½ pounds, fitted with a 36-inch by 17½-pound rider plate on top of the floors with 4½ by 3 inches continuous angles. The frames are 6 inches by 3 inches by 14 pounds, channels spaced 24 inches apart and continuous to upper deck, with web frames of 12 inches by 22 pounds channel, spaced every 24 feet. Solid floors are fitted on every frame, 20 pounds in the machinery space and 18 pounds elsewhere, and are secured to the vertical keel by 3 inches by 4 inches double angles. Deck beams are of channel section, 10 inches by 22 pounds on main deck, and 6 inches by 14 pounds on upper deck, all spaced four-foot centers and secured to frames with substantial brackets. Three channel stringers are fitted in the lower hold, one on each side and between decks. The shell plating is as follows:

Garboard 19 pounds to 16 pounds at ends; bilge and side plating, 17 pounds to 14 pounds at ends; shear strake, 60 inches by 20 pounds, and 17 pounds at ends; between deck plating, 10 pounds. The vessel is constructed with two complete steel decks, and is fitted with three gangways on each side for handling freight. The stern post is a steel casting, and the rudder frame and stem are forgings.

The passenger accommodations are very complete, and all conveniences for a large passenger business are provided. The main cabin on the upper deck is finished in mahogany, and has 42 staterooms, with the dining room at the forward end. The galley and crew's quarters are directly under the dining room, on the main deck. Aft of the engine room on the main deck is a large smoking room, with connection to the main cabin by a grand stairway, all finished in mahogany, similar to the main cabin. Pilothouse and officer's quarters are on the boat deck, on which are also located 16 staterooms similar to those in the main cabin. The accommodations for second class passengers are under the main deck aft. The steamer has accommodations for 200 first and second class passengers, and is licensed to carry 2,000 excursionists.

The machinery consists of an inverted, direct-acting, triple expansion, surface condensing engine, with cylinders 21 inches, 34 inches and 58 inches in diameter, and 40-inch stroke, designed by the Craig Ship Building Co., and built in their own shops. The high pressure and intermediate cylinders are fitted with piston valves, and the low pressure cylinder with a double-ported slide valve. All valves are worked by Stephenson double-bar link motion, and

Figure 29. *George M. Cox* after the 1933 refit for the new Isle Royale Line. Appearance at the time of loss. U.S. Army Corps of Engineers Canal Park Marine Museum Collection.

The framing of the engine consists of three cast iron housings of box section in front and back, the latter being fitted with guide surfaces provided with water back for circulation of cooling water. The bedplate is cast iron of box section, cast in one piece, with five main journals.

The lower main journal boxes are cast steel, lined with anti-friction metal, as are also the cast iron caps which form the upper part of the bearings. The crank shaft is of wrought iron, 12 inches in diameter with steel crank pins and cast steel webs. Line and propeller shafting is wrought iron, provided with forged couplings and supported by suitable spring bearings. The thrust bearing is of the horseshoe type, with adjustable shoes. The propeller is four-bladed, solid cast iron, 12 feet in diameter and 19 foot pitch.

Owing to the large amount of lime in the waters of Lake Michigan, a surface condenser was fitted to obviate any trouble with the scaling of boilers. The condenser is separate from the main engine, and is of the cylindrical type, with steel shell fitted with composition tube sheets and composition tubes tinned inside and out. The cooling surface is 2,500 square feet

All the pumps are independent of the main engine, and with the exception of the circulating pump, were furnished by Dean Bros. of Indianapolis, Ind. The air pump is of the simplex vertical type, 12 inches by 24 inches by 18 inches; and the main and auxiliary feed pumps are of the Admiralty duplex type, 8 inches by 5 inches by 12 inches. Two duplex pumps, 5$\frac{1}{2}$ inches by 5$\frac{1}{4}$ inches by 7 inches, and one simplex pump, 4 inches by 4 inches by 5 inches are also fitted for general water service and for pumping from the bilge. Water is circulated through the condenser tubes by a centrifugal pump, with a 10-inch suction and discharge, driven by a 6-inch by 6-inch vertical, direct-connected engine, supplied by the Morris Machine Works of Baldwinsville, N.Y.

Steam is generated by four water tube boilers with an aggregate heating surface of 7,500 square feet. These boilers were tested to 450 pounds hydrostatic pressure, and are allowed a working pressure of 225 pounds.

The *Puritan* is lighted throughout with electricity, generated by two 15 kilowatt direct-connected General Electric Co. generators, located in the engine room. She is also fitted with steam steering engine and a Hyde steam windlass. Her anchors are of the Baldt stockless type, and weigh 2,840 pounds each.

have adjustable cutoffs, actuated by screws in the arms of the reverse shaft. The reversing gear is direct connected with a steam cylinder 11 inches diameter by 16 inches stroke. All pistons are fitted with cast iron spring rings, the high pressure and intermediate bodies also being cast iron and the low pressure being cast steel. Piston rods are machinery steel, secured to piston by tapered ends and nuts, and to crossheads by cottars. Crossheads are cast steel recessed for crosshead pin boxes and fitted with composition slippers. Connecting rods are wrought iron, the upper end being forked with crosshead pins shrunk in. The crank pin boxes are cast steel lined with best anti-friction metal.

Taken altogether the *Puritan* exemplifies the highest class of vessel for the trade in which she is employed, and is a credit to both her owners and builders.

Although she has only been running altogether about six weeks she has already broken the record for the run between St. Joseph, Mich., and Chicago, beating the best time of the whaleback steamer, *Christopher Columbus,* thus ranking her as one of the fastest boats on Lake Michigan. Her time for the run was 3 hours 11 minutes, making an average of 19¾ miles per hour....She now averages 108 revolutions with 200 pounds of steam.

The triple-expansion engine of *Puritan* was rated at 1,700 indicated horsepower (Certificate of Consolidated Enrollment and License, Puritan. May 23, 1924).

Operational History

John H. Graham, of Graham and Morton Transportation Company, was a prominent businessman connected with the passenger pleasure resort service out of Chicago and the fruit traffic from Michigan. Graham and Morton had built a line of palatial steamers primarily for the summer passenger service between Chicago, St. Joseph and Benton Harbor. In addition, the vessels also carried freight between these cities as well as to Milwaukee (Mansfield 1899: 2: 245).

Graham and Morton Transportation evolved as a stock company in 1880 or 1881 from the partnership between J. Stanley Morton and J.H. Graham, formed originally in the early 1870s. By 1899, the Graham and Morton Transportation Co. had grown to be the largest single business on the docks at Benton Harbor and Chicago, employing more than 100 persons in the summer (Mansfield 1899: 2: 246).

After *Puritan*'s launch in 1901, it made a trial run on Maumee Bay with William A. Boswell as captain and Louis Sebastian as chief engineer. On board were George Craig, representing the builders, master mechanic Cady Markely, E.E. Roberts, designer of the four water-tube boilers and who represented the Marine Boiler Works of Toledo, and other invited guests (Hamilton n.d.).

Graham and Morton Co. was anxious for the delivery of the new vessel. When *Puritan* left Toledo for Chicago on June 15, carpenters were on board completing their work. The ship was placed on the daily Chicago-to-Holland run shortly after the company took title on June 28, 1901. Typically, *Puritan* remained on this run until the end of the fruit season, when it sometimes ran from Chicago to Benton Harbor during the winter (Hamilton n.d.).

The first temporary port of enrollment was Toledo. When the

Graham and Morton Transportation Co. took delivery, the port of record according to enrollment documents was changed to Grand Haven, Michigan. W.A. Boswell was the master of record, and remained so when the ship was transferred to the ownership of J.H. Morton on December 27, 1902.

Puritan was reboiled in 1905. The Roberts boilers were replaced with four newer 11x10-foot Scotch boilers built by Johnston Bros. of Ferrysburg, Michigan (Hamilton n.d.). Recent field observations of these boilers reveal they were constructed with steam drums, an unusual feature for Great Lakes vessels.

A new enrollment was issued for *Puritan* in February 1908, reflecting a 26-foot increase in length. The lengthening took place in Manitowoc under the direction of George Craig, the designer and builder (1908 Certificate of Enrollment; Hamilton n.d.). The revision increased the gross tonnage from 1,547 to 1,762.20, and the net from 1,052 to 1,267. The registered depth increased from 21.9 feet to 26.6 ft. W.A. Boswell was again listed as master. It is unclear whether the depth change indicates an actual structural modification or was an artifact of a change of measurement procedures. There were some vessels structurally altered to accommodate automobiles. More research is needed to clarify this point for *Puritan/Cox.*

Puritan was one of several Great Lakes ships summoned to serve in World War I. There were at least five of the Lake Michigan passenger-steamer fleet called to U.S. Naval service: *Theodore Roosevelt, City Of South Haven, Virginia, Manitou* and *Puritan* (*Fort William Daily Times Journal* April 9, 1918).

Figure 30. *George M. Cox* as *Puritan* in March 1920 after service in World War I. U.S. Army Corps of Engineers Canal Park Marine Museum Collection.

Puritan was purchased by the U.S. Navy in April 1918 and commissioned November 20 of the same year (U.S. Department of the Navy 1970: 5: 405; *Lake Carriers' Association*

Figure 31. *Puritan* with the temporary bulkhead in place to allow passage through canals for ocean service in World War I. U.S. Army Corps of Engineers Canal Park Marine Museum Collection.

Annual Report 1918: 149). The ship's enrollment papers were surrendered October 23, 1918 (Consolidated Certificate of Enrollment and License *Puritan*. July 7, 1920). In Naval service, *Puritan* was designated SP-2222. It was the third vessel of that name to serve in the U.S. Navy.

The passenger steamers were principally used to bring U.S. troops back home after the Armistice (U.S. Department of the Navy 1970: 5: 405). *Puritan* was modified for naval service at the Krafts Shipyard in South Chicago, where it was fitted out for ocean service and camouflaged.

Most Lakes passenger vessels had to be structurally altered to allow passage to the ocean. Contemporary photographs indicate the bow of *Puritan* was severed to allow passage through the canal system to the Atlantic (Figure 31). The cut was made immediately forward of the pilothouse, and both sections were apparently bulkheaded to make the passage, or perhaps the smaller bow portion was simply loaded and carried through the passage.

The details of *Puritan*'s military career are unclear. The *Dictionary of American Fighting Ships* (U.S. Department of the Navy 1970: 5: 405) indicates that the ship served as a troop transport, and it was later reported that the ship had spent some of its time operating in the English Channel (Toledo Blade May 29, 1933). Some sources state that *Puritan*, along with other Lake passenger steamers, served as a minelayer in the North and Baltic seas (*Lake Carriers' Association* 1933: 35-36). Dana Thomas Bowen recorded that *Puritan* was used as a training ship for recruits (Bowen 1952: 308). Another writer stated that *Puritan* saw no action or service at all, but spent the time laid up in the Boston Navy Yard (Hamilton n.d.). Further historical research is needed to clarify *Puritan*'s military service.

Apparently, after *Puritan* was decommissioned, it was sold to a private company and rebuilt to resume the Lake passenger trade. The rebuilding took place at the South Chicago Drydock in the spring and early summer of 1920 (Hamilton n.d.). *Puritan* was redocumented on July 7, 1920, to the Chicago, Racine and Milwaukee Line, whose agent of record was James F. Gallagher of Michigan City, the same agent who served the Graham and Morton Transportation Co. before the war (Consolidated Certificate of Enrollment and License, *Puritan*. July 20, 1920).

The newly rebuilt passenger steamer was chartered to the Michigan Transit Co. of Chicago, which purchased the vessel outright in May 1924 (Consolidated Certificate of Enrollment and License, *Puritan*. May 23, 1924).

The Michigan Transit Co. utilized *Puritan* in the "Direct Overnight Service to Cool Northern Michigan Summer Resorts" (Advertisement that appeared in the *Chicago Herald and Examiner* June 24, 1925). Triweekly express service left Chicago Mondays, Wednesdays and Saturdays at 6 p.m., with the first run of the summer season on June 27. The towns served were: Ludington, Hamlin Lake, Epworth Heights, Manistee, Onekama, Portage Point, Frankfort and Crystal Lake, with service extended to Glen Haven and Traverse Bay on Wednesdays. *Puritan* served on this resort run with the steel steamer *Manitou*. Both vessels accommodated vacationers' cars (*Chicago Herald and Examiner* July 8, 1926).

In the severe storm of December 6, 7 and 8, 1927, *Puritan* broke from its moorings in Muskegon Harbor and drifted around with no one aboard. Buffeted by 65-mile-per-hour winds, *Puritan* dragged its winter moorings – steel cables fixed to large concrete blocks that had been buried six feet deep – and came to rest against an abandoned pier at East Lake. The huge concrete blocks that were dragged by the ship prevented serious damage to the hull when the ship hit the pier (*Detroit Free Press* December 9, 1927). The same storm sank the canaler *Kamloops* on Isle Royale.

The resort and passenger cruise vessel *Puritan* was idled in 1929, just before the demand for recreation cruises and passage to the northern Michigan resorts was virtually eliminated by the Great Depression. The ship was docked at Manistee (Hamilton n.d.).

After the idle time at Manistee, *Puritan* was purchased by Isle Royale Transportation Co. The Enrollment Document for the purchase (May 22, 1933) registered the name change from *Puritan* to *George M. Cox*. The Isle Royale Transportation Co. was an Arizona corporation headed by the man for which *Puri-*

tan had been renamed.

George M. Cox was a millionaire ship builder and brewer from New Orleans and a large stockholder of the Duke Transportation Company. The new owner had refitted *Puritan* in a grand manner. "I never had to shine shoes, but if I did I would try to do it better than the other fellow, and I am going to follow this same procedure with these boats," he said after the refitting and renaming of his company's newest boat was complete. "The boats are elegantly equipped, and everything that can possibly be done will be offered for the passenger's pleasure. The ships, however, are going to remain clean – there'll be no gambling or disorder – if we have to sink them first. Our purpose is to supply two ships, and perhaps more, where every facility will be offered for clean and wholesome amusement and plenty of good times" (*Manistee News Advocate* May 25, 1933).

There was much excitement regarding the newly appointed *George M. Cox*. On May 23, the ship, decorated with a new coat of white paint and carrying the International Code of Signals, left the moorings at Arthur Street in Manistee to move down to the Michigan Transit docks. Hundreds of people visited the ship as it lay at the dock, the crew finishing last-minute preparations for departure on *Cox*'s first voyage in more than two years. The ship was slated to leave for Chicago the next morning with George Johnson as captain and Arthur Cronk (appears as Kronk in most other references) of Houghton or Hancock, Michigan, as first mate. The refurbished vessel met with approval from its many visitors and well-wishers. "Entirely repainted, inside and out, the fine appearance of the ship won the favorable comment of those who inspected it" (*Manistee News Advocate* May 24, 1933).

Wreck Event

The first voyage of *Puritan* as the newly appointed *George M. Cox* was also to be its last. On May 25, 1933, the ship left Chicago bound for Port Arthur to begin its new route in the passenger trade between those two cities. Intermediate stops were planned for Houghton and Isle Royale.

The steamer left Saturday, May 27 from Marquette at 2 a.m. bound for Houghton with namesake George M. Cox and 124 others aboard (*Daily Mining Gazette* May 27, 1933). The captain was George Johnson of Traverse City and the first mate was Arthur Cronk. There was also an eight-piece orchestra aboard ready to join in the festivities anticipated on the maiden voyage (*Manistee News Advocate* May 24, 1933).

Cox arrived in Houghton and tied up at the Peninsula dock around noon after its 10-hour run. The vessel was opened for inspection, and hundreds of local residents toured the finely appointed cruise ship (*Daily Mining Gazette* May 28, 1933).

George M. Cox left Saturday afternoon, May 27, 1933, for Isle Royale, but *Cox* ran hard aground off the west end of Isle Royale sometime before 6 p.m. Saturday evening while those on board ate dinner. The steamer *Morris S. Tremaine* intercepted a wireless SOS message from the stricken ship, and the first word reached Houghton about 8 p.m. Word of the disaster was received by Capt. Fred Sollman of the Portage Canal Coast Guard via Ft. William. The Coast Guard left immediately for the wreck site (*Daily Mining Gazette* May 28, 1933).

Capt. M.L. Gilbert, marine superintendent of the Isle Royale Transit Company in Ft. William, was receiving fragmentary reports of the wreck by wireless from ships in the vicinity. The ship had struck a reef in thick fog, and George M. Cox and three women passengers were reported aboard *Tremaine*. Gilbert described *George M. Cox* to the press as an unusually seaworthy craft with a hull of steel. He went on to reassure those concerned that "the boat was commanded by Capt. George Johnson of Traverse City, a veteran Great Lakes shipmaster" (*Daily Mining Gazette* May 28, 1933).

On the 28th, the story of the wreck appeared in the newspapers. The New Orleans *Times-Picayune* carried a detailed report prominently mentioning the president of Isle Royale Transit Co., a resident of New Orleans:

> Four persons were injured, one seriously, in the wreck, the first on the Great Lakes this season, but no lives were lost. The four, with George M. Cox of New Orleans...and a

Figure 32. *George M. Cox* hard aground at Rock of Ages, Isle Royale circa May 27, 1933. U.S. Army Corps of Engineers Canal Park Marine Museum Collection.

nurse were brought to Fort Williams by the freighter *M.S. Tremaine* and placed in a hospital....

Mrs. Cox said Sunday afternoon that she talked with her husband Sunday morning at Port Arthur, Canada, by long distance telephone and that he suffered no ill effects from his harrowing experience.

The *George M. Cox*, making her first trip of the season, was en route to Port Arthur, Ont., from Chicago to pick up

250 Canadian residents and take them to the Century of Progress Exposition at the latter city. Thirty-two of the persons aboard on the out bound trip were passengers....

Plowing through a heavy fog, the steamer, with its passengers at dinner, struck an extended ledge of rock a short distance from Rock of Ages Lighthouse with such force that her engines and boilers were ripped loose. The impact threw the passengers to the salon floors and sent tables and chairs crashing against the walls.

Keepers of the Rock of Ages Light said they saw the spars of the steamer above the low-hanging fog and made frantic but futile efforts to attract the vessel's attention with the siren. A few minutes after the vessel struck she had broken open and filled with water until her top decks were awash.

Only the fact that the Lake was calm enabled the keepers of the light and the crew of the steamer to transfer everyone to small boats and rafts and avoid loss of life.

A description of the wreck was given by the 23-year-old ship's staff nurse, Adeline Keeling, who was taken to Port Ar-

Figure 33. Stern view of *Cox* aground at Rock of Ages. Note starboard lifeboats in place. U.S. Army Corps of Engineers Canal Park Marine Museum Collection.

thur with Cox, the injured passengers and crew (*New York Times* May 29, 1933):

"There was a heavy thud, followed by a series of crashes," said Miss Keeling. "The passengers were at dinner at the time. I saw a heavy buffet slide across the floor and crash into tables and a partition. I was in my stateroom and was thrown against a door and stunned. The stewardess, Beatrice Cote, helped me to my feet, and was herself knocked down in the second crash. She injured her back.

"There was no panic, but the steamer listed heavily to port and the passengers and crew rushed to starboard. It was impossible to lower the starboard boats because of the list of the vessel, but the port boats were lowered and ferried us all to the lighthouse."

Capt. George Johnson, whose actions had been termed heroic in his hometown newspaper (*Traverse City Record Eagle* May 29, 1933), recounted the wreck events (*Superior Evening Telegram* May 29, 1933): "We hit a reef while going at a speed of 17 knots. The impact was severe, causing a large hole to be torn in her side. It listed to 90 degrees and the ship's stern submerged in about four minutes, I should judge." A similar quote of Johnson's appeared the next day in the *Daily Mining Gazette* (May 30, 1933) with one difference: the speed was given as 10 knots.

Although no casualties resulted from the wreck, some injuries were sustained by crew members. Beatrice Cote, a stewardess from Manistee, Michigan, suffered an injured back. John Gancarz, deck hand from Freesoil, Michigan, injured his legs, hand and shoulder. George Williams had a head injury that was a scalp wound. Alex Mack, from Portland, Maine, broke a leg and injured his hand (*Superior Evening Telegram* May 29, 1933). Other reports indicate that Mack's injuries were severe burns, rather than a broken leg. George M. Cox himself was among the injured (*Manistee News-Advocate* May 29, 1933), but the inclusion of Cox on the injured list may have resulted from his accompanying the injured to the hospital. Other sources state that Gancarz' injuries were severe scalds (*Fort William Daily Times Journal* May 30, 1933).

Heroic deeds had been observed during the stranding and evacuation of *Cox*: Rita Little refused her seat with the other women in the lifeboat and assisted Deck Mate M.L. Gilbert in loading three more lifeboats before leaving the deck. Alex Mack, with a broken leg, also gave up an early seat in the lifeboats and only left after all the women had been taken off the stricken vessel. Bar steward Zoeller tied a rope around himself and searched the ship to insure no passengers remained trapped (*Manistee News Advocate* May 29, 1933).

Departure from the stricken ship was orderly; the crew was apparently well disciplined. There was some confusion, but no panic after the crash. Members of the crew moved among the passengers and quieted their fears (*Manistee News Advocate* May 29, 1933). Wireless messages were immediately sent out and the radio was manned until the water quieted the transmitter. The ship was safely abandoned in 40 minutes under the direction of Capt. Johnson, who was the last to leave the ship (*Traverse City Record Eagle* May 29, 1933). The removal of 89 passengers and 32 crew from *Cox* makes this one of the largest mass ship abandonments and rescues recorded in the history of Lake Superior.

Five life boats were lowered on the port side; the boats on the starboard side were not launched because of the extreme port list. The passengers were loaded into the ship's lifeboats and towed to Rock of Ages by lightkeeper John Soldenski's motor launch. The passengers took turns warming themselves in the limited quarters of the lighthouse, and they were served hot coffee by the wife of the lightkeeper (*Cleveland News* May 29, 1933).

The operational procedures of the U.S. Coast Guard at Portage Canal Station and aboard the cutter *Crawford* offer some insight into the *Cox* rescue operations. About 8 p.m. the Portage Station received the following telegram from Port Arthur: "Steamer *George M. Cox* aground on Rock of Ages. In bad shape. Want assistance" (Letter from F.C. Sollman, Officer in Charge, Portage Station to John Hanson, Bureau of Navigation and Steamboat Inspection June 7, 1933). Within 10 minutes a lifeboat and crew left the station. The Portage crew arrived at the wreck site at 2:15 a.m. the morning of the 28th. All passengers and crew had been removed from the wreck and were safe on Rock of Ages.

The Portage crew transported 43 persons from the lighthouse to Washington Island hotel dock on Isle Royale and returned to Rock of Ages. Captain Johnson requested the removal of baggage from the wreck, and 71 bags, suitcases and other baggage items were taken aboard the lifeboat and transported to the lighthouse, arriving there at 8:40. Twenty crew members were transported from the lighthouse to *Crawford* with some of the baggage, then 12 more of the *Cox* crew were transported to Washington Harbor.

The Coast Guard cutter *Crawford* received word of the wreck at its dock at Two Harbors at 6:10 p.m., May 27, from *Tremaine* as it was transmitting a message to the Port Arthur radio station addressed to the Portage, Michigan, Coast Guard Station. *Crawford* left immediately making all due speed. During the trip the ship's log indicates that the speed was increased when additional weights were placed on the governor to increase the engine's revolutions. The officers of *Crawford* assumed that human lives were at stake.

Crawford arrived on site at 5:35 a.m., May 28, and anchored in three fathoms of water. Five minutes later the officer of the North Superior Coast Guard was aboard to brief the officers of *Crawford*. Captain Johnson was consulted on the disposition of the passengers and crew. Johnson responded that he wanted them taken to Houghton, Michigan. The *Cox* crew and passengers were loaded aboard, and the cutter proceeded to Washington Harbor to pick up the people who had been transferred there. The Coast Guard lifeboat from Grand Marais had engine trouble and was towed to the Singer Dock in Washington Harbor by *Crawford*. The ship encountered dense fog on the way to the dock, finally arriving at 8:55 a.m. In an hour, all remaining people were loaded and *Crawford* was under way to

Houghton. The total aboard was recorded in the *Crawford* log as 113 (Log of the U.S. Coast Guard Patrol Boat *Crawford* May 27, 28, 1933).

Almost immediately, speculation and opinions regarding the crash were offered to the press. Captain John Hope Clark of *Isle Royale*, *Cox*'s planned running mate, stated that *Cox* had to cope with currents especially strong at that time of the year, in addition to fog conditions.

It is said that the light at Rock of Ages reef is equipped with a theoretically efficient fog whistle, but it is located in a so-called "silent zone," so that even if the whistle is operating, it may not be heard more than two or three miles away (*Manistee News Advocate* May 29, 1933).

The area of Rock of Ages reef, where the wreck occurred, was generally known to be a particularly hazardous region. When the cutter *Crawford* approached the reef on its rescue mission, the engines were slowed and the radio direction finder was used for navigation because the area was recognized as having a local magnetic attraction, so it was not advisable to rely on compass course for the last 15 miles approaching the light. In addition, because of the fog conditions, a double watch had been posted on the bow (Log of *Crawford* Sunday, May 28, 1933).

Early reports indicated that *Cox*'s first officer was in charge when the wreck happened, but the captain had taken over and directed the evacuation of the ship (*Traverse City Record Eagle* May 29,1933). There had been praise for the officers of the sunken steamer (e.g., *Detroit Free Press* May 30, 1933), but there would also be many questions. A federal inquiry was convened to answer them.

The federal inquiry was held in Houghton and directed by Capt. John Hanson, steamboat inspector, and Alfred Knights, boiler and machinery inspector. Both men were from Marquette and represented the U.S. Bureau of Navigation. They would be joined by Capt. F.J. Meno of Detroit, supervisor of the eighth district. The inquiry convened May 30, 1933, the same day the stranded *George M. Cox* was abandoned to the underwriters as a total loss (*Daily Mining Gazette* May 30, 1933).

The first witness called before the inquiry was Capt. Johnson, who testified that First Mate Arthur Kronk had changed the course he had set without his authority after the ship had cleared Portage Lake Ship Canal (*Detroit Free Press* May 31, 1933). Captain Johnson stated he set the course for Fort William at NW ¼ N, which is the charted course from the canal to the Canadian port city. He then retired and left the first mate in charge. Johnson remained in his cabin until 5 p.m. when they encountered fog on a calm sea. The *Daily Mining Gazette* (May 30, 1933) carried the captain's testimony:

"The sounding of the Rock of Ages fog siren was well determined," Captain Johnson said, "at 5:20 p.m., exactly one hour before it piled up on the reef. Continuing on a course one point north of the charted course, the vessel proceeded at a moderate speed until 6:10 p.m. when the fog siren on Rock of Ages became more distinct," the master testified.

"Discovering that we were near abreast of the light, owing to a greater speed than I had anticipated, we received an alarm signal from the Rock of Ages lighthouse and immediately I put the wheel hard to starboard and steered west for eight minutes....At 6:18, feeling assured we were at least two and one half miles westward of the lighthouse, I hauled slowly to the northwest in order to get a bearing on Rock of Ages Light. We struck at 6:20 p.m." Visibility at the time the *Cox* hit the reef was about one-quarter of a mile or about 1,500 feet, according to Capt. Johnson, who said the boat's speed at that time was about 10 miles per hour.

The change of course was not the only problem attributed to Kronk in the testimony. Kronk was allegedly one of the first of the crew to get into a lifeboat after the wreck. "One witness said that Kronk set out with one woman in his boat, but that he was ordered back to the steamer and additional passengers were placed in the boat" (*Detroit Free Press* May 31, 1933).

Others substantiated the captain's recounting of the events. John Nelson, the wheelsman on duty when the vessel left the canal, and M.L. Gilbert Jr. agreed with the captain's testimony. "Nelson stated that when the *Cox* left the canal he was steering northwest one-quarter north, and about 55 minutes out from the canal he was directed to change the course to northwest one-half north. When he was asked who gave him that order, Nelson answered: 'Mr. Kronk'" (*Detroit Free Press* May 31, 1933).

First Officer Kronk was called to testify late in the day, and he had not finished by the time of adjournment at 9:15 that night. The inquiry reopened at 8 the next morning:

The first mate admitted that the course had been changed from NW ¼ N to NW ½ N after leaving the canal, but he had not been questioned regarding who was responsible for the change. He said that he sighted top of Rock of Ages lighthouse about 5, and the light bore NNW when first seen, and it appeared about three miles away.

After sighting the light Kronk stated that he reported to the master, who took charge of navigation after that time. He said that the captain hauled to the west for about five minutes and then brought the ship back on a WNW course.

Questioned by Captain Hanson regarding the lowering and manning of the life boats after the crash, Kronk admitted that the life boat of which he was in charge was the first over the deck, and that he was the first officer off the boat. The inquiry was adjourned at this point in the interrogation (*Daily Mining Gazette* May 30, 1933).

Some additional information on the course change appeared in another paper:

Captain Johnson was again questioned Tuesday night [May 30] and said he asked Kronk about the change in course when he assumed command at 5 p.m.

"I asked why he changed the course," the captain told the investigators, "and he replied that I had advised him to steer chart courses whenever possible to obtain the correctness of our compasses on all chart courses."

Johnson's testimony brought up the question of the accuracy of the compasses aboard *Cox* and the influence of local deviations, two questions that concerned the investigators:

Replying to this line of questioning, Capt. Johnson admitted that the *George M. Cox* steered a good course over the entire route from Manistee to Chicago and north as far as Houghton. In the vicinity of Isle Royale, Captain Johnson said he believed there were some variations due to local magnetic disturbances, but when questioned admitted that he had not looked up the charted variations for that course on the map. First Mate Kronk said that in his opinion there was a one-eighth deviation to the west in the *Cox*'s compasses on a northerly course (*Daily Mining Gazette* May 30, 1933).

During the second day of the investigation (Wednesday May 31), Kronk maintained that he had remained at his post until the last, and that he assisted in lowering and loading lifeboats before leaving the ship and departing for shore with 17 men in his lifeboat (*Detroit Free Press* June 1, 1933). He also maintained that he did not change the course of *Cox* while in command between the time they had left Portage Lake Ship Canal and the time he turned the ship over to Capt. Johnson (*Daily Mining Gazette* June 1, 1933).

Emotions were running high during the investigation. Kronk had gotten into an "impromptu fistic argument" with Capt. M.L. Gilbert, vice president and general manager of the Isle Royale Transit Co. The encounter took place in the lobby of the Douglass House Hotel, where the investigation was being held (*Daily Mining Gazette* June 1, 1933).

Later during the afternoon questioning, stress of the proceedings were reflected:

While being re-questioned this afternoon, Mr. Kronk created some commotion when he broke down and cried, and, slamming his fist down on a desk, shouted that he was being "framed by a dirty bunch of crooks!" (*Detroit Free Press* June 1, 1933).

The findings of the *Cox* investigation were not announced until July 8, 1933. The board found both Capt. Johnson and First Officer Kronk guilty of "reckless navigation in a fog and inattention to duty." Both men were stripped of their officer's papers by the U.S. Steamboat Inspection Service (*Daily Mining Gazette* July 9, 1933; *Manistee News Advocate* July 10, 1933). Because no time period was mentioned, presumably the revocation of their papers was permanent. The *Cox* inquiry decision marked the second time Kronk had lost his papers; they had previously been suspended for 90 days for negligence in the loss of the freighter *Kiowa* in 1929 (*Detroit Free Press* June 2, 1933).

Salvage

George M. Cox had been reconditioned at a cost of $80,000, and was valued at $150,000 when lost (*Traverse City Record Eagle* May 29, 1933). Other sources place the value of the vessel at $200,000 (*Daily Mining Gazette* May 30, 1933). The ship was declared a total loss; uninsured liability to the company was about $40,000 (*Daily Mining Gazette* May 30, 1933).

Beginning the day after the wreck, groups of sightseers cruised out to the wreck, and many photographs were taken of the stranded ship, its bow poised 110 feet in the air. Some furnishings and other items were removed from the wreck while it could still be boarded. Six high-backed oak chairs ended up in the Douglass House of Houghton, the same location where the wreck investigation took place (*Daily Mining Gazette* April 26, 1980). The chairs had been removed by members of the Hancock Naval Reserves and were placed in the Naval Armory until the building was taken over by Michigan Tech in 1980 (*Daily Mining Gazette* July 22, 1980). These chairs are now part of the museum collection of Isle Royale National Park.

Four men were left on guard at the site until the company decided the disposition of the wreck (*Manistee News Advocate* May 29, 1933). Records of professional salvage efforts are scanty. The salvage tug *Strathbuoy* visited the site on the 29th or 30th and reported: "the bottom of the steamer was torn out, the engines jolted from their moorings and the vessel is listing toward deep water, with the likelihood of sinking in the first heavy storm" (*New York Times* May 29, 1933). The salvage barge *Strathmore* may have also operated on site.

Some salvage was carried out with its recovered materials being stored in the Booth Fisheries Dock at Port Arthur. On September 5, 1933, the running mate of *Cox, Isle Royale*, cleared Fort William on the last run of its season loaded with the equipment salvaged from *Cox* (*Canadian Railway and Marine World* Oct. 1933: 495).

Three of the men who were left to guard the site were returned to Houghton on June 2 to testify in the federal inquiry. A seaplane was chartered to make the run to the island and retrieve the crewmen. Their reports indicate they were undertaking some light salvage operations while guarding the wreck. They reported that the compass and charts had been recovered along with some gas masks. The plane also brought 400 pounds of baggage from the island with the crewmen (*Daily Mining Gazette* June 2, 1933). It is most likely the luggage had been recovered since the departure of *Crawford,* and was the result of the guards' salvage activity.

The wreck was abandoned to the underwriters on June 6, 1933 (*Daily Mining Gazette* June 6, 1933). The Enrollment and License for the Coasting and Foreign Trade (number 31) for *Cox* was surrendered in Chicago on July 18, 1933. There was a May 17 endorsement of a preferred mortgage for a total of $95,000 due to mature June 1, 1933 (National Archives Record Group 41).

George M. Cox remained in position on the reef until early July. The strong box, reportedly containing more than $200,000 in stocks, bonds, money and jewelry, was salvaged by two Portage Entry men, Arthur and Emil Tormala. The safe was raised from 35 feet of water and taken to Marquette, Michigan, July 11 (*Daily Mining Gazette* July 11, 1933). They reported that the ship was breaking up fast and had already broken in two; the stern was sinking.

The advent of scuba diving 25 years later brought heavy attrition of artifacts from the wreck site. The wreck sites of Isle Royale became diving attractions in the 1960s and '70s. Local divers held formal artifact collecting expeditions in the mid-1970s. An example, relating to *Cox*, is the Minnesota School of Diving pamphlet telling of their recoveries in August of 1972:

> Thirty-nine years after her descent, a team of 20 sport divers from Minnesota School of Diving explored the wreckage [of *George M. Cox*]. They dove in 1½- to 2-hour intervals three times a day, almost every week-end in August of 1972. Found were tea kettles, silverware, dishes, port holes, running lights and a multitude of other souvenirs... all evidence of the hard crash that night in 1933 on the Rock of Ages Reef.

Most portable artifacts have been removed from the site. Despite the losses of portable artifacts, *Cox* is still a primary diving attraction at Isle Royale and was rated as the second most visited diving site at Isle Royale National Park (Stinson 1980: 15).

Chester A. Congdon: History

Construction

Chester A. Congdon was built as *Salt Lake City* for the Holmes Steamship Company of Cleveland, then managed by W.A. Hawgood. The new steamer was of the 10,000-ton capacity class and measured 532 feet in length, 56 feet in beam with a depth of 26 feet. The gross registered tonnage was 6371.49, and net tonnage was 4,843. While under construction, the Chicago Ship Building Company numbered the hull 74. The steel bulk freighter had 32 telescoping hatches nine feet wide, on 12-ft. centers, with three compartments of 3,700, 3,100 and 3,400 tons, for a total capacity of 10,200 tons. The ship carried a crew estimated at 19.

The Chicago Ship Building Company departed from its tradition of launching its vessels on Saturdays when *Salt Lake City* slid down the ways; it splashed into the Calumet River on Thursday, August 29, 1907. The new bulk freighter was given U.S. Registry Number 204526 when it was enrolled September 11, in Cleveland.

The huge steel bulk freighter was powered by a triple-expansion engine with cylinders of 23.5, 38 and 63 inches on a 42-inch stroke. The engine received its steam from two induced-draft Scotch boilers 14 feet 6 inches x 11 feet 6 inches. Both the engine and boilers were built by the American Shipbuilding Company of Cleveland. The engine produced 1,765 indicated horsepower.

Operational History

The first owner of *Salt Lake City* was the company that had it built: the Holmes Steamship Company of Cleveland, Ohio. The Holmes Company operated the boat until 1911, when it was sold to the Acme Transit Company of Ohio, managed by

H.B. Hawgood (May 13, 1911, Certificate of Enrollment).

On February 2, 1912, *Salt Lake City* ownership was transferred to the Continental Steamship Company of Duluth, G.A. Tomlinson, President. A change of name to *Chester A. Congdon* was registered by D.W. Stocking, Secretary of the Continental Steamship Company, on April 1, 1912. Chester A. Cong-

Figure 34. 532-foot long bulk freighter *Chester A. Congdon* as it appeared at the time of loss in 1918. U.S. Army Corps of Engineers Canal Park Marine Museum Collection.

don was a prominent Duluth lawyer and financier who had made a fortune in mining and grain interests.

On August 10, 1912, *Chester A. Congdon* ran aground while waiting for fog to clear. The ship drifted onto a shoal about four miles north of Cana Island on Lake Michigan, and damaged several plates (*Lake Carriers Association* 1913: 18; 1912: 9).

Congdon ran aground again in October 1915. The ship was drawing 19 feet 6 inches of water, and it rubbed both bilges hard while going through Grosse Pointe channel during a period of low water. The grounding sheared several rivets, which opened some seams, and the vessel began leaking (*Bulletin of Lake Carriers Association* Nov. 1915: 62; May 1915: 18).

Wreck Event

The newspaper that contained the first report of the wreck of *Chester A. Congdon* carried the news on page 10; the headlines and front pages that day were devoted to the news that World War I had ended (*Fort William Daily Times Journal* Nov. 7, 1918).

The voyage that would end with one of the most costly marine disasters on the Lakes began on November 6, 1918. At 2:28 a.m. *Congdon* left Fort William, Ontario, downbound to Port McNicoll with a cargo of 380,000 bushels of wheat (*Lake Carriers Association* 1918: 142). Other sources list the cargo as 400,000 bushels (*Fort William Daily Times Journal* Nov. 12, 1918), and 350,000 bushels (*Cleveland Plain Dealer*, Nov. 8,

1918). The grain had been loaded at the Ogilvie and Pacific elevators (*Fort William Daily Times Journal* Nov. 12, 1918). *Congdon* had done a one-day turnaround. The ship arrived on November 5 and cleared downbound on the 6th (*Duluth News Tribune* Nov. 6, 1918).

Congdon proceeded a little way past Thunder Cape, where the ship encountered a heavy sea whipped up by a southwest gale. At 4 a.m., Capt. Autterson turned his ship and retreated seven or eight miles to calmer water, anchoring until 10:15 a.m. By then the wind had abated, although the sea was still running. The captain ventured out again, but after passing Thunder Cape, a thick fog set in. A course was set for Passage Island at 10:40 a.m., and the ship held a speed of nine knots. The captain's intention was to run for 2.5 hours at that speed and stop if the fog held (*Lake Carriers Association* 1918: 142-143). "I figured on stopping on account of fog until we could locate something. At eight minutes after 1 in the afternoon she fetched up – grounded (from the captain's account, *Fort William Daily Times Journal*, Nov. 12, 1918).

The ship's officers had not heard the Passage Island fog signal before they struck the southerly reef of Canoe Rocks (*Lake Carriers Association* 1918: 143). Captain Autterson described the events that followed:

We immediately lowered boats and sent one boat over to Passage Island, about seven miles, to try and secure some assistance from the lighthouse keeper, if possible. We were on Canoe Rocks. Then the second mate took another boat, a fisherman's launch, from Canoe Rocks into Fort William. He had two fishermen with him. The launch became disabled, and they did not reach Fort William until 6 Thursday morning (Nov. 7) (*Fort William Daily Times Journal* Nov. 12, 1918).

The second mate brought the first news of the wreck to Fort William. Apparently, *Congdon* had no wireless aboard, or it was disabled when the ship struck. The historical accounts indicate no messages were transmitted from *Congdon*.

As soon as word of the disaster reached Fort William, J. Wolvin, manager of the Canadian Towing and Wrecking Company, dispatched the wrecking barge *Empire* and the tug *A.B. Conmee* to the site. The tug *Sarnia*, with additional equipment, was being prepared to follow soon (*Fort William Daily Times Journal* Nov. 7, 1918).

First reports of damage to the stricken ship indicated that the vessel, although damaged, might be saved. "Her forepeak, Nos. 1 and 2 starboard tanks and No. 1 port tank are full of water" (*Cleveland Plain Dealer*, Nov. 8, 1918). It was hoped that lightering would be all that was necessary to refloat the vessel. The lightered grain was to be placed aboard the barge *Crete* (*Cleveland Plain Dealer* Nov. 9, 1918).

The most serious obstacle to refloating *Congdon* would prove to be the weather. When the lightering tugs and barges initially left for the site, the weather had been "calm and thick" (*Cleveland Plain Dealer* Nov. 8, 1918), but this did not last long. Two days later, by Friday, strong winds had blown up. The crew was removed from the wreck sometime that day, November 8, and was placed aboard the barge *Empire*. As the wind blew from the southeast at gale force, reaching a speed of 55 miles per hour (*Lake Carriers Association* 1918: 143, *Cleveland Plain Dealer* Nov. 10, 1918), the crew was sheltered on the barge in protected waters at Isle Royale (*Port Arthur Daily Chronicle* Nov. 8, 1918).

No loss of life resulted from the wreck. One serious injury, however, did occur before the lightering operations were concluded, due to the fierce gale that drove the salvage vessels and crew to shelter at Isle Royale. Wireless operator Thomas Ives of the barge *Empire* was transported to the hospital in Port Arthur with a mangled thigh, which was smashed when he caught his leg in a hoisting gear. He was taken to port on one of the attending tugs (*Port Arthur Daily Chronicle* Nov. 7, 1918).

The messages of the wreck that reached land on November 9 relayed the news that *Congdon* had broken in two, and that the stern had sunk in deep water. The tugs had stood by as long as possible, but there was nothing they could do, although they stayed at the site until heavy seas were breaking over the wreck (*Fort William Daily Times Journal* Nov. 9, 1918). The steamer had broken in two aft of the No. 6 hatch sometime Friday night (Nov. 8th). The forward end remained on the reef in 20 feet of water, but was in very bad condition (*Fort William Daily Times Journal* Nov. 12, 1918; *Lake Carriers Association* 1918: 143; *Cleveland Plain Dealer* Nov. 10, 1918). The 36-man crew of *Congdon* returned to Fort William, arriving on the tug *Conmee* Saturday morning, November 9 (*Fort William Daily Times Journal* Nov. 12, 1918). The captain, along with Superintendent Close who had arrived from Duluth to investigate the accident, both visited the wreck on Sunday morning and salvaged personal effects from the bow section.

The ship was declared a total loss. The newspapers noted that four-fifths of the cargo would be lost (*Fort William Daily Times Journal* Nov. 12, 1918). The crew arrived in port in time to participate in the Nov. 11 armistice celebrations. The survivors of the *Congdon* wreck paraded in the streets carrying the ship's flag, and a large crowd fell in behind them (*Fort William Daily Times Journal* Nov. 11, 1918). "We expected to be somewhere on Lake Huron today," said one of the crew, "instead of back again at Fort William" (*Fort William Daily Times Journal* Nov. 12, 1918).

The wreck of *Chester A. Congdon* was a tremendous financial loss. When declared a constructive total loss, officials

Figure 35. *Chester A. Congdon* aground at Canoe Rocks, Isle Royale November 1918. U.S. Army Corps of Engineers Canal Park Marine Museum Collection.

placed the value at more than $1.5 million. Although the owners carried insurance of $365,000 on the hull and $369,400 in disbursements, the wheat cargo alone at $2.35 per bushel was worth $893,000 (*Lake Carriers Association* 1918: 143). Contemporary accounts labeled *Congdon* the largest loss ever sustained on the Great Lakes, surpassing the loss of *Henry B. Smith*, wrecked in 1913 (*Lake Carriers Association* 1918: 138; *Canadian Railway and Marine World* 1918: 567; *Cleveland Plain Dealer* Nov. 10, 1918).

Congdon's cargo of wheat had been owned by the Wheat Export Company (*Canadian Railway and Marine World* 1918: 567). The lightering operations were only able to remove about one-fifth of the cargo, some 50,000 to 60,000 bushels. The amount remaining was described in the *Fort William Daily Times Journal* (Nov. 12, 1918):

> What it means in wheat – four-fifths of the whole cargo of 400,000 bushels is unsalvageable, meaning a total loss of 320,000 bushels. In money – at $2.24 a bushel, $716,000. In flour – net weight, 97,950 barrels, or 195,900 bags. Made into number 1 pure white flour, allowing 33 percent

shrinkage, 100 pounds of wheat equalling about 66 pounds of pure white flour, this four-fifths lost cargo represents 79,200 bushels, or 158,400 bags with a retail flour value of $918,720. In bread – number of standard loaves that could be made from this amount of wheat, 14,139,200 loaves. Allowing nine inches as the length of a standard loaf of bread, the lost wheat on the *Congdon*, if converted into loaves, would reach 6,025.75 miles, or more than twice the distance from Montreal to Vancouver. Computing that one person can subsist on a loaf of bread a day, this amount would be enough to feed the present population of the Dominion for two whole days, or afford sufficient (loaves) for one meal for the whole of the population of Great Britain and Ireland.

Salvage

John Bell, an agent for the Great Lakes Transportation Company, and who investigated other Isle Royale wrecks (*Monarch* and *Glenlyon*), announced on November 29, 1918, that James Playfair, apparently a private investor, had purchased *Congdon*

Figure 36. *Chester A. Congdon* aground. View is from the bow showing the break in the hull aft of the Number 6 hatch. U.S. Army Corps of Engineers Canal Park Marine Museum Collection.

Figure 37. View from the deck of the grounded *Chester A. Congdon*. U.S. Army Corps of Engineers Canal Park Marine Museum Collection.

and intended to raise the wreck in the spring (*Lake Carriers' Association* 1918: 143).

By late November, the bow was reported in 50 feet of water (*Fort William Daily Times Journal* Nov. 29, 1918). The Lake Carriers Association stated that recoveries of forward-end equipment had already been made (1918: 142-143). Playfair reportedly paid $10,000 for the wreck, outbidding U. Wolvin, who had done the original salvage work (*Port Arthur News Chronicle* Dec. 13, 1918). This same report said that when Playfair's crew arrived at the wreck site (presumably in December), "they found that it had completely disappeared, having washed off the rock on which it rested."

Chester A. Congdon was one of 45 steel and iron vessels that became total losses on the Great Lakes between 1902 and 1918. *Congdon* was the largest of those lost during that time. In 1918 alone, the year of *Congdon*'s demise, a total of 21 vessels were lost from all causes in the Great Lakes. There were 10 wooden steamers, one steel bulk freighter (*Congdon*), six barges, the forward end of one steel passenger steamer, the forward end of a steel bulk freighter and two new mine sweepers belonging to the French government lost that year (*Lake Carriers Association* 1918: 141).

Emperor: History

Construction

When the steel bulk freighter *Emperor* was launched on December 17, 1910 (*Port Arthur Daily News* April 8, 1911), it was the largest ship ever built in Canada (*Duluth News Tribune* April 9, 1911). It was built as hull number 28 by the Collingwood Shipbuilding Co. of Collingwood, Ontario, for James Playfair's company, the Inland Lines Ltd. of Midland, Ontario. Playfair would eventually build up a substantial fleet of Lakes carriers, and *Emperor* was his first large vessel. Evidently Playfair had a penchant for giving his ships names that related to royalty, for in later years he would own vessels with names like *Empress of Midland, Empress of Fort William* and *Midland King* (Greenwood 1978: 53).

The length of *Emperor* was 525 feet, breadth 56.1 feet and depth 27 feet. Molded depth was 31 feet and the draft could go as deep as 27 feet. The gross tonnage was 7,031 and the regis-

Figure 38. 525-foot long, Canada Steamship Lines' bulk freighter *Emperor*, the largest ship built in Canada at the time of launch. U.S. Army Corps of Engineers Canal Park Marine Museum Collection.

tered tonnage was 4,641. The original registry number assigned to the vessel at its home port of Midland was 126,654. The Transcript of Register states that *Emperor* had one deck, two masts, was schooner-rigged with a plumb bow and elliptical stern.

The new ship was built of steel and designed on the arch-and-web frame system of construction to create an unobstructed cargo hold under the 30 hatches. Each of the hatches was 9 x 36 feet wide and placed on 12-foot centers. There was an ore chute at each hatchway (*Railway and Marine World* Jan. 1911: 89). The ship had 11 bulkheads; the engine room was 67 feet long.

The hull was equipped with seven side-ballast and water-bottom tanks with a capacity of 5,021 tons (Transcript of Register). The tanks were directly connected with 7-inch steel suction pipes. A combination header connected to sea valves and ballast pump allowed the ship to rapidly take on or discharge ballast water. There was no separation between the side and bottom tanks.

The pilothouse, captain's and mates' quarters were forward; boilers and engine were aft with the crew's quarters. Between the forward and aft superstructures, the deck was clear, free of spars and other obstructions in order to allow rapid loading and unloading of its bulk ore cargo (*Canadian Railway and Marine World* Feb. 1911: 188).

Emperor was powered by an inverted, triple-expansion steam engine built by the Collingwood Shipbuilding Co. The engine had cylinders of 23, 38.5 and 63 inches on a 42-inch stroke and received steam at 180 pounds of pressure from two Scotch boilers 15.5 feet in diameter and 12 feet in length. The engine produced an indicated horsepower of 1,500 (Transcript of Register) at 82 revolutions per minute. Registered nominal speed was 10 knots. By the time the vessel sank, its normal speed loaded was 11 knots.

The last recorded major hull modifications were done in 1944. The Canada Steamship Lines Co. installed new side tanks and tank tops at a cost of $140,000 (*Toronto Globe and Mail* June 5, 1947).

Operational History

Emperor was launched December 17, 1910, but was not ready to go into commission until April 1911 (*Port Arthur Daily News* April 8, 1911). By the time the ship was ready for its first trip, the captain selected was G.W. Pearson, and G. Smith was chosen to be the chief engineer for the season (*Canadian Railway and Marine World* March 1911: 283).

The huge bulk carrier's first season commenced with a major incident. The ship broke its main shaft in Thunder Bay, Lake Huron, and was towed to Detour, Michigan (*Canadian Railway and Marine World* June 1911: 573; *Port Arthur Daily News* May 26, 1911).

The broken shaft on the first trip out was not the most serious mishap to befall *Emperor* during its first season. While anchoring in the Canadian canal at Sault Ste. Marie, the ship rode over its anchor, causing it to tear a hole in the bow. The freighter sank the few feet to the bottom blocking the channel. It was released, and after temporary repairs were made, proceeded on to Midland, Ontario (*Canadian Railway and Marine World* Nov. 1911: 1085).

A court found the canal employees to blame for ordering the flooding of the lock without inquiring if the vessel was ready. The court stated it believed that it was customary for the master of a vessel to sound one blast of the whistle as a signal to the canal authorities to begin flooding. Although the officers were exonerated, the responsibility was placed on the watchman on board who "happened to be a deck hand and, therefore, irresponsible" (*Canadian Railway and Marine World* Dec. 1911: 1187). The court added that it believed it necessary for masters of all vessels to have copies of the regulations governing the operation of locks and canals.

In May 1916, James Playfair sold *Emperor* to the Canada Steamship Lines Ltd. of Montreal, Quebec. Playfair was listed as the sole owner of the 64 shares of the ship (Transcript of Register).

Another incident occurred October 29, 1926, when *Emperor* was grounded on Major Shoal near Mackinaw City, Michigan. The ship was released unharmed at 4 that afternoon after jettisoning 900 tons of ore (*Detroit Free Press* Oct. 27, 1926). It is not known how *Emperor* dumped the ore.

The 1926 ore season closed November 17. The season had been the busiest on record for the industry at Hamilton, Ontario, with an average of 10 ore carriers a month unloading at the docks of the Steel Company of Canada. The last ship of the season to bring down a cargo that season was *Emperor* (*Detroit Free Press* Nov. 20, 1926).

In 1936, *Emperor* lost a rudder (*Toronto Evening Telegram* June 4, 1947). A man was washed overboard at the same time. *Emperor* ran aground in 1937 off Bronte, on Lake Ontario, and was soon released (*Toronto Evening Telegram* June 4, 1947).

Wreck Event

Emperor struck Canoe Rocks off Isle Royale June 4, 1947, and sank in about 30 minutes. Three officers and nine crew were lost. The following account was developed from the official investigation of the disaster conducted by Canadian officials on June 6 and July 2 and 3, 1947:

Emperor had brought up a load of coal and unloaded at the coal docks at Ft. William. The freighter had immediately moved from the coal docks to the Port Arthur Iron Ore Dock to load ore. The loading of ore took six to seven hours. The first mate had supervised the loading and took the watch after they cleared the breakwall.

The doomed ship was laden with 10,429 tons of bulk iron ore (removed from the Steep Rock Mine) stowed in its five holds when she cleared Port Arthur at 10:55 p.m., June 3, downbound for Ashtabula, Ohio. The ship's draft was 21 feet 3 inches forward and 21 feet 9 inches aft.

The steamer was in seaworthy condition and well-equipped with suitable charts and sailing directions for the intended voyage. *Emperor* was also carrying a gyro compass, echo meter, sounding machine, ship-to-ship and ship-to-shore telephone and the "latest modern type of Marconi direction-finding equipment," in addition to the usual compasses and other equipment. *Emperor*, however, did not carry a full crew. There was no third mate.

The weather was good, the wind light and visibility excellent. These favorable conditions held for the short voyage. The navigation lights of Passage Light and Blake Point should have been clearly visible. Passage Island Light should have been visible from Trowbridge Light outside Thunder Cape, and Blake Point Light should have been visible for at least an hour before the wreck occurred.

The watch sequence established that Capt. Eldon Walkinshaw had the watch until midnight when the first mate, James Morrey, took over. He had the watch from midnight to 6 a.m., and spent that time seated in a chair in the front of the wheelhouse. Evidence brought out that Morrey was in charge of loading the vessel in port before departure during most of the six hours he normally would have been off duty and, as a result, was probably overtired during his watch and fell asleep.

Figure 39. Port side view of *Emperor* as it appeared when lost in June 1947. U S. Army Corps of Engineers Canal Park Marine Museum Collection.

According to the testimony of J. Leonard, wheelsman, who was on duty the watch before the accident, the courses were plotted by the first mate at Thunder Cape. The course steered from Welcome Islands to Thunder Cape was 138 degrees true with a two-degree alteration to pass the steamer *Battleford*. Leonard, who was inexperienced in the upper Lake region (this was his first time steering downbound from the Lakehead), believed the course was altered to 98 degrees true abreast of Trowbridge light. The mate did not take a four-point bearing, a bearing on the light, nor did he use the radio beacon on Passage Light. Leonard went off watch at 4 and stated Passage Island Light was 10 degrees off the port bow. He turned the wheel over to J. Prokup. The mate did not check the course at the watch change.

There was no record of the ship's course until it passed Welcome Island at the mouth of Thunder Bay. At Thunder Cape Light, the normal downbound course should have been set to 98 degrees true; however, the court determined that the course was not set until the ship was abreast of Trowbridge Light, some three miles beyond Thunder Cape Light.

Emperor struck Canoe Rocks shortly before 4:15 a.m. According to various accounts, the ship stayed afloat from 20 to 35 minutes.

By the time the first reports of the wreck appeared in the newspapers the survivors were already in Fort William, having been rescued by the U.S. Coast Guard crew aboard the 125-foot, 250-ton cutter *Kimball,* under the command of Lt. C.R. Clark. *Kimball* had been in the vicinity of Isle Royale repairing navigation lights and was headed to the Coast Guard base at Cleveland by way of Canoe Rocks when the distress message from *Emperor* was intercepted. It took them about 35 minutes to reach the wreck (*Houghton Daily Mining Gazette* June 4, 1947).

Kimball picked up 21 survivors and the body of the first cook, Evelyn Shultz, of Owen Sound, Ontario. The survivors were brought to the Fort William City Dock on the Kaministiquia River at 8:30 a.m. They were taken from there to the Salvation Army Hostel. Some of the survivors moved to the Royal Edward Hotel. By the evening of the 5th, all would be residing there with Canada Steamship Lines picking up the bill (*Fort William Daily Times Journal* June 6, 1947). The company gave each wreck survivor $100 for clothes and essentials. The survivors were transported to *Emperor*'s downbound destination aboard a Canadian Pacific Railway sleeping car provided by Canada Steamship Lines.

Soon after the cutter arrived, the survivors began to relate stories of their grim struggle. There had been no panic after the ship struck. Eleven of the crew were still missing, including the captain, who was last seen on the bridge of his wrecked ship (*Winnipeg Free Press* June 4, 1947).

Two lifeboats were launched, one from each side of the ship, but both ran into difficulties. The one on the starboard side lost a bilge plug, and when the 10 sailors aboard were rescued, they were knee-deep in water. The port lifeboat pulled away from the wreck but was sucked under by the ship when it went down. Four men were clinging to it when *Kimball* arrived. The suction from the sinking ship also pulled crew members below the icy waters – some said they had been drawn down 30 to 40 feet as the freighter sank. Second Mate Peter Craven of Port McNicoll, Ontario, said he was pulled under twice by the suction (*Winnipeg Free Press* June 4, 1947).

Seven men were rowed to safety on Canoe Rocks by the starboard lifeboat that returned to pick up other survivors. The men on the rocks were taken off by a motorboat launched from *Kimball.* Two men, suffering from shock and exposure, had to be carried aboard the cutter (*Port Arthur News Chronicle* June 4, 1947; *Montreal Gazette* June 5, 1947).

Exposure to the waters of Lake Superior is serious at any time during the year. On the day the wreck occurred, there was little relief for those lucky enough to get out of the water because the air temperature read in the mid-30s on that "summer" day. In fact, it was the coldest June 4 reading in Michigan's history (*Houghton Daily Mining Gazette* June 4, 1947).

"It was lucky that we were on the west side of Isle Royale," Lieutenant Clark of *Kimball* said. "We had intended to go along the east side. We received the call about 4 a.m. and we were under way at 4:17, and were picking up survivors at 4:50. I was told by one of the survivors that suction took one of the lifeboats under. The two halves of the *Emperor* must have sunk in a hurry" (*Port Arthur News Chronicle* June 4, 1947).

When *Kimball* left the site with the survivors, the only trace of the ship above the water was the mast jutting some 15 feet above (*Minneapolis Star* June 4, 1947). However, pictures taken after the wreck show that the top of the pilothouse was exposed.

Chief Engineer Merritt Dedman, a 63-year-old veteran of 32 years on the Great Lakes, was awakened when the ship struck and told the following story to the press:

"I didn't have to have anyone tell me something seriously was wrong. I threw on my clothes and went down to the engine room. I listened as I ran down a passage. The engine started to race and I knew then that the propeller was gone. It was a case of waiting with our fingers crossed until the captain gave the order to abandon ship. He wasn't long; about 10 minutes, I would say. (Dedman got into the starboard lifeboat and found himself up to his knees in water.) We picked up several men in the water and cruised around until we were picked up by the U.S. Coast Guard cutter" (*Port Arthur News Chronicle* June 4, 1947).

Peter Craven, the second mate, related his experiences during the sinking:

"As the ship began to list sharply the captain gave his abandon ship order. The first boat was lowered and floated without too much trouble and men piled down ropes to get in while others jumped into the water. I jumped in and managed to get in the second boat but she was capsized by suction of the sinking ship. Most of the missing were in or about this second boat. Down we went. When I came up I reached the surface a moment before the boat came up overturned. (He climbed on the boat with Louis Gale and Ed Brown.) We were a wet, cold bunch as we waited for the rescue ship to reach us. I'm still shivering. Gee, that water was cold" (*Port Arthur News Chronicle* June 4, 1947).

Bill Randall, a wheelsman, was on watch near the bow of the ship. He also gave his account to the newspapers (*Port Arthur News Chronicle,* June 4, 1947): "It was pitch black and I couldn't see a thing, but I knew something serious had happened. I noticed the ship begin to sink almost immediately at the bow." He knew it was "only a matter time" before they went under. "I would say the men kept remarkably calm. I don't think they realized we were sinking as fast as we were. When the time came to abandon ship, things began to happen so fast that no one had much time to get scared." He said water was "up to the winches" when the order to abandon ship was given. He saw the captain rush from the wheelhouse as waves came over the side and toppled him on his back. "I didn't see him after that" (the same source states that not one of the survivors saw Capt. Walkinshaw in the water).

Randall noted one pathetic scene. He saw Paul Perry, a watchman, walking at the stern with his suitcase in his hand. Apparently Perry could not swim, for he made no attempt to jump overboard with the others. "He didn't say a thing. He just stood there and went down with the ship."

Only one account mentioned exploding boilers. Night Steward Art Laframboise said he was cooking a meal when the ship struck. He rushed out and helped launch a lifeboat.

"I helped pull two men into the lifeboat, and they were still jumping from the sinking freighter when the boilers exploded. Instead of drawing us in, the force of the explosion pushed us out....That was lucky. I was careful to steer the lifeboat straight away from the ship as she went down, otherwise, if we had been traveling in a parallel direction, I don't think we'd have made it. A few hundred feet ahead we saw a rock sticking out of the water, so we made for it and discharged our cargo. Then we went back to pick up some more survivors....By this time the ship had gone down. On the way over to the Coast Guard cutter we picked up the body of the first cook, Mrs. Shultz. Her clothes were torn and I figured she went down with the boat, and then was blown to the surface when the boilers exploded" (*Montreal Gazette* June 5, 1947).

The Albrecht account below contradicts what Laframboise thought happened to Shultz. Albrecht was on the aft deck with all three of the women when the ship went down and saw them aboard a lifeboat. This was apparently the port lifeboat that capsized from the suction of the ship sinking.

Nick Tonita would remember his first voyage as a sailor. "I jumped over the side. I went under pretty deep and when I came up I hit my forehead on the overturned lifeboat. Then I swam to a mattress and stayed on it until the other lifeboat picked me up. The water was like ice" (*Fort William Daily Times Journal* June 4, 1947).

The *Minneapolis Star* (June 4, 1947) carried the experience of Ernest Albrecht, 18, a coal passer who was the youngest of the 21 survivors. Albrecht was preparing to go to bed when he learned the ship was going down. When he heard the news he dressed rapidly, grabbed a life jacket and rushed to the after-deck, where he helped lower the two lifeboats. He waited until the three women cooks were aboard and started to follow them.

"Before I got into the boat I was standing by the after house.

Then the ship gave a lunge and water came gushing over like a waterfall. The port lifeboat was thrown against the after house bulkhead, with several persons in it. I thought my time had come as the boat threatened to pin me to the cabins, but luckily I was just bruised and cut a bit. The next thing I knew I was in the water, floating with the jacket. The port lifeboat was overturned and a few feet away. I couldn't swim in that water, it was so cold, so I drifted to the boat and hung on it until I saw the cutter coming."

Emil Savereux, deck hand, said, "I was bounced out of my berth from a sound sleep when the crash came." He added, "I ran down into the dunnage room. There the second mate told the men to put on life belts and prepare the lifeboats to be lowered. I then jumped into the water...a sinking section of the ship drew me and the second cook, Mabel Cochrane, under the water. The suction was bad, but I fought my way to the surface and came up in a life ring....I was later picked up by a lifeboat and brought to safety" (*Fort William Daily Times Journal* June 4, 1947).

The survivors were a hardy lot. Young Albrecht, who was just starting his career as a Lakes sailor, said from his hospital bed that he was planning to ship out again in a few weeks. Perhaps he summed up the attitude shared by some of the other survivors, and many of those who had made their living on the Great Lakes, when he said, "We can't let one little shipwreck get us down" (*Fort William Daily Times Journal* June 4, 1947).

Shortly after the survivors returned safely to Fort William, the search for the missing was resumed. *Kimball*'s Lt. Clark and his crew of 12 left port about 11 o'clock the morning of June 4 to "hunt around Canoe Rocks for survivors and bodies" (*Port Arthur New Chronicle* June 4, 1947).

Alan J. Linfoot, general agent, announced that Canada Steamship Lines had chartered another vessel, *Coastal Queen*, owned by the Northern Engineering Company, to go to the wreck site to continue the search and also to attempt recovery of bodies still trapped on board the wreck. *Coastal Queen* had a diver, E.J. (Doc) Fowler, aboard. Fowler was a veteran diver who was employed by Pigeon River Timber Company and was on loan to C.S.L. (*Fort William Daily Times Journal* June 5, 1947). Small launches were also aboard *Queen* to enable the many small bays and inlets of Isle Royale to be searched. The charter vessel left at 6 p.m. (reported elsewhere as 3 p.m.) on the 4th and diving operations were planned for that evening (*Montreal Gazette* June 5, 1947; *Toronto Globe and Mail* June 5, 1947; *Fort William Daily Times Journal* June 5, 1947).

Kimball's crew found the body of another woman during the search they conducted after returning to the site the afternoon of the disaster. It was identified as that of Marie Tobachuk, a porter. She was found about four miles from the site, floating upright, supported by her life jacket (*Fort William Daily Times Journal* June 5, 1947). The Coast Guard returned her to Fort William that evening (*Montreal Gazette* June 5, 1947). The two lifeboats and a company raft were also reported in the same general area.

At first there was some confusion regarding the number and identity of the missing from the wreck. The official company list of the dead and missing released from its corporate headquarters in Montreal named only 11 persons. Company officials in Fort William stated that there were indeed 12 missing or dead. The 12th missing crew member was J. Prokup (also Proykop and Prohupof), a wheelsman. Prokup had replaced J. Sepchuk, who left the ship the night before it sailed. Sepchuk had surprised everyone when he walked into the company headquarters on the day of the wreck to pick up his pay (*Toronto Globe and Mail* June 6, 1947; *Montreal Gazette* June 5, 1947).

Emperor's crew usually consisted of 35, but two men were left behind when it departed Fort William on its last trip (*Montreal Gazette* June 5, 1947).

Malcom Melsaacs (or McIsaacs, *Winnipeg Free Press* June 5, 1947) and Melville Anderson were the two men on the normal *Emperor* crew roster not aboard when the ship took its last voyage. Anderson, a wheelsman, had been suffering from eye trouble and stayed ashore (*Fort William Daily Times Journal* June 5, 1947). A day earlier, the same paper stated that a fireman and third mate were not on the ship.

This would have been Melsaacs' second trip on the Lakes. His luck had changed for the better. As a salt-water sailor, he was torpedoed three times during the war (*Fort William Daily Times Journal* June 4, 1947).

James Buzzie was not as fortunate as those who had missed the boat. Buzzie, who was among the missing, shipped aboard *Emperor* as a coal passer on June 3 – the ship's last night afloat (*Fort William Daily Times Journal* June 4, 1947).

Capt. Norman Reoch, operating manager of Canada Steamship Lines, told the newspapers that his company's ships had the most modern safety devices obtainable, and apart from that,

> "*Emperor* was one of the most seaworthy ships in the company's lines. We feel that our fleet is one of the best-maintained fleets on the Great Lakes. There has been more safety practice on the Great Lakes in the past 10 years than ever before, in view of the fact that operators are endeavoring to obtain lesser premiums on insurance rates – and with telling results" (*Toronto Globe and Mail* June 5, 1947).

Reoch's comments were in response to those made by Harry Davis, president of the Canadian Seaman's Union (*Toronto Globe and Mail* June 5, 1947). The night of the wreck, Davis had called for an immediate investigation into the sinking, and demanded that the C.S.U. be represented on any board set up that would probe the worst Lake tragedy in five years. "Too many Lake ships are far too old to be sailing with such heavy cargoes as ore, and altogether too many safety regulations are being violated. It is high time to call a halt to the needless tragedies." He stated that the union had always fought for adequate safety regulations and would continue to do so. "We of the union mourn the loss of these men along with their relatives. We consider, however, that the best memorial to those lost in this tragedy is to ensure such future calamities shall not take place" (*Montreal Gazette* June 5, 1947). Captain Reoch, however, labeled the Davis statement as that of "an opportunist," and stated that Lake ships are inspected periodically by the British Corp Register (a classification society) and approved by the Steamship Inspection Service, Ottawa (*Toronto*

Globe and Mail June 5, 1947).

Three investigations were soon opened regarding the cause of the disaster. One was begun by the U.S. Coast Guard under the direction of Lt. Cmdr. S.D. Larue, inspector, from Duluth. The Coast Guard was required to make an investigation, because the incident happened in U.S. waters. The other inquiries were the ones by the Steamship Inspection Branch of the Canadian Transport Department (this would be a preliminary investigation, with a formal inquiry to follow), and the Canada Steamship Lines, to be conducted by H.R. Baxter, of Toronto, shore captain for the company (*Toronto Globe and Mail* June 6, 1947). There may have been a fourth inquiry; it was reported that the Fort William coroner was also investigating the cause of the accident (*Houghton Daily Mining Gazette* June 5, 1947).

The most informative document of the many inquiries into the wreck is that of "The Preliminary Inquiry into the Circumstances concerning the Sinking of the S.S. *Emperor*; Conducted by Capt. W.N. Morrison, Supervisor and Examiner of Masters and Mates for the Department of Transport, Province of Ontario on the 6th day of June 1947" (Canadian Archives). Ten of the survivors were interviewed under oath and the questions and answers are contained within this document.

The Canadian Legislature expressed its concern over the wreck. More navigational aids were urged in the Commons as a result of *Emperor*'s loss. T.L. Church led the discussion. Church declared that there were no aids to navigation on the Lake at the spot where the ship struck the reef, and he asked what the government was going to do to protect shipping. Transport Minister Chevrier replied that if Church knew the facts, he would not make the statements he did (*Montreal Gazette* June 6, 1947).

Apparently the Canadian Seaman's Union also conducted an inquiry on the wreck. A report of its findings was released June 18, and excerpts and company responses appeared in the press (*Montreal Gazette* June 19, 1947). In the union's report, T.G. McManus, national secretary, charged that an officer of *Emperor* had disregarded warnings that the ship was nearing dangerous rocks, and that, due to "rusty davits, the crew had difficulty in launching lifeboats." According to McManus, survivors of the sinking told the union that the ship had been sailing short one mate since the beginning of the season, and the chief and second mates had shared the missing mate's wages between them. The union charged further that, contrary to the regulations of the Canada Shipping Act, no lifeboat drills had been held aboard *Emperor* that season. McManus went on to say that "facts revealed by investigations conducted by the union" had moved the union to request the government to include C.S.U. representatives in the government inquiry board that was investigating the sinking. The union wanted unlicensed survivors to be called as witnesses during the inquiry.

Capt. Norman J. Reoch issued a statement in response to the union's report on behalf of Canada Steamship Lines (*Montreal Gazette* June 19, 1947). He declared the report "false and irresponsible."

The formal investigation to be done by request of Transportation Minister Chevrier was announced (*Montreal Gazette*

June 19, 1947). Justice F.H. Barlow of the Supreme Court of Canada presided, Capt. F.J. Davis and Angus G. McKay acted as assessors, Hugh Plaxton of Toronto acted as counsel for the Transport Department. The investigation opened at the Osgoode Hall, Ottawa, July 2. Representatives of the Canadian Seaman's Union had been invited to attend.

The court findings were announced July 26 (in Court Documents):

> Honourable Lionel Chevrier, Minister of Transport, today announced the findings of the investigation into the stranding and sinking of the S.S. *Emperor* in Lake Superior on June 4 last with the loss of 12 lives. The report places the blame for the wreck on James Morrey, the first mate, "who did not keep proper watch." In this connection, the report expressed the opinion "that the system which prevailed, which required the first mate to be in charge of the loading of the ship during the period when he should have been off duty, resulted in his becoming over-tired, suffering as he was from loss of sleep." James Morrey was drowned when the vessel sank.

The ill-fated vessel had loaded 10,429 tons of iron ore and had sailed from Port Arthur at 10:55 p.m. on June 3. The captain was in charge of the watch till midnight when the first mate, James Morrey relieved him for the midnight until 6 a.m. watch. The evidence indicated that the first mate was overtired and the report emphasizes the fact that "James Morrey was a man of wide experience on the Great Lakes, that he was most efficient, and that he had an excellent record previous to this unfortunate accident."

Recommendations of the Court of Investigation are as follows:

1. We recommend that some system be evolved, either by employing a third mate or otherwise, if feasible, to prevent a mate or other officer from taking charge of a ship when he is suffering from loss of sleep or is in a state of exhaustion by reason of his duties. We find that the eight-hour day prevails with the engine room officers and crew but not with the officers in the forward end. We cannot understand why the eight-hour day should not prevail throughout the ship, and we would so recommend.

2. The evidence does not disclose, and so far as we know there is no requirement by which a ship is equipped with a system of electrical gongs, throughout the ship, to be used in case of a disaster, such as collision, fire or grounding. We recommend that a regulation be passed requiring all Lake vessels to be so equipped.

3. In our opinion, the evidence does not disclose that sufficient lifeboat and fire drills were held to familiarize the changing crew with their proper stations and proper duties, in order that the same may be carried out speedily and efficiently. We recommend that lifeboat drill and fire drill be held weekly during the summer season and that at least twice during the navigation period, apart from the spring inspection, that lifeboat drill and fire drill be

held in the presence of and under the supervision of, an officer from the Department of Steamboat Inspection.

4. In view of the submissions made we have given consideration to whether or not wooden lifeboats should be used. We are of the opinion that wooden lifeboats are far superior to any other.

The evidence submitted before the Court of Investigation showed that the vessel was in a good and seaworthy condition as regards hull, machinery, lifesaving and other equipment. All necessary charts and sailing directions were on board and in addition, the following equipment in excess of Department of Transport regulations had been installed: gyro compass, echo sounding machine, ship-to-shore radio telephone and radio direction finder.

The Board of Investigation fully exonerates the master, Captain Eldon Walkinshaw, and says: "We are of the opinion that under all the circumstances he did everything possible most promptly and efficiently." He sent out a distress signal by radio immediately after the vessel struck, in response of which the United States Coast Guard vessel *Kimball,* located nearby, came to render assistance. In this connection, the report says "We cannot commend too highly the action of the captain and crew of the *Kimball* for the prompt assistance which they rendered." As a result, 21 of the crew were saved. Most of those who lost their lives were in the second lifeboat which was being launched and was sucked down when the *Emperor* sank.

Newspaper stories at the time of *Emperor's* loss compared the high shipwreck concentration at the northeastern end of Isle Royale to Keweenaw Point and Whitefish Point, which had been known as the "Graveyard of the Great Lakes" (*Port Arthur News Chronicle* June 4, 1947). Most of the wrecks that occurred at Keweenaw Point were ships driven ashore during storms. The wrecks on Whitefish Point have been due primarily to vessels converging into the narrow channel leading out of the Upper Lake, and then colliding, usually during fog. The Isle Royale wrecks have been principally attributed to a "combination of storms and mistaking the travel routes, the latter, in former days particularly, being due to magnetic disturbances which sometimes affect the steamer compasses in that area" (*Port Arthur News Chronicle* June 4, 1947.)

The loss of *Emperor* was the worst disaster on the Great Lakes since the year 1942, when three incidents were recorded: 25 drowned in a launch in Georgian Bay, 14 elsewhere in a tug and 18 in a barge in Lake Erie. *Emperor's* demise was the first event on Lake Superior resulting in a loss of life since 1940, when the steamer *Arlington* went down in a gale with the loss of one crew member. The worst year on Lake Superior prior to the *Emperor* wreck was 1927, when *Kamloops* disappeared in a storm with 22 crew aboard (*Houghton Daily Mining Gazette* June 4, 1947). The worst year since the turn of the century on the Great Lakes was 1913, when a two-day November storm wrecked 13 vessels and 240 people drowned. It was estimated that, since the turn of the century, more than 100 ships have gone down on the Great Lakes, and more than 2,000 seamen have lost their lives (*Winnipeg Free Press* June 4, 1947).

Emperor was the most recent large ship to be wrecked on Isle Royale.

Salvage

The first diver to view the remains of the *Emperor* was E.J. (Doc) Fowler. On Thursday, June 12, 1947, Fowler made three dives of about 30 minutes duration in an attempt to recover some of the bodies of those still missing from the wreck (*Port Arthur News Chronicle* June 14, 1947). The dives had been planned to take place during the original search operations carried out by *Coastal Queen* after the wreck, but weather conditions did not allow them to be done.

There are no records of commercial salvage on *Emperor*. Soon after the advent of scuba diving, *Emperor* became a popular diving attraction in Lake Superior. The continued exploration of *Emperor* led to the discovery of what Fowler sought. In 1975, the clothed and preserved remains of one of the crew was discovered by sport divers in the area of the engine room (*Houghton Daily Mining Gazette* Sept. 2 and 3, 1975). The body was discovered by members of the Inland Divers Club of Duluth and was reported to the National Park Service. Park headquarters said that no further diving attempts to recover the remains were planned due to the depth and the difficulty in reaching the remains (*Daily Mining Gazette* Sept. 3, 1975). The remains were reportedly removed by Canadian divers and sunk in deep water. Occasional reports of additional remains have reached the Park Service. However, none have been verified.

Kamloops: History

Construction

Kamloops was built in England by Furness Shipbuilding Co. Ltd. at its shipyard at Haverton Hill on Tees in 1924. Built for Steamships Ltd. of Montreal, Quebec, Canada, for use in the Great Lakes package trade, the single-screw, steel freighter was designed as a canaller, with dimensions appropriate for passage through the Welland Canal system. Its primary intended function was to transport package freight, but it could also carry bulk cargo.

The specific vessel type in the Great Lakes known as "canallers" began with the opening of the Welland Canal in 1829. These vessels were built close to the maximum dimensions that would allow their passage through the locks. The original locks required a ship's length to be less than 110 feet, the beam no more than 22 feet and a draft of less than eight feet. The Welland Canal was expanded to accommodate a nine-foot draft in 1850, and a 10-foot draft in 1872 (Murphy 1966: 393). By 1887, improvements permitted vessels up to 256 feet long, 44 feet wide with a draft of 14 feet (nearly double in length over those of 1829) to clear the locks and canal system from Lake Ontario to Montreal (Mills 1910: 226-7).

Kamloops had a length between perpendiculars of 250 feet,

molded breadth of 42¾ feet and a molded depth of 26½ feet. Its deadweight capacity was 2,400 tons on a 14-ft. draft (*Canadian Railway and Marine World* July 1924). *Kamloops* was of the vessel type built to the maximum possible canal dimensions.

At each improvement of the locks, the older vessels became obsolete because of their increasing competitive disadvantage with the larger ships. Had *Kamloops* not wrecked on Isle Royale in 1927, it might have become outdated when the canal improvements begun in 1913 were completed. The Welland Canal in 1932 allowed vessels to pass measuring 715 feet long with a draft of 30 feet. The locks could accept vessels with a beam of 80 feet (Murphy 1966: 394). However, *Lethbridge,* the sister ship of *Kamloops*, survived until it was scrapped in 1961, two years after the larger Saint Lawrence Seaway opened (Greenwood 1973: 125).

Steamships Ltd., the company that ordered both sister ships built, was a subsidiary of Canada Steamship Lines Ltd., and all of its principal company executives were also officers of Canada Steamship Lines. Steamships Ltd. was incorporated in November 1923, stating its purposes as "to carry on the business of transportation of passengers, freight, etc., towing, wrecking and salvage in or over any of the navigable waters within or bordering on Canada, and to or from any foreign port, and various other businesses connected therewith" (*Canadian Railway and Marine World* August 1924: 422-3).

The first of the two new ships slid down the ways on May 20, 1924, after being christened *Kamloops* by Agnes Black, daughter of the Canada Steamship Lines superintendent. *Lethbridge* followed on June 14. A fairly complete description of *Kamloops* was published in *Canadian Railway and Marine World* in July 1924 (p. 370):

> *Kamloops* is built on the longitudinal system of framing, with upper, shelter and forecastle decks. The double bottom, extending all fore and aft, and the peak tanks, are arranged for water ballast, and a water-tight cofferdam is fitted at the sides of [the] fore hold to give added protection to the cargo to meet the severe conditions of the service. The captain's accommodation and chart-room are in house on [the] forecastle deck, with [the] steering wheel in [the] teak Texas house above. Special attention has been given to the accommodation[s] for the officers and crew in [the] forecastle, and engineers and firemen in [the] deck-house aft. The whole of the accommodation is heated by steam radiators, and electric lighting is to be installed. A powerful steam windlass is fitted in [the] forecastle, and special pockets are arranged in the hull to house the anchors. The cargo gear, consisting of four sampson posts, each having one 5-ton derrick, is operated by one 8x12-inch and two 7x10-inch steam cargo winches, and mooring arrangements are carried out by means of four 6x10-inch steam mooring winches. A hoisting gear, consisting of 13 winches driven through shafting by a double-cylinder vertical steam engine, will be fitted in the upper 'tween decks for discharging cargo. A steam steering gear will be fitted in [the] after 'tween decks and controlled by shafting from

Figure 40. *Kamloops*, a canaller built for the package freight trade as it appeared at the time of loss. U.S. Army Corps of Engineers Canal Park Marine Museum Collection.

[the] wheelhouse forward and boat deck aft. The propelling machinery consists of a set of triple expansion inverted marine engines, having cylinders of 18, 30, and 50 inches diameter, and a stroke of 36 inches. Steam is supplied by two single-ended boilers 13.6 feet in diameter by 11 feet long, working at a pressure of 185 lbs.

The Canadian Transcript of Register (Nov. 7, 1926, Montreal) gives additional information on *Kamloops'* registry record and construction. Apparently, the ship remained under British registry No. 154 until 1926. There is a mistake in the recording of the official number on the Transcript of Register, as two registration records exist for *Kamloops* in the Public Archives of Canada. One register with overstamps reads: "Registery Of Shipping May 26 1926 Marine and Fisheries;" "Registery of Shipping Dec 27 1927 Marine and Fisheries;" and "Registery of Shipping Jun 30 1937 Dept. of Transport" (RG 12 Vol. 3028) gives the official number as 147682. The other, apparently a later version of the Transcript of Register, with two overstamps, reads: "National Revenue Canada 20 Jan 1926 Registrateur Maritime Montreal, P.Q." and gives the official number as 147,687. The earlier one (147,682) is probably correct.

According to the registers, the ship had two decks and two schooner-rigged masts, fore and mizzen, and was classed as clincher-built, with an elliptical stern. The hull contained five bulkheads, four of which were water-tight, and six water-ballast tanks with a capacity of 699 tons. The depth of hold from the tonnage deck to ceiling at midships was 24.3 feet, with the depth from the top of the deck at the side amidships to the bottom of the keel 26.65 feet. The hull had a very sharp chine. The round of bilge was 8.3 tenths of a foot.

The triple-expansion engine and the Scotch boilers were made specifically for *Kamloops* by Richardson, Westgarth and Co. Ltd. of Hartlepool, England, and rated at 1,000 indicated horsepower. The engine could push the ship at an estimated speed of 9½ knots.

The tonnage particulars give a perspective on hull volume configuration. A total of 2,226.09 tons are recorded under the tonnage deck. In addition, the forecastle measured 49.72 tons, and the deck houses 125.73 tons, including two tons for access of hatchway. Thus the ship's gross tonnage totaled 2401.54. Deductions yield a register tonnage of 1,747.79 tons.

Kamloops completed its builder's trial on July 5, 1924, and proceeded to Copenhagen to load the first cargo, which was bound for Montreal. The ship went on to Houghton, Michigan. The vessel, along with its sister, would run regularly between Montreal and Fort William, Ontario, carrying package freight west and grain east (*Canadian Railway and Marine World* Oct. 1924: 527).

Operational History

Kamloops' first season on the Lakes started late, when its maiden upbound passage began on September 13, 1924 (*Detroit Free Press* Sept. 14, 1924), under Capt. William Brian and engineer T.W. Verity (*Great Lakes Red Book* 1925: 51). The new package freighter had arrived from Copenhagen shortly before its sister ship *Lethbridge,* which reached Montreal on September 18 (*Canadian Railway and Marine World* Oct. 1924: 527). A cargo of pebbles was brought from Denmark for the Calumet and Hecla Mining Company in Calumet, Michigan. Here the crew which sailed on the maiden voyage was replaced by a crew of Lake sailors (*Calumet News* Aug. 24, 1924; Dec 14, 1927). *Kamloops* passed Port Colborne on the Welland Canal on September 22 downbound for the first time (*Detroit Free Press* Sept. 23, 1924).

The first season set the pattern for *Kamloops,* whose owners continued to operate as long as possible each season. The canaller weathered a severe storm on its last downbound run of the 1924 season on December 13 and 14 when winds of 50 to 60 miles per hour and a temperature of six degrees below claimed at least one vessel believed wrecked near Eagle Harbor on the Keweenaw peninsula. After the storm, *Kamloops,* along with *Midland Prince, Midland King* and *Lethbridge,* each with a load of grain, were all reported downbound on Lake Superior, while other vessels were laid up in the shelter of Isle Royale (*Marquette Daily Mining Journal* Dec. 15, 1924). The four ships soon became trapped by ice in the St. Marys River, and two tugs of the Great Lakes Towing Company were dispatched to assist them. Those four vessels were the last of the 1924 season to pass through the locks (*Marquette Daily Mining Journal* Dec. 17, 1924).

The 1925 season began for *Kamloops* in April, when it cleared Sault Ste. Marie on the 20th at 3:30 upbound, and again on the 23rd downbound (*Detroit Free Press* April 21, 23, 1925). In October the freighter was held up with 10 others of the grain fleet during a downbound run by the grounding of *W.H. Daniels* in the Welland canal aqueduct (*Detroit Free Press* Oct 12, 1925). The remainder of the season was uneventful.

The first downbound run of the 1926 season began May 3, when *Kamloops* cleared Detroit at 3 a.m. (*Detroit Free Press* May 4, 1926). The ship ended its third season like the first – stuck in the ice. This time there were not four ships stuck in the St. Marys River, but more than 100. The 100 ships were caught in the channel near Neebish Island on December 3, the same location where *Kamloops* had been trapped earlier. That event was the largest ice jam in the history of Upper Lakes shipping, according to contemporary references. The soft ice halted all progress of the steamers, and even the powerful tugs made only slow headway through the slush that in places was 12 feet thick. The problem was increased by the fact that there were about 2,000 people aboard the jammed ships, and supplies ran short (*Detroit Free Press* Dec. 4, 1926).

The weather worsened, and a 35-mile-an-hour northeast wind pushed the temperature to 12 below zero, turning the slush to ice. Every available tug in the vicinity was summoned, and the steel car ferry *Sainte Marie* was brought out to assist in the

struggle to free the trapped fleet. Truck loads of food were shuttled to the ships by the tugs (*Detroit Free Press* Dec. 5, 1926).

On December 5, seven inches of snow fell, further complicating the rescue effort, which at this time was assisting 40 upbound and 65 downbound boats in the channel. The shortage of coal became critical on some vessels, and efforts were begun to purchase coal from the upbound carriers because none was available at the Sault. During this blockade more vessels left Port Arthur loaded with grain to get their last run in before the ice got too thick to be broken by the harbor tugs (*Detroit Free Press* Dec. 6, 1926). These vessels fell in behind those already ice-bound in the St. Marys River.

The upbound fleet was released the next day, but the number of trapped downbound vessels grew to 70. The principal obstruction was *Coulee,* which was stuck nearly crosswise in the channel. Ten thousand tons of coal were purchased by the Lake Carriers' Association, whose members were losing an estimated $50,000 a day as a result of the ice jam, although Sault merchants were making $15,000 a day from providing supplies to the inert grain fleet (*Detroit Free Press* Dec. 7, 9, 1926).

By December 7, the number of blocked Lake carriers reached 90. Experts arrived in growing numbers, as representatives of companies and the now idle grain elevators joined the effort. *Coulee* was released, but the next ship in line, *General Garretson,* became trapped, halting further rescue efforts for that day (*Detroit Free Press* Dec. 8, 1926).

The trapped grain carriers, now more than 100, began moving down the river December 8, but were held up for another 12 hours (*Detroit Free Press* Dec. 9, 1926). Twenty-six freighters were freed on December 9 (*Detroit Free Press* Dec. 10, 1926). However, *Kamloops* was not one of the fortunate vessels, being 39th in line (*Detroit Free Press* Dec. 9, 1926). In a list of vessels freed from the ice on December 10 that was published in the *Detroit Free Press* (Dec. 11), *Kamloops* is not mentioned, and therefore must have been released on the 11th after being trapped in the ice for nine days. It was *Kamloops* last voyage of the 1927 season.

Open water was visible April 7 for the first time of the 1927 season at Port Arthur, when an ice breaker opened a channel for the downbound freighters (*Cleveland Plain Dealer* April 8, 1927). *Kamloops* cleared Sault Ste. Marie upbound for the recently opened Port Arthur during the first run of the new season on April 20 (*Cleveland Plain Dealer* April 21, 1927). The vessel was reported in Fort William on April 22, and had cleared downbound on the 23rd (*Cleveland Plain Dealer* April 23, 24, 1927). *Kamloops* cleared the Sault at 9 a.m. on the 25th (*Cleveland Plain Dealer* April 26, 1927).

Kamloops was technically under new ownership the 1926 season. On October 11, Canada Steamship Lines bought the vessel from Steamships Ltd. On October 28, 1926, the registry listed a mortgage dated October 19 for $50,000,000 (although the amount seems unlikely), loaned at six percent yearly interest by Montreal Trust Company.

The dealings between steamship companies and the various financial institutions have not been researched by historians. The relationship between Steamships Ltd. and Canada Steamship Lines Ltd. should interest historians studying the development of capitalist enterprise on the Lakes, for the officers were the same for both companies, and the addresses of their principal places of business were the same. The details of this arrangement should shed light on the business practices of ship owners of the period.

Wreck Event

The last trip of the 1927 season would be *Kamloops'* final trip. The doomed vessel cleared Port Colborne, Ontario, on the Welland Canal upbound on December 1 at 9:30 a.m. (*Detroit Free Press* Dec. 2, 1927). The ship passed Detroit at 11:30. Apparently *Kamloops* passed through the Soo on December 4 in the company of *Quedoc,* a 345-foot bulk freighter (*Owen Sound Daily Sun Times* Dec. 13, 1927). From Sault Ste. Marie, Capt. Brian wrote his wife in Toronto, saying that the weather was very bad and that he was going out to anchor his ship (*Ibid.* Dec. 14, 1927). Mrs. Brian expected her husband home for the winter season six days later on Saturday, December 10.

The giant freeze-up of vessels the year before was still fresh in memory as the 1927 navigation season drew to a close. A rumor had circulated from Buffalo that Lake ships, fearing another blockade, would end their season on November 30, but executives of Canada Steamship Lines denied the rumor. A company official was quoted in the *Fort William Daily Times Journal* on November 29: "We will run our ships as long as the weather holds good, and as long as there is grain to carry. The experience we had last year does not deter us because we realize that a thing like that may not happen again for another 50 years." The executive's declaration would prove ironic on two counts: Company vessels would be lost in 1927, and others would end their season icebound in the very same channel as the year before (*Detroit Free Press* Dec. 15, 16, 1927).

The day following the executive's statement, a 36-mile-an-hour northeast wind began, causing the upbound vessels to shelter overnight on November 30 at Whitefish Point and the Welcome Islands. The temperature was 8 degrees F at Duluth, 10 degrees F at Port Arthur, and storm warnings were raised at the Soo. The temperature continued to drop as a massive cold front advanced from the northwest (*Sault Daily Star* Dec. 1, 1927). This cold front would be closely followed by a worse storm.

Insurance rates were raised at midnight, November 30, reflecting the increased risk of late-season navigation. The rates were raised again on December 5, and underwriters ceased all coverage by midnight on the 12th. Navigation aids and lightkeepers were removed from the Lakes by that time (*Sault Daily Star* Dec. 1, 1927; *Owen Sound Daily Sun Times* Dec. 1, 1927).

Meanwhile, the Booth Fisheries' steamer *America* was reported to have arrived at Port Arthur on December 3, ice-covered after passing through the storm. The vessel carried a load of salt and was to return to Duluth with a cargo of salted herring (*Port Arthur News-Chronicle* Dec. 3, 1927).

The storm increased as the second front arrived, sweeping Lake Superior with high winds on December 5. Upbound vessels, including *Kamloops*, had been delayed and anchored at Whitefish Bay. The downbound grain fleet had weathered the

storm at Fort William. *Valcartier,* the first ship to reach the Soo, arrived heavily laden with a thick coating of ice, and reported temperatures of 40 degrees below during the storm (*Sault Daily Star* Dec. 6, 1927).

The financial pressure of the December 5 increase in the insurance rates had prompted furious activity at the Lakehead grain port. Eighteen ships of the grain fleet were loaded by the Port Arthur elevators, which worked at maximum capacity to clear the fleet before the insurance rates went up. All but three made it before the rate changed (*Port Arthur News Chronicle* Dec. 6, 1927).

Storm signals were raised once again on December 7 as a northeast wind began blowing at 20 to 30 miles per hour. The temperature dropped to 10 degrees below at Port Arthur. The passenger steamer *Assiniboia* was loading flour to begin its downbound voyage as soon as the weather cleared (*Port Arthur News Chronicle* Dec. 7, 1927). The next day the same paper announced that no vessels had entered Port Arthur or Fort William for the last 36 hours (*Ibid.* Dec. 8). The winds would soon exceed 60 miles per hour, and later 80 before the storm subsided.

The storm became a major blizzard. The weather remained at sub-zero levels with lows of 10 to 38 degrees F below zero reported. The gale was responsible for at least eight deaths in Alberta. More than 30 people on land lost their lives during this storm (*Detroit Free Press* Dec. 10, 1927), which was so severe that train service between St. Paul, Winnipeg and Minneapolis was suspended on the 7th (*Fort William Daily Times Journal* Dec. 8, 1927.

The situation on the Lakes grew worse as the storm raged the 7th and 8th. Damage reports began filtering in on the 9th: the bulk freighter *Agawa* was aground in Lake Huron, being pounded to pieces; all efforts to rescue the 23 stranded crew members were thwarted by the weather. At least 20 other vessels were in distress or missing. Seven downbound grain ships were overdue at Detroit. Winds of 84 miles an hour broke four vessels and a passenger steamer from their moorings at Detroit. An unidentified boat (which turned out to be the bulk freighter *E.W. Oglebay*) ran aground at Shot Point; *Martian,* another bulk freighter, ran aground in Thunder Bay; *Altadoc* was aground at Keweenaw Point. In Lake Erie three steamers ran aground with a total of 81 men aboard (*Detroit Free Press* Dec. 10, 1927). In all, five vessels were eventually declared a total loss by the underwriters – *Kamloops* was among the missing.

The steel package freighter *Winnipeg* arrived in Port Arthur on Friday the 9th with the news that the crew had seen *Kamloops* at Whitefish Bay on Tuesday (Dec. 6). When the storm first broke, *Winnipeg* had laid up in Whitefish Bay, but left during a lull. At the upper end of the Lake, thick fog slowed its progress and an anchor was set. The early morning light revealed that *Winnipeg* was only a few hundred yards from rocks and had just narrowly missed becoming a casualty of the storm. *Winnipeg* arrived in port covered with tons of ice on the deck, white with frost.

A crewman of *Winnipeg* described his five-day ordeal (*Port Arthur News Chronicle* Dec. 10, 1927):

"I have never seen anything like it in my 20 years of sailing. The storm was bad enough, but to get a combination of gales, fogs and 20 [degrees] below zero weather all at the same time is something that has given many a mariner nerves this last few days.

The same report stated that a gang was at work unloading the ship and cutting away tons of ice so that "the steamer, like a good many more, will make 'one more trip' to the east before the close of navigation."

By December 12, grave concern was mounting regarding the fate of *Kamloops*, which was now overdue at Ft. William. No word of the ship had been received other than that brought by *Winnipeg; Kamloops* carried no wireless. [Wireless was not required on all Lake ships at this time, although many carried them as safety equipment. Wireless was required on all vessels carrying 50 or more persons (*Sault Daily Star* Ontario Dec. 14, 1927).]

At least three other vessels were missing: *Saskatoon,* a Canada Steamship Lines package freighter; *Brookton,* a bulk freighter also owned by CSL; and the tug *Champlain* (*Owen Sound Daily Sun Times* Dec. 12, 1927). All but *Kamloops* would soon be located.

News of another victim of the storm circulated: *Lambton,* a steel canaller similar to *Kamloops*, was discovered wrecked on Parisienne Island in Lake Superior (*Sault Daily Star* Dec. 12, 1927; *Fort William Daily Times Journal* Dec. 12, 1927)

The ordeal of the survivors of the wrecked vessels *Altadoc, Agawa* and *Lambton* give a view of the conditions that *Kamloops* faced. The Coast Guard dory that attempted the removal of *Altadoc's* crew became frozen in the ice and was freed only after 16 attempts by the cutter *Crawford* to break a lane to the boat. *Agawa's* crew was trapped aboard without food or heat for three days, and during that time the stranded vessel was covered with ice four to six feet thick. The captain, who retired after that voyage, reported being battered by 40-foot waves that swept away the smokestack, spars and top deck (*Detroit Free Press* Dec. 12, 1927). Two suicides were reported aboard *Lambton* by crew members unable to withstand the severe conditions. These deaths, reported as suicides, may have been attempts to swim to shore.

A search for *Kamloops* began in earnest December 12. *Islet Prince*, commanded by A.E. Fader, began searching the north shore (*Ft. William Daily Times Journal* Dec. 12, 1927). The government tug *Murray Stewart* left from the Soo to join the search (*Sarnia Canadian Observer* Dec 13, 1927). W.J. King, assistant manager of Canada Steamship Lines, announced that his company was in communication with officials in Ottawa and had requested the use of a government plane to aid the search (*Owen Sound Daily Sun Times* Dec. 12 1927).

Speculation on the whereabouts of *Kamloops* centered on Isle Royale. Captain R. Simpson of *Quedoc* arrived at the Soo and discovered *Kamloops* still on the unreported list. He gave the following account (*Owen Sound Daily Sun Times* Dec. 13, 1927):

The *Quedoc* passed upbound December 4. Beside her was the *Kamloops* upbound loaded with package freight, with

21 [sic] men aboard, and captained by William Brian. The *Quedoc* was leading, and the *Kamloops* was one-quarter of a mile astern. At 10 o'clock Tuesday night [Dec 6], the lookout on the steamer *Quedoc* suddenly saw a dark mass ahead, and gave the alarm immediately. The *Quedoc* turned sharply to avoid running head on into the rocks at the same time blowing the danger signal to the *Kamloops*. A north gale was blowing, there was a heavy sea and it was rough going. The visibility was poor, on account of frost fog, and it is not known if the *Kamloops* saw the rock or heard the signal. The *Kamloops* has not been seen or heard of since. She had no wireless aboard.

Finally the weather cleared, and there was no wind on December 12 when the last grain carriers of the season departed the Canadian Lakehead (*Owen Sound Daily Sun Times* Dec. 13). All departing vessels had been alerted to watch for wreckage. Searching vessels benefited from the fair weather, however, there was still no trace of *Kamloops* (*Sault Daily Star* Dec. 13, 1927).

A report circulated that the lost ship *Kamloops* was aground at Keweenaw Point. Brock Batten, the CSL general agent at Port Arthur, reported that the Coast Guard at Eagle Harbor had been requested to search the Point. Evidently that agency had been contacted by the Chicago-based marine insurance underwriters (*Port Arthur News Chronicle* Dec. 13; *Calumet News* Dec. 13). The cutter *Crawford* was unable to respond because of heavy ice in the harbor, and damage to its props incurred during the rescue of the *Altadoc* crew. The Keweenaw was searched by lifeboat to no avail (*Detroit Free Press* Dec. 14, 1927; *Houghton Daily Mining Gazette* Dec. 14, 1927; *Calumet News* Dec. 14, 1927; *Sault Daily Star* Dec. 15, 1927). The Keweenaw was searched by the tug *Champlain* (*Ft. William Daily Times Journal* Dec. 14; *Owen Sound Daily Sun Times* Dec. 14, 1927). Both searches would prove futile.

Apparently, the rumor that *Kamloops* was aground on Keweenaw Point had originated at the American Soo, relayed to Buffalo and then to Chicago, from whence it was forwarded to the steamship company (*Port Arthur News Chronicle* Dec. 14). The search for *Kamloops* on the Keweenaw Peninsula was unsuccessful, and the ship's whereabouts remained unknown.

Three hundred square miles of water and more than a thousand miles of rugged coastline had been searched with negative results (*Owen Sound Daily Sun Times* Dec. 15 1927). As hope for the safe return of *Kamloops* and its crew dimmed, speculation of Lakes sailors and captains began to appear in the regional press. "Either her cargo shifted and she keeled over, or she ran aground on some rocks and was wrecked" (*Ft. William Daily Times Journal* Dec. 14, 1927). Another paper (*Houghton Daily Mining Gazette* Dec. 14, 1927) added:

Marine men agree that the only hope for the safety of the *Kamloops* is the chance it might have made a successful run to the north Canadian shore where it either ran ashore or is laying to in some isolated harbor, probably frozen in or has run aground somewhere on the Keweenaw.

Kamloops was carrying a heavy cargo. Included in the cargo was valuable machinery, made in England for the Thunder Bay Paper Company (*Ft. William Daily Times Journal* Dec. 14, 1927). There was also a full deck load on board. Captain Harry Lavers of the steamer *J. Frater Taylor* described seeing *Kamloops* during his downbound trip (*Owen Sound Daily Sun Times* Dec. 14 1927):

> I passed quite close to the *Kamloops* somewhere between Caribou Island and Michipicoten Island, and while it was blowing fairly hard at that time, I did not think there was any danger, although I thought about her safety after we had passed her. There was another freighter going with her, but she was some little distance away, and I could not say what boat it was, but I know that one of the two boats was carrying quite a heavy deck load, and I am of the impression that it was the one nearest to us, which would be the *Kamloops*.

The ship seen by Lavers accompanying *Kamloops* must have been *Quedoc*. The deck load described may have been a factor in the sinking of *Kamloops*. Ice was discussed as a possible factor in its loss, as the possibility of finding a trace of the ship or of the survivors making it to shore grew more grim (*New York Times* Dec. 15, 1927):

> It is believed that the missing vessel, fighting against the mountainous waves which swept Superior last week, foundered when the weight of ice formed by the huge waves as they dashed against the vessel in sub-zero weather made the ship unmanageable and brought disaster while she was far from port or sheltered inlet.

A "well known mariner" later added (*Sault Daily Star* Dec. 17, 1927):

> The *Kamloops* went up the Lake with a deck load of fence wire...and I am of the opinion that this is what swamped her. The wire was piled high, and water washing over the deck would immediately freeze there. It would be impossible to remove it, and the cargo and ice would make one huge, heavy and solid mass. It would be impossible to remove the ice or the deck load under such conditions. Other boats have nearly come to grief in Lake Superior from the same cause. I suggest this as being responsible for the loss of the *Kamloops*, and I believe I am right. The *Kamloops* became over weighted with the wire and ice and turned over and sank.

The speculation of the mariners of the Lakehead was somewhat different (*Port Arthur News Chronicle* Dec. 16, 1927):

> Unless something unforeseen has happened, broken steering gear or sprung plates, the *Kamloops* could have made some beach or shore line, is the general opinion of mariners. The *Kamloops* was a staunch vessel, heavily loaded perhaps, but nonetheless the ship could have been able to weather the storm, or seek shelter. Mariners do not think the Captain of the *Kamloops* would allow sufficient ice to form on their decks to put her in danger of sinking. He probably knew his position and, if danger of that kind had

arisen, it is more than likely the Captain would have made a run for shore to beach his vessel, is another opinion.

As more time passed without a trace of wreckage, and hope was reluctantly abandoned, the general feeling grew that *Kamloops* would remain a Lakes mystery (*Sault Daily Star* Dec. 14, 1927). The Coast Guard ceased its search of the Keweenaw in the face of heavy seas and ice, and suggested concentrating efforts on the shores of Isle Royale and Manitou Island (*Houghton Daily Mining Gazette* Dec. 16, 1927). The *Islet Prince*, which had seen no wreckage, was called back to port by CSL officials. Evidently, no planes were employed in the search for *Kamloops* (*Port Arthur News Chronicle* Dec. 15 1927). *Midland Prince* and *Murray Stewart* had also been unsuccessful (*Owen Daily Sun Times* Dec. 13, 1927).

Company officials, however, remained optimistic. Alex Auld, Canada Steamship Lines superintendent in Toronto, issued a nress dispatch, saying, "We have every hope of hearing from the *Kamloops* yet." He pointed out there was no probability of the ship's food supplies giving out and, as it had no wireless, there was nothing to indicate it was not lying in some sheltered spot inaccessible from land. Auld also said there was "not the slightest" possibility that the boat's cargo had shifted, causing the ship to turn turtle (*Ft. William Daily Times Journal* Dec. 16, 1927).

Isle Royale and Manitou Island represented the last shred of hope for the searchers. Captain Henry Gehl of the tug *Champlain* believed every bay of Isle Royale should be inspected. "I would like to give the Isle the once-over to be certain. It might be that some member or members of the crew got ashore and are wandering about the island. It must be made certain that no one is on the island before the search for the missing steamer is given up as hopeless," he said (*Port Arthur News Chronicle* Dec. 16, 1927).

Capt. Gehl was not alone in his belief that survivors might be on Isle Royale. Another tug captain, Sam Wright, said that practically every tug captain, mate and engineer was ready to start a close search of the shore of Isle Royale, and the waters and islands between Port Arthur and the big island, to ascertain the fate of the freighter *Kamloops*. Wright believed that the missing ship would be found ice-locked on the inner side of Isle Royale between Washington Harbor and Gull Rocks, a stretch of 15 miles of sheer rock where there is no shelter for ships, or else in one of the numerous bays and island-sheltered nooks that extend from Gull Rocks to the outer point of the island (*Port Arthur News Chronicle* Dec. 17, 1927). The prospect of finding survivors still alive on Isle Royale was considered remote (*Daily Mining Journal*, Marquette Dec. 16, 1927).

The Fort William agents of Canada Steamship Lines informed the Eagle Harbor Coast Guard that they planned to charter the Dominion Towing and Salvage tug *James Whalen*. The tug was to leave Port Arthur on Friday, December 16 to search for *Kamloops*, proceeding to Isle Royale first and then to Keweenaw, circling the end of the peninsula and Manitou Island (*Daily Mining Journal*, Marquette Dec. 17, 1927).

One newspaper report, if accurate, changes what is known of the last days of *Kamloops*. According to the *Port Arthur News*

Chronicle, December 17, 1927, the crew of *Martian* said that it had almost collided with *Kamloops* in heavy fog on December 9. This is the only reference located regarding any such occurrence, and may be a case of mistaken identity.

Further efforts to find the missing boat would be undertaken by the company. Tug *James Whalen,* carrying extra food and warm clothing, left Fort William on the night of December 19, three days later than announced, to search for *Kamloops* (*Owen Sound Daily Sun Times* Dec. 20, 1927). Indications are that this search was a combined mission, for the tug would also pick up lighthouse keepers ending their season (*Ibid* Dec. 21, 1927). The reason for *Whalen's* delay from the first notice of its pending search on December 16 was not stated in this reference. Apparently it was involved in channel clearing operations (*Owen Sound Daily Sun Times* Dec. 22, 1927).

Company officials received a telegram from *James Whalen* on December 21 saying the tug had made a circuit of Isle Royale without finding any trace of the missing steamer. "That the *Kamloops* was flung against some jutting boulder, cracking in two and sinking almost immediately, now appears the logical solution to the mystery" (*Houghton Daily Mining Gazette* Dec. 22, 1927).

James Whalen, with two Canada Steamship Lines captains aboard, searched around Manitou Island and off Keweenaw on the south shore of Lake Superior. The tug returned to Port Arthur about 10 p.m. on the 22nd and reported no trace of *Kamloops*. *Whalen's* return marked the official close of the 1927 navigation season (*Port Arthur Daily News Chronicle* Dec. 23, 1927; *New York Times,* Dec. 24, 1927).

During *James Whalen's* search for *Kamloops,* public concern mounted. Citizen pressures to find the missing canaller grew, as did the number of rumors. Letters and editorials on the ship appeared in newspapers in increasing numbers. One popular editorial topic was the need to change regulations to require that all boats carry wireless equipment (e.g., *Sault Daily Star* Dec. 23, 1927; *Port Arthur Daily News Chronicle* Dec. 23, 1927).

Assertion of the continued possibility of the ship being ice-bound in a remote area was frequently mentioned in letters to the editor (e.g., *Owen Sound Daily Sun Times* Dec. 24, 1927). The suggestion that the government should patrol the coast by airplane again appeared. Pressure was also exerted on the government to continue the search with ice-breaking tugs, although none were available at the west end of the Lake. Telegrams had been sent by the Port Arthur Chamber of Commerce and private business leaders to the Minister of Marine and Fisheries in Ottawa urging that government tugs be employed. These people were assured by the Ministry that it had been in constant touch with the owners of the vessel "with the idea of leaving nothing within reason undone to ascertain the whereabouts of the missing ship" (*Port Arthur News Chronicle* Dec. 20, 21, 1927).

Rumors circulated widely. The charge that the Canada Steamship Lines was dropping the search and not doing all it could was raised in Fort William and Port Arthur. The company responded through W.J. King, assistant manager of the company (*Owen Sound Daily Sun Times* Dec. 22, 1927):

The feeling that Canada Steamship Lines were not pushing the search for the *Kamloops* as vigorously as they might, was said by W.J. King to be absolutely without foundation, and that on the contrary, everything humanly possible was being done to find some trace of the vessel and its crew.

On December 23, the rumor that *Kamloops* had been located by some fishermen caused a great deal of excitement in the Lakehead port cities. Supposedly the missing ship was ashore on Manitou Island. *James Whalen* was once again chartered by Canada Steamship Lines, this time for a "roving commission" (*Detroit Free Press* Dec. 25, 1927). Again, there were two Canada Steamship Line captains aboard to supervise the search (*Sault Daily Star* Dec. 24, 1927). The captains had been authorized by the company to visit any part of the Lake that in their opinion should be looked over, to keep the tug out as long as there was any hope and otherwise direct operations.

"They have full liberty to go wherever their judgement dictates and to stay out as long as they think there is any use. They can even go as far east along the south shore as Marquette," said Brock Batten, agent for the Canada Steamship Lines.

Isle Royale waters will again be visited by the *Whalen,* making the third time they have been inspected on behalf of the owners of the *Kamloops* (*Port Arthur News Chronicle* Dec. 24, 1927).

The Canada Steamship Lines head offices at Montreal flew its flag at half mast on Dec. 24, 1927, a gesture in memory of *Kamloops'* crew (*Ft. William Daily Times Journal* Dec. 24, 1927).

James Whalen was out three days on the final active search for *Kamloops.* It returned at 5 p.m. on December 26, again without sighting a trace of the missing vessel. It had been a thorough search, primarily due to a period of calm weather. The principal search area was around Manitou Island. The only signs of life had been a wolf and an eagle. *Whalen* had circled Pie Island and Angus Island opposite Thunder Cape. The Canoe Rocks area of Isle Royale was also searched. In all, more than 500 miles were traveled in the search, which was the first time Christmas Day stillness had been pierced on mid-Lake Superior (*Owen Sound Daily Sun Times* Dec. 27, 1927; *Port Arthur News Chronicle* Dec. 27, 1927; *Sault Daily Star* Dec. 27, 1927).

On December 22, 1927, Arthur Magnan, registrar for the Canadian Marine and Fisheries, Registry of Shipping, closed *Kamloops'* official registry.

The losses of the season were summarized and the *Marquette Daily Mining Journal* provided a picture of what mariners of the next season might expect (Dec. 24, 1927):

The bet with the Storm King lost again, the navigation season has come to a close with the wreckage of five steamers and hundreds of thousands of bushels of grain wasted on Lake Superior's and Lake Huron's bleak waters and shores; one ship, the *Kamloops,* presumably on the bottom of Lake Superior with 20 men, two women and valuable cargo; and the expense of another ice blockade on the debit side of the shipping ledger.

The fad of last-tripping claimed four victims this year, landmarks which will be pointed out in 1928 when the merciless wire ticks out again the order for "that last cargo."

Events of 1928: Discovery of Members of the Crew of *Kamloops*.

By the beginning of the new year, there was little mention of the loss of *Kamloops*. In January, the Ontario Workman's Compensation Board judged the crew lost and were waiting for receipt of the official report so compensation to the widows and children could begin (*Owen Sound Daily Sun Times* Jan. 12, 1928; *Detroit Free Press* Jan. 17, 1928). It was known that there were two women aboard *Kamloops* during its final voyage. Jennet Grafton and Alice Bettridge were the first and assistant stewardesses. This was to have been the last season on the Lakes for Grafton; it was the second season for 22 year-old Bettridge (*Owen Sound Daily Sun Times* Jan. 12, 1928).

The opening of the 1928 navigation season began April 17, when *James Whalen* began breaking ice at the Lakehead port (*Ibid.* April 17, 20). The Canada Steamship Lines planned to have the first ships out of port begin looking for evidence of their missing vessel. The company intended to systematically search the north shore of Lake Superior and the entire shore line of Isle Royale. The cutter *Crawford* would be dispatched from Eagle Harbor to begin its search as soon as the weather and ice conditions allowed movement. Some writers held to the slim hope that some of the crew may have survived the winter.

Ship crews were not the only ones on the lookout for *Kamloops'* wreckage. A number of pilots flew into Port Arthur and reported seeing wreckage, at first thought to be the missing vessel. The wreckage was not that of *Kamloops,* but *Lambton* (*Fort William Daily Times Journal* May 16, 1928).

Insurance claims on the missing vessel were settled in February. The net collection of the insurance on the ship was $214,009.05 (Letter from the Montreal Trust Company to Canada Steamship Lines, Feb. 8, 1928, Queens University Archive, Kingston). The hull and machinery were insured for a total of $168,100 (Letter from Montreal Trust Co. to Canada Steamship Lines, Feb. 4, 1928). There were 13 companies carrying hull and machinery insurance and 20 companies involved with disbursements insurance on *Kamloops*.

On May 26, the electrifying news that the fishermen of Isle Royale had found bodies believed to belong to the crew of *Kamloops* reached the newspapers (*Calumet News* May 26, 1928; *Detroit Free Press* May 27, 1928). The cutter *Crawford,* which postponed entering the dry dock in Duluth at Marine Iron and Shipbuilding for repairs, went to investigate. Two bodies had been reported found by David Lind (*Duluth News Tribune* May 27, 1928).

The U.S. Coast Guard Cutter *Crawford,* flying its flag at half-mast, returned the sailors of the missing freighter to Port Arthur. Captain Christianson and executive officer Lt. Woods of *Crawford* provided the details of the recovery.

The bodies, both wearing life preservers with "*Kamloops*" stenciled on them, were reported located near Twelve O' Clock Point on Amygdaloid Island (sic) on the north shore of Isle Royale. They were found along with wreckage of the lost steamer. Fragments of superstructure, including the top of the wheelhouse, a spar with a flag on which was printed *Kamloops* and a lifeboat, were found in the area between Green Isle and Hawk Island.

Captain Christianson stated that the wreckage includes all of the boat's hatches, half a lifeboat and five or six pairs of oars. The beach is covered with medicine, candy, tooth paste and foodstuff carried by the steamer. The reason the steamer was not found until Saturday was because ice on the little bays is just beginning to melt. Indications are that the steamer *Kamloops* can not be very far from Isle Royale (*Duluth News Tribune* May 28, 1928).

It is unlikely the bodies were on Amygdaloid Island. It would have required a southwest wind, rare in the winter, for the bodies to have drifted toward Amygdaloid Island. Many contemporary sources erroneously reported Amygdaloid as the location of the bodies. Apparently, Twelve O' Clock Point was believed by some to be located on Amygdaloid Island – it is actually located near Todd Harbor on Isle Royale.

The same paper reported that four other ring buoys, marked "*Edward Chambers,*" were found among the wreckage. It was believed that these were carried aboard *Kamloops* as cargo (also reported in *The Evening Telegram* [Superior] May 28, 1928).

At Sargent's Funeral Parlor, where the bodies were taken, they were searched for any evidence that might indicate the identity of the sailors. There was no material to furnish a clue on one body; the other, however, did produce an identification:

It is thought that the name of one of the men is J. Journeault, for on his body was found a letter, addressed to him in care of the Sault Canal post office, written in French. In his pockets also were found a $10 bill and a check for $60 made out in his favor by the Canada Steamship Lines (*Fort William Daily Times-Journal* May 28, 1928).

Journeault's body was sent to L'Islet, Quebec, for burial. The unidentified sailor was buried in Riverside Cemetery at Port Arthur. Brock Batten, Canada Steamship Lines representative, made burial arrangements. He selected the caskets for both men and secured the cemetery plot for the unknown sailor (*Port Arthur News Chronicle* May 28, 1928). Batten made every effort to show respect for the unidentified employee. The funeral was held at the Riverside Cemetery, and the minister of the First Presbyterian Church officiated. The pallbearers were four Canada Steamship Lines captains (*Ft. William Daily Times Journal* May 29, 1928).

The discovery of the bodies and wreckage prompted the Canadians to mount an air search of the area to locate the other crew members and the wreck itself (*Owen Sound Daily Sun Times* May 29, 30, 1928). Ontario government hydroplane *Nightingale* searched the Amygdaloid Island coast, but located no additional wreckage. The pilot reported much ice still in the bays of the area, which delayed the deployment of a search party. In this account, Capt. Martin Christiansen of the coastal steamer *Winyah* reported seeing wreckage in the area between Hawk and Green islands. The captain also speculated that the wreck was in deep water, and accounted for the fact that the ship sank on the north side of the island because of a possible mishap to the rudder (*Port Arthur News Chronicle* May 31, 1928).

A detailed description of the probable location of *Kamloops* was published in the *Calumet News* (June 1, 1928; cf. *Houghton Daily Mining Gazette* June 1, 1928). This report indicated that the loss was not Amygdaloid Island, as was frequently reported in the press. Captain Christianson of *Crawford* was quoted as believing that the wreck was "lying on a rock just off Twelve O'Clock Point on Isle Royale, within 300 feet of the little unnamed bay where [were found] the bodies of two members of the crew and considerable wreckage identified as that of the *Kamloops*...in rather shallow water and the ice packs of the winter had torn off the roof (of the pilothouse)."

Legislative ramifications of the loss of *Kamloops* were being felt at this time. The sinking of the CSL steamer was used as an example of the need for additional lifesaving stations at the upper end of the Great Lakes and also to substantiate the argument for the requirement of wireless sets on all commercial vessels. Those arguments were presented to the House of Commons by D.J. Cowan of Port Arthur-Thunder Bay and R.J. Manion of Fort William (*Port Arthur News Chronicle* June 1, 1928).

American interests were also represented in the discussion of the opening and closing of the Great Lakes navigation season. D.P. Quinlan was sent by President Calvin Coolidge to investigate the controversy that came about when small shippers on the Lakes charged that the operators of the larger fleets and the Great Lakes Carriers' Association delayed the opening of the 1928 season to benefit themselves. There were 80 civil suits against the operators pending in Cleveland (*Duluth News-Tribune* June 19, 1928).

Quinlan indicated that the government would control the opening and closing dates of the navigation season and would provide equal rights to all vessel operators and would safeguard as much as possible the lives of seamen and vessels. *Kamloops* was used as the example of a wreck that might have been prevented if governmental restrictions had been in effect.

> It is the belief of Mr. Quinlan that weather conditions in the future will control the opening and closing of navigation. Heretofore, it has been a practice among large vessel owners to insert in their shipping contracts clauses which declare the date of navigation open or closed. Many of these contracts are made without reference to weather conditions....The findings of the government inspection will be presented to the Secretary of War who will issue executive orders to district U.S. engineers relative to navigation dates (*Duluth News-Tribune* June 19, 1928).

On June 4, six more bodies of *Kamloops'* crew were found, again by fishermen. News of the discovery was relayed to the port cities from Isle Royale by the captain of *Winyah*. Brock Batton of the Canada Steamship Lines dispatched the tug

Champlain to recover the remains, which were found close to Twelve O'Clock Point (*Ft. William Daily Times Journal* June 5, 1928; *Port Arthur News Chronicle* June 5, 1928). The tug had four CSL captains aboard to supervise the search and shipped a gasoline launch for searching the shallow bays and inlet. The bodies were decomposed, but one appeared to be that of a woman (*The Calumet News* June 5, 1928).

At first, the woman, reportedly found attired in nightclothes, was believed to be stewardess Netty Grafton of Southampton (*Owen Sound Daily Sun Times* June 6, 1928). The woman was later identified as Alice Bettridge, the assistant stewardess, an identification based on the fact that the body had a set of natural teeth; it was known that Netty Grafton had false teeth (*Port Arthur News Chronicle* June 7, 1928). The report that Bettridge was found in her nightclothes was denied. Brock Batten stated, "She was fully dressed and wore a sweater and a coat" (*Ft. William Daily Times Journal* June 7, 1928). This evidence supports the belief held at the time by many that the bodies found were the occupants of a lifeboat that made it to shore. All had been found with lifebelts.

Three other bodies were identified based on pocket contents (*Owen Sound Daily Sun Times* June 7, 1928; *Port Arthur News Chronicle* June 7, 1928; *Port Arthur News Chronicle* June 8, 1928). The identified bodies were returned to their families for burial, except for Gauthier, whose address could not be determined. The two unidentified sailors and Gauthier were buried in the Riverside Cemetery in a central plot over which the Canada Steamship Lines erected a bronze tablet commemorating the wreck victims (*Ft. William Daily Times Journal* June 6, 13, 1928). Although reported, the tablet was apparently never erected.

A ninth body was found inland some distance from shore, believed to be the remains of Honore (Henry) Genest, first mate. The body had no lifebelt, although one was found in the vicinity. It was surmised that the first mate was able to make it to shore and remove his lifebelt before succumbing to the elements (*Ft. William Daily Times Journal* June 14, 1928).

The theory that some of *Kamloops'* crew may have made it to shore, and there died of exposure, gained support. Those who adhered to this view argued for a complete search of the inland region of Amygdaloid Island (*Houghton Daily Mining Gazette* June 7, 1928).

Capt. H.J. Brian, brother of the captain of *Kamloops*, was influenced by this possibility. When he was not able to identify his brother among the bodies found, he mounted an independent search party to find his brother's body. The tug *Ruth B*, captained by George Burns, was chartered (*Port Arthur News Chronicle* June 13, 1928).

Brian's search was based on some strong evidence. The fact that a lifeboat had been found and the bodies had lifebelts on indicated that there was at least some warning of the disaster. Searchers had reported finding papers in the pockets of the victims as well as other items that had not been water-soaked. Most believed they perished from the cold and not hunger, because of the large amount of food found on the shore (*The Calumet News* June 15, 1928).

Brian's search took place June 14 and 15. He and his search party returned to Port Arthur on June 16 to report that they had found no further remains (*Owen Sound Daily Sun Times* June 16,1928). The private searchers did, however, report finding evidence of what they believed to be "shelters and resting places that might have been erected by members of the crew of the wrecked steamer" (*Port Arthur News Chronicle* June 16, 1928). He stated to the newspaper that a shelter of shrubs and brush was found 400 feet from the shore, and Henry Genest was found in it. There was also a quantity of candy, particularly peppermint lozenges, in the shelter.

> "I am positive that no bodies are along the shore line, after a thorough search. I came to Port Arthur with the idea in mind that they would all be found in the bush, and I go away with the same belief. I am positive the entire crew got away safely from the *Kamloops* and that they had lived, some of them possibly, for days."

A fisherman living near Todd Harbor, the place where most of the wreckage came ashore, informed the searchers that on a night in December, the date of which he is not certain, he heard a ship, not far in the distance give four blasts of her whistle. At 3:30 o'clock next morning, the fisherman says the whistle blew continuously about an hour.

The CSL Company had sent a party of five "experienced bushmen" to search the island, who were apparently still in the area during the Brian search and returned after Brian had issued his report (*Ft. William Daily Times Journal* June 15, 18, 1928). The party returned to Port Arthur, and Brock Batten issued the following report (*Port Arthur News Chronicle* June 19, 1928):

> This party made a very thorough search of the whole vicinity....They went up and down the shore line for a couple of miles on either side of the apparent location of the wreck and they went inland a couple of miles, over the same frontage. Their report is that they saw no trace whatever of any of the crew having survived the wreck and spent any time on shore.

Capt. Brian did not respond directly to the statement of the other searchers. However, he did give some additional comments after the Canada Steamship Lines statement was published (*Owen Daily Sun Times* June 20, 1928):

> Captain Brian says that in his own search he found a set of false teeth and a woman's wig, which he was informed tallied with Miss Grafton. Miss Betteridge [sic] had natural teeth. The captain thinks that the finding of the wig and teeth would suggest that they were from one of the bodies already recovered. He is of the opinion that one of the bodies having male attire and already buried is that of Miss Grafton of Southhampton.

> Explaining further his belief that many of the crew reached shore alive, Captain Brian offers the statement that he found articles from the wreckage of the boat carried up onto the shore, farther he says than they could have been

washed by the waves, and also in condition to suggest that they had been tampered with by human hands. Had these human hands been of the fishermen who remained late on the island, reports of their finding would have early reached the outside world last fall. No such reports have been heard. The articles in question were principally boxes of candy, and the captain believes some of them were used as food.

The discrepancies between Brian's reports and the searchers hired by Batten only added to the mystery shrouding *Kamloops'* loss. Apparently the public felt that Canada Steamship Lines was not doing everything possible to recover the missing crewmen, and was perhaps even hiding something.

Brock Batten, who served as company spokesman and director of the search and recovery operations undertaken by Canada Steamship Lines, issued a statement to the newspapers detailing the efforts that had been made to learn the fate of the missing crew. The account of Batten's comments to the press was carried in the *Port Arthur News Chronicle* (June 21, 1928):

> Mr. Batten particularly explained why the officials of his company feel certain all members of the *Kamloops'* crew met their death when the steamer went to its doom, and why they do not credit suggestions that they reached shore alive to perish afterwards of hunger and exhaustion.

> Asked particularly with regard to Henry Genest...,"It is possible Genest did reach shore alive," said Mr. Batten. "The evidence seems to indicate that he was tossed up on the bank and succeeded in walking or crawling a short distance back. I do not believe he was, however, the occupant of a life boat. He was more likely washed over from the ship. This is the opinion of our captains, who have had the experience to know what might be happening at such a time. We all believe the most plausible explanation with regard to the others whose bodies have been found is that they were working at the lifeboat which has been found among the wreckage when they were engulfed. We do not believe they ever entered the lifeboat. If they did the chances were all against them getting ashore, because of the backwash of the waves and the nature of the shore line. One man in a safety suit might be thrown up where he could get a footing if he were carried by a particularly high wave, but those in a boat could not be so fortunate. Genest apparently was the only one on the *Kamloops* who had donned a safety suit. If any of the others had done so, their bodies would most likely have been found, as they would thereby at least have been kept floating. The safety suit would keep a man afloat, but would not save him from exhaustion or exposure to the cold. It was 30 below zero at that time and snowing."

> Asked with regard to reports that shelters have been found at Isle Royale which might have been used by members of the missing crew, Mr. Batten pointed out that Isle Royale for many years had been a camping and tourist resort and the working ground of fishermen, and the finding of a rude shelter had no significance. It might have been built by anyone at any time.

Batten listed the various search and recovery parties that the company had dispatched: the *Midland Prince*, the week-long survey of the north shore by *Islet Prince*; tug *Whalen* searched when it went out to get the lightkeepers and circled Isle Royale closer to shore than *Midland Prince* was able to reach; *Whalen* searched a second time, going all the way to Keweenaw; *Crawford* made two trips to the island to recover bodies and made limited searches each time. The last search expedition was by the five men who searched the island.

They reported to us yesterday they had carefully examined 15 miles of shore line and on a front of four miles, two miles either side of the wreck, had worked inland for about two miles at distances apart of only 10 feet and could find neither bodies nor evidence that anyone from the *Kamloops* had been ashore to live. They are of the opinion that there is no reason to continue the search.

...Friends of the missing ones and the public may rest assured that every effort is being made, as it has been made, to continue fullest information regarding the crew of the missing steamer, and to hide nothing (*Port Arthur News Chronicle* June 21, 1928).

The next day the same paper ran an editorial comment on Batten's statement that gives some insight into the public sentiment (*Port Arthur News Chronicle* June 22, 1928):

Even though the statement comes at what we consider a rather late date, it will nevertheless be welcomed by the public. The attitude taken by the officials of the Canada Steamship Company toward the public was not by any means satisfactory. The loss of the ship involved much more than the interests of the company....The public was entitled to a frank statement of what the company was doing, the extent of the search that was taking place at the time it was being made.

...But this knowledge was not given them. The whole proceeding was surrounded with mystery.

The same unsatisfactory procedure was followed when the U.S. cutter *Crawford* brought the dead bodies of two of the ill-fated crew of the *Kamloops* to Port Arthur. Orders were issued to dock attendants to close the docks and not permit any person to approach. The undertakers were given orders to give out no information. The newspapers were compelled to get information from whatever source they could in regard to the finding of the bodies. When other bodies were brought to port, every possible precaution was taken to prevent information getting to the public.

This attitude of the company could not but arouse suspicion in the public mind that there was something to hide. However unfounded this suspicion might be, it continued, and Mr. Batten can count himself extremely fortunate if it is dissipated by the statement he just made of the measures taken by the company to deal with the situation when it first arose and subsequently when the remains of the unfortunates were found.

Batten's statement did not dissipate the public feelings, at least with some of the people directly involved. Capt. Brian, who had returned to his home town of Kingston, returned to Port Arthur a few days later to mount another search of the island for his missing brother and the other crewmen (*Ft. William Daily Times Journal* June 22, 1928).

The final search for the bodies of the crew of *Kamloops* left June 23 for the wreck site. Capt. Brian, who organized the search, had little to say regarding the expedition other than that he had procured the participation of James Higgens of the Canadian Forestry Department to take charge of the actual operations in the woods and that he planned to be out with the party of seven men for six days.

When asked to explain his belief that there were bodies to be found in the woods, proving that some of the crew of the *Kamloops* reached shore alive, Capt. Brian said he needed nothing more than the recent official statement from the Canada Steamship Lines, wherein it was admitted that the body of Mate Henry Genest had been located 100 yards from shore under conditions which indicated that he had reached there alive (*Port Arthur News Chronicle* June 23, 1928).

Capt. Brian and the search party returned to Port Arthur after six days. Nothing was found to shed further light on the fate of the steamer and its crew (*Detroit Free Press* June 30, 1928).

An official crew list has never been located. Press reports of the number aboard included 20, 21, 22, 27 and 29; the most frequently cited totals for the crew were 20 and 22. A roster of 20 people was compiled from crew lists published in the *Port Arthur News Chronicle* on December 15, 1927, and again on June 6, 1928, and the *Fort William Daily Times Journal* of Dec. 15, 1927:

Captain William Brian, Toronto (Kingston)
First Mate Henry Genest, St. Thurbie
Second Mate J. Poitres, L'Islet
Watchman P. Lalonde, no address
Watchman J. Journeault, L'Islet
Wheelman Leon Laroche, St. Antoine
Wheelman Victor Latham, Sarnia
Deck Hand R. Tooley, Toronto
Deck Hand M. Mckay, Fort William
Deck Hand G. Gauthier, Quebec
Deck Hand A. Morton, Toronto
Chief Engineer J.A.C. Hawman, Collingwood
2nd Engineer R.E. Eashney (Dashney), Coldwater
Oiler Robert Owen, Toronto
Oiler Fred Brown, Collingwood
Fireman Andy Brown, Collingwood
Fireman Harry Wilson, Port Arthur
Fireman Sam Lamont, Phelpeston
Steward Netty (Jennet) Grafton, Southampton
Assistant Steward Alice Bettridge, Southhampton

There was no mention of the *Kamloops* tragedy in the press until the following year. In January it was reported that a note from one of *Kamloops'* crew had been found a month earlier. Louis Coutu, a trapper, found a bottle containing the note at the mouth of the Agawa River in Canada. The first news of the find reached Sault Ste. Marie by way of another trapper, who reported that the note said, "We are freezing to death." At first considered a ghastly hoax, the family of Alice Bettridge identified her writing on the note (*Detroit Free Press* Jan. 22, 1929; *The Evening Telegram* [Superior] Jan 22, 1929).

Coutu arrived in Sault Ste. Marie soon after the news of his discovery. At first he refused to divulge the contents of the note, saying "the people of the Sault don't give me anything for nothing. If they want something I've got, they can pay for it or go without." The trapper eventually did turn the note over to Capt. Brian. Brian took it to the parents of Alice Bettridge, who identified the writing as that of their daughter (*The Evening Telegram* [Superior] June 22, 1929).

Through the efforts of Thom Holden, the text of the Bettridge note has come to light from interviews with Alice Bettridge's relatives. In November 1976, two brothers, a sister and a sister-in-law were interviewed in Sarnia and Southhampton. Apparently the exact contents of the note were not published by the contemporary press. Surviving relatives of Alice Bettridge recalled the note saying, "I am the last one alive, freezing and starving on Isle Royale. I just want mom and dad to know my fate. Alice Bettridge." Present whereabouts of the note are unknown. Family members believe it no longer exists.

Discovery of *Kamloops*

The location of *Kamloops* remained one of the mysteries of Lake Superior until August 21, 1977. On that date Minneapolis sport diver Ken Engelbrecht spotted the dark shadow of the wreck during an exploratory dive searching for *Kamloops*. Engelbrecht, along with dive partner Randy Saulter of Mounds View, was carrying out a systematic search in the area known as Twelve O'Clock Point. The dive team had been directed to the possible site of the wreck by Roy Oberg, captain of the *Voyageur II*. Oberg had made a fathometer tracing several years earlier in the area that indicated a shipwreck lying on its side (Press release by Ken Engelbrecht and Thom Holden, 1977).

The wreck was found while diving off Ken Merryman's boat *Heyboy* on the second day of the search. On earlier dives, bits of cargo, such as a brass barrel and a ladder, were sighted. Then, "enough pipe to fill a semi-truck." On the last dive of the weekend, Engelbrecht, at a depth of 195 feet, "saw this really big shadow, the *Kamloops*, and this other shadow coming out of it, which was the flagpole. I got a really big rush and started trucking over there" (*Minneapolis Star* Oct. 13, 1977).

The next dives on the wreck were done September 5 and 6, 1977, but there was some doubt that the wreck was indeed *Kamloops*.

> The real proof, he [Ken Merryman] said, came after the second dive when pictures, on close inspection, showed the ship's name peeking out through the years of accumulated rust and underwater debris on the freighter's stern....

The wreck lies on a steep slope. The stern is toward shore,

about 195 feet below the surface at its shallowest point. One of the first things the divers check is the condition of the rudder and propeller; they seem to be intact.

The divers go to the back deck and examine a large wooden wheel. It's apparently an auxiliary steering wheel for emergencies, because the main steering equipment would be in the pilothouse near the bow of the ship....

They note that the glass in a skylight over the engine room is intact, snap some more pictures and move forward along the 250-foot ship....

They see other artifacts: The inside of a cabin, a string of new shoes to be sold in some Canadian store, a drum with steel cable neatly rolled on it, a running light that looks in good condition.

They can't make it to the pilothouse at the front – it's too deep. But they get about two-thirds of the way forward and they can see the pilothouse, with its top shorn off [its roof was found in the 1920's along with other debris].

The best theory about the sinking...according to Holden, is that the ship lost its steering and drifted at the mercy of the storm.

"It's quite possible that the final disaster occurred because of a massive ice buildup" on its deck caused by waves crashing on the freighter and freezing in the bitter cold, he added. He emphasized that the theory isn't proven....

Merryman said what they've been able to inspect of the ship bears that theory out. "All the other wrecks around Isle Royale have their bows smashed up and pointed to shore," Merryman says. The *Kamloops* has her stern to the shore and it's intact. The bow, 270 or more feet below the surface, retains its secret (*Minneapolis Star* Oct. 13, 1977).

Later dives by those and other divers add to what is known of the last moments of *Kamloops*. A party led by John Steele filmed the wreck in 1978. This expedition discovered that the engine telegraph was set at the "Finished With Engines" position, indicating that the engines may not have been operational at the time of sinking, or that the vessel was laid to before the disaster. Steele's party made the following speculations based on their observations:

> In the position of her last sighting and in the raging storm, a guy wire attached to the port side of *Kamloops'* stack snapped or tore free. The stack, no longer secure and positioned only by gravity, toppled to the starboard side shearing off the ventilators and crashing overboard breaking through the starboard railing atop the stern cabin.

> The coal-fired, forced-draft engine could not function without the stack. The crew was forced to "finish" the engines. If there had been power available, they would have been put on "Standby" not "Finished With Engines." *Kamloops'* power plant was shut down before she sank. With no power, she was at the mercy of the raging storm, and the northeast gales tossed and blew her toward Isle Royale.

> She hit Isle Royale broadside, smashing her starboard

bow. Temporarily, she remained fixed on the reef; quickly taking on water she rapidly sank bow first to rest at the foot of the reef.

The crew probably thought themselves safer aboard rather than facing the icy seas and subzero temperatures. They probably hoped she would remain foundered on the reef, leaving a potential for rescue. However, the opened cabin door may indicate a hasty departure of crew members as they realized their doom....The other 12 crew members probably remain trapped in the stern house, yet to be opened (Schuette 1979: 41).

Because of the hazards involved with conducting air dives to the depth of *Kamloops*, particularly in frigid water, a decision was made by the Submerged Cultural Resources Unit not to document the site using dives. In 1985 the opportunity to visit the site was offered by Michigan State University/Sea Grant using the sea link submarine from the Research Vessel *Seward Johnson*. *Seward Johnson* was not able to deploy over the site so the focus of their visit was turned to other research objectives. In 1986 a very successful mission was carried out on *Kamloops* using two miniaturized Remote Operated Vehicles. The latter was a joint venture of the National Park Service and National Geographic Society.

Dunelm: History

Construction

Dunelm was a steel package freighter built by the Sunderland Shipbuilding Company of Great Britain. The ship was registered at Sunderland, Official number 123950. The propeller was built in 1907 for Dunelm Ltd., also of Great Britain. Hull No. 246 had a keel length of 250 feet, beam of 43.2 feet and a depth of 23.5 feet and was built to pass through the Welland Canal. *Dunelm* was 2,319 gross tons and 1,481 net tons with a capacity of about 3,000 tons (*Toledo Blade* Dec. 8, 1910).

The British-built steamer was powered by a triple-expansion engine with cylinders of 19.5, 33 and 54 inches in diameter on a 36-inch stroke. The two Scotch boilers were 12.6 feet x 11.6 feet. The engine was built by Northeastern Marine Engine Works.

Dunelm, although never registered in Canada, was managed by James Playfair in association with the Canadian companies Richlieu & Ontario Navigation Company of Montreal, Quebec, and Inland Lines Ltd. of Hamilton, Ontario. In 1913 these were merged with Canada Steamship Lines Ltd.

There has been little research into the operational history of *Dunelm*, other than the incident that occurred at Isle Royale. It is known, however, that *Dunelm* was wrecked en route from Sidney, Nova Scotia, for England in 1915. The boat was primarily involved in the trading between the Canadian Lakehead and the lower Lake ports (from notes on file at the Institute for Great Lakes Research).

Wreck Event – Stranding at Isle Royale

Underwriters were notified on December 7, 1910, that the Inland Navigation Company package freighter *Dunelm*, downbound from Ft. William to Goderich, Ontario, with a load of wheat flour (*Toledo Blade* Dec. 10, 1910; Wreck Register, Record Group 12 Vol. 1007: 121), was ashore at Isle Royale. The first reports of the stranding were received in Port Arthur by wireless from the steamer *F.B. Squire;* apparently *Dunelm* was not equipped with a wireless (*Daily Mining Gazette* Dec. 9, 1910). The position of the stranding was first given as Blake Point near where *Monarch* was lost in 1906 (*Detroit Free Press* Dec. 8, 1910). *Dunelm*, like some other shipwrecks of Isle Royale, was wrecked on its last scheduled trip of the season.

The stranded vessel was reported in bad shape, and James Playfair summoned the Canadian Towing and Wrecking Company of Port Arthur to its aid. *Dunelm* was in command of Capt. C.R. Albinson, with J.A. Nicol as chief engineer and a crew of 18. The first reports gave no indication of whether there was loss of life (*Toledo Blade* Dec. 8, 1910).

The captain and 21 crew all arrived at Port Arthur on the afternoon of December 9 aboard the tug *Whalen,* with reports of the condition of their vessel. The wreckers had been driven away by heavy weather. The steamer was lost in a snowstorm while trying to get through Passage Island gap. Fourteen feet of water stood in the engine room, but the hull compartments were dry. "They report the steamer is resting easily on the rocks, but in an exposed and dangerous position should a heavy sea come up. The hull is badly punctured forward. The lighter *Empire* is standing by ready to start work" (*Detroit Free Press* Dec. 10, 1910).

The owners, after viewing *Dunelm*, gave up hope that the ship could be saved, and the wreck was abandoned to the underwriters on December 14. The value of the loss was placed at $100,000 (*Detroit Free Press* Dec. 15, 1910). The next day the underwriters announced they were taking salvage bids on a no-cure, no-pay basis (*Toledo Blade* Dec. 15, 1910). (In this account the captain of *Dunelm* is listed as Featherston.)

The Canadian Towing and Wrecking Company took the contract, and Capt. Morrison was put in charge of the operations. The work was carried out in the face of heavy waves that continually pounded the wreck. It was feared that the waves would push *Dunelm* off the reef's edge to sink in the 500-foot depths. (This report accurately gives the location of the wreck as Canoe Rock rather than Blake Point.) The weather grew colder and the salvage vessels became covered with ice, making the difficult salvage job that much harder. Some days nothing could be done, and at times the salvage efforts seemed hopeless (*Detroit Free Press* Dec. 21, 1910).

On December 21, Port Arthur received the wireless message that *Dunelm* had been freed and was safe at anchor in Duncan Harbor. The ship would be towed to Fort William and would be the first vessel to use the new dry-dock facilities that had just recently been completed. In the Dec. 21 account, *Dunelm*'s cargo was listed as general merchandise (*Detroit Free Press* Dec. 21, 1910; *Detroit Free Press* Dec. 29, 1910).

Sarah Moore Morrison, wife of Capt. Morrison's son Neil,

wrote the following poem commemorating the stranding and salvage of *Dunelm* (originally published in a book of poetry by Sarah Morrison titled *Scenes and Hours* [from notes in the Michigan Technological University Archives by Neil F. Morrison and published in the *Fort William Daily Times Journal* and *Nordic Diver*, Winter 1975.]

> At the head of navigation
> Of our Great Lakes waterway,
> Stand Port Arthur and Fort William
> Looking out to Thunder Bay.
>
> In the busy sailing season
> Vessels come, unload and fill,
> But they tie up for the winter
> When the ice-bound Lakes are still.

Figure 41. Package freighter *Dunelm* aground at Canoe Rocks, Isle Royale December 1910. U.S. Army Corps of Engineers Canal Park Marine Museum Collection.

> Yet one Christmas at Port Arthur
> People gathered at the quay:
> Why should they be there on Christmas –
> What was there for them to see?
>
> Bitter cold it was that morning
> When the *Dunelm* stood at dock.
> Salvaged after two weeks' effort,
> Stranded on a ledge of rock.
>
> Stranded where the Great Lakes' *Monarch*
> Met her doom some years before
> On Isle Royale in Lake Superior,
> Broke in two, sank aft and fore.

> On her last trip of the season
> And her last forever more.
> But the *Dunelm* held together,
> She was floated, towed to shore.
>
> And the people hailed her gladly,
> And they hailed the rescue crew,
> Glad to have them home for Christmas,
> After all they had been through.
>
> In the cold and stormy weather
> They had stayed when hope was slight,
> They had worked with skill and patience,
> They had laboured day and night.

> Sheathed with ice the rescued freighter
> Had a dignity new born;
> She looked stately at her moorings
> On that clear, cold Christmas morn.

Figure 42. *Dunelm* under tow after release from the stranding at Canoe Rocks. U.S. Army Corps of Engineers Canal Park Marine Museum Collection.

Chapter V

Shipwrecks of Isle Royale: Archeological Record

This chapter consists of a series of analytical descriptions of each of the principal shipwreck sites at Isle Royale. For each site a depiction of the remains on the Lake bottom is developed through graphics and narratives. Empirical observations in the narrative are interspersed with references to those aspects of the historical record that most influenced our approach to data recovery in the field. The best way to understand any preconceptions held by this research team in its interpretation of the archeological record is to read, in its entirety, the historical record section of this report, which identifies all of the archival elements thought pertinent to the archeological analysis and site interpretation.

The historical record has been isolated to this chapter to emphasize an overall philosophical approach to Historical Archeology. Archives and oral accounts were used to establish that major wreck events had occurred and to indicate contemporary notions about what happened and why. A chain of evidence was then developed to support a constantly evolving explanation for how each ship was transformed into an archeological site due to the wreck event and subsequent post-depositional processes, whether natural or cultural in nature.

In each case, the archeological record is seen as the hard evidence that confirmed, controverted or augmented the historical record. In many instances, on-site observation also suggested new areas of inquiry. Establishing a range of expectations from the written and oral traditions enabled identification of more fruitful lines of inquiry much quicker than would have been possible in a totally inductive framework. Generic and specific research questions are explicitly stated in the research design section of this report (Chapter I). The analyses presented address most of those questions and in all cases were guided by them.

The amount of time devoted in the field to each site varied dependent upon several factors. The intact vessels, for the most part, received less attention than the ones that were broken and scattered. In a dispersed wreckage field the archeological record requires more explaining; i.e. more discussion is necessary to establish the identity of each piece of vessel fabric. The more intact the wreck, the less time needed to ascribe function or significance to specific pieces of structure or machinery.

Additionally, in the decision-making process about time allocations in the field, more weight was given to those sites representing vessels without plans and to the older wooden vessels, which, coincidentally, ended up being the same ships. Also, wood usually breaks in discrete units and individual components retain much of their original form, much like pieces of a jigsaw puzzle. In contrast, steel plates in a high-energy site buckle, fold and adopt shapes that are generally irrelevant to the process of archeological reconstruction. Consequently, more latitude was given to the illustrators in portraying fine details of dispersed metal wreckage than dispersed wooden pieces. One may expect, therefore, that the details in the portrayal of the twisted structural remains of *Glenlyon*, for example, may not match the level of accuracy inherent in drawings of *Chisholm, Cumberland* and *Monarch*. In the case of *Algoma*, a decision was made to document only a representative sample of the wreckage fields, because it would have been extremely expensive and time consuming to produce a high-resolution map of this widely scattered site, much of which lies in deep water.

As with all archeological endeavors, the provenience of the material remains and the judgment of the researchers determine where "sites" begin and end. For this report, artifactual material that was spatially continuous or contiguous was seen as composing one site, regardless of the nature of the cultural material itself. Consequently, the wrecks of *Cumberland* and *Chisholm* are treated as one site because their remains overlap spatially on the Lake bottom. These two ships are, of course, treated separately in the historical record chapter (IV). *Emperor* and *Dunelm* are also treated as one site for the same reason; it is only the analysis of the remains that ascribes separate identities to the wreckage of *Emperor* as opposed to the nearby anchors and other residues attributable to the *Dunelm* stranding event. The latter event did not end in complete loss of the vessel, but did result in a limited amount of material residues.

The one exception to the rule in the manner in which sites were defined for this presentation is in the treatment of a piece of ship structure located off Cumberland Point several miles from the main concentrations of *Cumberland* wreckage. There is compelling evidence that this piece of structure is indeed a portion of

Figure 43. Members of the NPS/National Geographic Society survey team drop an ROV unit into Lake Superior from aboard the *Beaver* near the wreck site of the *Kamloops*. NPS photo by Ann Belleman.

119

Figure 44. Preparing for surface-supplied video dive. NPS archeologist Toni Carrell is in diving helmet, assisted by Larry Murphy. NPS photo by Daniel Lenihan.

Figure 45. Toni Carrell reads the printout of the side-scan sonar unit. NPS photo.

Figure 46. Two NPS divers use baseline trilateration techniques to retrieve data from an Isle Royale wreck site. NPS photo.

Figure 47. District Ranger Jay Wells prepares a line for mooring a buoy to a wreck site for the use of visiting recreational divers. NPS photo by Daniel Lenihan.

Figure 48. Underwater investigators were equipped with scuba gear, measuring instruments, drawing materials and individual lighting units. During early years of the project (1980-83), NPS divers used cumbersome surface-monitored black-and-white video and full face masks. NPS photo by Daniel Lenihan.

Figure 49. In 1986, the British Broadcasting Corporation (BBC) filmed SCRU team operations at various wreck sites in Isle Royale National Park. Footage was eventually used in the popular "Discoveries Underwater" documentary series. NPS photo by Larry Murphy.

Figure 50. ROV unit investigates the *Kamloops* wreck site during its 1986 operation. ROV photo by Emory Kristof courtesy of National Geographic Society.

Figure 51. Keith Moorehead of National Geographic Society and Wayne Bywater of Northeastern Underwater Services with ROV units on deck at Rock Harbor. NPS photo by Ann Belleman.

Figure 52. Beam knees and shelves of the *Chisholm*. NPS photo by Larry Murphy.

Figure 53. NPS diver swims past the boiler of the *Cumberland*. NPS photo.

Figrwue 54. NPS archeologist Toni Carrell over segment of paddle wheel from the *Cumberland*. NPS photo by John Brooks.

Cumberland, which was deposited there after the wreck event, and because it was convenient from an organizational point of view, it was included as part of the *Cumberland/Chisholm* site description. In all, this section will include nine site descriptions encompassing 11 separate shipwreck events.

Observations

Although the specific problems identified for each site in the research design are addressed in the context of the individual site discussions in this chapter, there are some observations that can be made related to issues identified in the general problem statement.

First, the material remains of vessels at Isle Royale give the impression of industrial intensity even more than is indicated in the historical record. There is little in the way of recreational vessels or vessels designed solely for passenger excursions represented in either the major shipwreck population or the number of small craft wrecks, which are primarily fish tugs. This is not necessarily compatible with expectations because there was significant resort-oriented activity at Isle Royale as evidenced from examination of land-based sites and the historical record.

Regarding the role that Isle Royale played in Lake Superior navigational history: it is clear that it was more than just that of a natural obstacle to shipping. At least one of the major shipwrecks (*America*) was intimately tied to the island, and many of the smaller wrecks were tied to fishing or support activities of the island population. Resource extraction was a major motive for prehistoric and historical human activity in the area followed temporally by recreation and leisure values that eventually predominated, resulting in the island becoming a national park.

The number of modern wrecks associated with the bulk trades is remarkable. It is rare to work in an area in which there is such a disproportionate amount of post-1900 shipwrecks. Even considering the shorter history of maritime activity compared to the Atlantic seaboard, for example, the fact that there are no known shipwreck sites representing sailing vessels would not be predictable from the historical record alone. This disparity is additionally noteworthy when one considers that steam vessels had much greater flexibility in coping with navigational problems associated with shipping environments with limited sea room; i.e. they could maneuver without dependency on wind conditions. If one were only to use the visual remains at Isle Royale and never open a book or visit an archival collection, the impression would be one of steam mayhem. It would suggest to the viewer that something about the nature of steam applications on Lake Superior (perhaps differential capital investment from that associated with sail) was resulting in increased risk-taking ventures than under sail. The preponderance of steam vessels could also be the result of the formation of shipping lanes after the decline of sailing vessels. It is not at all clear that this situation is replicated on the eastern and western U.S. seaboards. In Florida, California, Cape Cod and numerous other areas investigated by this research team, it would be extremely unusual to have no sailing vessels represented in a shipwreck population of 10 major vessels. Even if the answer is that "they haven't been found yet" at Isle Royale, it is still noteworthy that the first 10 located are all steam, and it is unlikely that a comparable population of sailing vessels has thus far escaped detection.

Some other general observations derived from examination of the material record has to do with post-depositional processes. The lack of superstructural remains from the vessels is notable, as is the fact that in all the 10 complete major losses at Isle Royale, including the "intact" sites, the pilothouse remains in place only on *Congdon*. This would not have been predicted before examining the sites. Although it is understandable that lighter structural remains would be less well-represented in the archeological record than the heavy hull components, it is surprising that in a fine preservation medium such as cold, fresh water, almost nothing related to superstructure remains. The lesson this leaves the viewer with is that superstructure, which is the least well documented part of a vessel in construction plans, is also going to be the least well-represented under water. It is also the part of the ship that is the most dynamic in an architectural sense, because it changed the most over time. These modifications are, of course, the signatures of adaptive behavior to meet exigencies of social change and vessel use. The ability to compare the modifications against the original intent, for function and form evident in the hull construction, is what is lost when one loses superstructural remains.

Another general observation that can be made is that wooden vessels of the construction dates as represented at Isle Royale (1871-1890) tend to break apart in a very predictable fashion. They disarticulate along the turn of the bilge into fairly large discrete units. The point of greatest variability in the wreck process on the hull of the vessel is the bow, which is not well represented in any of the three wooden ships wrecked at Isle Royale.

There is much to suggest from the individual site analyses in this chapter that ice damage is a significant factor in the site-formation process, preceded only by the short period immediately following the wreck event in which the ship is often in a high-energy zone, and by those processes which can be related to human activity – "C transforms" in the sense of Schiffer (1976: 12-19).

There are two points at Isle Royale where there is a clustering effect for shipwrecks. One is Canoe Rocks and the other is Rock of Ages. It is not surprising that ships tended to pile up in these areas because they represent points where either course changes were taking place, or that a vessel was at most risk just prior to making a course change to avoid Isle Royale. The composition of the concentration at Canoe Rocks, however, has implications for understanding the economic dynamics of the period of vessel losses.

All the shipwrecks in the vicinity of Canoe Rocks were downbound from Port Arthur or Fort William. The locations, time of loss, cargo and type of vessel closely fit the model of Lake Superior shipwreck distribution developed by Hulse (1981).

The spatial distribution model of Hulse links site location to transportation, rather than settlement. The model reflects the cultural history generally and the transportation industry specifically. The shipping industry was structured by trade routes, industrial development and the physical environment. Hulse demonstrated that shipping is a non-random, culturally patterned phenomenon, and consequently shipwrecks will similarly be patterned and non-random in their distribution (Hulse 1981: 2).

The typical downbound navigation route from Port Arthur and Fort William contains four course changes after leaving Thunder Bay. The first two are made to avoid Isle Royale. The first course change is made at the mouth of Thunder Bay as Pie Island and Thunder Cape are passed. This course alteration aims the vessel directly for Passage Island, the shortest route around the north end of Isle Royale. Navigational errors in setting and maintaining this course contributed directly to the Canoe Rocks and vicinity wrecks. The second alteration occurs immediately after clearing Passage Island and corrects for the shortest course to Whitefish Point. The construction of the lighthouse on Passage Island in 1882 greatly diminished the potential for wreck occurrence at the second course change; consequently, there are no known wrecks after that date in the area.

The known sites on Canoe Rocks reflect the heavy bulk traffic of the late-19th to mid-20th century. The shipwrecks of Canoe Rocks – *Emperor, Congdon, Dunelm* as well as *Monarch* (wrecked on The Palisades just in-shore of Canoe Rocks) – were all carrying Canadian cargoes, and all but *Congdon* were Canadian vessels. The location of these wrecks reflects the growth of Canadian freight trades, primarily iron ore and grain.

Canadian grain production moved westward in a similar pattern as that of the United States (see Chapter III). Port Arthur and Fort William, Ontario, became the major Canadian ports on Lake Superior soon after the completion of the Canadian Pacific Railway, which connected Port Arthur with Winnipeg in 1883. Prior to this date, most Canadian grain was shipped out of Duluth.

Continued settlement of the Canadian Northwest and the growth of grain production was ensured by the construction of additional raillines. Port Arthur and Fort William were the principal grain shipping ports of Canada until about 1920. These ports diminished in importance as a result of the development of the Pacific coast route, becoming a viable alternative to the Lakes route after the completion of the Panama Canal in 1914. Port Arthur and Fort William, however, remained important grain exporting ports well into the mid-20th century (Nute 1944: 140, 316). *Monarch* (1890-1906) carried grain, flour and package freight on its last voyage. *Congdon* (1907-1918) was loaded with wheat when it was wrecked. *Dunelm*, stranded in 1910, carried a load of wheat flour.

Iron ore shipped from Lake Superior's Canadian Superior port cities never reached the magnitude shipped from the American ports. Ore bodies comparable in size to those on the south shore of the Lake were not discovered on the north shore. The source of iron ore shipped out of Port Arthur and Fort William was the Steep Rock mine west of Port Arthur in the Atikokan district. The mine was discovered just before 1940; mining operations began in 1942 after the Steep Rock Lake was drained. A new ore dock was built at Port Arthur for the trade (Nute 1944: 155-6). *Emperor*, sunk in 1947, was carrying 10,000 tons of Steep Rock Mine ore.

The other principal export of the Canadian Lakehead was lumber. There are no wrecks currently known on the north side of Isle Royale with a load of lumber. Basing a prediction on the pattern of ship loss that develops from those in the vicinity of Canoe Rocks, it is likely that one exists, yet to be discovered.

Algoma and *Kamloops*, vessels wrecked well away from either end of the island, were the result of severe storm activity and possibly equipment failure in the case of *Kamloops*. *Glenlyon* was wrecked while seeking shelter from a storm. Outside of the attributes of cargo and general location, the final position of these ships could not have been predicted from the distribution model.

On the south end there also is a concentration of shipwrecks. Three vessels are wrecked in close proximity over a period of 44 years. *Cumberland* and *Cox* wrecked on Rock of Ages while downbound from Canadian ports to Duluth/Superior. Because of participation in the passenger/package trade on the north shore, their final location could have been anticipated. *Chisholm*, in contrast, was a bulk freighter that had left Duluth downbound with a cargo of grain for Buffalo. The ship was caught in a storm and released its tow, which was a schooner carrying a cargo of lumber. *Chisholm* was lost as a result of navigation error while searching for its consort around the south end of Isle Royale. Its location could not have been anticipated by the generally accurate shipwreck distribution model of Hulse. Some shipwrecks occur as a result of activity not anticipated in a general distribution model.

Cumberland/ Chisholm: Site Description and Analysis

Site Location

The wrecks *Cumberland, Chisholm* and *Cox* are on a shallow reef southwest of Rock of Ages lighthouse on the south end of Isle Royale. The vessels are within a square, 3,000-feet on a side, with its geographic center at 47°51'28"N and 89°19'32"W. The center is 3.9 statute miles from the starboard-hand nun buoy at Cumberland Point on a true bearing of 275 degrees. It is 336 degrees true from the starboard-hand nun buoy southwest of Rock of Ages lighthouse and 222 degrees from the lighthouse, a distance of 4,000 feet (useful for chart plot). On site location is best from North Rock: the site is 258 degrees true, 2.4 statute miles from the rock.

Site Description

The wreckage of *Cumberland* and *Henry Chisholm* are intermingled near the lighthouse at Rock of Ages reef. They represent two wreck events separated by 21 years, but because their remains overlap on the Lake bottom, they will be treated as one site in the archeological record. The historical background of these vessels leading up to the wreck events is presented in detail in Chapter IV.

In addition to providing a remarkable museum-like exhibit on

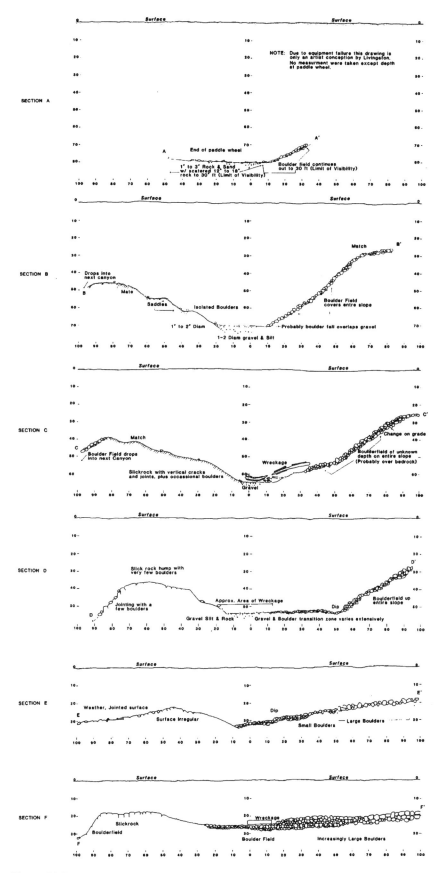

Figure 55. Environmental cross section of the *Cumberland/Chisholm* site. Data gathered by NPS archeologists Larry Nordby and Jim Bradford. Drawing by Ernesto Martinez.

late-19th century wooden vessel construction, the *Cumberland/Chisholm* remains, when closely examined, reveal much about both wreck events and the subsequent post-depositional processes. First impressions of this site by divers have been characterized by phrases such as "mass confusion" and "huge jumble of timbers." What at first appears to be a hopeless jigsaw puzzle makes good sense, however, when attributes peculiar to each vessel are discerned, and the whole is reduced to manageable size on paper. Given the constraints of underwater visibility and the large size of the site, divers can never see more than a small fraction of the wreckage at one time. This makes accurate mapping critical to obtaining an understanding of the site.

It is apparent from a brief perusal of the site map in Figure 65 that the two vessels comprising the site are broken into several large, discrete units. Most of these structural elements are spread through a single underwater ravine that ranges in depth from 20 to 80 feet. The exceptions are the rudder of *Chisholm* located part way down the reef, the portion of hull on which the *Chisholm* engine rests (V) in 140 feet of water and a disarticulated piece of hull (IV) that lies next to it at 150 feet of depth. These latter pieces are at the bottom of a drop-off that fringes the rock reef that in turn surrounds the main wreckage field in shallow water. To gain a perspective on the site in its general environmental context, Figure 55 has been provided.

Attributing these various hull sections to one vessel or the other becomes easier when several selective factors are recognized. The most remarkable contrast between the remains of the two vessels is size. The following table is a general comparison of the two vessels as built:

Table 4 – *Cumberland/Chisholm* Comparison

Dates	Gross Tons	Length	Beam	Depth
Chisholm				
1880-98	1775.3	256.5	39.3	20.3
Cumberland				
1871-77	629	204	26	10.7

Although both vessels had two decks, *Cumberland* was a side-wheeler, and *Chisholm* was a propeller-driven bulk freighter (see Figure 56). The length to depth ratios are: *Cumberland* 1: 19; *Chisholm* 1: 12.6. The length to beam ratio for *Cumberland* is 1: 7.8, indicating a long, narrow hull configuration when compared to the beamier *Chisholm*, with a ratio of 1: 6.5.

129

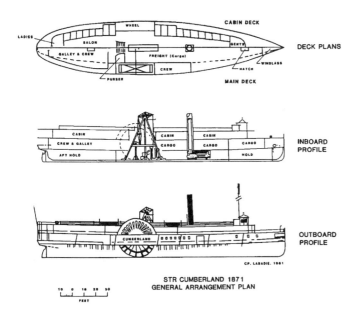

Figure 56. Conjectural general arrangement plans of *Cumberland*. Drawings by C. Patrick Labadie.

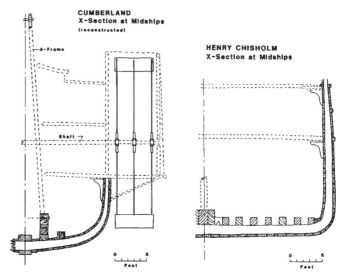

Figure 57. Comparative midship cross sections. Drawings by C. Patrick Labadie.

The higher ratio of *Cumberland* reflects the desire for speed in the passenger trade. *Cumberland* probably would have drawn about six feet of water and *Chisholm* 12 to 14 feet.

The comparison of the documented dimensions of the two vessels indicates that the scantlings of *Chisholm* would be significantly larger than those of *Cumberland*. This observation was supported by the examination of the wreck remains on the site. The remains of the two vessels could be separated on the basis of the single attribute of size alone. The remains of *Chisholm* are massive compared to *Cumberland* (Figure 57).

Cumberland remains are characterized by split frames that were employed in the construction process (Figures 58, 59, 60). The futtocks are separated by a spacer block and are quite distinctive. *Chisholm*, in contrast, had the more common solid, triple-futtock framing from the keel to the turn of the bilge (Figure 63), double futtocks from there to the weather deck and a single-frame timber that continued up to become a stanchion of the bulwark. At all points in the hull, this style of construction can be easily distinguished from the split frames and associated architectural attributes of *Cumberland*'s wreckage.

Another useful diagnostic element is the diagonal strapping that was used to provide longitudinal hull support in *Chisholm*. At any point where the broken hull sections expose the interface between the molded face of the frames

and outboard planking on the side of the hull, this metal strapping is evident. The strapping intersects itself at 90 degrees and forms a sort of rigid steel basket weave over the hull side augmenting the longitudinal strength of *Henry Chisholm*. No comparable feature exists on the *Cumberland* hull pieces. In its stead, the builders of the latter vessel used an unusual arch support that is built into its ceiling plank layout to deal with the common problems of sagging and hogging in large wooden ships (Figures 59, 60). Truss rods provided the transverse sup-

Figure 58. Structural elements related to stern of *Cumberland*. Note split-frame construction with separated futtocks on the central segment. These pieces are outboard side up. NPS photo by Larry Murphy.

Figure 59. Hull structure of *Cumberland*. Note that a structural arch for longitudinal support was built into the ceiling planking. NPS photo by Larry Murphy.

port needed to cope with the special problem of wheel guard sag in side-wheelers and evidently formed part of the longitudinal support system as well.

In some cases, the task of separating out hull pieces was greatly facilitated because enough of a particular section was intact that two rows of vertical or "hanging" knees were evident, indicating the piece was part of *Chisholm* (Figures 64, 66). The knees on *Cumberland* were sawn and elongated (dagger knees), whereas the larger knees of *Chisholm* are natural (i.e. made from "compass" timber) and noticeably broad.

That some third, undocumented wreck also occurred at this site is a possibility that must be addressed in this discussion, but one that can be quickly dismissed. The same thematic traits in construction that permit distinguishing these ships from each other also indicate that they are the only two vessels represented in the wreckage field. This becomes a certainty beyond reasonable doubt when we fit the pieces together on paper and find

that we are left with no duplication of parts in the final picture, nor any elements not readily attributed to either vessel.

Cumberland's remains are evident in the northern part of the ravine where they trail off into deeper water. *Chisholm* dominates the southern portion of the ravine and slightly overlaps *Cumberland* (Figure 65). None of the wreckage in the deep water where *Chisholm*'s engine is located can be attributed to *Cumberland*.

When all the hull sections making up the site are sorted and

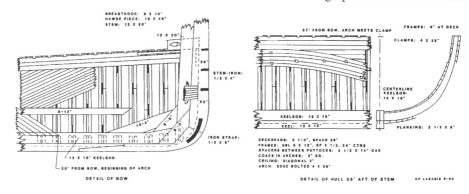

Figure 60. Port bow structure of *Cumberland* found at the entrance to Grace Harbor. Drawing by C. Patrick Labadie.

Figrure 61. *Chisholm* engine at depth of 140 feet. NPS photo by John Brooks.

Figure 62. Archeologist Larry Murphy examining propeller of *Henry Chisholm*. NPS photo by John Brooks.

reconstituted into their original form as two ships, several other observations can be made. The most intriguing is the fact that much of *Cumberland* is not represented on the site. What had seemed an endless field of shipwreck remains does not in fact represent the two vessels in their entirety. Also, as is typical of all the wrecks of Isle Royale, little of the superstructure of either vessel is present on the site.

A comparison of the reconstituted *Chisholm* to the original ship shows that approximately 50 feet of the port side of the hull is missing, mostly from the bow area. All of the rest of the vessel is represented with the glaring exception of part of the bow and all of the superstructure. Similarly, no significant portion of *Cumberland*'s superstructure is evident on the site, but, unlike *Chisholm*, a very significant portion of its hull is also absent.

Once the initial separation of the remains on the basis of size was completed, researchers turned their attention to a compari-

Figure 63. Hull bottom remains of *Henry Chisholm*. Centerline keelson is on the right and bilge keelson and broken paired vertical frames on the left. NPS photo by Larry Murphy.

Figure 64. View of main and spar deck beam knees and shelves of *Chisholm*. Note their large size compared with the structure of *Cumberland*. NPS photo by Larry Murphy.

son of individual components. The components were approached in categories, such as propulsion elements, auxiliary machinery, hull architecture, cargo handling machinery, superstructure and cargo. The latter categories of cargo and superstructure were of no assistance, because no superstructure attributable to either vessel could be located and no evidence of cargo was observed.

Propulsion elements

Propulsion elements, particularly engines and boilers, could be easily separated. The vessels had distinctive propulsion machinery: *Chisholm* was a screw steamer, powered by a compound engine and Scotch boilers (Figure 68), whereas *Cumberland* was a side-wheeler powered by a walking beam engine and firebox boiler (Figures 56, 67). Although the specific type of boiler was not historically documented for *Cumberland*, it could not have been a Scotch type. Scotch boilers appeared on the Lakes after the loss of *Cumberland*. It is unlikely that propulsion elements of the two vessels could be confused.

The compound engine of *Chisholm* was located intact in 150 feet of water sitting upright on its mounts within the detached stern portion of the wreck (Figures 61, 69). An examination of the structure related to the stern portion revealed the unmistakable characteristic hull architecture of *Chisholm*. A comparison of the shallower remains with those found with the engine of *Chisholm* allowed quick separation of the two wrecks based on scantling size and construction technique. This would have allowed the separation of the two wrecks even in the absence of historical documentation of their dimensions.

The steam plant of *Chisholm* presents a unique opportunity to study an example of Great Lakes technology in a formative

stage. The engine is still connected to the shaft and screw, much like it might be arranged in a museum display. It is a double-expansion, inverted, vertical, direct-acting steam engine with

Figure 65. Main and spar deck beam knees and shelves of *Chisholm*. NPS photo by Larry Murphy.

cylinders of 30 and 56 inches in diameter and a 48-inch stroke. The two cylinders pushed the *Chisholm* at almost 9 knots.

The engine, number 128, was built in Cleveland by Globe Iron Works the same year as the hull. Upon examination, one is struck by the ornate quality of the steam jacket around the cylinders, which contains wrought iron borders and diamond designs in the center of each cover. The engine cylinders are mounted on top of iron supports cast in the shape of columns. The supports between the columns are in the shape of circles.

This is the earliest steam engine extant of the Isle Royale shipwrecks, and its ornate embellishments reflect a time when the designers of steam engines were concerned with both func-

tion and aesthetics. (A discussion of the cultural context of machinery decoration in the Eighteenth and Nineteenth Centuries relevant to the interpretation of the steam engines of Isle Royale can be found in Kasson 1976.) None of the other engines of the ships of Isle Royale shows the same regard for aesthetics on the part of the designers. In other wrecks, e.g. *America*, the embellishments have been executed by the men who used the machines, rather than the designers.

Chisholm's propeller has four blades; the two lower ones are broken (Figure 62). It is uncertain if the blades were broken as a result of the initial wreck event or the trip down the slope after the stern section separated. It is most likely that the two lower blades were broken as the stern settled. The first historical accounts of the wreck indicated that the bow was aground with the stern over deep water. The break up of the wreck occurred as the stranded vessel was buffeted by two storms in quick succession (*Detroit Free Press* Oct. 26, 27, 1898, see Chapter IV).

The propeller shafts and shaft log are in their normal position. The tail shaft is flanged to a thrust shaft. The thrust shaft has a single collar that articulates with the thrust bearing mounted on a pillow (or plummer) block, which is tied into the centerline keelson. The single-collar thrust bearing was sufficient for the relatively low rpm of *Chisholm*'s engine (Figure 69). Multiple-collar bearings came into use later to dissipate the increased thrust and friction of the more powerful triple-expansion engines and larger hulls. A typical example of the multiple-collar thrust bearing may be seen on the shaft of *Glenlyon* (Figure 95).

Figure 67. Firebox boiler similar to that on site from *Cumberland*, which did not have a steam drum as depicted in this illustration. U.S. Army Corps of Engineers Canal Park Marine Museum Collection.

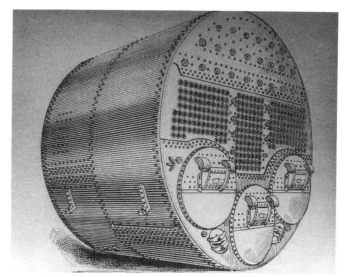

Figure 68. Single ended "Scotch" boiler similar to those carried on the other Isle Royale vessels. U.S. Army Corps of Engineers Canal Park Marine Museum Collection.

The rudder of *Chisholm* (Figure 71) is in 70 feet of water immediately upslope from the engine. The visible steering chain is attached through a block to one of the two tiller arms on the rudder stock.

The rudder is typical of those fitted to contemporary wooden propeller-driven vessels. Figure 70 shows the position and attachment of the rudder on a similarly constructed bulk freighter of the period. The rudder is not hinged on a gudgeon and pintle arrangement common in earlier vessels, but rather, the rudder stock is suspended from a rudder carrier that is inboard of the horn timber. The lower end of the rudder stock rests and pivots on the rudder shoe. The rudder shoe is a flat, iron casting attached to the underside of the keel extending about four frames forward of the stern post, and aft beyond the screw to support the base of the rudder.

Chisholm had two iron rods extending from the horn timber as additional support for the rudder and shaft. One rod was attached to the lower side of the horn timber positioned aft of the screw and forward of the rudder. This rod, which supported the aft end of the rudder shoe, is not depicted in the example of Figure 70.

A second iron rod extending from the horn timber terminates at the aft end of the shaft log forward of the screw. This rod appears to be adjustable and was apparently used to relieve the tension of the bearing on the shaft.

Examination of the sternpost directly beneath the horn timber revealed Roman numeral depth marks. Numerals XII and XIII were on the upper edge of the sternpost. The numeral XIV was split between the sternpost and horn timber (Figure 72).

Portions of side-wheels were located on the other end of the site from the *Chisholm* engine (Figure 65). Obviously related to *Cumberland*, they indicated that wreckage scatter from this vessel lies generally to the north. A boiler and condenser were located between the paddle wheel fragments and the concentration of hull remains. The boiler and engine cylinder, which still remains in the hull of *Cumberland*, are separated by a distance of 270 feet. In the immediate area of the boiler there was also a piece of particularly heavy structure, which could be a portion of reinforced deck below the boiler.

Propulsion elements of *Cumberland* are spread along a distance of more than 400 feet. There are paddle wheels in 80 feet of water at a distance of 300 feet from the engine cylinder. A paddle wheel flange and three radii (or paddle wheel arms) are located on the hull side of *Chisholm* 135 feet in the opposite direction from the *Cumberland* engine cylinder (Section IV, Figure 65).

The paddle wheel segments (Figure 73) are connected to a cast-iron flange that forms the hub. The paddle wheels had an outer and inner circle or rim of wood (square) connecting and strengthening the paddle wheel arms or radii. The paddle arms were separated by 4-inch square blocks 2 feet 10 inches long behind the outer rim. The rim strengthened the outer circumference of the wheel at the edge of the floats.

The inner rim, 2 feet 6 inches below the outer rim where the buckets (or floats) were attached, was made of wood with a circle both on the inside and outside of the arms. There was no evidence of iron reinforcement on the circles of the paddle wheels of *Cumberland* as would be typical of western river practice – a reflection of the lack of floating obstructions on the Lakes that frequently damaged the western river paddle wheels.

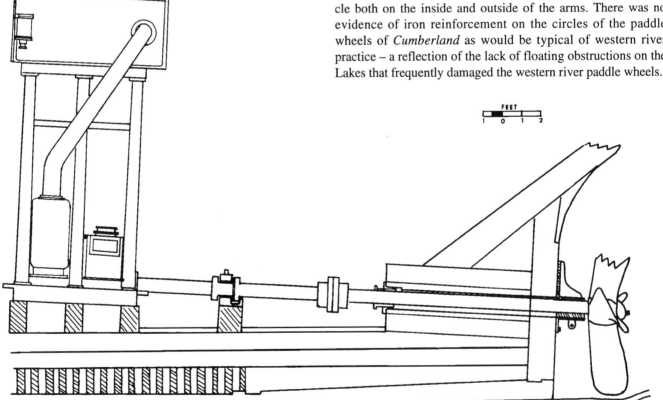

Figure 69. Tracing from 1881 plans of *Massachusetts*, a vessel very similar to *Chisholm*. The drawing corresponds to the remains of *Chisholm* in 140 feet of water.

The paddle floats were attached to the arms by three iron through-bolts. The dimensions of the extant floats or buckets are 1 feet 8 inches x 1 inch, and 7 feet long. A section of paddle wheel was located at a depth of 82 feet with buckets still attached (Figure 65).

Western river steamboat buckets were most often attached by an iron "U" rod or stirrup that bent around the arm and bolted through the bucket planks. This variation may be the result of the different environmental conditions of the Lakes and western rivers. The western river steamboat frequently damaged paddle wheel buckets on floating debris, and quick replacement was necessary. The U-bolt assembly practice allows quicker replacement, although it might not be as strong as the Lakes through-bolt attachment. The Lake paddle wheels were stronger in the buckets and weaker in the arms than the western river vessels. The western river practice strengthened the arms (the most difficult element to replace) and considered the bucket expendable.

The paddle wheels of *Cumberland* were estimated to be 26 feet in diameter. The arms are 12 feet long from the hub to the outer rim. A contemporary newspaper report gives the diameter of *Cumberland*'s paddle wheels as 30 feet (*Detroit Free Press* Oct. 4, 1871). The field observation estimate was based on the length of the arms attached to a partial flange. Given the 12-foot paddle wheel arm length, the complete flange would have had to be six feet in diameter to conform to the historical dimensions, which is unlikely. The contemporary diameter may have included the paddle wheel boxes in the 30-foot measurement.

The boiler on the site (Figure 74) is from *Cumberland*; of this there can be little doubt based on both archeological and historical evidence. The boiler is in proximity to the paddle wheels and quite removed from the engine of *Chisholm*. An explanation would have to be developed to account for the movement

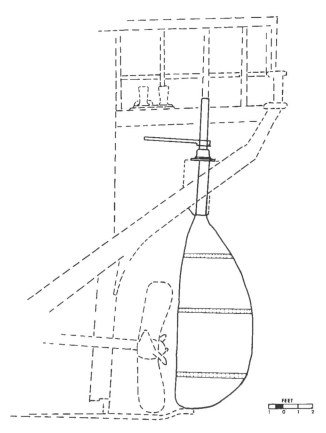

Figure 70. Arrangement of rudder from *Massachusetts* plans. The rudder and support is similar to that of *Chisholm*.

of the mostly rectangular boiler far from where it would have been located if it had been part of *Chisholm*. The possibility that another vessel could have deposited the firebox type boiler can be dismissed: there were no structural remains located that did not conform to either of the two vessels.

Historical evidence also supports *Cumberland* as the origin of the firebox boiler, although the records of what type boiler *Cumberland* carried and whether they were salvaged have not been located. A rectangular, multitubular firebox boiler would be expected on *Cumberland*. Firebox boilers were used extensively after 1850 on walking beam side-wheelers. Beam engines normally operated with less than 50 pounds of pressure, the pressure normally produced by a fire box boiler. Compound engines required 100 pounds of pressure or more, considerably in excess of the normal capabilities of a firebox boiler of the type located on site. Historical documentation indicates that *Chisholm* carried Scotch boilers at the time of

Figure 71. Rudder of *Henry Chisholm* at Rock of Ages Reef. NPS photo by Dan Lenihan.

loss and they were salvaged in 1901 (See Chapter IV).

The elements of propulsion other than the boilers located in the shallow area of the site can be attributed to *Cumberland*. The pressure vessel in the vicinity of the boiler appears to be a surface condenser, the type recorded for *Cumberland*, and of a size too small for the engine of *Chisholm*. Surface condensation came into general use in 1860 and resulted in a reduction in fuel consumption when coupled with higher steam pressures. A first-class vessel, built in the early 1870s like *Cumberland*, would generally have carried a surface condenser to reduce operating costs in the highly competitive passenger/package trade.

An iron cylinder 36 inches in diameter and about 4 feet long was also located near the largest concentration of *Cumberland* hull remains. This is much too small to be the main cylinder (*Cumberland*'s engine was 44 inches in diameter with an 11-foot stroke); it is probably the air pump.

Underneath the inverted main hull section of *Cumberland* (CU Bottom, Figure 65), the bottom of the main cylinder was located. The bottom of this feature can be viewed through a break in the hull planks. Nearby, mounted on the bottom of the hull, is a rectangular feature that contains a lobed shaft (resembling a modern gas engine cam shaft) of uncertain function. This may have been a part of the mechanism for operating engine and pump valves.

The last elements related to ship propulsion located on the site were the tops of the A-frames (Figure 75). The A-frames were wooden timbers, heavily fastened with iron, constructed in an A shape to support the overhead shaft or trunnion of the walking beam (Figure 56). The two A-frame tops were broken off just below the apex of the frame. Both fragments contain the walking beam shaft bearing.

The missing machinery of *Cumberland* presents a bit of a problem. No other fragments of the main cylinder, steam chest, walking beam, crank shaft, lifting and connecting rods, piping, boiler breeching or stack have been located. It is likely that most of the portable artifacts have been removed by divers, but the larger machinery that is missing is puzzling. Perhaps some of it could have been removed by the salvors when they were working on *Chisholm*, but the question remains as to why they only removed some pieces and not others. If they were interested in the recovery of scrap, then it is not clear why the firebox boiler was left. They certainly had the means to recover it – they salvaged the Scotch boilers of *Chisholm*. It is hard to imagine that they simply overlooked it, or did not locate the *Cumberland* boiler.

The salvors of *Chisholm* were

Figure 72. Roman numeral draft markings located on the horn timber of *Chisholm* at a depth of 130 feet. NPS photo by Larry Murphy.

Figure 73. Segment of paddle wheel from *Cumberland*. Note firebox boiler in upper right. NPS photo by Dan Lenihan.

apparently not interested in scrap, but only reusable elements with high resale value. The firebox boiler was not only out of date, but was also damaged beyond reasonable repair. The top of the boiler was ruptured. This was not likely the result of a boiler explosion – the shell is depressed inward. Because the salvors did not remove the boiler, it is unlikely they removed any of the other machinery. Perhaps there is large machinery yet to be discovered near the site.

Auxiliary Machinery

Another piece of machinery was located on the *Cumberland/Chisholm* site but cannot, as yet, be definitely attributed to either vessel. Figure 76 shows a reciprocating steam water pump of a type commonly used for boiler-feed water. The steam piston is

Figure 74. Firebox boiler of *Cumberland*. NPS photo by Dan Lenihan.

141

Figure 75. Top of A-frame that supported the bearings of the walking beam of *Cumberland*. NPS photo by John Brooks.

on the right of the pump and the piston of the water pump housed on the left. The spherical attachment above the pump piston is an air chamber. The air chamber serves to allow an even flow of water. Without the air chamber, or accumulator dome, the water would tend to pulsate because of the back-and-forth motion of the pump piston, which stops at the end of each stroke. When the piston moves forward water enters the dome and compresses the trapped air, which later forces the water out of the chamber when the piston comes to rest at the end of the stroke. This allows a steady discharge of water.

The pump is similar in design to those of a number of manufacturers. It is quite similar to the "Knowles Single Pump" and the "Blake Single Piston Pump" in common use in the latter part of the 19th century.

It is likely that the pump in Figure 76 is from *Chisholm*. Although unattached, it lies on a section of the port side of *Chisholm*'s hull. It is also likely that the pump is near its proper location on the vessel, in the machinery spaces and close to the boilers. In the immediate area of the pump other evidence of machinery is found. Above the steam cylinder of the pump and

to the left above the diver's head in Figure 76, a strongly reinforced through-hull fitting can be seen. The location of this fitting is above the main deck, and it is probably an overboard discharge. Some metal sheeting was found in the area (immediately below pump, north end of Section II, Figure 65), which may have been used to line the boilerroom.

A separated windlass with some decking attached was located on the bottom of *Chisholm*'s hull (Section II, Figure 65). Based on the dimensions, it is most likely to have belonged to *Chisholm*. In the immediate vicinity of the windlass is an anchor, which is wedged between the bottom of the hull and the starboard side. The wooden stock was all that could be reached to measure. The stock is 13 feet 8 inches long, indicating an anchor of a size more appropriate for *Chisholm* than *Cumberland*.

Along the limberway of *Chisholm*'s hull bottom 2½- and 3-inch-diameter iron pipe was located. This was bilge pump piping. A rod with two cup-like attachments was found on the port side of *Chisholm*. This is assumed to be the interior mechanism for a double-acting, hand-operated bilge or fire pump.

The last feature possibly associated with auxiliary machinery is also located on the assumed port side of *Chisholm* (Section I, Figure 65). A 10-foot-long, iron-capped cylindrical timber of unknown use was discovered. The base of the timber, which was 12 inches in diameter, was broken.

Hull Architecture

As discussed, the hull architecture of the two vessels is easily separated. The differences in scantling size and construction techniques is marked. The centerline frame dimensions of *Cumberland* are 12 x 14 inches including a 2-inch space between the futtocks, while those of *Chisholm* are 18 x 18 inches. On this basis alone, the remains of the two vessels can be distinguished; however, there are specific attributes of both vessels that bear close examination.

There are certain aspects of architecture that would be expected of a 200-foot class, side-wheel passenger vessel. Indications of guards, gangways, round stern, sharp bow and hull support should be notable in the remains.

A right-angle iron bracket was located on a section of the side of *Cumberland*'s hull (CU Side, near fantail, Figure 65). The bracket, which is on the outboard side of the hull, was used to support a section of the paddle wheel guards that ran longitudinally along the outside of the hull at the height of the lower edge of the paddle wheel box along the level of the main deck.

Guards (or sponsons) may have originally appeared on Fulton's eastern river steamboats. Fulton introduced them to prevent damage to the otherwise exposed paddle wheels. Eastern river guards were widest at the paddle wheel and tapered fore and aft. Later, in western river practice, guards were extended the full length of the hull to add cargo space to the main deck. In addition, the guards gave support to the outboard paddle wheel shaft bearing.

Great Lakes steamboats normally followed the eastern style of guards with the widest overhang at the paddle wheel and tapered ends. The maximum width of the guards was determined by the size of the paddle wheels and paddle boxes (housings).

Guards were extended to provide additional usable deck space and ease of cargo handling. Gangways normally opened on the guard level to facilitate cargo loading. Package freight could be wheeled from the dock across the guards, and into the cargo spaces on the main deck.

Judging from the size of the right-angle guard support brace, this portion of the hull was far forward or aft of the paddle wheel, in the area of minimum guard width. It is most likely that the hull portion with the brace attached is from the stern, rather than the bow. This speculation is based on the proximity of stern structure (sternpost and fantail) and the lack of bow structure anywhere within the main site concentration.

Along the upper edge of the side of the *Cumberland* hull, there are rectangular cutouts for the main deck beams. The main deck beams extended beyond the hull side and supported the guards. The right-angle braces or struts, which appear to occur in pairs on *Cumberland*, were located between the deck beam and hull side in the area of the largest overhang. One side of the brace was attached to the hull, the other attached to the beam with the iron brace between them forming the hypotenuse of the right angle. Examination of a portion of the bow of *Cumberland*, which was located in Washington Harbor, revealed that the main deck beams were extended over the sides in the

forward part of the hull.

The rounded structure visible in Figure 65 (fantail) is from the stern of *Cumberland*. This portion, with exposed cant beams, sternpost, centerline keelson and deadwood attached, can be seen on the map to the north of *Chisholm*'s hull bottom. The deck beams radiated from the sternpost to support the overhanging fantail. This portion of the stern would have been on the main deck level, even with and a continuation of the guards. This hull fragment was the overhang above the rudder.

Most of the *Cumberland* hull structure located on site comes from below the level of the main deck. All structure seems to come from the stern of the vessel. The sharply curved frames visible in Figure 58 are from the stern area between the keel and main deck in the aft third of the hull.

An interesting feature of the frames visible in Figures 58 and 60 is that the futtocks are separated by a 2 x 14-inch spacer block. The futtocks are made of 12 x 6-inch timbers. The frames are on 24-inch centers. A possible explanation for this feature is that the technique reduced dry rot in the frames. This is unusual for ocean and western river vessels as well. The hull was built by Melchanthon Simpson of Port Robinson, Canada. Historical research may produce some additional evidence for this construction style and the rationale for it. If historical

Figure 76. Double-acting, steam water pump on *Cumberland/Chisholm* site. Pumps similar to this were often used as boiler feed pumps. This one is in proximity to the machinery spaces of *Chisholm* and is likely from that vessel. NPS photo by Larry Murphy.

research is unproductive, examination of other wrecked vessels produced by the builder will be the only source of comparative data. This construction is apparently not unique with *Cumberland*, but it is rare on the Great Lakes, known only from brief mention in historical references.

Cumberland carried cabins above the main deck, as was the practice on the Great Lakes after the appearance of *Great Western* in 1839. Figure 56 is a drawing of the general arrangement plan of *Cumberland*. A steamer of the dimensions of *Cumberland* would have had about 60 cabins, plus parlors and a large ladies' cabin aft. The crew's quarters would most likely have been below decks.

There were no structural features located on site that could be attributed to deck structures. Few elements of deck structures have been located from any of the wooden vessels. Deck structure was of lighter construction and easily demolished and separated from the hull during, or soon after, the wreck event.

The construction of *Chisholm* was of much heavier scantling than *Cumberland* (Figure 57). The floor frames are composed of three 6-inch-wide members. Each 18 x 18-inch frame is spaced on 24-inch centers. There are two 6-inch futtocks on the sides of the hull and one 6-inch futtock above the spar deck, which formed the bulwark stanchion.

The hull of *Chisholm* has a large centerline keelson composed of six elements. The center keelson is 15 inches wide and 28 inches deep, the sister keelsons on both sides are 12 inches wide and also 28 inches deep. The centerline keelson contains two elements each 14 inches deep. The elements are fastened with $^3/_4$-inch-diameter iron drifts. The centerline keelson scarfs are not hooked, but are straight diagonals.

Next to the centerline keelson assembly is a transverse limberboard $2^1/_2$ inches thick and 12 inches deep. The limberway is a triangular cut on the bottom of the member.

On each side of the hull there are six side or floor keelsons and a bilge keelson. The side keelsons are 12 x 16-inch timbers on 28-inch centers. The bilge keelson is similarly constructed with two 5 x 11-inch ceiling planks and a single 5 x 9-inch plank edge-fastened at the turn of the bilge. The ceiling above the bilge is composed of 6 x 14-inch planks.

The hold floor is composed of 2 x 8-inch and 2 x 10-inch planks laid transversely. This upper layer overlies a $^3/_4$-inch thick layer of planks of smaller widths.

The height of the hold was 12 feet 6 inches and the height above the main deck was 7 feet 6 inches, which together equals the register depth of 20 feet 3 inches

The spar deck shelf, bulwark and rail detail is depicted in Figure 57. Close examination of the interior of the rail cap revealed it to have been painted pale green with a routed groove at the base, which was painted red. At regular intervals between the spar deck knees there were $5^1/_2$-inch-diameter cargo rings of $^3/_4$-inch stock attached to the ceiling planks.

Hull support

A detailed study of the hull support systems integrated into the wooden vessels of Isle Royale can reveal much of what was understood by mid- and late-19th century Lakes shipwrights

about the dynamics of the stresses that the hulls would be subjected to by the Great Lakes. Much can be learned about the technology of these vessels, as well as the interaction of ideas from other shipbuilding areas. The Lakes shipwrights borrowed methods and techniques from other areas as they developed and experimented with variations on their own to meet specific requirements imposed by the environment of the Great Lakes.

Fortunately, we have examples of three very different vessels to compare hull structure and support systems: *Monarch*, a propeller-driven passenger/package freighter; *Chisholm*, once the largest bulk freighter on the Lakes; and the side-wheeler *Cumberland*. All three had different hull support systems.

The hull of *Cumberland* was long and relatively narrow with a shallow depth. The registered length was 204 feet. The beam was 26 feet and the depth 10.7. Length-to-beam ratio is 1:7.8, and the beam to depth is 1:2.4. Length-to-depth ratio is 1:19. The hull was built to attain higher speeds with moderate power desirable for the passenger/package trade. Knowledgeable opinion of the period was that the longer the boat, the faster, and beam being equal, the same power would push a longer boat faster (Wheeling Bridge Case 1851: 385, 648 in Hunter 1949: 85-89). The theoretical hull speed of *Cumberland* is estimated at 19 knots.

The length-to-beam ratios of the western rivers peaked about 1850 at 1:7.9 and dropped to 1:6.0 in the 1870s, representing a shift in emphasis from speed to cargo capacity (Hunter 1949: 86). *Cumberland* represents the continued emphasis on speed in the passenger/package trade on the Lakes. Slower and cheaper propellers had the competitive advantage in cargo capacity, and were generally designed with much more beam, and lower length-to-beam ratio. The design of bulk freighters on the Lakes emphasized carrying capacity and cheap operation; speed was a secondary concern.

The machinery of *Cumberland* was located just aft of amidships. The heavy keelsons (engine keelsons) in the engine area amidship supported the machinery weight and stresses of the A-frames. In addition to the weight of the engine and boilers, the weight of the outboard paddle wheels exerted stresses on the hull. The concentration of weight in the center of the hull had the effect of correcting some of the hull curvature due to hogging.

The hull would still have the tendency to hog as a result of the reduced buoyancy from the decreased volume in the relatively sharp stem and stern areas of the hull, as well as the light scantlings necessary for the shallow draft design. The stresses from the long, narrow and shallow draft design of Lakes sidewheelers and the weight of machinery made hull reinforcement necessary. In most of the middle-size vessels of *Cumberland*'s class, structurally integrated arched trusses running fore-and-aft were the common method of longitudinally strengthening the hull. These trusses were tied into the deadwood at the bow and stern, and rose above the gunwales, often above the paddle boxes amidships. The hull-truss system of the paddle wheeler functioned much like the trusswork of a bridge forming a sturdy and well-supported longitudinal structure.

Cumberland, however, did not have the typical arched-truss support system. None is visible in the historic photograph

Shipwrecks of Isle Royale: The Archeological Record

(Figures 13, 14). An obvious question arose regarding the support structures of *Cumberland*'s hull. Several possibilities were considered. *Cumberland* could have longitudinal bulkheads like some of the western river steamboats, or some other hull-level support mechanisms. Rod and turnbuckle arrangements were possible, again, much like the "hog chains" common to western river vessels.

Examination of the vessel remains produced features that were a part of the hull strengthening system of *Cumberland*. No evidence of longitudinal bulkheading was observed, although additional keelson structures were added amidships in the machinery area to handle the increased weight and stress (Figure 57).

Elements of a longitudinal support system that were built into the ceiling planking were noted (Figure 59). These curved planks were tied into the stern deadwood and appeared to arch upward on the inside of the hull. Historical research has not shed any light on this construction technique. Measurements of the hull side indicate that the "ceiling arch" extended to, but not above, the main deck. Unfortunately, more documentation is needed on this feature before a definitive description of the construction technique is made.

A similar feature was predicted for the bow. This speculation was later verified when a portion of *Cumberland*'s bow was located. In July 1984, after the writing of the first draft of this section of the Isle Royale report, divers from the Submerged Cultural Resources Unit in association with Park Ranger Jay Wells located and videotaped the bow section of *Cumberland* in about six feet of water in Grace Harbor. A tip from Stanley Sivertson, Captain of *Wenonah* that "an old dock structure or perhaps a piece of wreckage had been sighted frequently by locals in the area" provided the clue to this major part of *Cumberland* structure. This wreckage is more than seven miles from the main site.

Later, Patrick Labadie and LaMonte Florentz relocated this site and diagrammed the construction details. This revised documentation is reproduced in Figure 60.

The bow wreckage is in two major pieces. The larger contains the stempost. There can be little doubt that this is the port bow of *Cumberland* because it has the unusual split-futtock frame construction and shares many attributes with the identified structure on Rock of Ages. The location of these bow fragments contributes additional information to the construction details of the inner ceiling arch support noted on the stern elements on the main site.

The bow section incorporated features that allowed a better understanding of the construction details of the support system. The frames at the bow were 5-inch sided by 12-inch molded at the keelson, tapering to 6-inch molded at the deck level with a space of 2½ inches between the futtocks. The spacers between the futtocks are of oak, 2½-inch sided and 14 inches long.

There was diagonal ceiling planking present forward and above the beginning of the arch. The arch began 20 feet aft of the stem post and was 4 x 36 inches, edge bolted with 3-inch square coaks present. The clamps were 4 x 32 inches, composed of three planks. It was observed that the ceiling arch met the clamps 57 feet from the stem. Deck beams, as determined from the cutouts at the main deck level, were 5½ inches square and placed on 24-inch centers between the frames. The presence of the deck beam cutouts indicates that the deck beams extended beyond the side of the hull the entire length of *Cumberland*.

The stem was 12 x 26 inches and the stemson 12 x 20 inches. There were three iron straps across the stem, which were of ½-inch stock, 4 inches wide. An 8 x 10-inch breast hook was present. The hawse piece was 16 x 48 inches.

Additional features associated with the inshore bow area include 1½-inch rod and iron sheeting. The iron rods lend support to the conjecture that *Cumberland* contained a longitudinal hog-truss system in addition to the transverse trussing in the midship section. The iron sheeting was an external hull cladding for ice protection.

Captain Sivertson also recalled fishing over what he believes to be the rudder of *Cumberland* outside of Cumberland Point. "Trolling" SCRU team members behind a boat for several hours on two occasions did not produce any finds in this regard, but Park staff and sport diver volunteers have been encouraged to continue the search along the wreckage trail.

A second feature located on the main site connected with hull strengthening was a 7½-inches-square, 20-foot-long king-post with a square iron cap to which an iron rod with a turn buckle was attached. The king post was a support member for a section of hull connected to the post by the iron rods, which were called "hog chains" in many areas.

Both 1- and 1½-inch iron rods were located in association with *Cumberland* on the site. Fittings that appear to be for the attachment of hog chains were located on the engine keelsons. Hog chains were typically used on western river steamboats to add hull support longitudinally and, on side wheelers, transversely. It is not clear whether this feature, located in proximity of the amidship engine mounts, was a portion of a transverse chain used to support the guards and the shaft blocks of the paddle wheels, or was part of a longitudinal hog-chain system. Generally, iron rods were used in association with the A-frames, but the presence of the king post is evidence of a more complex arrangement on *Cumberland*. Iron rods were also noted on the A-frame tops found on site (Figure 75). The two sizes of iron rod may indicate that both transverse and longitudinal hog chains were employed. It is unknown how common the use of hog chains was beyond their common association with A-frames on the Lakes.

The hull support system of *Chisholm* has already been mentioned. Beside the keelson and ceiling arrangement, *Chisholm* used a network of iron strapping for additional longitudinal hull support. The sided or outside face of the frames were rabbeted at a 45-degree angle to the keelson to receive the criss-cross of 5-inch wide and ½-inch thick diagonal iron straps. The iron straps were riveted together where they cross in the spaces between frames. The common practice was to secure the top of the diagonal strapping with rivets to a horizontal belt course below the bulwarks. This feature, composed of ¾-inch-thick, 10-inch-wide iron strapping, was observed on *Chisholm*. This sheer belt can be seen at the ends of the hull sections (I and III) on Figure 65.

145

Apparently, some ocean vessels used diagonal strapping over the entire hull, including the bottom, but the practice in the Lakes was to extend it under the turn of the bilge only enough to fasten securely. Observations on site indicate that *Chisholm* followed the Lakes practice.

Typically, iron strapping was also secured to each frame with a drift. This feature was not observed on the wreck, although it was a common practice and was required by various registers and certifying agencies. The 1876 International Board of Lake Underwriters requirements for diagonal strapping stated: "all straps are to be fastened with bolts, one to each timber of the frame; one to the ceiling or planking in each room between the frames; and one to each crossing....The fastening of iron to iron to be hot-riveted; and all other bolts riveted or nutted on the wood."

Contemporary accounts of *Chisholm* described the diagonal strapping:

…iron straps run down the sides and under the turn of the bilge, and fasten to the long frames under the bottom and bolt through the bands when they cross and outside of the frames under the planking *(Chicago Inter Ocean* Sept. 24, 1880).

Site Formation Processes

The remains of *Chisholm* are principally in four large sections. There are 177 feet of the bottom on the shallower portions of the site. Below, there is a second section of bottom 47 feet in length. A total of 227 feet of *Chisholm*'s original hull length of 256 feet remains on site. The portion missing is the bow, which is only represented by the windlass and anchor and some associated frames west of the bow of *Cox* (Figure 112).

Examinations of the structural elements of the vessel remains indicate the original location of the principal structural elements in the hull, and reflect that the sequence of formation process, such as salvage attempts, storms and ice heaving, worked in concert to produce the remains seen on site.

Although the hulk apparently reached a deep resting place before the high-energy action at the surface could break it into smaller pieces, it is disarticulated and positioned in a fashion that would have been difficult to predict. Consider the fact that Section V (Figure 65), which comprises the engine and extreme stern flooring of *Chisholm,* is facing southwest in 150 feet of water, while section IV, which was part of the original starboard side and bottom where it articulated with the fantail, is facing the opposite direction. The piece of wreckage lying under the engine floor timbers is part of the fantail itself. The matching stern section of the hull for the port side is still a part of a larger section of the side (I) that is located above in the shallow water ravine. Apparently, the port side broke through the stern gangway. This conclusion can be reached by process of elimination: II is the hull bottom and section III is associated with the starboard side, because it is the only piece short enough to fit the puzzle yet not exceed the length of the *Chisholm* if added to IV, which is part of the stern.

The assumption that IV is the starboard stern can be further justified by examination of the northern end of the piece. The

arrangement of shelves, knees and so forth indicate that it was coming to a narrow juncture with the deadwood in the stern. With all the pieces restored, the end product would be as illustrated in the midship cross section (Figure 57).

Historical documentation informs us that the vessel ran aground in 12 feet of water, with the stern floating over 40 feet of water *(Detroit Free Press* Oct. 23, 1898). The bow was damaged severely enough by the grounding to dislodge hull planks. When the ship was abandoned, it was listing "4 feet" *(Ft. William Daily Journal* Oct. 21, 1898). The wreck was broken up by two storms, which struck in quick succession, the first only four days after the wreck, and the second three days later *(Detroit Free Press* Oct. 26, 1898).

The positioning of the hull pieces allows the development of a probable sequence of events. The stern section was broken off as a result of the still-buoyant stern section of the hull being worked by the storm waves. The hull was probably grounded from the bow to below the boilers. Historical records do not state to which side the vessel was listing, but indications are that it was to port, because hull damage caused from the boilers appears to have been on that side, and the deep portions of the wreck show more extensive damage to the port side in the stern section. What probably took place was the boilers tumbled out of the port side as the stern section broke off. The most damaged section of the port stern was in the area just aft of the gangway. The starboard gangway is still visible in section IV. The boilers would have slid down the slope, while the hull, relieved of the weight of the machinery and stern structure, became more buoyant and continued to move to the port (north), pushed by the waves and wind.

As the stern section slid down the face of the reef, the rudder shoe struck with enough force to dislodge the rudder and push the horn timber upward, breaking the fantail. The lighter stern and fantail pieces reached the bottom of reef before the stern section of the hull bottom, which still contains the engine. This stern section (V) is resting on structure that is from the port side of the stern. The large piece of wreckage just off the port side of the bottom hull (IV) is a major portion of the starboard part of the stern and fantail. The end containing the knees and gangway (northern end) was forward on the starboard side.

The hull was presumably more heavily damaged on the starboard bow, probably a result of being the first point of contact with the reef. The starboard side, now free both bow and stern, separated along the bilge as the hull pivoted on the remains of the bow. The starboard side was probably originally deposited in shallower water and later pushed northward and down the slope into the gully by ice movement.

The storms, principally from the northwest *(Detroit Free Press* Oct. 26, 1898), continued to buffet the still-connected port and bottom. As the vessel moved, the bow was breaking up. It apparently dropped the anchor and deck section carrying the windlass northward to the upslope location above their current position. The port side must have separated after the hull bottom turned almost 180 degrees with the bow facing south and the stern portion of the bottom to the north.

The depositional sequence of the 177-foot-long bottom section, the port side, the anchor and windlass in the shallow portions of the site might have taken place over a longer period of time. The bottom was the first element to arrive in its present location, with the anchor coming to rest at its present location at the port bilge. The windlass evidently was the next element to be located in its present position on top of the bottom. The port side was the last piece of *Chisholm* to find its way down the incline to the bottom of the gully. After the port side was in position, a piece of paddle wheel of *Cumberland* came to rest on it. All the shifting of the elements was probably the result of ice movement.

Diagnostic features can be used to establish the articulation of the hull pieces. The principal diagnostic feature of the large bottom portion (II) is the doubled floor keelsons on the north end of the section, which are likely associated with strengthening of the machinery spaces.

The features on the section of hull side that is in proximity to the bottom (I) that indicate that the stern is to the north are more definitive. The water pump and through-hull fittings on the north end of the piece reflect the boiler spaces. There is an iron beam in the vicinity. Historical documentation indicates that *Chisholm* had iron beams below the boilers for support. In addition, documentation indicates that the boiler spaces were sheathed with iron. Iron sheeting, riveted together, was located in close proximity to the beam. This sheeting is of a style of construction appropriate for sheathing for fire protection:

> The iron beams under the boilers, and the iron house over and around the boiler, with the iron coal bunkers, are sure protection against fire…(*Chicago Inter Ocean* Sept. 24, 1880).

(No indication of the iron coal bunkers was located).

There are indications that the bow was the southern end of this portion of port hull. The mooring fairleads on the southern end of the piece appear to be bow associated. Directly behind the fairleads is a chain plate assembly. Seventy-five feet to the north along the gunwale (under the paddle wheel segment) is a second set of chain plates. The location and distance are what would be expected for the fore and main mast of *Chisholm*. The reason the mizzen chain plates are missing is that they were placed higher on the cabin structure in the stern, and no cabin structure remains on site.

The second side section in the shallow area of the site (III) has no clearly diagnostic attributes, except it lacks both bow and stern features. The main indication that this is the starboard side is found on the hull side in deeper water. The hull and fantail section (IV) associated with the stern bottom section has considerably more of the starboard side connected to it. The beams and gangway are clearly starboard side. The assumed starboard side (III) in shallow water is 200 feet in length, including the diagonal-strap sheer belt, while the port hull side (I) is 230 feet in length. The port side would simply be too long for the vessel's dimensions if added to the starboard fantail section.

The last of the diagnostic elements to be considered is also in the deeper section. The stern bottom section is resting on remnants of the port side. Virtually all of the stern hull structure is represented.

Questions arose as to those portions of the vessel missing. All the fore and aft cabin structures are absent. In addition, the towing bitts, which would have been stepped into the horn timber, deadwood and the main deck, are not represented. There is also about 25 feet of bow that was displaced from the central site concentration. Other elements missing are the main and spar deck beams. None were recognized anywhere on site. They must have all been pulled out when the sides of the hull separated from the bottom. The main deck may not have originally been planked, but would have had the beams in place, whether planked or not.

The remaining fragments of *Cumberland* exhibit more extensive alterations by formation processes than *Chisholm*. The relatively intact structural elements of *Chisholm* can be attributed to heavier construction and the diagonal strapping that tended to hold the sides together. *Chisholm*'s bow, lacking the iron strapping, appears to have come apart as separate elements.

Less than 100 feet of *Cumberland* bottom was located on site. Apparently the hull separated between the engine and boilers, as did *Chisholm*. The boiler and bow structure maintained enough buoyancy to be moved a hundred feet to the north before the boilers and other machinery dropped out. The bow section was able to float the 7.5 miles into Grace Harbor. The offshore hull elements show evidence of movement by ice. Some of the hull sections show ice scour damage. Ice movement must be considered a major formation process in the shallower sections of *Cumberland*.

Cumberland, with a draft about half that of *Chisholm*, originally broke up in the shallower sections of the reef. Storm and ice movement are undoubtedly responsible for the vessel fragments being moved off the edge of the reef into the gully in which they now lie. Both of the vessels moved basically northward during and after the wreck event. This may be the best indicator for the direction to concentrate future survey efforts.

The remains of the vessels are a particularly rich source of information on wooden steamers of this period. As has been demonstrated, there are many details of construction techniques and steam technology that may only be answered by examination of the material record. Even when one is fortunate enough to have construction drafts and blue prints of a particular vessel or, as in the case of *Chisholm*, plans of a similar vessel, many details were omitted. They were considered too obvious and common to have been included in plans and have already slipped from our current understanding of our technical heritage.

The side-wheeler contained numerous common and some very rare features. The split-frame construction is apparently rare. The details of the hull support system will be of interest to historians and students of marine technology, as well as serving as a comparison. *Chisholm* has already contributed to the details of known technology through its nearly complete engine and drive train. In addition, the use of iron beams for boiler support and other technical details of construction are not represented on the blueprints of the similar vessel of Figures 69 and 70.

A last glance at the wreckage of the *Cumberland/Chisholm* site leaves us with a tantalizing thought for future research:

where is the rest of *Cumberland*? The reconstruction of *Cumberland* parts available in the known site boundaries indicates that some very interesting materials related to this wreck have neither been found on the site nor been accounted for in the historical record of salvage. Is it possible that more large machinery and intact pieces of *Cumberland* bow wreckage are waiting for discovery some place between the boiler and the bow in the deep waters leading up to Rock of Ages light?

Algoma: Site Description and Analysis

Location

Algoma is directly offshore of Mott Island on the northeast end of Isle Royale. The center point of the known wreckage is computed at 48°06'41"N and 88°31'55"W. This point is approximately 2¹/₃ statute miles from the starboard-hand bell buoy at Middle Island Passage on a true bearing of 53 degrees, 4¹/₈ statute miles on a true bearing of 31 degrees from the white daymark at Saginaw Point, and approximately ⁷/₈ of a mile on a true bearing of 61 degrees from the radio mast on Mott Island. The point can be reached by rounding the starboard-hand bell buoy at Middle Island Passage, traveling a distance of 2¹/₃ miles, and lining up on the Mott Island radio mast with a true bearing of 240 degrees.

The steel steamer *Algoma* was wrecked at Greenstone Rock, Mott Island, on the north end of Isle Royale in November 1885. It blundered onto offshore rocks at the south end of the 1¹/₂-mile island and was subsequently driven onto the rugged and exposed shoreline by heavy seas and easterly winds of gale force. Because the shoreline is studded with irregular ledges and rocks, the ship's steel hull broke up immediately, and even the stern portion, which remained relatively intact, rested on an uneven bed of pinnacles and ridges. The ship's upper works were entirely shattered by the breaking seas and driven into three narrow coves. There is no shelter at the site from easterly or southerly winds, which enjoy a clear sweep of the open Lake for a fetch of anywhere from 50 to as much as 200 miles.

In the shallower water near the shoreline, three depressions or gullies lead into deeper water from the three coves, and the wreckage of *Algoma* rests principally in those gullies, separated by shallower rocks and ridges reaching out from shore. The fractured wreckage was likely pushed into the gullies from the ridge tops by ice action. The remains of the ship are, as a result, largely found in three main fields. The remaining wreckage lies dispersed in deeper water immediately offshore, ranging from 50 to about 150 feet of depth. The inshore portions are from 6 or 8 to 50 feet deep.

An unusual quality about the *Algoma* wreck is that it is broken up in a different manner from most steel ships. The hull is not so much torn apart as it is disassembled. The component parts of the vessel are intact for the most part, but few are attached to anything else. As a result of this, most of the wreckage of the ship consists of collections of parts that are structural elements, lying in random groupings as the topographical features of the Lake bottom and natural forces arrange them. Only in a few places are there assemblies large enough to refer to as a section of the vessel. The peculiar quality of the *Algoma* wreck is thought to have resulted from the failure of the fastenings, the steel rivets by which its frames and plates were held together. It is interesting to note, however, that *Algoma*'s sisters, *Alberta* and *Athabasca,* had long successful careers lasting more than 60 years after *Algoma*'s loss; as far as is known, these vessels never had problems resulting from rivet-failure, and they were broken up for scrap in the late 1940s. *Algoma* was barely two years old at the time of its disastrous loss.

Historical records indicate that repeated salvage work was done on the *Algoma* wreck. The ship's machinery, including engines, boilers and auxiliaries, was removed in 1886. Duluth newspapers mention the removal of large quantities of scrap steel in 1903 (see Chapter IV). Both of these salvage jobs undoubtedly involved the use of divers and explosives, but archeologists could not distinguish the effects of dynamiting from those of a century of waves and ice. The tangible evidence of salvage work lies not so much in the remains of the ship, but rather in what is missing. There are no machinery parts at the site at all. The boilers, engines, windlass and all of the auxiliaries are gone. There is no evidence of anchors, chains, propeller or shafting, and it must be assumed that all of those elements were removed. There are few steel rails left from the cargo; the large quantity known to have been carried aboard was probably removed by the same salvors. The major machinery is known to have been used in the construction and outfitting of the steamer *Manitoba* in 1889, but it is not clear whether or not that included all of the ground tackle (anchors and chain, windlass, etc.) and auxiliaries.

The configuration of the bottom near shore is quite dramatic. There are distinct ridges and gullies, rocky pinnacles, ledges and holes until a depth of about 50 feet is reached, and then the bottom becomes flatter, with a gentle steady slope downward. In general, the 50-foot depth lies about 200 feet from shore; the bottom slopes to 100 feet deep about 300 feet from the beach.

The three fields of wreckage nearest the shore have a wide variety of ship parts. There are angles, bars, beams, flat floors and hold-pillars from the framing; steel plates of various thicknesses from the shell; masts, gaffs and tackle from the rigging; and specialized fittings such as davits, fairleads, gangway doors and cargo-handling gear. Inasmuch as the ship was carrying mixed freight at the time of its loss, it is speculated that the debris also includes portions of the cargo, but that premise proves difficult to substantiate. There are also remnants of personal effects from passengers and crew as well as articles of the ship's outfit, such as cabin-fittings, china, kitchenware and engine room tools liberally distributed about the heavier items and lying in all of the depressions and cracks in the rocks. Most of these lighter artifacts are broken by the movement of rocks and ice, or worn by the abrasion of sand and gravel, especially in the "high-energy zone" of the shoreline, where the constant action of a century's waves has left it mark.

There are no known shipyard plans of *Algoma* or its 1883 sisters, but shipbuilding texts of the period offer clues about the details of *Algoma*'s design. Most of the elements of construction and the dimensions of component parts were dictated by Lloyds' Rules of Ship Construction – strict standards adopted by the steel shipbuilding industry almost world-wide during the 1870s and 1880s, resulting from research by United Kingdom shipbuilders, owners, classification societies and marine underwriters. The Rules specified appropriate sizes of beams, plates, frames and so forth, according to the length or tonnage of a vessel. Parts of *Algoma* measured at the wreck site all fit the recommendations of Lloyds' Rules, and the ship's design seems, as a result, to have been very "standard." The construction shows many distinctly British features and, although the vessel's sister ships are no longer in existence, similar features may be observed in the steel steamer *Keewatin*, which was also built in Scotland for the Canadian Pacific Railway Company at a later date (1907). The *Keewatin* is preserved as a museum at Saugatuck, Michigan, and offers a very useful comparison for a number of the Isle Royale wrecks.

Besides the rivet failure that is evident in all parts of the *Algoma* wreck, another interesting characteristic is the relative simplicity of its framing. All of the framing members are built up of a few standard parts. It is clear that the steel shipyards of the 1880s had a limited field of standard steel shapes with which to work, and from a narrow assortment of sheets, angles and bars they had to produce all of the complicated shapes and forms necessary to frame a ship. The frames, as a result, were all built up of sheets cut to the appropriate shapes, with inner and outer edges reinforced by 3 x 3-inch angles. With those simple components, frames of any variety could be fabricated and riveted together. Longitudinal stringers and transverse deck beams were made of 3 x 6-inch bulb-angles. Aside from pipes, which were used for stanchions and pillars, almost every piece of framing on board seems to have been fabricated from those three basic pieces of steel stock. Standardized castings were used for fairleads, mooring bitts, davits, fittings and machinery parts, but virtually none for the fabric of the hull.

The most northerly of the three fields of wreckage contains several distinct features of *Algoma*'s stern. Among them are the after mast and sections of the ship's sides, along with much nondescript hull material. This field is nearest to what is called "Algoma Beach," the small cove pictured in historical views of the wreck where the whole stern lay for some time after the accident. This field extends from about 10 to about 60 feet of water.

The second field of wreckage lies about 100 feet west of the first and includes more hull parts, fender-strapping from the ship's sides, frames, the gaff from the after mast, the ship's steel rudder, gangway doors, and much small debris such as broken crockery. It must be assumed that large quantities of artifacts were removed from this area by divers in previous years. The site has always been regarded as rich in artifacts, and this field demonstrates the fact. It lies between the shoreline in about 30 feet of water.

The third field of wreckage is another 100 feet west of the second. It is also rich in cultural materials and small ship parts, but contains a large section of the after end of the bottom, including an assembly of frames, keelson and steel-plating from under the engine room. It is one of the most significant portions of wreckage because it communicates much about the framing scheme of the vessel, and it is one of the only assemblies left that shows multiple components still fastened together. The proximity and depth of the frames demonstrate that it came from the machinery spaces, probably right under the engines. In this same area are also more gangway doors, framing, long sections of shell plating, piping, railroad iron, boat davits, rail stanchions from the hurricane deck, tools and chinaware. Some rigging was also observed here, with wire rope and jib-hanks from a staysail, presumably the one carried on the after mast.

About 150 feet west of the third field of wreckage, a large section of the ship's spar deck was found lying in about 50 feet of water, sheltered by a ridge of rocks. The piece measured about 35 by 50 feet and consisted of numerous deck beams all tied together

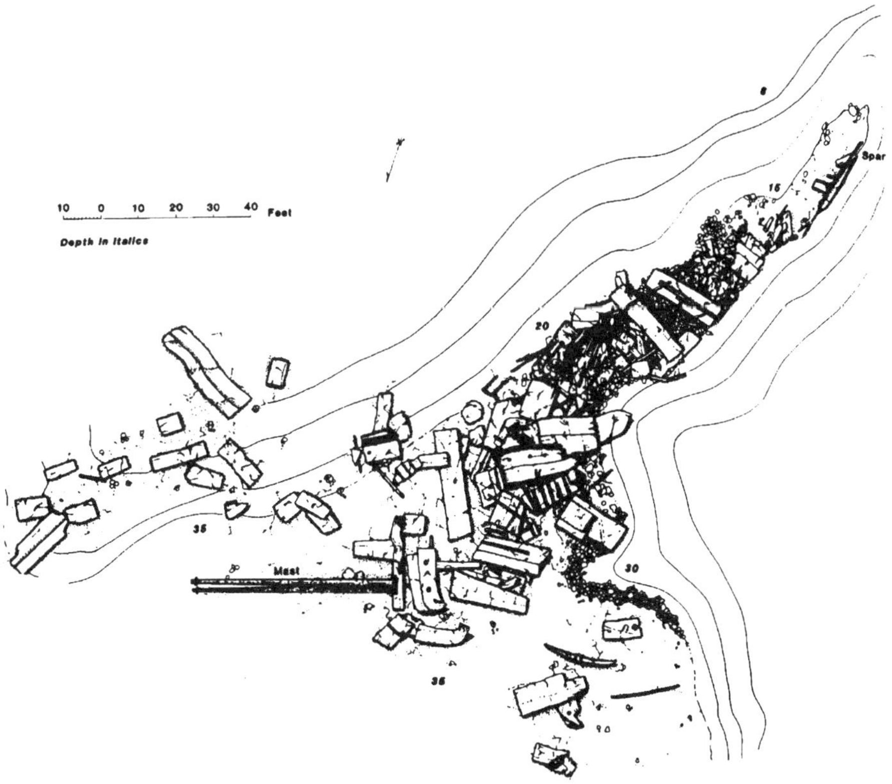

Figure 77. Sample portion of *Algoma* wreckage field. Drawing by Larry Nordby.

by the steel stringer-plates on either side, with a portion of the deck-planking still attached. The section is inverted; the planking lies on the underside of it. This is the only place where wooden parts of the wreck are still preserved, as far as is known, and their preservation is probably due to the fact that the deck-section is inverted, with the heavier steel beams holding the deck-planks in place. The deck section showed curvature at its sides, suggestive of the hull's shape near the bow. If this piece proves to be from the bow, it would be the only portion of the forward half of the ship found in shallow water. All other wreckage in the three nearby fields is presumed to have come from the midships or stern sections of the ship. There are many distinctly stern features found there, and a careful examination revealed no definite bow features at all.

The location of the forward half of *Algoma* has puzzled divers and historians for decades, because it is clear that all of the wreckage found along the shore to date consists of stern features. Field work at the site during the 1985 field season included the use of remote video equipment that enabled archeologists to examine a large area of the bottom to a depth of 450 feet of water in search of the ship's bow. The search turned up no evidence of the missing half of the ship, and so the mystery deepened. Some effort was made by sport divers and volunteers to search a large area to the west of the three known fields of wreckage, but nothing of the bow was found there, although wind conditions at the time of the 1885 accident suggested that buoyant portions of the wreck would have likely drifted in that direction.

Diving on the wreck during 1986 permitted re-examination of deeper portions of the site, and videotapes were made of several features in 120 feet of water in scattered locations directly offshore of the three shallower fields. Several large sections of hull-plating were observed that were indistinguishable from pieces found in the shallower locations. One section, however, proved to be a large piece of vertical bulkhead, with distinctive vertical stiffeners on one side and horizontal stiffeners on the other side. Inasmuch as the entire stern of the ship is known to have been either broken up along the shore or salvaged commercially, no section of bulkhead as large as this could have migrated from there to deeper water. That suggests, therefore, that the bulkhead must have come from the bow half of the ship, and that the entire bow must have broken up like the remainder of the wreck and not drifted down the shore from the site of the stranding at all, which supports some of the observations based on historical documentation in Chapter IV.

The deeper part of the site also contains elements of the ship's superstructure, some of it definitely from the forward portion of the ship. The galley stack, with a distinctive weather cap, appears in historic photographs just abaft the ship's pilothouse – the stack has been seen lying with the deeper pieces of wreckage. The forward mast is there, too, and at least one of the ship's wooden lifeboats. All of these elements are removed by several hundred feet from the deck section believed to have come from the forward part of the ship, and there is no clear explanation for their having become so far separated. It is possible that the deck section retained some buoyancy with the

wooden planking attached, and that it simply floated ashore. There have been no other features found in the deeper water that can be definitely attributed to the bow of the ship, such as anchor windlass, anchors or chains, pilothouse equipment or the stem or hawse pipes, all large and durable pieces that should have survived. Some may yet be found, but it is likely that the reusable items were recovered by salvors. Sport divers who visited the site during the 1960s may provide some clues, but it is highly unlikely that the removal of such heavy materials could be attributed to their activity. It is just as unlikely that such easily recognized features could have escaped discovery if they were still at the site.

A more thorough examination of the *Algoma* wreck site will undoubtedly provide more clues about the events that followed the ship's loss in 1885, and explain the present dispersion and condition of the wreckage. A site map and more complete documentation would be useful because the wreck is so randomly dispersed, because so many of the features are not easily recognized by most lay divers and because the orientation of the component parts is so confusing. It seems likely, despite further study, that much of *Algoma*'s story will remain a mystery.

Monarch: Site Description and Analysis

Site Location

Monarch is directly offshore on the west side of the northeast point of Isle Royale. The northeast point on the island is known as Blake Point, and the area immediately onshore from the site is known as The Palisades. *Monarch* is 1.2 statute miles from Locke Point on a true bearing of 76 degrees. The site is on a true bearing of 84 degrees from the starboard-hand nun buoy off Locke Point and 251 degrees true from Blake Point Light. The magnetic bearing is 255 degrees (compass) from the site to Locke Point and 90 degrees (compass) from the Locke Point buoy to the site. The site can be readily located in the water by rounding the Locke Point starboard-hand nun buoy and setting a course of 90 degrees (compass) to The Palisades and lining up on the characteristic features of the cliff. The site is located at 48°11'20"N and 88°26'3"W.

Site Description

If one has viewed many wooden shipwrecks splayed open on the bottom, and especially if one has recently seen the *Cumberland/Chisholm* site, the first reaction on seeing *Monarch* might well be, "So where are the knees?" There are various substitutions for hanging knees in marine architecture but, when present, these old friends provide quick and easy indicators for identifying hull sides and their approximate location on the original vessel.

Other diagnostic features of structural elements must be used to identify and position hull sections. The knees familiar on the *Cumberland/Chisholm* site are replaced by beam shelves on

Monarch. Such comparisons and contrasts are informative of the changes and development of marine architecture that occurred during the time period represented by the wooden ships of Isle Royale.

The wreck of *Monarch* begins in less than 20 feet of water in front of The Palisades area and extends in a generally westerly direction to a depth of more than 70 feet at the stern section of the hull (Figure 79). The structural remains of the vessel within

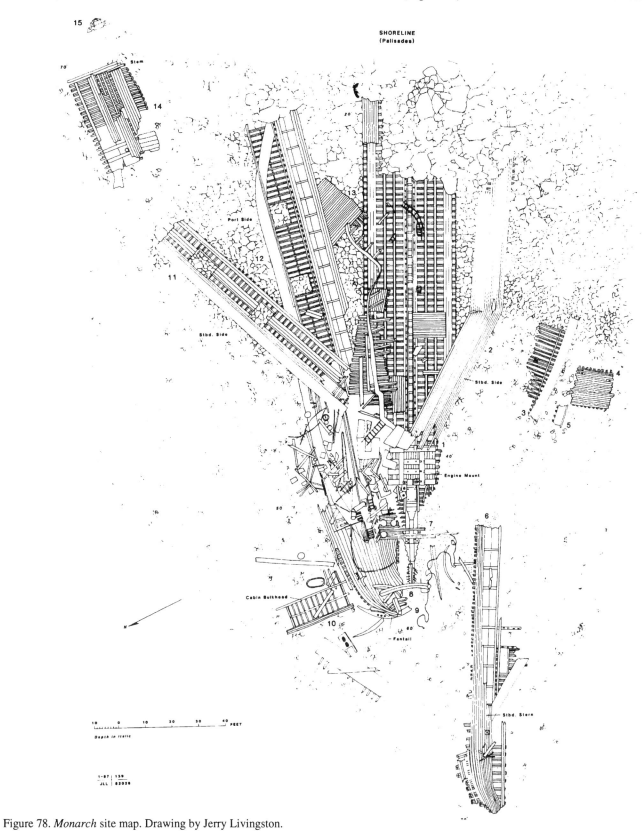

Figure 78. *Monarch* site map. Drawing by Jerry Livingston.

the central wreck concentration consist of at least 15 elements (Figure 78). The principal site scatter covers an area of about 1.5 acres. The arrangement of the components gives the appearance of a vessel that has "opened up" and separated along lines of structural weakness. Components have shifted from their proper alignment and may reflect the activities of the 1908 salvage operations, as well as natural site formation processes.

Large disarticulated portions of hull lie near the major bottom piece with the multiple keelson structures exposed. The engine mounts and shaft bearings are visible where salvagers have relieved them of the weight of the triple-expansion engine they once supported. The boilers, propeller and most other salvageable steam machinery were also removed by contemporary wrecking crews.

What is not immediately apparent from examining the site first hand is how much of the ship is missing in the known wreckage field. Much as in the case of the *Cumberland/Chisholm* site, one feels an enormous "presence" from the massive wooden timbers, and the site assumes a maze-like quality when the farthest a diver can see is 20 to 30 feet. The site is only turned into an understandable entity when subjected to the measuring tapes and protractors of an underwater mapping operation.

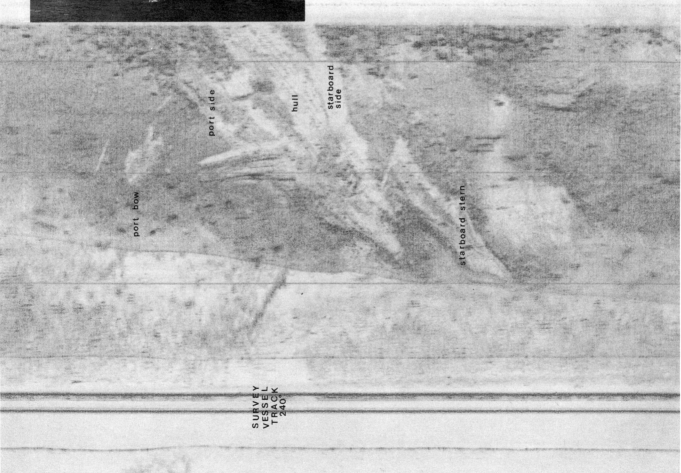

Figure 79. Top photo is of Palisades Cliff in the area where *Monarch* struck. The remains of *Monarch* visible on the side scan sonar printout are arranged in this graphic to show how they lie on the steeply sloping shoreline below the cliffs. NPS photo by Jerry Livingston.

When the wreck material is reconstituted on paper into a ship, it becomes evident that the better part of the bow section, some 100 feet of hull and 60 feet of starboard side are not represented on the site. The parts missing on the site, except the portion of port bow, are roughly equivalent to the portion sticking above the water's surface in the historic photographs (Figures 21, 22). Spurred on by the knowledge gained of how much ship was missing from the map, Park Service divers in 1982 discovered a previously unknown wreckage trail extending north and northeast of the site. Significant portions of wreckage, scattered over a halfmile in that direction and to depths of at least 150 feet, have now been located. No attempt was made to develop a detailed map of this scatter, because the depths and extent of the material distribution would make it too time consuming to study for the information returns gained. Further exploration dives should be productive and add to what is known about this site.

Hull Architecture

The hull remains of *Monarch* are an interesting and valuable example of the maritime architecture of wooden Great Lakes passenger/package freight vessels and represent the refinements of a long tradition of wooden shipbuilding in the region. The heavily constructed oak hull produced a strong, rigid vessel that incorporated a combination of iron-reinforcing systems.

The largest single element on the wreck site is the bottom of the hull. It is 155 feet long and extends from the aft deadwood, just forward of the sternpost in 70 feet of water, shoreward to a point about 20 feet deep. An anchor is located just off the farthest extension of the port bilge keelson.

The bottom contains a centerline keelson, four side keelsons (two port and two starboard) and the bilge keelson on each side. The centerline and bilge keelsons are heavily strengthened, made up of multiple elements.

The double futtock frames are 10 x 12 inches and set on 24-inch centers. Ceiling planking from the turn of the bilge to the lower edge of the sheer strap below the main deck is 4 x 8 inches. The center keelson was constructed of 14 x 14-inch timber, and the sister keelsons, two on each side, are 11 x 14 inches and 12 x 11 inches, the smaller outboard. The 2-inch reduction of the outboard sister keelson provided a step for the transverse planks that made a flat floor in the cargo hold on each side of the centerline keelson to the bilge.

The side keelsons are 14 x 11 inches and 12 x 11 inches. The bilge keelson contains three elements: a 12 x 11-inch keelson with an 11-inch-wide and a 16-inch-wide ceiling plank rein-

forcing the turn of the bilge.

The center keelson was capped with two planks laid on edge that tied together the base of the 8 x 8-inch centerline stanchions. The stanchions were secured at the base with through

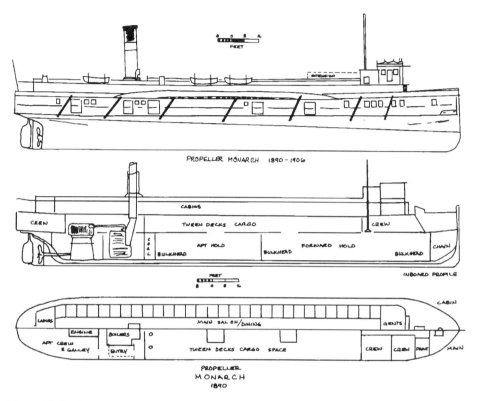

Figure 80. Conjectural general arrangement plans of *Monarch*. Drawings by C. Patrick Labadie.

bolts, some of which are still in place. The keelsons were joined by hooked scarfs.

The side keelsons were capped by a plank somewhat narrower than the keelson. This arrangement provided a support for the hold floorboards, some of which are still in place. A bilge limber hatch was located about a third of the distance forward from the stern on the port side. This hatch was the access to the bilge pump intake, which was found intact with the strainer (rosebox) still in place.

The aftermost feature of the stern portion of the bottom is the deadwood, which reinforced the sternpost. The iron fasteners that secured the planking of the stern to the deadwood are in place. The sternpost itself is missing, as are other hull timbers that formed the stern and fantail. A piece of the fantail was located, and is number 9 in Figure 78.

The rudder has not been located. The only other construction element connected with the stern was a heavy iron-reinforced timber, which is the rudder shoe (this piece is not depicted on the map, Figure 78, but is shown in Figure 81). The rudder shoe was attached to the sternpost and supported the base of the rudder.

A portion of the starboard side of the hull was found lying outboard side up and is identified as number 2 on the map. Examination of the structure showed it to have collapsed inward with the edge that would have been attached near the bilge line located away from the hull. The hull broke longitudinally on

Figure 81. Timbers heavily reinforced with metal from near the stern of *Monarch*. This portion is the rudder skeg that supported the lower end of the rudder. NPS photo by Larry Murphy.

the starboard side close to the bilge line above the bilge keelson and just below the gangways on the upper edge. The sheer strap can be seen on the edge closest to the hull in its current position. A portion of a rub rail is located on the forward edge of this section, which indicates that it is a forward portion of the hull. In the historical photographs of the vessel, this rub rail can be seen extending from the stem part way to the stern, and its presence gives the structural location of this portion of hull. There are iron hull patches on this hull section.

Sections 3 and 5 are similar and probably from the same location on the hull. The notable feature of these pieces is the half-round, canvas-covered railing on the edge farthest from the hull. White paint is still visible on this rail. The rail was originally located on the inboard side at the cabin deck level and is the top of the gunwale. Both pieces are inboard side up and stripped of both exterior and interior planks.

Section 4 is a piece of hull lying outboard side up. The possibility of it being a section of decking is discounted because the paired timbers are set the same distance apart as the hull frames, clearly indicating it is hull construction.

Section 6 is the starboard stern. The piece is lying inboard side up, and on it can be seen two of the iron hull-support members: the sheer strap and the stern terminus of the truncated iron arch. Together, section 1 and section 6 represent about 195 feet of the starboard side from the turn of the bilge to the main deck level. There is more of the starboard side of the hull than hull bottom present on site.

The piece of decking (Number 7) lying across the stern between the thrust-bearing mount and stern shaft-bearing is part of the cabin (upper) deck and was from the area above the coal bunkers. The identifying characteristics of this piece are three round holes visible in the port side (north) of the segment. Iron rings with the same diameter as these holes were located on site (Figure 83). The rings were constructed to support two covers. Examination of the artifact concentration in the vicinity produced examples of the two covers that fit inside the rings, indicating they were coal scuttles. The smaller was an iron grate, and the larger was solid, much like a manhole cover. The top cover would have been flush with the deck when in place. Removed, the coal bunkers could be vented through the inner grate.

154

Figure 82. Hull structure and brass fixtures in the rarely visited portion of *Monarch* at a depth of 130 feet. NPS photo by Larry Murphy.

Hull section 8 is the port stern, which mates to the starboard hull piece (12) and the deadwood. It is lying inboard side up. The position of this piece and the general configuration of the large hull sections give the appearance that the stern may have been pulled apart. The separation may be the result of a natural break as the hull "relaxed," but it also may reflect salvage activities to ease engine removal. The stern may have been pulled apart by tugs, which explains the displacement of the 100-foot-long starboard section of the stern. Section 9 is a portion of the fantail construction.

Section 10 is part of the stern crew quarters that would have been between the main and cabin deck aft. This section is of lighter construction than other segments of the hull and is pierced by two port hole openings. The port holes have been removed. Port holes

Figure 83. Scattered wreckage of *Monarch* off the port side of the hull. In the center are hardwood cargo winches and two iron rings that were coal scuttle hatch coamings. NPS photo by Larry Murphy.

155

were only found on the stern of the vessel after the modifications to the pilothouse and lengthening of the Texas deck. Earlier photographs taken prior to the modifications show square windows in the aft crew quarters.

Near Section 10, off the port side of the hull, is the main artifact concentration. A bath tub is indicated on the drawing because this feature is easily recognizable to sport divers, and, in fact, it has become the subject of countless photographs with the predictable "diver-in-tub" artistic composition. The area was photographed and videotaped to serve as a base line for monitoring future artifact attrition.

Component Number 11 is a portion of the starboard hull side and is lying on top of the port side of the hull, outboard side up. There are two side cargo hatches, or gangways, located in this section. The two gangways indicate this hull segment is from the forward hull side under the arch.

Component 12 is the port side and clearly shows the arch and sheer strap assembly. The piece is positioned nearly parallel to where it would have been attached, and it is inboard side up. The section broke just below the metal sheer strap, leaving a few feet of hull side above the turn of the bilge on the port side. One section of hull in the forward area (Number 13) is outboard side up. This hull section must have been in place prior to the separation of the port side from the bottom. This section of the hull may be a portion of the bow that was broken away soon after the wreck. There are gouged sections on the hull planks that may be the result of the initial wreck event. It is unlikely that the gouges were caused by post-depositional ice movement because none of the structure around the damaged planks shows any similar damage.

The remaining two sections, 14 and 15, are from the bow. The larger is a 40-foot section of the whole port bow assembly. The straight timbers of the fore portion were part of the stem post. The curved timbers to the right articulated with the bow deadwood and centerline keelson. An important feature of Section 14 is the forward junction and tie-in of the arch support and sheer strap.

The triangular piece lying off the forward edge of the bow section is a deck hook. The indicators of the deck hook are the two half-round indentations to the rear of the piece. They were probably cut to fit windlass mounts. A similar section can be observed on the foredeck of *America*. This structure is inverted.

Parts of the vessel structure that are not represented in the site remains are the upper cabins, pilothouse and decking of the vessel. The only trace of the cabin work located was some metal deck railing found in the forward portion of the bottom.

There are no indications of the transverse beams of the two decks; they seem to have been completely stripped out.

Hull Support

The *Insurance Underwriters' Vessel List* (1890) referred to *Monarch*'s hull as having "oak construction strongly reinforced with iron." *Monarch* was indeed "strongly reinforced with iron," with three principal iron hull components: the main arch ("hog truss" or "truncated" arch on both sides of the hull), the sheer strap (below the main deck level) and the gunwale girder that ran along the promenade or cabin deck level.

The main arch is attached to both the bow and stern deadwood. For the remainder of its span, the arch is attached to the vertical frames that run from the keel to the gunwale. This is a much heavier design than found on most contemporary vessels. Frequently, only every other or even every fourth frame ran the full height to tie into the arch.

Monarch's iron or steel arch was composed of ¾-inch thick stock, 36 inches wide. Prior to the use of iron or steel for the arch, they were constructed entirely of wood. Earlier arches were composed of several layers of heavy oak timbers with mortises for the vertical frames. The metal arch reinforcing of *Monarch* is on both sides of the hull frames. Where the arch enters the hull, it is beneath the hull planks. Portions of the arch may be seen above the level of the promenade or cabin deck in Figures 19 and 20. The arch is constructed of iron and runs

Figure 84. Forward end of starboard stern section of *Monarch*. This section is inboard up with the metal sheer strake clearly visible. The photo is looking aft. NPS photo by Larry Murphy.

along both the inside and outside of the vertical frames. Its shape is slightly flattened and extends just above the deck rail, thus sometimes referred to as a "truncated" arch.

It may be that the metal reinforcing in the hull of *Monarch* was steel, rather than iron. *United Empire* was reported to have

Figure 85. Metal sheeting likely associated with boiler room of *Monarch*. NPS photo.

had steel arches (*Chicago Tribune* March 23, 1883; May 21, 1883; *Chicago Times* May 27, 1883). It is likely that *Monarch*, which was built later, did as well. As of the time of the field work on *Monarch*, there was no easy method to determine the composition of metal underwater. Contemporary accounts, like modern ones, often used iron and steel interchangeably and are not reliable. "Iron" or "ferrous" are used in this report with the realization that the material referred to may be steel. When there is a high certainty that steel is used, it will be so labeled.

There apparently was a box girder arrangement at the level of the cabin deck rail. This girder is made up of two iron plates that run from the stern to the arch, and from the bow to the arch, forming a continuous iron-clad deck rail. This girder provided additional longitudinal strength.

The sheer strap ran the length of the hull inside the frames under the main deck level. This feature is visible on hull sections 6 and 12 in Figure 78. This member, unlike the others, is made of a single layer of iron sheeting, riveted together and tied to the inboard side of the vertical frames (Figure 84). The material seems to be the same stock as the main arch: ³/₄-inch

thick and 36 inches wide. Two widths have been riveted together to give a sheer strap width of about 72 inches.

An inside framing of timbers tied the top and bottom of the sheer strap into the frames, and a vertical frame was laid over the joints of the iron sheets making up the strap on every fourth frame. This detail can be seen in the site map and also in Figure 84. The details of the forward junction of the arch and sheer strap are located on the port bow section, segment 14.

There is no evidence of the sheer strap on the outside of the hull. It has been suggested that this member was included in the ship construction for protection from ice, but that was not the case. This strap is on the inside of the frames above the normal water line, and the hull was planked with 4-inch-thick oak hull planks.

The three support systems provided a particularly strong, rigid hull. This is reflected on the wreck site by the large size and structural integrity of the various hull elements that have survived.

Iron was used in two additional instances within the *Monarch* hull. The centerline stanchions were tied together with iron strap for additional longitudinal strength. These stanchions may be seen on the site map (Figure 78), and the straps appear as the long ribbon-like element running along the inner port edge of the hull bottom. The stanchions were torn out, and some are held up above the bottom, still supported by the iron strapping that ran along the upper portion of the port and starboard edge of the timbers. The stanchions are on 4-foot centers, except in the stern section where they are closer together, and may have been used as additional support for the boiler deck. The angles that were made into the strap suggest that it ran from the aft deadwood, up under the boiler deck and along the underside of the main deck beams to be tied into the bow. The bow section of the stanchions has not been found and was probably torn off with the bow when the ship broke during the wreck.

Another major use of iron in *Monarch*'s construction was to line the boilerroom. A section of this lining may be seen in Figure 85. The practice was fairly common on Great Lakes steamers as a precaution against fire. A similar section of sheeting was located on *Chisholm* (Figure 65).

Propulsion Elements

The stern portion of the hull remains is particularly interesting because the engine and machinery mountings are still in place. The largest feature is the engine mount or bedplate. It is made of cast iron and attached to the large engine bed timbers built into the floor frames (Figures 86, 87).

Apparently the engine was removed with little difficulty by the 1908 salvors. It was simply unbolted from its bedplate. The threads on the mounting bolts show little damage and are still clearly visible. One of the most obvious features of the engine mount is the main shaft bearing to the stern of the mount.

Proceeding along the drive train toward the stern, another machinery mount is visible. The mount is a very large, single timber with four holes (Figures 78, 88). This is the mount for the thrust bearing. A thrust bearing was necessary to minimize the pressure against the internal crankshaft bearings of the engine and the engine mounts. The thrust bearing transmitted the push of the screw to the hull through this heavily constructed fea-

ture. The thrust bearing, a high-cost and reusable item, must have been salvaged with the engine and shaft. A second shaft bearing is located aft of the thrust-bearing mount. Thrust bearings may be easily observed on *Glenlyon* and *Chisholm* (Figures 95, 69). The *Glenlyon* bearing is a multi-collar type and that of *Chisholm* the earlier single-collar type.

Located near the hull, in the area off the engine mount is a 5-foot-long, upright iron pipe (Figure 89). The pipe is riveted together and connected to a box-like, through-hull fitting. This is the overboard discharge for the circulating pump of the con-

Figure 86 (top) & Figure 87 (bottom). Two views of the engine mount and main bearing of *Monarch*. NPS photos by Larry Murphy.

Figure 88. Illustrator Jerry Livingston drawing details of thrust bearing mount, looking toward the stern. NPS photo by Larry Murphy.

denser. An intact example may be seen on the port side of the engine room of *America*.

Auxiliary Machinery

A manually operated, double-acting water pump is located in the engine room area (Figure 90). This would have multiple uses aboard a vessel like *Monarch*. The pump was used as an auxiliary feed pump for the boilers, a fire pump or an emergency bilge pump. A wooden handle was inserted through the top allowing two people to operate the pump. This pump is similar to one located on the bow of *America*.

This artifact concentration area also contains machinery, including a water pump with a flywheel. An example of the cargo winches found on the site is

Figure 89. Overboard discharge pipe for the condenser. NPS photo by Larry Murphy.

visible in Figure 83. The winches were mounted along the centerline above the main deck. An iron A-frame supported the end opposite the large iron roller. The winches were mounted in pairs above the gangways and were friction turned by a line shaft with a smaller friction roller that fit between the iron rollers of the two cargo winches. They were used to lower and raise package freight from the main deck to the hold. Several wraps of rope were passed around the slowly turning hardwood roller that functioned as a friction drum. A long portion of the line shaft with the smaller rollers was also located within the hull structure.

The 14-inch-diameter wooden friction-drums were 6 feet 8 inches long and turned on a 3.5-inch-diameter shaft. A six-spoke wheel 2 feet 8 inches in diameter was still attached to one end of the drum. The spoked wheel, which was turned by a friction drum mounted on a long shaft, was made in two pieces. The inner section appeared to be a casting that included the spokes. The 9-inch outer, flat rim was attached by rivets.

In Figure 91 (left center) a portion of a steam radiator may be seen. Great Lakes vessels used boiler steam piped throughout the living and working quarters for heat. Steam radiators, much like ones used in buildings, were the local heat genera-

tors. Similar intact examples containing three elements were located on *America*. One intact specimen is in the social hall of *America*.

Figure 90. Manually operated water pump. These pumps were used as bilge pumps or fire pumps. A similar pump is located in-place on the bow of *America*. NPS photo by Larry Murphy.

Cargo

The assemblage of artifacts in the stern area is interesting and informative. Cargo, machinery and ship's fittings are found in close proximity. Figure 91 shows some of the cargo and fittings. Five boxes, containing either rivets or threaded bolts, are still intact. The bolts and rivets have corroded together to form a solid mass the shape of the packing box. Broken China and brown bottles are strewn over the area. The brown bottles are of the type frequently used for beer, but curiously, some of these are packed completely full of grain and stoppered with cotton (Figures 91, 93). There has been some speculation that these were beer bottles of the salvors that were somehow filled with grain. It is more likely the bottles contained grain samples. It has also been suggested that the samples were seed grain. Most likely the bottles contain samples of the cargo grain.

Formation Processes

The remains give some indication of the wrecking process. The vessel was apparently listing to port on the bottom as the breakup occurred. Most of the artifacts and sections are on the

Figure 91. Artifact scatter off the port side of the *Monarch* hull. There are four boxes of cargo in the right center. The contents were rivets and bolts. Bottles and chains are also shown in lower right. To the left is a portion of the ship's steam radiator. NPS photo by Larry Murphy.

Figure 93. Bottles in the area of cargo concentration on *Monarch*. Many of these bottles were filled with grain and stoppered with cotton. NPS photo by Larry Murphy.

kiwit Bay and protects its waters from all but northeast winds.

Site Description and Analysis

Glenlyon came to rest astride of the shoal, on an apparent heading of about 255 degrees in November 1924. The wreckage lies in two principal fields; the bow lies inside the shoal ridge and the stern on the seaward. Parts of the fragmented hull are spread along a linear distance of more than 900 feet, with smaller pieces somewhat further afield. In general, all of the propulsion machinery lies in shallow water associated with the remains of the stern, on the seaward side of the reef. The majority of the wreckage lies in less than 50 feet of water; much of it can be seen from the surface under the right conditions of lighting and water clarity (Figure 92).

Most elements of the wreck are easily identified despite the disarticulated nature of the remains, because most parts, although greatly transformed in appearance, are not far removed from their structural location in the vessel. Bow features lie at one end of the field and stern features at the other. Historical documentation indicates that there were no large-scale commercial salvage operations on the wreck. No significant portions of the vessel were noted as missing from the site. The only contemporary salvage was directed toward removal of the cargo of wheat. No trace of grain could be found during the field work at the site.

The stern of *Glenlyon* rests seaward, or to the east of the shoal which bears its name, in depths varying from about 20 to more than 100 feet. Furthest from the shoal (and in deepest water) are the ship's aftermast and small portions of the hull from the stern, lying about 100 feet east of the larger portions of the stern. In this area is a small steel structure, which may be a stern deck house that was added in 1918 (*Canadian Railway and Marine World* 1918: 126).

Nearer the shoal in shallower water is a field of wreckage covering an area 100 feet wide and 300 feet long, and including what is essentially the whole after end of the ship. At its northern extremity, the field includes heavy but discrete items from the fantail of *Glenlyon*, such as a spare propeller blade, cast iron mooring bitts, a deck capstan with the drive shaft attached and the twisted remains of the fantail itself; the rudder, its shaft and the bearing-collar are still held in the tangled steel of the fantail's shell plating.

Moving up the reef face, the next section of wreckage is the most impressive single piece, and it consists of the whole engine room section of the bottom, with keel and frames to the margin-plate at the turn of the bilge, the main engine and several auxiliaries, the tailshaft and propeller and a large section of

port side, which is the deeper side of the hull. The hull sides broke away from the bottom higher above the bilge line on the port side, and the side left in place served to trap many artifacts on the port side of the hull. The extent and nature of the salvor's activities are not known, but the stern area appears to have been separated and moved with the aid of surface vessels.

Glenlyon: Site Description and Analysis

Site Location

Glenlyon is on a shallow reef, known as Glenlyon Shoal, north of Menagerie Island on the south side of Isle Royale near Siskiwit Bay. The charted vessel position is 0.7 statute miles from the Menagerie Island light on a true bearing of 62 degrees. It is on a true bearing of 169 degrees from the western point of Schooner Island and 124 degrees true from the starboard-hand nun buoy ("N"2") in the Malone Bay entrance channel. The site can be located by running a course of 169 degrees true from the west end of Schooner Island a distance of 2.2 statute miles. *Glenlyon* is at 47°57'8"N and 88°44'53"W.

The wreck site is an exposed and treacherous ridge of submerged rocks one-half mile northeast of Menagerie Island Lighthouse on Isle Royale's easterly side. The rocks are the northernmost features of a ridge that runs eight miles in a southwest-to-northeast direction from Houghton Point and includes Menagerie, Long, Castle, Siskiwit and Paul islands, plus a long string of reefs and shoals. The whole string encloses Sis-

Figure 94. Archeologist Dan Lenihan examining the triple-expansion engine of *Glenlyon*. The engine lies on its port side in 30 feet of water at Glenlyon Shoals. Photo by Mitch Kezar.

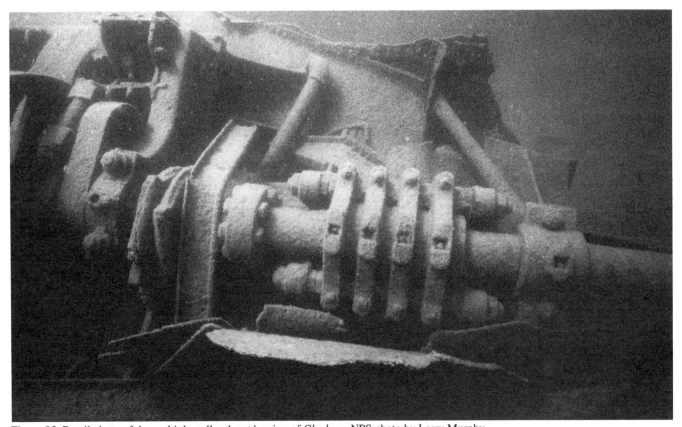

Figure 95. Detail photo of the multiple-collar thrust bearing of *Glenlyon*. NPS photo by Larry Murphy.

the port side. A smaller portion of the starboard hull side is present to the north of the engine. Prior to the 1985 field work, an intact port hole was observed on the port hull side below the engine. The port hole glass and storm cover were removed by

Figure 96 (above) & Figure 97 (below). Views of *Glenlyon* steam engine and main shaft from the top. NPS photo by Larry Murphy and Mylar field drawing by Jerry Livingston.

looters in either 1984 or early 1985.

From a diver's perspective, the engine is massive, and it towers above the crankshaft in a jumble of huge castings and forgings. The columns that once supported the huge cylinder-chest have been broken. As a result, the cylinder-chest is lying collapsed onto the crankshaft, and all of the connecting rods are bent out of shape. The cylinder-chest lies over at an angle of about 90 degrees from vertical, leaning to the port side.

The thrust bearing with its four collars is visible directly to the stern of the engine (Figures 94, 95). The propeller shaft has been broken, and the tailshaft and propeller are twisted about 30 degrees out of line to the port. This twist may be the result of the engine block and hull bottom assemble sliding down the reef and bending the shaft. The cylinder chest is over some of the port side of the hull, indicating that the hull had collapsed before the engine moved to its present location. Two of the four blades of the iron propeller have been sheared off at the hub, and a third blade has been broken in half. It is not clear whether they were broken off when the ship struck the reef or at some time afterward. The missing portions of the propeller blades were not found at the site. It is most likely that the blades were broken during the wreck event.

The engine is a direct-acting, inverted, vertical, triple-

expansion steam type, which was developed in the mid-1880s and introduced to the Lakes in the steel steamer *Cambria* in 1886. This design became the standard for most commercial steam vessels everywhere between 1890 and about 1930. In the remains of *Glenlyon*, the three cylinder-heads with diameters of 20, 32 and 54 inches may be clearly distinguished (Figures 94, 96, 97). A large air pump was run off the moving connecting rods and still attached to the starboard side of the engine. The pocketed jacking gear used to turn the engine during repairs is also notable (Figure 94). The large size of the gear indicates that it may have also served as a flywheel.

Several other auxiliaries lie in close proximity to the engine in the chaotic scatter of the engine room debris; among them are the steering engine, which the ship's construction plans show on the main deck just aft of the engine room bulkhead; various steam pumps for sanitary water, boiler feed, ballast water, bilge suction and fire fighting; the refrigeration compressor or "ice-machine;" the electrical generator ("light plant"); and numerous tools and parts. Most of the apparatus appears whole, relatively undamaged and gives the impression it would be easily operable. The engine room remains lie heaped in a 50-foot-long pile. The engine and engine room are in a position that affords a remarkable opportunity for a detailed study of early 20th century steam technology on the Great Lakes.

Alongside the engine room wreckage is a 70-foot section of

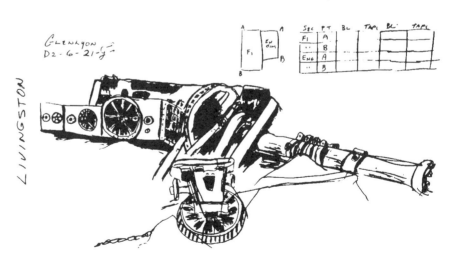

the ship's hull that formed the port side of the machinery spaces, from the afterpeak bulkhead to the boilerroom. It is pierced with several through-hull fittings for water intakes and ballast discharge, which are all lying exposed; the hull section is inboard up. On the reef directly below the low pressure cylinder head is an overboard discharge valve and pipe, much like the one remaining upright on the site of *Monarch* (Figure 89).

Near this section are several other sections of shell plating, bulkheads and decking from the after end of the ship, and a very heavy length of iron pipe, which seems to have been the main steam line from the boilers to the throttle valve on the engine; the measurements correspond to that element in the vessel's original shipyard drawings. Sections of ballast piping may also be seen in the vicinity; they are similarly large, but of a lighter gauge of pipe.

Further to the west, but still on the seaward side of the ridge, are two more areas of hull wreckage. The first consists of many sections of bottom and side plating and frames, and the second

Figure 98. Larry Murphy detailing the anchor pocket of *Glenlyon*. Photo by Mitch Kezar.

is an 80-foot length of the spar deck from the starboard side, with a pair of mooring bitts still standing near the outboard edge. The decking is presumed to have come from just forward of the boilerhouse, where such a pair of bitts are shown on the vessel's plans.

In the shallower water right on the reef ridge lie the ship's two water-tube boilers, one entirely fragmented and the second with its shell torn off, but with the furnaces, smoke chests, tubes and sheets all standing intact. The remains of the latter boiler stand above the reef and reach to within 10 feet of the surface. This boiler is probably the shallowest piece of wreckage on the site, and its weight and bulk is substantial enough that visiting dive charter boats use this feature as a convenient mooring aid.

On the inside (west side) of the ridge that forms Glenlyon Shoal is the forward portion of the ship, from all appearances considerably more than half of the length of the hull. As one swims to what would have been the starboard side of the vessel along a wreckage trail extending into deeper water, deep gouges become apparent in the smooth rock face of the ravine. It is obvious that those scars are not a result of the initial impact, because they are too deep (below the waterline of the original vessel) and are probably a function of ice moving pieces of wreckage around during the winter. At some points, rusted bolts can be found in these cracks. This forward portion of the wreck extends access more than 600 feet of Lake bottom, but the greatest part of it consists of one mass about 300 feet square. Spread here are sections of bottom, side and deck; beams, hold pillars (stanchions), frames, piping, angles and shell plating. One steel mast lies draped across about 120 feet of debris, twisted grotesquely so that it is no longer easily recognized. There are also heavy steel gangway-doors and the davits that were used to lift them, 'tween-decks cargo winches and the line shafts to which they were connected and deck machinery from the spar deck. The forecastle and forepeak portion of the bow (Figure 98) lies relatively intact for about 30 feet of its length, with the immense steam windlass still firmly rooted in place. The chains are paid out across the windlass and through the hawse-eyes to a pair of stockless anchors. The chain links measure 6 x 9 inches. A steam capstan also lies nearby, as does a mooring winch, both remnants of the forecastle deck above the windlass room. At least three pairs of bitts are also lying within 50 feet of the site, more parts of the forecastle deck.

Some of the plating and trim from around the bow illustrate unusual attention to fine craftsmanship; they have a yacht-like quality about them, despite husky businesslike proportions. Some historians observed that the Wheeler shipyard failed because of its particularly costly craftsmanship and its uncompromising standards. Comparison of *Glenlyon* with other steel ships at Isle Royale tends to support that claim, although *Glenlyon* was built 15 years earlier than the other steel freighters there, and its workmanship may be more representative of 1890s standards than it is of any particular shipyard's; when compared with other Isle Royale wrecks, though, it is most reminiscent of *Algoma*'s Scottish artistry, and contrasts perceptibly with the utilitarian style of *Emperor*, *Kamloops* and *Congdon*.

Near the wreckage of the forecastle there is a single intact cabin structure standing upright amidst literally thousands of tons of ship parts. The cabin appears to be part of the Texas or officers' quarters from abaft the pilothouse. There is no simple explanation for its survival, as it is of far lighter construction than the portions of broken hull around it. This cabin was apparently added in 1918 (*Canadian Railway and Marine World* 1918: 126) for officers accommodations. Its separation from the surrounding wreckage may be the result of being relatively lightly attached to the structure, which enable it to separate as a unit. The cabin now contains no artifacts and the portholes have been removed.

Continuing in a southwesterly direction, other sections of the ship's hull may be found as much as 300 feet beyond the large concentration. The large field lies under a pair of ledges, but the remainder is spread across a flatter rock bottom. Recognizable pieces of structure include identifiable portions of side, with shell plating, vertical frames and distinctive longitudinal stringers; spar decking, in some cases with mooring bitts on it; and double-bottoms. This scattered material probably came from the midships portion of the hull that lay originally on the shallower part of the reef.

Site Formation Processes

The extreme distance between features of the *Glenlyon* wreck proved to be 960 feet; the ship measured only 345 feet in length. The condition and orientation of the wreck is almost certainly a result of the movement of ice floes over the site. Historic accounts describe the ship lying on the shoal and slowly beginning to break up. Witnesses say that the decks rose amidships, which indicated that the ship's bottom was caving in, and with rigid vertical I-beam stanchions running down the centerline, it forced the decks up. Not long afterward, the ship's back broke just forward of the boilerhouse, and the integrity of the hull failed. Once the ship broke, the two halves began to settle on either side of the reef, the bow to the inside and the stern to the outside; the heavy boilers settled out into the shallow water on the rocks, along with portions of the collapsed midships section of the hull. Those lighter parts of the hull that lie in the shallowest water were the easiest moved by drifting ice, and they are the ones that seem to have been carried farthest. The bow and stern portions of the ship ended up somewhat protected from the ice by the rocky ledges against which they came to rest, and they have consequently moved little since the sinking. Considering the alignment of the islands and shoals in the Menagerie group, there is only one direction in which ice could logically drift, and that is toward the southwest. It is logical to assume that any further, undiscovered parts of *Glenlyon* lie in that direction, probably consisting of the lightest parts of the ship's fabric or those that came to rest in the shallowest part of the shoal.

The fractures of the hull structure may also be the result of decades of ice action. Many of the steel shell-plates have simply been torn apart. Some failure has been along seam lines, but much is through the plates. Other than *Algoma*, the wreckage of *Glenlyon* is the only metal wreck of Isle Royale that has been completely broken up. Other wrecks have not been disarticulated to the extent of *Glenlyon. Glenlyon* is also the shallowest of the metal wrecks, except for the bow portion of *Cox* is also severely fractured and dispersed. The relatively small size of the structural remains of these two wrecks reflects the powerful destructive forces active in the shallow waters of Lake Superior.

Another aspect to be considered in the fracturing of the Isle Royale vessels is the variation of steel used. A comparative metallurgical analysis of the steel compounds used in construction coupled with the nature of natural impacts would give insight into the use-lives of vessel hulls of the Lakes for periods represented by the Isle Royale shipwrecks.

America: Site Description and Analysis

Site Location

America is in the channel between Thompson Island and the main island, known as North Gap, out of Washington Harbor at the south end of Isle Royale. The vessel is 0.7 statute miles from the northeast tip of Grace Island on a true bearing of 331 degrees. The vessel is marked by a privately maintained obstruction buoy in North Gap channel. *America* can be located in the channel by rounding the northeast end of Thompson Island entering Washington Harbor, using the white daymark beacon

Figure 99. NPS SCRU diver Ken Vrana examines the fine-lined bow of the north shore steamer *America*. Photo by Mitch Kezar.

on Thompson as a point of reference, on a true bearing of 119 degrees and traveling a distance of 0.2 statute miles. The position of *America* is 47°53'39"N and 89°13'15"W.

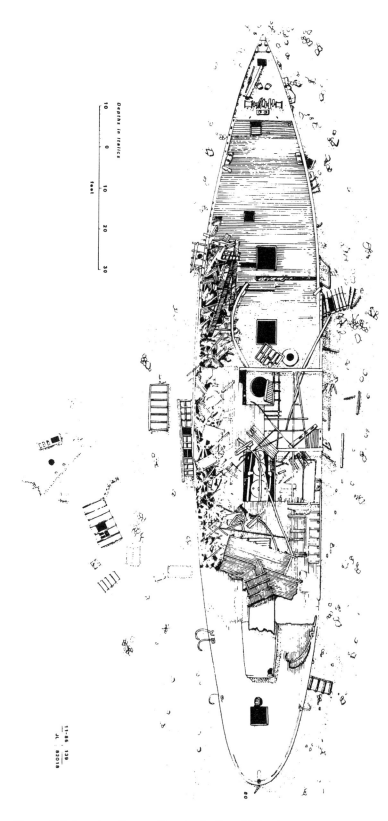

Figure 100. *America* site map. Drawing by Jerry Livingston.

Site Description and Analysis

The wreck event that resulted in *America* finding a final resting place against a steep underwater cliff in the channel to Washington Harbor is well documented. Considerable changes in the vessel remains have occurred due to both natural and cultural transformational processes; but, in a comparative sense, *America* is a very intact and accessible shipwreck. Sport divers have devoted more dives, by far, to the exploration of *America* than any other site at Isle Royale. It is renowned well beyond the regional diving population as a spectacular dive.

The heavy recreational activities have contributed significantly to site transformational process. Normally, contemporary salvage is the major source of human-induced change to a historic wreck site occurring after the initial sinking. In the case of *America*, both initial salvage efforts and later attempts to raise the hull resulted in some notable effects on the site, but slow vandalism over the years by sport divers before the Park asserted management control has resulted in the vessel being largely stripped of portable artifacts.

The most visually dramatic post-depositional effects on the site, however, were a function of natural forces at play on the wreck over the years. Major ice build-up in Washington Harbor and North Gap channel has torn away or crushed the majority of bow superstructure and the forward hull above the main deck level. The bow is just under the surface and the lowest point of the stern is in 75 feet of water. Impact from ice is apparent to a depth of at least 30 feet (Figure 101).

Post-depositional effects accounting for the major structural changes to the vessel are from ice damage. There is also evidence of purposeful modification from salvage efforts. The vessel's archeological value has been considerably diminished by removal of portable artifacts by sport divers.

The hull of *America* has both a stern and port list. Measurements of the hull-list angle were taken at various points on the ship. Readings were taken with a small plumbline and 180-degree protractor affixed to a square, plastic slate. The device provided a direct reading of degrees of slant angle from vertical. The stern list is between 21 and 24 degrees and seems to be somewhat more pronounced at the bow, where there is a 26-degree port list, a result of the combination of bottom topography and a 2-foot 8-inch deadrise in the hull.

A swim over the hull from bow to stern brings many features into view (Figure 99). The windlass is the most imposing of the shallower deck features. Historical records indicate the steam powered windlass is the original.

The windlass has two friction drums or warping-ends on each side. These were used to tighten the mooring lines. Two horizontal mooring pipes, which are parallel to the deck and extend through the hull and resemble the hawse pipes, are located forward of the windlass. The mooring lines were run through the pipes and wrapped

168

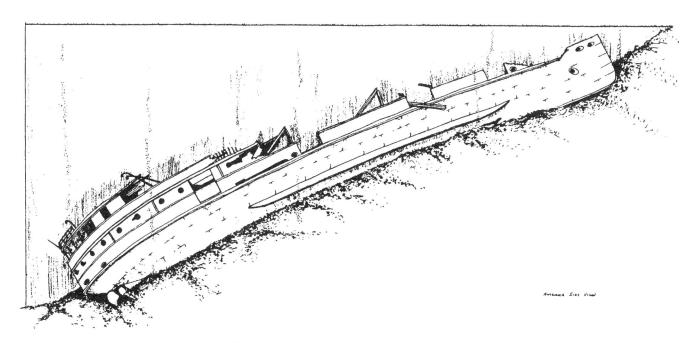

Figure 101. *America in situ* in the North Gap of Washington Harbor, Isle Royale. Perspective view from starboard stern. It is rarely possible to see the whole ship from this point. This illustration is a composite drawing from several dives. Illustration by H. Thom McGrath.

around the slowly turning friction drums to move the ship along the dock, or tighten the lines. The loose band toward the center of the windlass from the warping ends around the cylinder is the brake.

The windlass was enclosed on the main deck just forward of the saloon deck and pilothouse. Ice damage has removed the forward structures and wooden portion of the side of the hull. Forward of the windlass is a small hatch at the forepeak. This is the chain locker in which the anchor cable was kept. *America* carried two anchors of 2,100 pounds and 1,900 pounds. The 1928 Hull Inspection recorded that both anchors were fitted with 60 fathoms (360 feet) of anchor chain. The 1965 salvors reported 200 fathoms of anchor chain in the chain locker (Marshall Salvage Report to Carlock Dec. 3, 1965, on file Isle Royale National Park). Apparently the salvors removed the chain; the locker is now empty. There is no record as to the present location of the anchors, which were removed by the Corps of Engineers during WWII (J.R. Marshall 1974, 1986 interview with Holden; Capt. Alfred Sorenson 1982 interview with Labadie).

On the port side just forward of the windlass is a double-acting pump. This pump was mentioned in the 1928 Hull Inspection report and was termed a fire pump. A similar pump was located on the site of *Monarch* (Figure 90).

The pilothouse and forward cabins were removed by ice. It is uncertain

how far toward the stern ice impact to the cabin and boat deck went prior to the abortive 1965 salvage operations. The salvor's reports indicate they removed much of the superstructure. The report states they removed "a great deal of the damaged superstructure....A large portion of the damaged second deck...opening the area over the engine...and the area around the opening...has been shored" (*Duluth News Tribune* Oct. 25, 1965).

On the other side of the bulkhead of the galley area and social hall are the engine spaces. There is a passageway through the bulkhead at the top of the galley stairs. Directly on the other side was a 4-foot-wide hallway with a doorway on the star-

Figure 102. View up the main stair case from the floor of the social hall. The stairs are partially blocked by collapsed stern cabin bulkheads. NPS photo by Toni Carrell.

169

Figure 103. View of the purser's cabin showing file boxes and silt accumulation – a potential diving hazard encountered in the interior of *America*. The purser's cabin was directly aft of the social hall. NPS photo by Toni Carrell.

larger features will be discussed as if one immediately faced the stern on the port side of the engine and continued in a circular route around the stern of the engine and forward up the starboard side.

The most imposing sight as one reaches the bottom and faces the stern is the large silver-painted pipe that must be passed. This pipe is the overboard discharge for the condenser and is connected to the outside hull through a discharge valve. An example of this arrangement can be viewed on *Monarch* (Figure 89). The condenser is the large rectangular-shaped feature on the port side of the engine. There is a similar pipe that goes between the condenser and the low pressure cylinder of the engine. This is the eduction pipe and routes the used steam from the engine to the condenser.

Immediately to the right is a dual-acting, steam-driven water pump. The 1928 boiler inspection report describes the pumps of *America* as having a 4-inch diameter and 8-inch stroke. This is the bilge pump, and it may have been the last piece of machinery operated on the vessel. The bilge pump was overcome by the rapidly rising water from the pierced hull as the ship sank. The long hole in the hull that sank the ship is in the vicinity of the engine and boiler spaces and can be viewed on the outside of the hull at the turn of the bilge on the starboard side. On the inside, just below the bilge pump near the very bottom of the hull, is the bilge injection pipe and the sieve-like rose box. Also in this area are the injection pipe and valve for the condenser. The larger valves close to the bottom of the hull near the forward of the engine are seacocks.

Proceeding toward the stern, the electric generator or dynamo is on the right and just ahead is the switch and fuse panel. The generator supplied the ship's electric power and was controlled by the knife switches on the switchboard. Many of the switches have been removed as souvenirs.

At the stern of the engine, the shaft connection can be seen. Along the stern bulkhead are broken shelves and racks for spare parts and tools. Around the engine on the starboard hull is another pump. On the engine cylinder casing is painted an American flag. Historical documentation indicates that the crew of *America* was well known as a competent and proud bunch. The fact that they painted the flag on the engine reflects this contemporary characterization of them. A comparative study of the mechanical revisions and decorative embellishments done by engine crews on the various Great Lakes vessels could tell us much about the behavior of people in a completely technological work environment, if approached from an anthro-

board side that was one of the normal accesses to the engine spaces. The other was forward on the same side opposite the high pressure cylinder. The missing bulkheads of the engine spaces were evidently removed by the 1965 salvors.

Bulkheads exist for what once were the chief engineer and assistant engineer cabins on the starboard side of the engine. In addition, the baggage room and stewards' quarters bulkheads are partially intact.

The engine room of *America* is a remarkable example of turn-of-the-century Great Lakes marine engineering and offers a well-preserved, three-dimensional display of engineering details mostly unavailable from written documents of the period. The virtually complete engine room is fully plumbed, with asbestos insulation still present on most of the pipes. All accessories, valves and some of the steam gages remain. A swim through the engine room is a step into the technological past, without the filters of restoration or interpretation. An understanding of *America*'s engine room is informative and helpful in understanding the machinery remains of the more broken up vessels of Isle Royale. It is also a useful place to start in developing an understanding of the much larger and more complex machinery spaces of the larger intact vessels of Isle Royale. *Emperor*, for example is a much larger and more complex version of *America*'s engine room.

The engine room of *America* can be entered by dropping feet-first through the grated walkway near the forward port corner of the engine. A brief description of the machinery and

pological perspective. The Great Lakes is one of the few places that have an environment conducive to the preservation of this kind of information.

The engine controls are on the starboard side of the engine, and the engine was operated from that side. There are two additional pumps on the forward engine room bulkhead that separates the engine spaces from the boilerroom. These pumps are the boiler pumps, one the main and the other the auxiliary. Above the starboard pump is a control panel containing valves and gages for boiler feed. The remaining valve handles on the seven pipes were painted red. Above the feed pumps and the feed-water control panel is the main steam-gage panel with holes to mount six gages. Again, this panel, which is often looked at by the engineers, has been decorated with a hand-painted star and was outlined in red. Egress from the engine room is the same location as the entrance.

Going out of the engine spaces and proceeding forward brings the boilerroom into view. The boilers are intact, they did not explode as the vessel sank. There is no breeching present, and the stack, pilothouse, Texas and cabin decks are missing forward of the boilerroom. Only a few beams and frames exist above the engine room.

The stack was removed by the 1965 salvors. Their salvage report to the Park superintendent gives the following information:

The remains of the ship's funnel, weighing some seven tons, were severed from the boilers with a cutting torch, and with the assistance of the cruiser, drifted over the side. This exposed the steel room over the engine and boilers.

On the port side directly forward of the engine are the remains of a Ford Model T truck that was being transported as cargo. The vehicle is hardly recognizable after being stripped by divers. Intermixed in the wreckage on the port side forward of the Model T is a hardwood roller with an iron wheel attached. Nearby is a leather belt of the same width as the iron wheel attached to the roller. This wood and iron roller is identical to the friction drums located on *Monarch* (Figure 83). They were used to handle cargo. A rope was passed around the slowly turning hardwood drum, and cargo was lowered into or raised from the hold. The leather belt is a conveyor belt and was undoubtedly used to drive the drum, probably by an electric motor. The drums were turned by a shaft running fore-and-aft.

Forward of the boiler spaces is the coal bunker, still containing coal. The coal scuttles, which are round insertions into the deck, can be seen in the diagram on the starboard side. The port scuttle is hidden under the deck wreckage. Nearby is a hatch cover. This is not original, but constructed and left by the 1965 salvors. Across the deck in the port wreckage are three corrugated pipes, one with a small hatch cover still attached. These were also part of the 1965 salvage efforts.

There is a 5-foot by 6-foot 4-inch hatch on the centerline forward of the coal bunker. This was a cargo hold. On the bottom of the hold is tar that has spilled out of buckets, some of which are still present. There are also packing-box remains, but most everything else has been removed.

There is another similar hatch about 12 feet forward of the

cargo hold. This was the hatch access to the crew's quarters, and there are stairs leading down. The wooden crew's bunks remain. The smaller hatch that is off-center to the port also leads to the crew's quarters. This hatch, which may have been originally a vent or dumbwaiter before the 1911 alterations, is a vent and exit for the crew's quarters.

One additional piece of *America* wreckage has recently been located. In October 1984, Park Ranger Ken Vrana and seaplane pilot Tom Wunderlich observed what appeared to be a piece of a vessel's pilothouse on the side of Washington Harbor opposite the hulk of *America*. Closer inspection by Park staff indicated what is probably the roof of *America*'s pilothouse at a depth of 15 feet. They report it being 10 x 12 feet with a 2-foot square "manhole" on top.

George M. Cox: Site Description and Analysis

Site Location

The wrecks *Cumberland*, *Chisholm* and *Cox* are on a shallow reef southwest of Rock of Ages lighthouse on the south end of Isle Royale. The vessels are within a square, 3,000-feet on a side, with its geographic center at 47°51'28"N and 89°19'32"W. The center is 3.9 statute miles from the starboard-hand nun buoy at Cumberland Point on a true bearing of 275 degrees. It is 336 degrees true from the starboard-hand nun buoy southwest of Rock of Ages lighthouse and 222 degrees from the lighthouse a distance of 4,000 feet (useful for chart plot). On-site location is best using North Rock: the site is 258 degrees true, 2.4 statue miles from the rock. The wreck of the passenger steamer *George M. Cox* lies less than a mile east of the *Cumberland/Chisholm* site on a separate ridge of Rock of Ages Reef, just south of the southernmost tip of Isle Royale, in depths ranging from 15 to approximately 85 feet.

Site Description

The wreckage lies in two main fields, with the bow half of the ship scattered on a flat shoal, and the nearly intact stern portion on the side of a gently sloping ridge about 150 feet southeast (Figure 104). None of the superstructure remains in the shallower water, but some of the upper deck framing may be seen in the deeper water associated with the stern wreckage.

The bow portion of the ship has been fragmented by the action of waves and ice, so that it now covers a field approximately 350 feet in length, with some sections of hull another 200 feet away to the east. Most of the bow lies in shallow water, varying from 15 to little more than 25 feet in depth, although smaller portions have been swept from the shoal into deeper water surrounding it – probably the result of drifting ice or currents. Relatively strong currents, which swept over the reef in a southwest-to-northeast direction, were observed during field work at the site.

Historical photographs show *Cox* perched on the reef with its

Figure 105. Forepeak and chain locker of bow of *George M. Cox.* NPS photo by Toni Carrell.

bow high in the air and its stern underwater (Figures 32, 33). Island residents and commercial fishermen reported that the ship rested in that position for many days before the strain broke the ship's back, and the hull was broken cleanly in two just forward of the boilers. When the delicate equilibrium that held the ship on the rocks was destroyed, the stern began a slide backward into deeper water, and the bow settled on the reef to begin its collapse and disintegration.

Before the ship broke up, wholesale scavenging was done on board, including the removal of bedding, foodstuffs, hardware and tackle by local fishermen and others. Heavier equipment was removed by commercial salvors. The ship's 10 metal lifeboats were among the items removed at this time. An examination of the wreck site indicates that other more extensive salvage was also attempted, although its extent is not clear from either historical documentation or observations on the site. Heavy cables may be seen, for example, around the ship's four Scotch boilers, and it appears that there was some effort made to raise them. It is not known when this was attempted, but it could have been in May 1933, when the salvage tug *Strathbuoy* was on site (*New York Times* May 29, 1933). There is also a large wooden timber associated with heavy cable in the wreckage of the bow, and it may be inferred that this is a remnant of

some commercial salvage work. The timber is about 16 feet long and 6 x 10 inches in cross section, with iron work at one end. It appears to be a boom from some sort of derrick. Aside from those two elements, there is little tangible evidence of large scale salvage work on the wreck, and the orientation and condition of the wreck may be attributed entirely to natural causes. The exception is the removal of smaller artifacts by sport divers, which has been noticeably thorough. Virtually none of the thousands of fittings and furnishings associated with the passenger and crew quarters can be found on the site.

The array of wreckage on the reef offers some fascinating insights into the ship's structural characteristics and into the circumstances of its loss. Probably the first, most obvious and most enduring impression of the ship is its very light construction. The structural elements are all lightly built by comparison with other ships of the Isle Royale population, although contemporary accounts considered it to be heavily built and one of the strongest vessels of its class afloat (*Marine Engineering* 1901: 458-460). It would be of considerable interest to compare *Cox* with contemporary vessels not considered heavily built.

The frames of *Cox* are small in cross-sectional dimension, the keel is built up of light steel plates and the floors are very narrow. The shell plating is correspondingly thin. Everything about the hull construction suggests a smaller vessel than *Cox.* Indeed, the ship originally was smaller. It was built 233 feet in length and later lengthened to 259 feet in 1908; it was originally fitted with two decks and was later given a third.

All indications are that *Cox* was originally built for speed. The hull form was a deep "V" configuration with considerable deadrise, much like in a yacht. The ship was clearly designed for speed and not for carrying capacity, and it had unusually fine lines as a result. The desire for speed is further evidenced by the four large boilers, which were more than adequate for a 259-foot craft, and unusually powerful for the ship's original 233-foot dimension. In the first six weeks of operation, the vessel broke the record for the run between St. Joseph, Michigan and Chicago. The average speed was 19³/₄ miles per hour, which gave it a ranking of the one of the fastest boats on the Lakes (Ibid.).

The ship's design had nothing to do with its running up on Rock of Ages Reef, but it certainly contributed to the vessel's loss as a result of that incident. Major portions of *Cox*'s hull bottom may be seen on the reef, and much of it shows clear evidence of contact with the rocks. The bar keel, which extends seven inches below the ship's bottom, is made up of several plates riveted together. The keel is folded over at right angles to starboard for a distance of at least 50 feet where the ship slid onto the reef. The ship's bottom is dished and ruptured on the port side where it apparently ran over the rocks. It must have caused immediate and massive flooding. One section of the bottom along the centerline is caved in more than a foot, perhaps the point on which the vessel balanced so precariously before it broke in half. This section of bottom appears to have articulated with the section of the hull under the boilers, which is either fragmented or missing.

The forepeak section of the bow, about 20 feet in length, lies near the shallowest part of the reef, largely intact to the collision bulkhead (Figure 105). The ship's distinctively oversized hawse eyes are both there, although the starboard one, along with the attached hawse pipe, has been wrenched away from the shell plating. Both anchor chains run through the hawse eyes to their respective anchors, which lie close by. It was reported that the original Baldt stockless anchors of *Cox* each weighed 2,840 pounds (Marine Engineering 1901: 458-460). The anchors are painted white, like the rest of *Cox,* but there are also conspicuous traces of the ship's original emerald-green paint underneath, remnants of the old Graham & Morton era. *Cox*'s windlass is also lying 12 to 15 feet from the section of forepeak, in close association with the chains.

The forepeak stands about 45 degrees from vertical, and the lower portions of it are buried in gravel and rocks so that none of the forefoot can be seen. There would be some value in examining the extreme forward part of the ship's keel to determine exactly where the bow impacted with the shoal when *Cox* grounded. From all appearances, the first impact occurred just a few feet aft of the forefoot, and the ship seems to have glided swiftly up a gradual slope to wedge itself firmly on the rocks. It was reported that the ship was doing at least 10 miles per hour when it hit the reef (*Daily Mining Gazette* May 30, 1933). The inertia drove the ship well up on the reef.

An effort was made to establish the location of the ship's impact, and a shallow depression was found in the reef, which was about 30 feet to starboard (east) of the present day fore-and-aft axis of the stern portion of the wreck. There is reason to believe that the ship slid up into that depression when it ran aground, because the water on either side of the depression is too shallow to have admitted the ship without a terrible impact. Furthermore, numerous rivets from the ship's hull were found wedged in the cracks and crevices in the rocks of the depressed area, while none were observed on the rocks on either side. No gouged marks were found in the rock, however, which would

Figure 106. Larry Murphy drops through starboard stern gangway to examine interior of *Cox.* NPS photo by Toni Carrell.

have further substantiated the impact location.

The wreckage strewn in the shallow area on the flat of the shoal appears to represent the entire forward half of *Cox,* including the forepeak, keel and associated deep floors, the bottom and the sides of the hull. At least 10 discrete pieces of wreckage may be attributed to that part of the ship, varying from about 10 feet square to more than 70 feet in length.

Among the large sections of shell plating and frames is also a field of wreckage and debris extending nearly 100 feet in length, which includes steel pipes, columns, beams, angle-bars, cables and nondescript pieces. There are also machinery parts, some evidently associated with a large freight elevator known to have been installed in the ship. Although few of the pieces are joined together, many can be identified from *Cox*'s original builder's plans. The "midshipsection" of the builder's plans illustrates 7-inch-diameter pipe hold-stanchions under the main deck, 6-inch I-beams supporting transverse deck beams and "Z-bar" frames made up of steel angles. Components of each description were observed in the scattered debris on the shoal, and it may be assumed that they represent the framing of the whole forward half of the ship, which has been slowly and relentlessly disassembled by more than 50 years of natural site processes.

This portion of the bow wreckage is interesting because of the diversity of the remains lying there, and because of its easy access; the central concentration of remains, dubbed the "junkyard" by sport divers, lies in about 20 feet of water. It must have been staggering in its profusion, rich with the artifacts sifted by gravity from *Cox*'s salons and cabin, before it was picked over by divers and swept of its lighter debris by decades of currents, waves and ice floes.

Some of the debris in the area may be from cargo carried by the ship, as it is difficult to attribute some of it to the ship's structure. Virtually nothing is known, however, about the nature and extent of cargo carried by *Cox* on its last voyage. It is known to have carried large cargoes in its earlier days, and inasmuch as it was given a freight elevator during its 1932 reconstruction, it may be assumed that it was intended to carry heavy freight in its last role, too.

The stern portion of the *Cox* wreck consists of a little more than one-half of the ship's 259-foot length, lying substantially intact on a gently sloping bedrock bottom (Figures 106, 107). The ship lies on its port side, with a huge mass of tangled structural debris alongside on the port side and forward of the hull. The wreckage scatter includes machinery, structural elements from the hull and portions of superstructure and rigging. The dominant feature at the site is the ship's hull, which is impressive in its dimension, but still betrays a certain fragile quality by the extent of its distortion and the nature of its damage. There is also a distinct grace about the form and proportion of the stern, where there is enough integrity of the ship left to preserve some of its original beauty.

The stern measures 140 feet in length, and there are other sections alongside and underneath it which are 30 or 40 feet long. The keel is preserved unbroken, but the hull around it is twisted almost 90 degrees, so it is almost inverted at the fantail and nearly at right angles to the bottom at its forward extremity; specifically, the angles rotate from 195 degrees at the fantail to 290 degrees at the forward end. There are huge tears in the hull as a result of the exaggerated torsion (Figure 108). The tears correspond to structural features within the hull. One tear extends longitudinally for 70 feet, just to the starboard side of the keel, and another runs transversely about 20 feet from the rail to the keel, along the line of the afterpeak bulkhead. The longitudinal tear exposes the entire length of the propeller shaft, and the propeller itself has been wrenched from the stern-bearing. The propeller is displaced in a forward direction about 20 feet from its proper location, and although this was not confirmed by

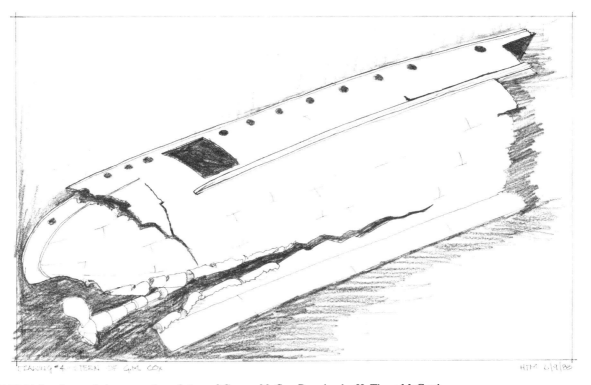

Figure 107. Field drawing, artist's perspective of stern of *George M. Cox*. Drawing by H. Thom McGrath.

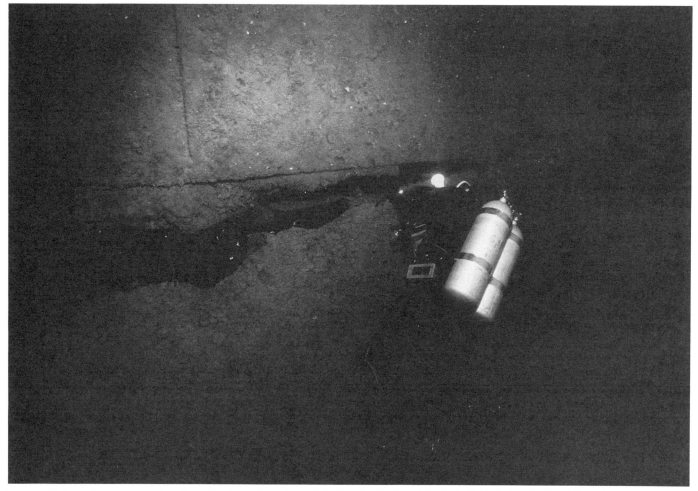

Figure 108. Larry Murphy examines the main shaft of *Cox* through the longitudinal crack in the hull. NPS photo by Toni Carrell.

field observation, it leads to the conclusion that the engine has been torn from its foundation in the hull, and also lies some 20 feet forward of where it should be. Some displacement of the engine was observed by the commercial salvors who visited the wreck in 1933: "The bottom of the steamer was torn out, the engines jolted from their moorings and the vessel is listing toward deep water...." (*New York Times* May 29, 1933).

Site Formation Processes

When the condition and orientation of the hull are compared with physical aspects of the Lake bottom in the vicinity of the wreck, they suggest a sequence of events that would explain many of the seemingly unconnected details. A process can be identified that leads from the historical photographs of the wreck event to the conditions observed during the recent field work.

Photographs and historical research show that *George M. Cox* rested on the reef approximately amidships following its stranding, with its stern under water and a list of about 10 degrees to port. A search of the reef led to a 10-foot deep spot in the middle of a six-foot shoal, and there is some possibility that *Cox* struck the sloping side of this ridge, to be funneled into the 10-foot groove or depression by its momentum. With its bottom badly torn, it filled quickly, and because it rested just for-

ward of amidships, the stern settled, lifting the bow high out of the water. The unsupported weight of the bow caused the hull to fail at the point where it rested on the reef; the immense tension on its structure would have focused at the sheer strakes, the bands of steel shell plate running along the ship's side just under the deck line. A historical photograph shows the hull failure to have been just forward of the boilers or almost precisely amidships. The bow settled on its port side in the shallow trough formed by the upper surface of the reef, and it went to pieces there, probably not long after the hull broke. The same photograph showing the ship broken in half does not show any sign of the bow portion in the shallow water nearby.

The stern half of the ship stood briefly on the slope of the reef, with its forward end resting in just a few feet of water and the aftermost portion jammed into the bottom supporting the whole weight of the wreck. Storm action caused the wreck to begin shifting, and it soon began to descend the slope astern of it. With the weight of the whole wreck borne by the projecting shapes at the stern, the propeller, rudder shoe and stern frame were all torn away as the ship moved backward down the rocky surface and turned slowly onto its port side, in the direction it was originally forced by the wreck event. Several parts torn loose in the descent indicate that the wreck moved more than

100 feet astern in the process, and about 30 feet to port as it rotated onto its side. The rudder shoe, for example, lies almost exactly 120 feet forward of its proper hull location, and under the starboard side of the wreck; the railings from the upper deck at the stern lie in the same area, and fully 150 feet forward of their original location on the stern of the ship (Figure 104). Both seem to have been torn off while the wreck lay some 120 feet forward of its present position and slightly to starboard. It was also during the backward slide that the propeller and shaft were forced through the bottom of the hull, leaving the terrible rent that is so dominant a feature of the ship's bottom today, and undoubtedly wrenching the engine from its mounts. Some historical accounts assert that the ship's engines were torn loose by the impact of striking the reef, but this seems unlikely, and certainly the long tear in the bottom plates did not occur at that time.

Figure 109. Steam drums atop Scotch boilers of *Cox*. Steam drums were not common features on Lakes craft. NPS photo by Larry Murphy.

The ship's four Scotch boilers (Figures 109, 110) lie just forward of the after section of the hull, and their support cradles or "saddles" lie still further up the slope, some as much as 30 feet away. Curiously, all four of the boilers are upright, despite

Figure 110. *Cox* boilers with nylon base line used for site mapping operations in place. NPS photo by Larry Murphy.

Figure 111. Interior of *Cox* aft of engine spaces. NPS photo by Toni Carrell.

wreck came to rest in its present position, because the remains of the deck structures lie around the stern wreckage, very near their appropriate locations. Even the remains of the smokestack can be seen just to the port side of the wreck, lying flattened on the bottom amid the shambles that were the cabins. Boat davits and other portions of the superstructure are easily distinguished in the same large field of wreckage. This appears to be the only Isle Royale wreck site with such extensive remains of wooden superstructure, although *Cumberland, Monarch, Algoma, Henry Chisholm* and *America* all had similar wooden cabins.

On the opposite side of the reef, at the foot of an abrupt drop off and in a long gully nearby, are other portions of *Cox* wreckage, including several steel tanks, a gangway door, sections of the ship's side and the one short section of bottom possibly associated with the boiler spaces, which may have come from the missing section of hull amidships. A part of the bulwark from the forecastle also lies there. Ice movement is the likely mechanism of movement for the structural elements

the fact that the stern portion of the wreck lies on its side. It appears that the section of ship's bottom, which supported the boilers, is completely broken up. The bottom of the hull may have been broken during the wreck event, and later by the weight of the boilers bearing down on the hull as the stern section moved down slope.

Evidently, there was an effort to salvage the boilers, which would explain the steel cable around the boilers at the site, as well as why the boilers are upright and the hull that contained them is on the port side. A section of bottom, with centerline keelson structure intact, was found lying a considerable distance from the boilers on the opposite (or east) side of the reef, in about 70 feet of water; inasmuch as it contained through-hull fittings that appear to have been associated with the boilers, it seems likely that it was the section of the bottom between the bow and the stern that supported the boilers. It is not known how this section of bottom became so far removed from the remainder of the wreckage, but the possibility cannot be discounted that the wreck was blown up by commercial salvagers to free up the boilers for salvage, although such an attempt was clearly unsuccessful. There was no other indications of explosion observed.

Cox's superstructure was apparently relatively intact until the

Figure 112. Ship knee located in a deep water ravine near the bow of *Cox*. This element is evidently from *Chisholm*. NPS photo by Larry Murphy.

located in this gully. Wooden framing members were observed that did not belong to *Cox* at all, but had the characteristics of *Henry Chisholm*'s hull construction. The distinctive shapes of the frames distinguished them as having come from a ship's bow (Figure 112). The attributes of the frames closely match those of *Chisholm* and indicate that the bow may have been completely disarticulated. Other wreckage is suspected to lie between the two sites, perhaps including portions of *Cumberland*'s missing bow.

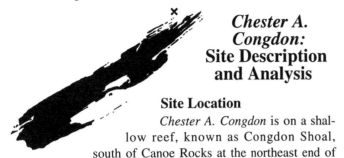

Chester A. Congdon: **Site Description and Analysis**

Site Location

Chester A. Congdon is on a shallow reef, known as Congdon Shoal, south of Canoe Rocks at the northeast end of Isle Royale. The charted position of the vessel is 2.0 statute miles from Hill Point on a true bearing of 14 degrees. It is 279 degrees true from the starboard-hand nun buoy at Locke Point and 271 degrees true from Blake Point Light. The site can be located in water by rounding Blake Point and setting a course of 271 degrees true and traveling a distance of 4.3 statute miles. *Congdon* is located at 48°11'36"N, 88°30'52"W.

Site Description

The site of *Chester A. Congdon* offers numerous exceptional exploratory dives to visitors and students of Lakes vessel technology alike. An interesting swim can be made from the bow (Figure 113), over the wreckage field to the top of Congdon Shoal, and then to the stern (Figure 114). Elements from the hull and deck that contained the first nine hatches lead up from the bow and across the top of the reef. Many of the shallower fragments show evidence of ice and wave impact in addition to the torn plates from the wreck event. There are bottom sections that show the scalloped shell plates, which appear as if they were draped over the frames, typical of grounding damage and heavy ice impact.

The aft section can be followed down to the engine room and stern cabins. The stern is laying at a very steep angle and drops quickly to a depth of 180 feet. There was no contemporary salvage on the stern. The only removal of material has been done through the actions of sport divers.

The bow can be penetrated through a number of entrances. The pilothouse and forecastle deck cabins can be entered through the doors along both sides. The room below and forward of the pilothouse is the sitting room, with the captain's quarters aft. The captain's office and living quarters can be entered on the forecastle deck. Much of the paneling is intact. The pilothouse has narrow oak strips on the walls and a white painted ceiling. The captain's quarters and the private quarters on the spar deck were walled with quartered oak.

The windlass room can be entered easily through the salvage hole in the deck. The hole, although it looks much like a hatch, is the result of salvage operations to remove the windlass. On the port side of the bow deck, the frame for the stairs leading into the windlass rooms can be seen. In the windlass room, the forward mounts for the windlass are in place. The chocks and bitts are also present.

Moving aft, the owner's staterooms and private quarters can be seen. This area, like the rest of the bow, was completely salvaged, but the bulkheads and some fittings are left. Immediately below on the lower deck are the chain locker forward, the dunnage and lamp room on the starboard, the hall and forward crew quarters on the port.

Congdon is an important and impressive site. It offers a relatively safe dive on the bow, where there are few portable artifacts. Divers wishing to penetrate the wreck can do so in the pilothouse and forecastle cabin. Deeper penetrations are more serious. The bow section can withstand heavy diver visitation with little additional impact. The mooring buoy should allow this to be done with a relatively high degree of safety.

The stern section, however, should

Figure 113. *Congdon* bow, artist's perspective. Drawing by Jerry Livingston.

be treated somewhat differently. The stern is a serious dive by any standards, and heavy diving may increase the attrition of portable artifacts that remain in the undisturbed engine and cabin areas. The *Congdon* stern, along with *Kamloops*, are the least dived sites in Isle Royale and, consequently, the best preserved – a result of their inaccessibility due to depth. Neither of these sites should be buoyed, and diving on them should not be encouraged.

Site Analysis and Formation Processes

Congdon, lost in November 1918, is the largest sunken vessel known in the waters of Isle Royale. The 532-foot vessel was lost in dense fog while making a timed run from Thunder Cape to Passage Island. Historic accounts indicate now that the ship hit the southern reef of Canoe Rocks at a speed of 9 knots (see Chapter IV).

The shoal that is now the resting place for the bulk freighter rises from 180 feet deep on the seaward side to a narrow point of solid rock, which is just under the surface. The reef drops quickly on the shoreward side to 110 feet deep. The ship apparently hit the southern edge of the shoal in 18 to 20 feet of water near the bow, with the stern over the deep water on the seaward side.

The first reports of damage stated that the forepeak, number 1 and 2 starboard tanks and number 1 port tank were full of water (*Cleveland Plain Dealer,* Nov. 8, 1918). The initial assessment was that the vessel could be freed, if the cargo was removed. These reports indicate that the original hull damage was not severe, probably only shearing of rivets and opening of seams in the bottom of the hull. Had there been significant distortion of the hull, more involved salvage operations than lighterage would have been initially discussed. Only lightering tugs and barges were involved in the first salvage attempt.

Unfortunately, a southeast gale interrupted the lightering operations. After a day of 55 mile-per-hour winds, the stern section broke and sank in deep water. After sinking, the stern was still attached to the bow section along the hull on the starboard side and deck plate, although the port side had been fractured. The stern hull section listed to starboard as it sank (Figure 36). The tearing of the hull was undoubtedly the result of the working of the still-buoyant stern section (some 400 feet of the hull) as it was buffeted by the waves created by the gale. The bow section was solidly aground, with the increased deadweight of the water in its flooded forward tanks. The first two tanks extended below the number 1 hatch (to frame 29). During the storm, the stern section acted much like a lever moved by the waves, which tore the port shell plates aft of the number 6 hatch.

Historical accounts indicate that the bow remained above the water for only a short period (Figures 35, 36, 37). By the end of November, the bow was reported to be in 50 feet of water, but salvage of forward-end machinery had already been made (*Fort William Daily Times Journal* Nov. 29, 1918; *Lake Carriers Association* 1918: 142-143). Examination of the bow section shows a virtually complete salvage operation, one that undoubtedly was conducted before the bow submerged. All machinery, steering and navigation gear, windlass, chains and anchors – even the sinks, tubs and toilets – were removed. A

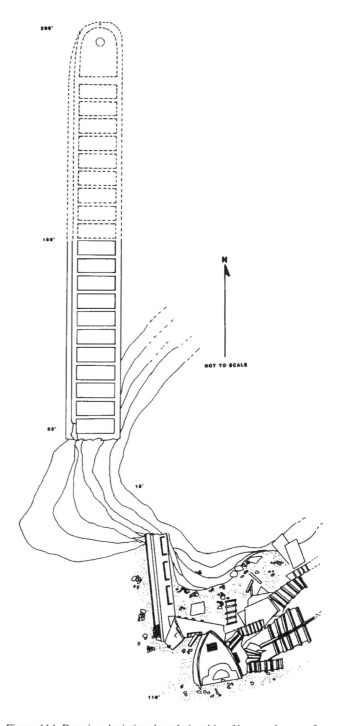

Figure 114. Drawing depicting the relationship of bow and stern of *Chester A. Congdon* on Congdon Shoal. Drawing by Jerry Livingston.

large, rectangular hole was cut in the forward deck to remove the capstan and lift out the windlass. Considering that only gas cutting technology was available at the time, there can be little doubt that this hole in the forward deck-plate was cut before the deck was submerged.

The bow section of *Congdon* sank upright at the base of a steep cliff with the stempost facing upslope, tilted up at an angle of 59 degrees and about 35 degrees to starboard, in 60 feet of water (Figure 113). The aft portion is 110 feet deep. The bow gives the appearance of having been cleaved from the rest of the vessel and is a singularly spectacular sight for divers.

Evidence of the sequence of events that led to the deposition of *Congdon*'s bow in such an unlikely position is to be found in the general area and on the bow itself. Steel hull construction techniques also contributed to the formation of this site.

The bow section is comprised of the first 24 frames of the ship. At frame 24, the blueprints show a reinforced, water-tight bulkhead from the keel to the forecastle deck at the aft end of the forward cabins. This tended to form the forward section of the vessel into a strong, integral unit.

After the stern sank in the gale two days after the wreck, the bow section was attached to the stern primarily along the bottom and lower side on the starboard side. The contemporary photographs show that both the port and starboard hull sides were severed, the port side at hatch 6, and the starboard, aft of hatch 9. The port side of the hull is raised in the air indicating that the rupture is complete on that side and that the separation extends to, and probably through, the hull bottom on that side. The principal attachment appears to be along the lower starboard side. There were probably stress cracks along the bottom and sides of the forward part as a result of the levering of the stern section prior to its sinking.

In the absence of historical documentation on the activities of the salvors, the separation of the bow portion must be considered as the result of natural forces. Although the bow was accessible and cutting torches were used to salvage the windlass, there is no indication that the salvors attempted to recover the bow portion intact.

A possible sequence of depositional events can be constructed based on the material remains. The port side separated first, with the bottom buckling and separating as the heavy bow portion began to sink. As the bow unit sank and began to slide down the steep underwater cliff, the port shell plates forward of the number 6 hatch (around frame 48) were torn loose from the port bow, both along the side of the hull and the bottom. Construction elements that can be attributed to this section of the ship can be seen on the top of the reef and along the slope above the bow to the north of the stem. As the bow gathered momentum, the starboard side remained attached to the stern long enough to turn the bow to the starboard as it moved downslope. The bow separated from the restraining starboard hull remnants and slid stern first down the cliff. Because of the last attachment of the hull being along the starboard side, and the configuration of the rock face, the bow portion shifted to the south as it descended.

Examination of the aft portion of the bow section reflects the events as described. Along the port side (Figure 124), the hull plates are sharply bent toward starboard. On the starboard side, the torn plates are bent both starboard and forward. There is a puncture on the starboard side of the bow that evidently is the result of detached hull elements sliding down the slope sometime after the bow had reached the bottom of the incline. Later, the starboard deck stringer plate and shell plates, including sections of the bottom, moved down the hill to their present location.

There is impact damage on the stempost of *Congdon*. The depression is 6 feet long, deep enough to displace the first two frames and crumple the shell plates. The stem is folded over to starboard. The area begins below the water line at the level of the lower hold-stringer. Although the damage is severe, it does not appear to have ruptured the plate seams. It seems unlikely that this damage was caused during the initial impact with the reef. If it had been, it would be expected that there would be further damage to the bow as the inertia of the ship forced the bow up and over the obstruction responsible for the stem damage. The forefoot of the bow is undamaged, indicating that it did not come in contact with the reef.

There are at least two possible explanations for the damage to the stem. It may have occurred earlier in the operating season, a result of a slow-moving contact with an obstruction. The damage was not severe enough to require immediate repair, but probably would have been repaired during the winter layover.

The second possibility is that the stem damage was done as the bow section moved down the steep slope during its sinking. If this is the case, the impact may have contributed to the turning of the bow and tearing of still-attached shell plates as the bow slid along the submerged cliff face. It is possible that further examination, mapping and identification of the hull fragments between the bow and stern section will lead to a more complete understanding of the wreck event and depositional sequence for this site.

Emperor/ Dunelm: Site Description and Analysis

Emperor and *Dunelm*, because of their proximity, will be treated together as two components of a single site.

The site lies to the northeast of *Congdon* on Canoe Rocks. *Emperor* is the second largest and most recent of the 10 major shipwrecks of Isle Royale. *Dunelm* was a stranding, and little remains to mark the site.

Site Location

Emperor is resting on the northeast end of Canoe Rocks located at the northeast end of Isle Royale. The charted position of the vessel is 1.9 statute miles from the starboard-hand nun buoy at Locke Point on a true bearing of 298 degrees. The site is 33 degrees true from Hill Point and 281 degrees true from Blake Point Light. The site can be located by rounding Blake Point and setting a course of 281 degrees true and traveling a distance of 3.5 statute miles. The vessel location is 48°12'02"N and 88°29'30"W. Historical coordinates were telegraphed to the Ottawa Department of Transport on June 4, 1947. These were given as: 48°14'06"N and 88°28'24"W. About 100 yards east of the *Emperor* bow are remains that are ascribed to the *Dunelm* stranding incident.

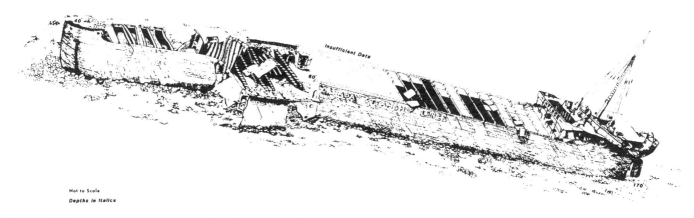

Figure 115. *Emperor,* artist's perspective. Drawing by Jerry Livingston.

Site Description

The stranding of *Dunelm* was the earliest of the known disasters (1910) that have left a material record on Canoe Rocks. The steel package freighter, like the other vessels of Canoe Rocks and vicinity, was downbound from Port Arthur. The freighter, carrying a cargo of wheat and flour, ran aground on the rocks during a December snowstorm. Salvors were summoned after the owners gave the ship up as lost. The Canadian Towing and Wrecking Company secured a "no cure-no pay" contract from the underwriters and eventually managed to free the vessel, despite heavy seas and severe cold.

What is probably the site of *Dunelm*'s stranding was located in 1982 by members of the Submerged Cultural Resources Unit northeast of the bow of *Emperor* on Canoe Rocks. The two anchors, chain cable and lifeboat frame (Figure 116) are all that mark the site.

It is not clear why the anchors and cable remain on the site. A prudent captain would surely have dropped anchors after grounding to ensure the distressed vessel did not sink and slide off into deeper water. The contemporary newspaper accounts state that there was concern that the waves would push the stranded vessel, with 14 feet of water in the engine room, off the reef into deep water (*Detroit Free Press* Dec. 21, 1910). The anchors and chain cable appear to have been dumped, rather than set. Anchors and cable are usually items that are salvaged because of the high resale value. In the historical record there is no indication of the reason for the salvors leaving the anchors on site. An explanation may be that the anchors and cables were dropped to lighten the ship. Follow-up documentation dives were conducted by volunteer Scott McWilliam and Park Ranger Ken Vrana in 1984. Following is an excerpt from their dive records.

The anchor stocks are six inches wide and tapered, being 12 inches deep at the base and eight inches deep at the top.

A large pile of chain lies around the anchors, and the payed-out chain runs approximately 30 degrees from the anchors.

The only other material remains in association with the anchors is the frame of what is most probably a lifeboat. The origin of the lifeboat remains is unknown. It is unlikely that the frame is from *Emperor*. Historical documentation indicates that there were two wooden lifeboats carried on *Emperor,* one port

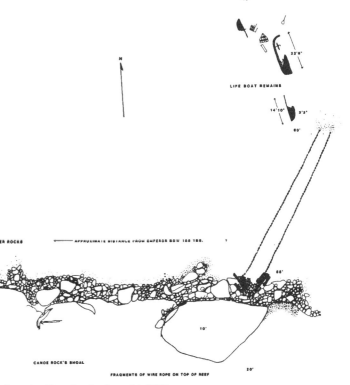

Figure 116. *Dunelm* stranding site. Drawing by Scott McWilliam.

and one starboard on the stern boat deck. Two lifeboats associated with *Emperor* were reported found in Todd Harbor soon after the wreck (*Toronto Evening Telegram* June 26, 1947). One of these boats is reportedly sunk in Pickett Bay and the other southwest of the NPS campground. Again, McWilliam's

Figure 117. Dan Lenihan recording the windlass of *Emperor.* NPS photo by Larry Murphy.

description from the 1984 dive:

> The writer measured the lifeboat from stem to stern and found it to be 22 feet 6 inches in length. A second piece of lifeboat was measured at the gunwale and found to be 14 feet 10 inches in length and the attached portion of hull 3 feet 2 inches at the widest point from the gunwale towards the keel. Flakes of white paint could still, upon close examination, be found.

The argument could be made that the anchors and lifeboat remains are not from *Dunelm* at all, but related to some other unrecorded wreck event. Although that is certainly possible, the fact that historical photographs of *Dunelm* aground and being towed (Figures 41, 42) show the lifeboats and anchors missing adds strong support for them being related to that ship. This hypothesis is further strengthened by the fact that all anchors and lifeboats associated with the nearby *Emperor* are accounted for.

Emperor is one of the most dived sites of Isle Royale. Stinson (1980: 15) rates the site as the third most visited shipwreck in the Park, however recent review by Vrana of Park diving-visitor registrations for the years 1980-85 indicates that *Emperor* is the second most dived site behind *America.* The continued popularity of this site can be attributed to the visual impact of this imposing site. The stern remains are nearly intact, while the bow has been subjected to serious ice impact, but is still quite recognizable.

The vessel is in two major sections (Figure 115). The bow is in shallow water ranging from 30 to 80 feet. The intact stern section starts in about 80 feet and goes to a depth of 150 feet at the propeller. The hull broke just forward of amidships. There are 17 of the original 30 hatches intact between the stern cabins and the hull break.

The stem and small portion of the bow is raised upward at a steep angle following the shallowing rock cliff face. Some of the wreckage appears to have been pushed beneath other elements, somewhat in an accordion fashion, although probably the result of collapsing, rather than occurring during the wreck event, according to historical accounts. The spar deck and forecastle deck are missing. Along with the deck structure, all traces of cabins, furnishings, head fixtures and artifacts are gone. This is a remarkable amount of material to have been removed from the site, whether from natural or cultural agents. There is also no evidence of the captain's cabin, furnishings, pilothouse or rigging to be found among the bow remains. The unaccounted for material includes at least eight sinks, three tubs and three toilets (as indicated in the blueprints).

The appearance of the bow section today is the result of the wreck event and natural processes. The structure is flattened and broken. Hulls sides are lying with hatch coamings on top of the ore. Undoubtedly ice has had the most impact to the remains. More than four decades of shelving pack ice riding over the rocks and shallow portions of the reef are considered to be the agent responsible for the structural breakage present.

The windlass and chain locker are present in the bow wreckage (Figure 117). The windlass was mounted on the main deck, beneath the forward crew's quarters. The starboard anchor is still shipped, although it has slipped out of the pocket. The port anchor looks as if the windlass disengaged and the anchor fell to the bottom. Neither anchor was intentionally dropped during the wreck event, according to historical accounts. Original specifications called for two 7,000-pound anchors and 180 fathoms of 2¼-inch (diameter) chain cable. Presumably, the original anchors and cable are the ones on site. Additionally the vessel carried a 2800-pound kedge anchor, which has not been located.

There are two tank-like structures mounted inside below decks on the hull. Their function is unknown. In the vicinity there are 5- and 6-inch-diameter air-supply pipes and 2-inch pipes for forward water service.

The deck winches are still mounted on the twisted, nearly vertical deck. These steam-operated deck winches were used as

Figure 118. Dan Lenihan examining the cargo of *Emperor*. The ship was loaded with more than 10,000 tons of Steep Rock Mine ore. NPS photo by Larry Murphy.

mooring winches and also to open and close the telescoping hatch covers. Near the port bitts, there is a square deck hatch that allowed access to the number 1 tank.

There are five fairly intact hatches aft of the bow structure (Figure 115). The holds still contain the reddish Steep Rock Mine ore (Figure 118). The hull sides have collapsed and the port side is twisted. Roller chocks and bitts are located on the spar deck level. The roller chocks were mounted on the outside edge of the deck and the bitts were even with and just forward of the edges of the forward hatch.

Within the port hull side, wires can be seen running longitudinally within the lightening holes of the frames. These wires connected the mate's and engineer's telegraphs forward in the pilothouse with those in the engine spaces. The whistle wires were also within this wire bundle.

The partially intact stern is an unforgettable diving experience. As one descends the buoy line, which is attached to a pad eye near the forward edge of the stern cabin roof, the ship's form materializes and the ventilators

Figure 119. Video operations on stern cabin of *Emperor*. Video diver Larry Murphy. NPS photo by Dan Lenihan.

Figure 120. Larry Murphy ascending the stern mast of *Emperor*. Mast has shifted to the stern and to port as a result of mooring dive boats to it. Port list is visible in photo. NPS photo by John Brooks.

come into view. The larger pair forward vent the boilerroom, the medium sized ones open into the engine area and the smaller vents go to the galley and crew areas. There is a small deck

Figure 121. Starboard stern cabins of *Emperor,* showing the state of preservation of Lake Superior shipwrecks. NPS photo by Larry Murphy.

structure also on the roof. Aft, the stern steering wheel is, unfortunately, missing.

Other features visible on the cabin roof include the engine skylight, which was probably blown out during the sinking, and the coal bunker. The coal bunker extends along the front of the stern cabin. The galley coal was carried in the smaller bin on the port side. It is curious that the ship left port with a partially filled coal bunker.

As one descends over the forward edge of the bunker and roof that covers the aft deck winches the vessel name may be viewed. *Emperor* is painted in black letters on a white background along the forward overhang of the roof (Figure 119).

Forward of the winches is hatch 30. The hatch covers were metal, and there were no canvas covers over the hatches. The battens are mostly intact. The corners of some of the hatches have been bent upwards, a result of the escaping air as the ship sank.

The stern is lying at an angle of 23 degrees from vertical with a three-degree port list. The mast has bent to the stern to 29 degrees from its normal stern rake of about 8 degrees, and

shifted to 18 degrees to port (Figure 120). The shifting of the mast is most likely the result of the practice of using the top of the mast as a convenient mooring location for dive boats. For many years a line with a buoy was attached to the top of the mast and a dive boat, sometimes several, would use it for a mooring line. The use of the permanent NPS mooring line will prevent further damage to the mast.

The stern cabin may be entered or viewed through the windows and doorways (Figures 121, 122). There is no glass anywhere, presumably blown out when the ship sank. On the port side the forward cabin contains six bunks and was the quarters for the deck hands. Proceeding to the stern, one can view the crew's dining room, kitchen and pantry areas. (Lake boats often do not follow the nautical terminology familiar to oceanic vessels.) Cooks' quarters were the aft-most cabin. On the stern the two spare prop blades are in place inside the bulwark (Figure 123). The stern winch, emergency tiller and bits are present.

Continuing around the stern to the starboard side, one can view the the aft-most cabin, which was a private dining area, with the officer's dining room forward. Both had two windows and a single doorway. A cabin with two bunks on the stern bulkhead is forward of the officer's mess and aft of the bathroom. Forward of the bathroom is the engine room entrance, the first engineer's cabin with a single bunk and the second engineer's cabin with

Figure 122. Bunks inside the starboard stern cabin of *Emperor.* NPS photo by Toni Carrell.

Figure 123. Dan Lenihan examining the spare prop blades on the stern of *Emperor*. NPS photo by Larry Murphy.

two bunks on the stern bulkhead. The forward cabin with four bunks was shared by the four firemen (Figure 124). Three firemen were lost in the wreck.

The engine room may be entered through the skylight. The emergency wheel and throttle are intact (Figure 137). The engine room is an important collection of a working engine room of a ship with nearly four decades of alterations and revision by the numerous crews that worked the vessel. This is a rich opportunity to collect data relevant to the anthropological questions concerning the interactions of people and a technological environment. The engine room of *Emperor* will provide a rich source of data for those in the future interested in such questions, as well as those of a historical nature. It is important that attrition and impact be limited in the machinery spaces of *Emperor*.

Site Formation Processes

There are remains of eight hatches between the relatively intact five forward hatches and the intact stern portion of the hull. This mid-ship section of the hull is clearly the most damaged.

The principal factors for this heavily damaged section are a combination of wreck events and natural features and processes. The general configuration is a result of the heavily damaged hull bottom settling on the contours of the rock cliff face. The dense, heavy cargo weighted down the floors as the hull sides twisted and broke in a seemingly haphazard way. The hull beams are torn, and some appear to be missing from the wreck concentration. Beam ends probably became detached during the wreck, and the collapse of the hull sides reflected the nature of the bottom damage as the ship ground to a halt.

The historical documentation, of which the Preliminary Inquiry (conducted by Capt. W.N. Morrison, June 6, 1947) is the most useful, gives some indication of the wreck events pertinent to the site formation process. The following is summarized from that document, which contains the testimony of 10 of the surviving crew members and officers. Most agree on the basic wreck sequence.

Emperor was under way at a normal running speed of about 11 knots when it struck Canoe Rocks. There was an initial "jar" and the ship continued to scrape along the rock for a short period. The Chief Engineer reported that the initial crash woke him up, and he found that the second engineer had shut off the engine because he had lost the shaft or wheel; i.e., damaged the prop. The chief tried to turn the shaft with the engine, but there was no resis-

Figure 124. View into the firemen's cabin, which is forward on the starboard side of the stern. There were three firemen lost in the wreck of *Emperor*. NPS photo by Larry Murphy.

Figure 125. NPS diver Ken Vrana surveys the *Monarch*. Photo by Mitch Kezar.

Figure 126. Larry Murphy tests the integrity of the wood on the *Monarch*. NPS photo by Daniel Lenihan.

Figure 127. The exposed parts of the *Glenlyon* are easily accessible to illustrator Jerry Livingston. NPS photo by Larry Murphy.

Figure 128. Larry Nordby and Toni Carrell team up to gather data on the *Glenlyon*. Photo by Mitch Kezar.

Figure 129. Daniel Lenihan passes by the engine of the *Glenlyon*. Photo by Mitch Kezar.

Figure 130. Sport diving is a major visitor use category at Isle Royale National Park. A visitor begins a descent on the wreck of *America* from a commercial charter boat. Photo by Mitch Kezar.

Figure131. Jerry Livingston is surrounded by his tools as he records data at the bow of the *Cox*. NPS photo by Larry Murphy.

Figure 132. An aerial view of the *America* as it lies in the North Gap of Washington Harbor. Photo by John Hoff.

Figure 133. A NPS team member inspects the windowless pilothouse of the *Congdon*. NPS photo by John Brooks.

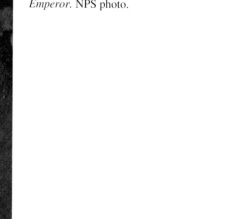
Figure 134. Dive team member at the stern of the *Emperor*. NPS photo.

Figure 135. Recording data at the bow of the *Emperor*. NPS photo.

Figure 136. Cargo in the *Kamloops*. ROV photo by Emory Kristof courtesy of National Geographic Society.

tance. Immediately, the forward portion of the vessel began to settle. Indications are that there was an initial jolt and the ship continued sliding along or over rocks. It is not clear how long

Figure 137. Auxiliary controls of *Emperor* in engine room. NPS photo by John Brooks.

this occurred, but one testimony said "4 or 5 minutes, maybe longer, before coming to a complete stop." There was one report that stated there was a slight starboard list. About 20 minutes later the stern sank rapidly. The stern section broke and may have rolled to starboard and then to port as it sank.

Reconciling the testimony of the survivors and the material record gives an indication to what likely occurred during the wreck event. Additionally, historical photographs (e.g., *Detroit Free Press* June 11, 1947) show the bow sank in just over 50

feet of water. The bottom of the pilothouse was under water, indicating a 50-foot water depth.

The first contact with the Canoe Rocks reef must have been at the very stern. The ship came close enough to the reef to cause the initial "jar" and shear off the propeller blades. Investigations of the screw of *Emperor* reveal that the hub is bare; the blades have been sheared off (Scott McWilliam personal communication). This explains why the chief engineer had no resistance on the shaft when he attempted to restart the engine. It is interesting to note that the contact with the reef was such that the rudder was not unshipped as is usual in wrecks. In fact, the rudder shoe does not appear to be bent at all, indicating that there was no contact with the reef. The prop blades were sheared off and probably remain in the location of initial contact, yet to be found.

At the initial contact with the reef, the ship, which had now lost power, began to slow rapidly. Survivors said they heard the sound of the hull scraping along the rocks for some time, apparently minutes. When the ship stopped and rapidly began to sink, it went down bow first, indicating a side, rather than bow contact with the reef. The stern does not seem heavily damaged, so the hull must have been in contact with the reef in the area of hatches 6 to13, the area of most damage.

Observations of the hull damage, which occurs mostly in the vicinity of hatches 6 to 13 from the bow, point to an initial contact with the reef along the starboard side, rather than a bow-on ramming of the rocks. A surprising aspect of the survivors testimony is the indication that the wreck was a series of jolts and scrapes, hardly what one would expect from the impact of a 525-foot vessel carrying more than 10,000 tons of iron ore moving in excess of 11 knots smacking into a rock reef. If the ship had hit in the bow the inertia would have carried it up onto the reef, and it could not have begun to sink in 50 feet of water. None of the survivors reported any shift to the stern as the vessel sank. According to testimony the pilothouse was visible from the lifeboats as the survivors rowed away.

The evidence points to *Emperor* hitting Canoe Rocks on the starboard side of the hull with a glancing blow. The pilot error responsible for the wreck was a course change, which should

Figure 138. Stern cabin of *Emperor* showing compression of the bulkhead as a result of the collapse of the stack. NPS photo by Larry Murphy.

have taken place at Trowbridge Light, being executed late. When the downbound course is plotted on a chart, it is evident that the later the change takes place, the more parallel the ship's course becomes to Canoe Rocks. The hull must have hit the rocks with a glancing blow to damage the prop blades first, and then sink bow first.

The hull broke as it sank, and, considering the relationship of the main hull pieces, it shifted to starboard. The rolling of the stern reported by some survivors is evidence that this occurred during the wreck event. The separated hull sides are closer together on the starboard side than on the port.

The breakup of the hull on the surface after the bow was down indicates some of the forces at work on the hull. The break happened after the hull was opened up sufficiently to rapidly sink the vessel. The hull bottom must have been nearly severed, putting the deck under considerable compression as the bow sank while the stern was still afloat. Some of the deck beams in the main damage area have been broken through the bracket plate on the port side. The rolling of the ship, and the hull twisting it represents, put tremendous torsion force on the hull. This force is evident in the way the hull sides in the main damage area are twisted both in and outward. The hull sides tended to collapse after the support of the deck beams was removed.

The stack of *Emperor* was probably loosened as the stern twisted and sank. The stack is still attached and lying to port. It fell with sufficient force to partially collapse the roof and port bulkhead of the stern cabin (Figure 138).

There is a crack in the bulkhead between the boiler and engine spaces. This, along with some of the natural collapse of wooden

cabin bulkheads, has led some to add credence to the story of the boilers exploding. The boilers are intact. The common-sense notion that hot boilers explode when submerged in cold water has not been substantiated in the wrecks of Isle Royale. The boiler of *Cumberland* is damaged, but the damage does not appear to be the result of an explosion. One of *Glenlyon*'s boilers is broken up, as is much of the steel hull. The other does not appear to have exploded.

The notion of exploding boilers on sinking steamers has been around for a long time. It was reported by at least one survivor that the boilers of *Emperor* exploded (the night steward in *Montreal Gazette* June 5, 1947, see Chapter IV). The rapid quenching of the hot boilers and fires would probably sound like an explosion in the midst of the stress of a shipwreck. Observations of the boilers themselves indicate this actually rarely, if ever, happens. In the case of *Emperor,* testimony by W. Gallagher, an engineer on duty when the wreck occurred, indicated that the boiler steam was "practically at the blow-off stage," and direct observation of the boilers of *Emperor* confirm they did not explode.

The fact that boilers rarely explode during shipwrecks was also noted in the Lake Carrier's Association bulletin (1938: 7):

> That boilers do not explode [during a shipwreck] has been known to Lake seamen...for years. Any number of steamers that comprised the old wooden fleet, submerged in rather shallow water were found, when raised, to have boilers intact. In recent years we have had several marked examples [of the same thing] furnished by steel bulk freighters....

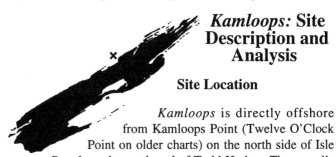

Kamloops: Site Description and Analysis

Site Location

Kamloops is directly offshore from Kamloops Point (Twelve O'Clock Point on older charts) on the north side of Isle Royale at the north end of Todd Harbor. The vessel's location is at 48°5'6"N and 88°45'53"W, which is 1.8 statute miles from the western tip of Hawk Island on a true bearing of 232 degrees.

Site Description and Analysis

As indicated in the historical record section of this report, the wreck site of *Kamloops* is more shrouded in mystery than any other wreck at Isle Royale. It is a classic case of "went missing," where a vessel disappears during a storm leaving no survivors. Bodies were eventually found at Isle Royale and speculation, ranging from reasoned to wild, abounded for many years, but it became clear over the years that the historical record itself is never going to satisfactorily answer the question of what happened to *Kamloops*. In August 1977, this became a question for historical archeology when *Kamloops* was discovered by sport divers off of Twelve O'Clock Point at Isle Royale. There is now a material record to work with and, much as in the case of a pathologist working on the remains of what had been a missing person, the archeologists adopted the role of sleuth, inevitably balancing written and oral perceptions of the past (history) with the hard facts of what can be seen, measured and felt.

So far, due to logistic and safety problems inherent in diving a site the depth of *Kamloops* (the wreck lies at a depth ranging from 180 to 260 feet), we have only been able to attain tantalizing glimpses of the remains, but already they have been sufficient to permit rejection of several theories of what happened to the ship and have suggested several new areas of inquiry. Let us review the major implications of the historic record that have bearing on reconstruction of the wreck event.

Kamloops was last seen by those who lived to report their observations December 4, 1927. Three people saw *Kamloops* from the bridge of *Quedoc*, another Lake vessel that was itself in peril from sea and weather conditions. It was several months later that flotsam associated with the ship began to be recorded at Isle Royale These residues included human bodies, life jackets, portions of a lifeboat and, significantly, some pieces of spars that would have indicated that the ship itself, and not just a lifeboat full of survivors, had played out a final drama at or near Isle Royale. There is also a second-hand oral history account by a fisherman friend of Roy Oberg that the fog whistles could be heard blowing all night at the end of the island when the ship went missing (Roy Oberg personal communication to Labadie). Although this oral account may sound weak on the face of it, the authors of this volume have learned to take very seriously the oral accounts of Isle Royale "old timers." At least

equal weight is given to their memories as is accorded to accounts of contemporary newspapers.

This still leaves the archeologist with only a few hard pieces

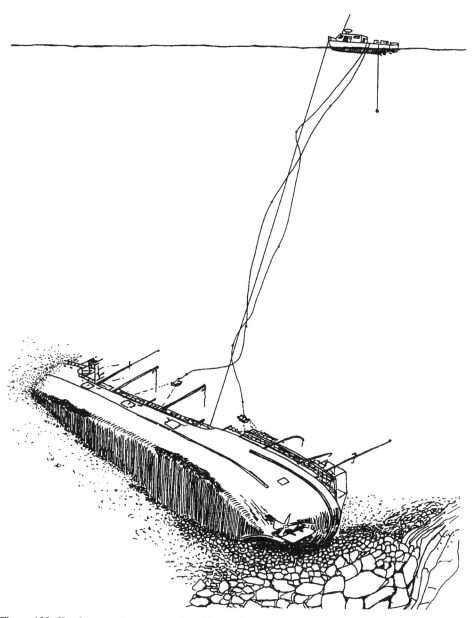

Figure 139. *Kamloops,* artists' perspective. Composite drawing by C. Patrick Labadie, Scott McWilliam, Jerry Livingston.

of evidence. One knows from history that a ship went down, but that leaves the questions of where, when and how. The where question was solved by empirical observations of sport divers in 1977. This reinforced earlier empirical observations by fisherman Milford Johnson Sr. that his nets were being caught in wreckage off of Twelve O'Clock Point and by Roy Oberg that his bottom scanner was indicating what looked like a shipwreck in the same area.

The question of when is not so easily dealt with, because any number of scenarios could have resulted in bodies and some

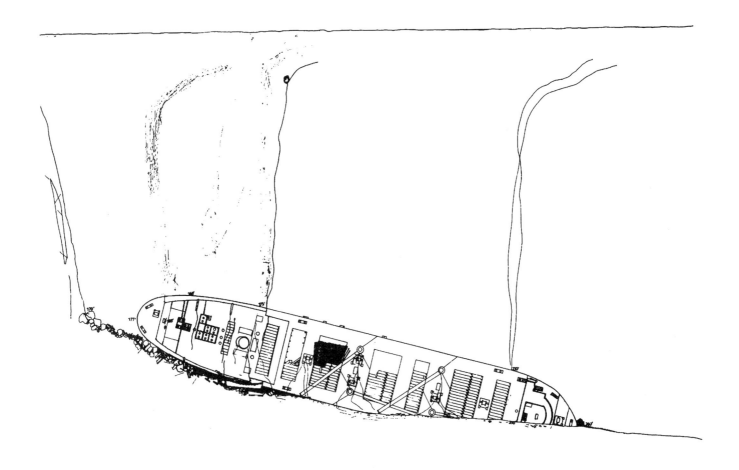

Figure 140. *Kamloops,* artist perspective. Drawing by Scott McWilliam.

spars being found at Isle Royale. Did the vessel go down in the violence of the storm? Did it lose power for some reason and drift into the island? Did it capsize from ice build up, or drift into the shelf ice and stay afloat near Twelve O'Clock Point for days, weeks or months?

The following are empirical observations made by the research team based on interviews with sport divers, deployment of remote operated vehicles in an NPS/National Geographic joint venture in 1986 and from personal observations of NPS divers who have briefly visited the site on several occasions. These will be treated as a material-evidence chain.

The largely intact vessel lies on its starboard side 400 feet from Kamloops Point with the bow pointing about 270 degrees on a magnetic compass bearing (Figures 139, 140).

Beginning from the stern, the following relevant factors have been noted. First we will consider those observations made by researchers through the eyes of the remote operated vehicle (ROV), which is our most reliable source.

1. Debris from the wreck, consisting of portions of the deck-cargo, was found 200 or 300 feet shoreward of the ship, indicating it capsized there before settling in deeper water. The debris lies at the foot of a 10-foot-deep ridge, but there is no solid evidence at this time that the ship struck that spot.

2. The rudder and propeller do not seem to be damaged. The rudder is on the centerline and properly fastened at top and bottom, and there is no damage to the shoe. There is about a 15-degree angle on rudder to starboard, but no evidence of grounding in this part of the ship.

3. Several of the scuppers in the stern had rubber hoses in them, probably indicating anticipation of a hard freeze. Hoses were ordinarily put in scupper pipes at time of winter lay-up to prevent bursting from extreme cold.

4. Davits on both sides were found empty; the port (upper side of wreck) davit has chocks still in place, some of the tackle still hanging in davits, guy-wires are also hanging. Both starboard davits are also empty, but the starboard lifeboat chocks are knocked down, indicating the probability that the starboard boat was intentionally launched. Historical records indicate that one boat was found near shore following the ship's loss, evidently the starboard one. The assumed port boat lies in about 230 feet of water near the wreck, where it seems to have fallen from the davits after the sinking. Because the ship appears to have rolled and slid down the slope on its starboard side, it may have had a starboard list for some time before its loss, which would

have precluded use of its port lifeboat.

5. ROV entered and explored bunker or coal chute (not absolutely certain which of the two), but did not observe stack breeching at deck-level; the smokestack has been reported missing, but we were not able to confirm this. We observed coal in bunker or chute, which indicates that the vessel did not run out of fuel.

6. Several engine room skylights were found opened, apparently by divers, and appear propped open on lower (starboard) side while held open by gravity on port (upper) side (Figure 141). The skylight over officers' mess also reported accessible by divers, although this was not observed.

7. At least one door was found open on the port side of the after deckhouse, probably an entry to the pantry or icebox.

8. The engine seems intact from ROV observations, although the chain fall was missing from the traverse bar which is used for lifting the pistons. Cylinder heads were observed, but at this point there is a very tantalizing clue that could not be positively confirmed. At the extreme end of the field of vision of the remote operated vehicle, it appeared that the head may have been removed from the high pressure cylinder, leaving the bare studs exposed. Many reruns of the videotape

of this portion of the ROV dive did not result in agreement on this observation by all the team. The importance of this point will be made clear in the analysis presented later in this discussion.

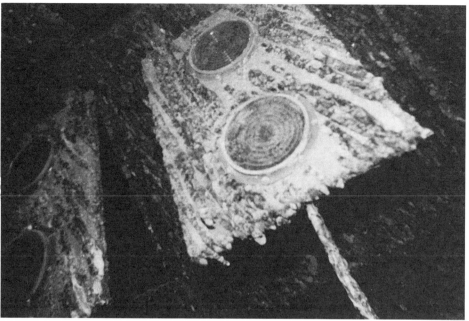

Figure 141. *Kamloops'* engine room skylights. ROV photo by Emory Kristof courtesy of National Geographic Society.

9. One human body was confirmed present in the engine room by the ROV. Reliable accounts by sport divers indicate there are more, with the number varying from two to five. The body observed and filmed by the robot vehicle seems to be in a sopafied state. This could not be confirmed by touch, but the appearance is white and appears textured. Adipocere formation is common for submerged corpses. This is a process in which soft tissues are converted into a soft waxy-type substance, frequently compared to soap. That this condition should still be noted after 50 years is remarkable, but apparently not unique in the Great Lakes, since at least one other case on an Isle Royale shipwreck is known. Again, there is not convergence from viewers of the tape regarding the issue of whether or not the clothing has survived intact. Although common sense would suggest this to be the case, and some divers have reported that at least one of the individuals was wearing bib overalls, this is not confirmed by the ROV. It is clear, however, that de-

Figure 142. *Kamloops'* stern wheel showing chain placed by sport divers. ROV photo by Emory Kristof courtesy of National Geographic Society.

composition was variable, neither the head nor feet remain on the corpse. The tibia and fibula of the legs extend out from the generic white mass of the body.

10. Divers have secured the emergency steering wheel with a padlock and chain (Figure 142); lamps and compass are missing from after binnacle, although the hood is in place and appears not to have been tampered with.

11. Examination of the ship's hull near the bow shows serious damage to shell plating at the turn of the bilge on the port side, extending approximately 50 feet from approximately from 65 to frame 50. The damage consists of dished and buckled plates and collapsed frames. The flat of the ship's bottom was not observed, but the damage did not appear to extend inward to the bottom. Although the damage was substantial, no ruptured plates were observed; the damage seen could account for leaks, but more than likely not massive flooding; other more serious hull damage is suspected. Inasmuch as the ship heeled over to starboard, damage on that side seems probable; this is further supported by the launch of the starboard boat, which suggests a starboard list, and therefore flooding on that side.

12. Portions of the ship's port side were viewed and the freight gangways examined. Those observed were still secured and presumed to be watertight. Stern details were also examined, including the propeller and rudder, and then the hull was viewed for some distance forward of the stern. Damage to the shell plating was observed at the turn of the bilge on the port side, extending from approximately frame 18 to frame 32. The damage was similar to that found at the forward end, consisting of stove-in plates and frames forced in about a foot or two. No actual ruptures in the shell plates were observed. Some corrugation of bottom plating appeared possible in the area, but was not confirmed.

13. Working toward the bow, little additional hull data was gathered, but the Mini-Rover was able to do a relatively thorough search of the forecastle and associated superstructure. The ship's pilothouse is missing, and it appears to have gone to pieces when the ship went down. Historical accounts indicate that portions of the structure were found near the shore. The false-floor and all of the instruments were also missing, except for a single vertical stanchion in the center of the pilothouse, the framing for a stairway at the starboard-side after corner of the house, a spotlight from the roof and a wood storage-box of uncertain use that was outside the house on the port side; both bridge wings are still in place. Lower portions of the superstructure appear undamaged. The Texas deck was examined on the port side. Deck details, such as a sounding reel, mooring bitts and rail stanchions, were observed. Examination of the structures offered no obvious clues about the vessel's loss.

14. Several features were observed indicating attrition from use by sport divers. Portions of the cargo had been stacked on the side of the ship, probably in preparation for removal (quart and gallon cans of paint in two crates), and the ship's two port-side navigation lamps were removed. It is not clear whether the navigation instruments were removed from the pilothouse or were lost at the time of the sinking.

15. Examination of hull at the forward end also revealed a plume of mud covering stem and anchor-pockets, preventing the observation of anchors or chains. Several of the portholes in the port side of the forecastle were found opened, presumably as a result of storm damage; fastners for the covers were seen inside, and while they did not appear broken or distorted out of shape, it is not thought likely that the ports were opened intentionally. The letter "K" was also viewed on the ship's port bow, painted in white.

There are two other observations about the *Kamloops* site that were made by sport divers, but not confirmed by this research team. If true, they may have a great deal of bearing on the reconstruction of the wreck event. The first is that at least one bow anchor chain comes out of the mud in which *Kamloops* bow is buried and extends seaward some distance. The second is that when found by divers the ship's engine room telegraph was set to "Finished with Engines" (both ordered and answered in this position), which indicates that the machinery was totally shut down at time of loss.

Analysis

The above empirical observations can now be used as a chain of evidence in concert with the historical record to allow a much more educated discussion of the *Kamloops* wreck event and the formulation of hypotheses that accommodate the most reliable aspects of the historical and material records.

1. Inasmuch as the ship lies at least 15 miles from the nearest point where it would have been safe under prevailing conditions, it must be assumed that it was disabled at the time of its loss and not under command. No experienced mariner would have purposely navigated a ship to that vicinity with northwest winds at gale force coupled with poor visibility. The nearest shelter would have been either in Thunder Bay or back behind the island via Blake Point.

   If the ship was disabled and drifting, its anchors should have been down; confirmation of the disposition of its anchors would provide valuable clues about the ship's condition at the time of its loss. Divers have reported that the ship's telegraph also shows evidence of the machinery being shut down (in "Finished with Engines" position); this, too, would substantiate the ship was disabled for some time before its loss. It would have been suicidal to let the ship lie so near a lee shore in the prevailing gale, if it could have possibly worked its way into open water.

2. If the steamer's high-pressure cylinder head was, in fact, removed, it would answer a basic question about the ship's loss: it would establish beyond a doubt that the ship was broken down from some hours before sinking, and it would explain why it ended up off Twelve O'Clock Point in so vulnerable and exposed a position. It would also suggest why some of the crew was at work in the engine room when the ship foundered. It would not explain the bottom damage.

   Damage to the ship's hull is not surprising, but the nature of the damage observed is not easily explained. It is clear that the ship struck bottom, and it would be easy to conclude that it struck the 10-foot spot only a few hundred feet from where it rests, but that appears to conflict with the material record. The ship lies with its bow "upwind" relative to the conditions at the time of its loss, and probably at anchor. If its bow was kept into the wind (as any responsible master would have done), then it would have struck the shoal stern-first. We know that did not happen, as is evidenced by the sound condition of its rudder and shoe. To have struck on its port side, it would have come ashore bow-on or nearly broadside. That could have been done only if the anchors were not out, which seems unlikely. The probability is, then, that it struck somewhere else. If it can be assumed that *Kamloops* struck subsequent to a breakdown, then the only place it could have struck is upwind, or some 20 miles away in the Welcome Islands.

The evidence seems to suggest that *Kamloops* battled the storm all the way across Lake Superior, but suffered some disabling accident to its engine, perhaps to the high-pressure cylinder, just as it reached the safety of Thunder Bay. It appears to have drifted into shoal water, damaging its port side so that it began leaking and developing a starboard list. In that condition and with its pumps going, it drifted downwind all the way to Isle Royale's windward shore, all the time with its anchors down. It would have fetched up just short of the rocks, apparently settling deeper and deeper. With daylight, a portion of the crew seems to have been put ashore on the starboard boat, while the engineer and a few others stayed aboard to pump and attempt whatever repairs were possible. Fishermen reported hearing distress whistles blowing all through the second night (see Chapter IV). After lying off the north shore of the island for some hours, the ship seems to have flooded so much that it finally laid over on its side and went down by the bow, plunging down the underwater slope and into the mud. The smokestack is probably alongside the wreck in the debris field. This conjectural sequence explains what is known of the vessel's loss and its present condition.

In addition to the richer understanding of the vessel itself and the wreck process, several other remarks can be made from the archeological investigation that deal with past depositional processes and Park management considerations.

Kamloops bears dramatic testimony to the preservation potential of deep shipwrecks in Lake Superior. The condition of inorganic and organic remains is astounding, significantly superior to what one may expect of the same ship and associated materials if they had never been lost, but tied to a dock in Duluth for 50 years. The siltation over the site is minimal, and apparently constant. The only active impacts to the site as an archeological/historical entity is the removal of certain enticing objects by sport divers.

One aspect of the past wreck natural deterioration process noted, but not expected, was the ridges of oxidization that appeared most dramatically on the ship's propeller. This phenomenon may be evident on other metal shipwrecks in fresh water, but none of the authors of this volume have recalled seeing this in the field or in the literature. The only exceptions are observations made during deep dives on *Titanic,* where these rivulets of oxidation formed dramatic displays and were called "rusticles" by the Woods Hole research team.

Kamloops is, in the archeological sense, a treasure trove, since it composes not only an intriguing remnant of an historic event in Lakes history, but because it contains a cross section of material culture that represents a synchronic snapshot of contemporary life in the region. "Package freight" is precious to the archeologist because it is a random reflection of subsistence needs. It is an intriguing place to dive, but there is some indication that its value as a time capsule for future generations will continue to diminish unless some restrictions are placed on access.

Epilogue

As this volume goes to press in 1994 it is interesting to reflect on developments since the 1987 publication of the technical report from which this book derives. The mooring buoys that were in the experimental stage back then have become a traditional element in Isle Royale's management activities. Park divers remove them at the end of each summer and replace them after the ice recedes in the spring.

The park now maintains a steady staff capability of five to six collateral duty divers. Park managers are making efforts to systematically monitor the wrecks and build a database to enable them to better understand visitor use on the sites.

Technical diving practices have become much more popular nationwide. Deeper wrecks, which were receiving minimal visitation by people using conventional air scuba, are now the subject of mixed-gas forays by recreational divers. Site attrition from vandalism has been minimal, but not eliminated. In some cases, such as the *Kamloops*, pilfering has increased.

Through the publication of the Isle Royale study and the attention focused on the park by the BBC series *Discoveries Underwater*, the lure of Isle Royale diving has increased. Between 500 and 600 divers register each year; a significant number in a remote park that has a comparatively small overall visitation rate. Park Ranger Nevada Barr has written an exciting mystery novel, entitled *Superior Death*, that centers on diving activities on the park's shipwrecks, particularly *Kamloops*.

The Abandoned Shipwreck Act of 1987 was passed into law by the U.S. Congress, codifying the role of historic shipwrecks as part of the nation's patrimony. This law has succeeded in taking historical shipwrecks in the territorial sea out of the hands of the Admiralty courts and put them in the domain of domestic preservation law. At the same moment the United States asserted title to these wrecks, it turned the jurisdiction over to the states with the exception of those areas administered by the National Park Service or Native American Peoples. Treatment by the states has thus far been somewhat inconsistent, since each jurisdiction attempts to put its own interpretation on the guidelines for implementing the law.

The SCRU has not yet had occasion to return to Isle Royale as it pursues its mission to generate models for submerged sites documentation throughout the National Park System and the Trust Territories. Although primarily focused on salt-water sites, some operations were conducted by SCRU at Pictured Rocks National Lakeshore and Apostle Islands National Lakeshore in Lake Superior and Sleeping Bear Dunes in Lake Michigan. The work at Pictured Rocks was assembled into an excellent report by Patrick Labadie for the SCRU report series, and Toni Carrell published a monograph on the *Noquebay* at Apostle Islands in the same series.

Isle Royale, however, was a proving ground for many of the methods and techniques and much of the philosophy that characterizes NPS underwater archeological endeavors nationwide. Impact of the study was also felt well beyond our own shores. The minimal printing of the technical report aimed at managers, universities and libraries generated comment far afield of its target audience. We had great interest shown from many state governments, other federal agencies and from as far away as Australia, India, the UK, Scandinavia and Central America. Our neighbors to the north had been actively managing shipwrecks in a pioneering manner under the stewardship of Stan McClellan at Fathom Five National (formerly Provincial) Marine Park. Our report greatly increased dialogue with them and the Canadian Park Service's very active underwater archeological team in Ottawa under the leadership of Robert Grenier.

Many, it turned out, had been wrestling with similar issues and were delighted to have the Isle Royale model as one viable option for dealing with the problem of managing historic shipwrecks on submerged public lands. A Swedish underwater archeologist wrote an extensive discussion of the merits of the USNPS approach to managing sites at Isle Royale and other parks in the International Journal of Nautical Archaeology.

The State of Michigan has moved ahead on its underwater preserve program, partly owing to the assumption of the State Archeologist position by John Halsey. A terrestrial archeologist, John lost no time in recognizing the unique value of Michigan's underwater heritage and moved aggressively to develop a proactive program. Dave Cooper became state underwater archeologist in Wisconsin and quickly brought his state into the forefront of state sponsored underwater research in the region. He also brought to bear the capabilities and resources of his former graduate program at East Carolina University.

Since completing the Isle Royale field operations in 1986, I have had the privilege of visiting some of the most spectacular shipwreck sites around the world. Truk Lagoon, Bikini Atoll, wrecks in the kelp beds off the California coast; all have great appeal in their own special way. But, for a world class diving experience on wrecks of unparalleled preservation in a setting of utmost beauty, Isle Royale is in a class of its own.

We have a wonderful historical and recreational resource in the shipwrecks of this park. How we treat them, both as managers and visitors, will determine their future. In the words of Roger Kennedy, Director of the National Park Service, "We borrow the parks from our children." Let's make sure that our generation can look back with pride to the manner in which we passed on the legacy of Isle Royale, from its pristine wilderness to its historical shipwrecks.

Daniel J. Lenihan

Bibliography

Abert, J.J. 1848 *Commerce on the Lakes and Western Rivers.* Letter from the Secretary of War, January 12, 1848. House Ex. Doc. No. 19. 30th Congress, 1st session.

Adams, Charles C. 1909 *An Ecological Survey of Isle Royale, Lake Superior.* Report of the University of Michigan for the Geological Survey, 1908. Wynkoop, Hallenbech, Crawford, Lansing.

Adams, James T. (editor) 1940 *Dictionary of American History.* Charles Scribner's Sons, New York.

Aitken, Hugh G.J. 1954 *The Welland Canal Co.* Cambridge, Massachusetts.

Albion, Robert G. 1938 *Square-Riggers on Schedule.* Princeton University, Princeton.

American Bureau of Shipping 1900 *Rules for Building and Classifying Vessels.* American Bureau of Shipping, New York.

1902 *1902 Record of American and Foreign Shipping.* American Bureau of Shipping, New York.

1917 *Rules for Building and Classifying Vessels, 1914-1917.* American Bureau of Shipping, New York.

American Fur Company Letters 1834-35 Microfilm copies from the New York Historical Society Collection, Glenn Black Laboratory of Archeology, Ohio Valley-Great Lakes Ethnohistory Archive, Indiana University.

Ancient Workings 1849 *Lake Superior Journal* 5(6):2. On file Marquette Public Library, Marquette.

Anderson, Romola and R.C. Anderson 1963 *The Sailing Ship.* Bonanza, New York.

Andrews, Frank 1910 *Grain Movements in the Great Lakes Region.* U.S. Department of Agriculture, Bureau of Statistics, Bulletin 81. Government Printing Office, Washington, D.C.

Andrews, Israel D. 1852 *Report on the Trade and Commerce of British North American Colonies and upon the Trade of the Great Lakes and Rivers.* Communication from the Secretary of the Treasury. U.S. Senate, Washington, D.C.

Arthurs, David 1982 Field notes and maps of Star Island reconnaissance survey on file, National Park Service, Southwest Cultural Resources Center, Submerged Cultural Resources Unit, Santa Fe.

Ashburn, T.Q. 1925 Transportation on Inland Waterways. *Transactions of The Society of Naval Architects and Marine Engineers* 33:67-90.

Avery, Thomas 1974 *The Mystery Ship From 19 Fathoms.* Avery Color Studios, Au Train, Michigan.

Babcock, W.I. 1899 System of Work in a Great Lakes Shipyard. *Transactions of the Society of Naval Architects and Marine Engineers* 7:173-188.

Baggley, George W. 1927 Report to Director, July 28, 1937. Document on file, National Park Service, Washington, D.C.

Baier, Louis A. 1955 *Contributions of the Department of Naval Architecture and Marine Engineering to Great Lakes Shipping.* University of Michigan, Ann Arbor.

Baker, W.A. and Tre Tryckare 1965 *The Engine Powered Vessel.* Crescent, New York.

Ballert, Albert G. 1962 *Bibliography, Great Lakes Research Checklist.* Great Lakes Commission, Ann Arbor.

Barkhausen, Henry N. 1947 *Great Lakes Sailing Ships.* The Ships and Sailing Albums Book 2. Kalmbach, Milwaukee.

Barnaby, K.C. 1962 *The Institution of Naval Architects 1860-1960.* Allen and Unwin, London.

1964 *A Hundred Years of Specialized Shipbuilding.* Hutchison, London.

Barry, James P. 1973 *Ships of the Great Lakes. 300 Years of Navigation.* Howell-North, Berkeley.

Barton, John Kennedy 1914 *Naval Reciprocating Engines and Auxiliary Machinery; Textbook for the Instruction of Midshipmen at the U.S. Naval Academy.* 3rd ed. rev. by H.O. Sticknay. Annapolis.

Bass, George 1983 A Plea for Historical Particularism in Nautical Archaeology. In *Shipwreck Anthropology,* edited by Richard A. Gould, pp. 91-104. School of American Research/University of New Mexico Press, Albuquerque.

Bastian, Tyler 1961 Trace Element and Metallographic Studies of Prehistoric Copper Artifacts in North America A Review. In *Lake Superior Copper and the Indians,* edited by J.B. Griffin, pp. 151-175. University of Michigan Museum of Anthropology Papers 17, Ann Arbor.

1963 Prehistoric Copper Mining in Isle Royale National Park, Michigan. Ms. thesis, University of Utah.

Bearss, Edwin C. 1966 *Hardluck Iron Clad. The Sinking and Salvage of the Cairo.* Louisiana University Press, Baton Rouge.

Beasley, Norman 1930 *Freighters of Fortune: The Story of the Great Lakes.* Harper & Brothers, New York.

Beckles, Henry aka Beckles, Wilson 1900 *The Great Company 1667-1871,* 2 vols. Smith, Elder & Company, London.

Benson, Barbara E. 1976 *Logs and Lumber: The Development of the Lumber Industry in Michigan's Lower Peninsula, 1837-1870.* Unpublished Ph.D. dissertation. University Microfilms, Ann Arbor.

Blue Book of American Shipping 1900 Marine Review Publishing, Cleveland.

Board of Engineers for Rivers and Harbors l930 *Transportation on the Great Lakes.* Transportation Series No. 1. War Department. Government Printing Office, Washington, D.C.

Board of Lake Underwriters 1866 *Rules Relative to the Construction of Lake Sail and Steam Vessels.* Matthews and Warren, Buffalo.

Bowen, Dana Thomas 1940 *Lore of the Lakes.* By the Author, Daytona Beach.

1952 *Shipwrecks of the Lakes.* By the Author, Daytona Beach.

Boyer, Dwight 1968 *Great Ships of the Great Lakes.* Dodd, Mead and Company, New York.

1971 *True Tales of the Great Lakes.* Dodd, Mead and Company, New York.

1977 *Ships and Men of the Great Lakes.* Dodd, Mead and Company, New York.

Brady, Edward M. 1960 *Marine Salvage Operations.* Cornell Maritime Press, Cambridge.

Brainerd, Winthrop 1986 Recommendations Concerning the Proper Disposition of Human Remains in National Marine Sanctuaries. Ms. on file, National Oceanic and Atmospheric Administration, Office of Ocean and Coastal Resource Management, Washington, D.C.

Brown, Oliver G. 1910 *Report of Inspection, Passage Island Light, Lake Superior, Michigan.* U.S. Department of Commerce and Labor, Bureau of Light-Houses, Washington, D.C.

Brown, W. Russell 1945 Ships at Port Arthur and Fort William. *Inland Seas* 11:45-51.

Bryan, William 1896 The Western River Steamboat. *American Society of Mechanical Engineers Transactions* 17:386-397.

Bryant, H.C., Thomas C. Vint, and John D. Coffman 1935 Report on Isle Royale, Part 1 Isle Royale Administration and Personnel Inspections and Investigations by Headquarters Officers, July 15, 1935. Document on file, National Park Service, Washington, D.C.

Bryce, George 1900 *The Remarkable History of the Hudson's Bay Company, Including that of the French: Traders of North-Western Canada and of the North-West, XY, and Astor Fur Companies.* London.

Bureau Veritas International Reporting of Shipping 1913 *Rules and Regulations for the Building and Classification of Steel Vessels Intended for Inland Navigation.* Bureau Veritas International Reporting of Shipping, London.

Burke, John A. 1975 Barrels to Barrows, Buckets to Belts: 120 Years of Iron Ore Handling on the Great Lakes. *Inland Seas* 31(4):266-277.

Butler, B.S. and W.S. Birbank 1929 *The Copper Deposits of Michigan.* U.S. Geological Survey Professional Paper 144, Washington, D.C.

Carrell, Toni 1983 *Shipwrecks of Isle Royale National Park, Thematic Group Nomination to the National Register of Historic Places.* National Park Service, Southwest Cultural Resources Center, Submerged Cultural Resources Unit, Santa Fe.

Carvel, John L. 1950 *Stephen of Linthouse: A Record of Two Hundred Years of Shipbuilding 1750-1950.* Alexander Stephen and Sons, Glasgow.

Celler, L. Craig 1975 Classified Structure Field Inventory Report and Historic Structure Worksheet. Documents on file, Isle Royale National Park, Houghton.

Chadwick, F.E. 1891 *Ocean Steamships: A Popular Account of Their Construction, Development, Management and Appliances.* Charles Scribner's Sons, New York.

Channing, Edward and Marion F. Lansing 1909 *The Story of the Great Lakes.* MacMillan, New York.

Chapelle, Howard I. 1935 *The History of American Sailing Ships.* Bonanza Books, New York.

1936 *American Sailing Craft.* Bonanza Books, New York.

1951 *American Small Sailing Craft.* W.W. Norton, New York.

1967 *The Search for Speed Under Sail 1700-1855.* Conway Maritime Press, London.

Christian, Sarah B. 1932 *Winter on Isle Royale: A Narrative of Life on Isle Royale During the Years of 1874 and 1875.* Private publication on file, Isle Royale National Park, Houghton.

Civilian Conservation Corps 1936-41 Camp Siskiwit Log. Document on file, Isle Royale National Park, Houghton.

1939 Civilian Conservation Corps Report, January 5, 1939, Part 1: Isle Royale Publicity, Statistics, Entertainment. Document on file, National Park Service, Washington, D.C.

Clowes, G.S. 1927 *Catalogue of the Collections in the Science Museum, South Kensington. Water Transport Sec. II. Merchant Steamers.* His Majesty's Stationery Office, London.

Cochrane, Timothy 1978 Memorandum to files re: George Mead Lumber Company logging operations on Siskiwit Bay, 1935-36. Document on file, Isle Royale National Park, Houghton.

1982 *The Folklife Expressions of Three Isle Royale Fishermen: A Sense of Place Examination.* Unpublished Master's thesis, Western Kentucky University, on file, Isle Royale National Park, Houghton.

1983 A Study of Folk Architecture on Isle Royale: The Johnson/Holte Fishery. Ms. on file, National Park Service, Southwest Cultural Resources Center, Submerged Cultural Resources Unit, Santa Fe.

Cockrell, Wilburn A. 1980 The Trouble with Treasure: A Preservationist View of the Controversy. *American Antiquity* 45:333-39.

Conary, Kate E.K. 1939 Interview in *Daily Mining Gazette,* June 21, 1939.

Cotter, John L. 1968 *Handbook for Historical Archeology, Part I.* Cotter, Wyncott, Pennsylvania.

Croil, James 1898 *Steam Navigation and its Relation to the Commerce of Canada and the United States.* William Briggs, Toronto.

Cumberland, B. 1913 Canoe, Sail and Steam: Early Navigation on the Great Lakes. *Canadian Magazine* 42:85-92.

Cummings, Calvin R. 1981 Cultural Resources Management: A Statement of Concerns from a Conservation Archeology Perspective. *Journal of Field Archaeology* 8(1):95-98.

Curr, Robert 1907 Lake Shipyard Methods of Steel Ship Construction. *Marine Review,* May 30: 40-42.

1908 Shipbuilding on the Great Lakes. *Transactions of the Society of Naval and Marine Engineers* 16:195-209.

Curtis, W.H. 1919 *The Elements of Wood Ship Construction.* McGraw Hill, New York.

Curwood, James O. 1909 *The Great Lakes: The Vessels That Plough Them: Their Owners, Their Sailors, and Their Cargoes, Together with a Brief History of Our Inland Seas.* G.P. Putnam's Sons, New York.

Cuthbertson, George A. 1931 *Freshwater, a History and Narrative of the Great Lakes.* Macmillan, New York.

Davis, Charles G. 1933 *The Built-Up Ship Model.* 1980 reprint, Edward W. Sweetman, Largo, Florida.

Delgado, James P. 1986 National Historic Landmark Study: USS *Monitor.* Ms. on file, National Park Service, Washington, D.C.

1987a *Nominating Historic Vessels and Shipwrecks to the National Register of Historic Places.* Bulletin 20. National Park Service, Washington, D.C.

1987b (editor) Maritime Preservation Edition. *The Journal of the Association for Preservation Technology* 9(1).

Denny, Archibald 1897 The Design and Building of a Steamship. *Cassier's Magazine* August:393-405.

Desmond, Charles 1935 *Naval Architecture Simplified.* Rudder, New York.

Detroit Historical Publishing Company 1877 *Marine History of the Lake Ports.* Detroit Historical Publishing, Detroit.

Dickinson, J.N. 1967 *The Canal at Sault Ste. Marie, Michigan: Inception, Construction, Operation and the Canal Grant Lands.* Unpublished Ph.D. dissertation, University of Wisconsin.

Dohrmann, Donald R. 1976 *Screw Propulsion in American Lake and Coastal Steam Navigation, 1840-1860: A Case Study in the Diffusion of Technological Innovation.* Unpublished Ph.D. dissertation, Yale University. University Microfilms, Ann Arbor.

Doner, Mary F. 1958 *The Salvager: The Life of Captain Tom Reid on the Great Lakes.* Ross and Haines, Minnesota.

Donovan, Frank R. 1966 *River Boats of America.* Crowell, New York.

Dorin, Patrick C. 1979 *The Lake Superior Iron Ore Railroads: The World's Heaviest Trains.* Bonanza Books, New York.

Dornfield, A.A. 1957 *Steamships: A Hundred Years Ago.* Chicago Historical Society New Series 4:148-156.

Dorr, E.P. 1876 *Rules for Construction, Inspection and Characterization of Sail and Steam Vessels.* By the Author, Buffalo.

Dustin, Fred 1932 A Summary of the Archeology of Isle Royale, Michigan. *Papers of the Michigan Academy of Science, Arts and Letter* 16:1-16.

1946 Isle Royale Place Names. *Michigan History* 16(4):681-722.

1957 An Archeological Reconnaissance of Isle Royale. *Michigan History* 41:1-34.

Eccleston, E.C. 1941 Report to Chief, Park Operations Division. Document on file, National Park Service, Washington, D.C.

Edwards, V.B. and Fred C. Cole 1945 Water Transportation on Inland Rivers. In *Historical Transactions 1893-1941,* pp. 400-422. Society of Naval Architects and Marine Engineers, New York.

Eliot, John L. 1985 Isle Royale: North Woods Park Primeval. *National Geographic* 167(4):534-550.

Engman, Elmer 1976 *Shipwreck Guide to the Western Half of Lake Superior.* Innerspace, Duluth.

Ericson, Bernard 1962 *The Evolution of Ships on the Great Lakes, Part I: Early History, Great Lakes and Great Rivers and Eastern Canadian Section.* The Society of Naval Architects and Marine Engineers, Pittsburgh Steamship Division, Cleveland.

Estep, H. Cole 1918 *How Wooden Ships Are Built.* Penton, Cleveland.

Evans, William H. 1967 Days of the Steamboats. *Parents Magazine.*

Fairbairn, William 1863 On the Construction of Iron-Plated Ships. *Transactions of the Institution of Naval Architects* 4:1-15. London.

1865 *Treatise on Iron Ship Building: Its History and Progress.* Longmans, Green, London.

Feltner, Charles E. and Jeri B. Feltner 1982 *Great Lakes Maritime History: Bibliography and Sources of Information.* Seajay Publications, Dearborn.

Finn, J. Leo 1979 *Old Shipping Days in Oswego.* Oswego County Board of Supervisors, Oswego.

Fitch, Charles H. 1888 *Report on Marine Engines and Steam Vessels in the U.S. Merchant Service.* U.S. Department of the Interior, Census Office, Washington, D.C.

Fite, Gilbert C. and Jim E. Reese 1965 *An Economic History of the United States.* Houghton Mifflin, Boston.

Fletcher, Daniel O. 1960 *A Study of Package Freight Carriers on the Great Lakes.* Unpublished Ph.D. dissertation. University Microfilms, Ann Arbor.

Fletcher, R.A. 1910 *Steamships: The Story of Their Development to the Present Day.* Sidwick and Jackson, London.

Fowles, Otton 1925 *Sault Ste. Marie and its Great Waterways.* G.P. Putnam's Sons, New York.

Fox, George R. 1911 An Ancient Copper Workings on Isle Royale. *Wisconsin Archaeologist* 10:75.

Franchere, Gabriel 1939 *Journal of his Voyage in the* Brewster *to Grand Portage, Isle Royale and the Anse in August, 1839.* Microfilm on file, Michigan Technological University Library, Houghton.

Frederickson, Arthur C. and Lucy F. Frederickson 1961-63 *Ships and Shipwrecks in Door County Wisconsin,* 2 vols. Sturgeon Bay, Wisconsin.

Gale, Phil 1987 Interview recorded by Toni Carrell and Ken Vrana, March 17, 1987. On file National Park Service, Southwest Cultural Resources Center, Submerged Cultural Resources Unit, Santa Fe.

Gilmore, James 1956 *The St. Lawrence River Canals Vessel.* The Society of Naval Architects and Marine Engineers, Montreal.

Gjerset, Knut 1928 *Norwegian Sailors on the Great Lakes.* Norwegian-American Historical Association, Northfield.

Goodrich, Carter 1961 *Canals and American Economic Development.* Columbia University, New York.

Gould, Richard A. (editor) 1983 *Shipwreck Anthropology.* University of New Mexico, Albuquerque.

Graham, C.S. 1958 The Transition from Paddle-Wheel to Screw Propeller. *Mariner's Mirror* 44:45-46.

Greenhill, Basil 1980 *Schooners.* Naval Institute, Annapolis.

Greenwood, J.O. 1973 *Namesakes II: A Sequel to Namesakes of the Lakes.* Freshwater Press, Cleveland.

Haber, Gordon 1962-65 Field report on Cemetery Island. Ms. on file, Isle Royale National Park, Houghton.

Hakala, D. Robert 1955 Isle Royale Primeval Prince: A History. Ms. on file, Isle Royale National Park, Houghton.

Hall, Henry 1880 *Report on the Ship-Building Industry of the United States.* U.S. Tenth Census, vol. 8:1-276. Dept. of the Interior, Washington, D.C.

Hall, John W. 1870 *Marine Disasters of Western Lakes During the Navigation of 1869.* Wetunis, Detroit.

Hall, Stephen P. 1976 *Duluth-Superior Harbor Cultural Resources Study.* U.S. Army Corps of Engineers, St. Paul District, St. Paul.

Hamilton, Frank E. n.d. *Notes on* Puritan/George M. Cox. Ms. on file, Richard J. Wright Collection, Bowling Green State University, Bowling Green, Ohio.

Harrison, John MacLean 1974 *The Fate of the* Griffon. The Shallow Press, Chicago.

Hatcher, Harlan 1944 *The Great Lakes.* Oxford University, London.

1945 *Lake Erie.* Bobbs Merrill, New York.

1950 *A Century of Iron and Men.* Bobbs-Merrill, New York.

Hatcher, Harlan and Erich A. Walter 1963 *A Pictorial History of the Great Lakes.* Crown Publishers, New York.

Havighurst, Walter 1944 *The Long Ships Passing.* MacMillan, New York.

1966 *The Great Lakes Reader.* Macmillan, New York.

Heden, Karl E. 1966 *Directory of Shipwrecks on the Great Lakes.* Bruce Humphries, Boston.

Henry, Alfred J. and Norman B. Conger 1907 *Meteorological Chart of the Great Lakes.* Summary for the Season of 1906. U.S. Dept. of Agriculture, Weather Bureau, No. 2. Government Printing Office, Washington, D.C.

Heyl, Erik 1965-69 *Early American Steamers.* 6 vols. By the Author, Buffalo.

Hill, Ralph N. 1953 *Sidewheeler Saga. A Chronicle of Steamboating.* Rinehart, New York.

Hill, Reubin 1987 Interview recorded by Toni Carrell and Ken Vrana, February 3, 1987, re: Lake Superior small craft construction on file, National Park Service, Southwest Cultural Resources Center, Submerged Cultural Resources Unit, Santa Fe.

Hoagland, Henry E. 1917 *Wage Bargaining on the Vessels of the Great Lakes.* University of Illinois, Urbana.

Hoge, Anna B. 1984 Interview recorded by Bruce Weber, July 19, 1984, re: Passage Island Lighthouse on file, Isle Royale National Park, Houghton.

Hodge, William 1884 *The Pioneer Steamboats on Lake Erie.* Bigelow Brothers, Buffalo.

Hohman, Elmo P. 1956 *History of the American Merchant Seaman.* Shoestring Press, Hamden, Connecticut.

Holden, Thomas R. 1974 Park Interpretation as an Environmental Communication Process with a Sample Interpretive Booklet Text on the Maritime Disaster History of Siskiwit Bay, Isle Royale, Lake Superior. Unpublished Master's thesis, University of Wisconsin, Madison, on file, Isle Royale National Park, Houghton.

1976 On The Rocks Isle Royale Style. *Nor´Easter* 1(1):2-4.

A Shallow Grave for the *America. The Nordic Diver* 1(2):1-5).

1985 *Above and Below: A History of Lighthouses and Shipwrecks of Isle Royale.* Isle Royale Natural History Association, Houghton.

Holecek, Donald F. and Susan J. Lothrop 1980a *Attitudes of a Scuba Diving Population Concerning Government Regulation of Underwater Resources.* Michigan Sea Grant Technical Report, Ann Arbor.

1980b *Shipwreck vs. Nonshipwreck Scuba Divers: Characteristics, Behavior, and Expenditure Patterns.* Michigan Sea Grant Technical Report, Ann Arbor.

Holecek, Donald F. and E. Thomas Smiley 1982 *Management Guidelines for Michigan's Great Lakes Bottomland Preserves.* Michigan Sea Grant, Ann Arbor.

Holte, Ingeborg 1984 *Ingeborg's Isle Royale.* Women's Times, Grand Marais.

Houghton, Jacob 1896 Letter to George A. Newett, Ishpeming, Michigan, November 22, on file, Isle Royale National Park, Houghton.

Hruska, Robert 1987 Personal correspondence to Ken Vrana 19 January 1987, re: Oskosh Public Museum activities on Isle Royale in 1964, on file, Isle Royale National Park, Houghton.

Huber, N. King 1975 *The Geologic Story of Isle Royale National Park.* Geological Survey Bulletin 1309. Government Printing Office, Washington, D.C.

Hull, William J. and Robert W. Hull 1967 *The Origin and Development of the Waterways Policy of the United States.* National Waterways Conference Inc., Washington, D.C.

Hulse, Charles A. 1981 *A Spatial Analysis of Lake Superior Shipwrecks: A Study in the Formative Process of the Archaeological Record.* Unpublished Ph.D. dissertation, Michigan State University. University Microfilms, Ann Arbor.

Hulse, Charles A. and Donald F. Holecek 1979 *Underwater Parks Symposium Proceedings.* Extension Bulletin E-1350. Michigan State University, East Lansing.

Humins, John H. 1985 The American Fur Company in the Old Northwest Territory. *Michigan History* 69(2):24-31.

Hunter, Louis C. 1949 *Steamboats on the Western Rivers: An Economic and Technological History.* 1969 reprint, Octagon, New York.

Hutchinson, G.H. 1914 The Handling of Coal at the Head of the Lakes. *American Society of Mechanical Engineers Transactions* 35:283-339.

Inches, H.C. 1951 Wooden Shipbuilding. *Inland Seas* 7:3-12.

1962 *The Great Lakes Wooden Shipbuilding Era.* The Great Lakes Historical Society, Vermillion, Ohio.

Inland Lloyds 1882 *1882 Vessel Classification of the Inland Lloyd's American Hulls.* Printing House of Matthews, Northrup and Company, Buffalo.

1890 *Inland Lloyds Vessel Register.* Inland Lloyds, Buffalo.

Innes, Harold A. 1930 *The Fur Trade in Canada.* New Haven.

Isle Royale 1854 *Lake Superior Journal* 10(4):2. On file Marquette Public Library, Marquette.

International Shipmasters Association Directory. 1925 International Shipmasters Association, Cleveland.

Ives, William 1847 *Survey Notes and Plats of the 1847 Survey of Isle Royale.* Microfilm on file, Michigan Technological University Library, Houghton.

Jackson, Charles T. 1849 *Report on the Geological and Mineralogical Survey of the Mineral Lands of the United States in the State of Michigan.* 31st Congress, 1st Session, House Ex. Doc. No. 5, vol. 3, Pt. 2.

Johns, Edgar 1965 Interview recorded by L. Rakestraw, September 30, 1965, on file, Isle Royale National Park, Houghton.

Johnson, Milford Jr. 1986 Interview recorded by Ken Vrana, August 23, 1986, on file, National Park Service, Southwest Cultural Resources Center, Submerged Cultural Resources Unit, Santa Fe.

1987 Interview recorded by Toni Carrell and Ken Vrana, February 3, 1987, on file, National Park Service, Southwest Cultural Resources Center, Submerged Cultural Resources Unit, Santa Fe.

Johnson, Myrtle 1986 Interview recorded by Ken Vrana, August 23, 1986, on file, National Park Service, Southwest Cultural Resources Center, Submerged Cultural Resources Unit, Santa Fe.

Johnson Brothers Brochure ca. 1940 Launch and Boat Service, Rock Harbor, Isle Royale. On file National Park Service, Southwest Cultural Resources Center, Submerged Cultural Resources Unit, Santa Fe.

Johnston, Paul 1983 *Steam and the Sea.* Peabody Museum of Salem, Salem.

Kasson, John F. 1976 *Civilizing the Machine: Technology and Republican Values in America 1776-1900.* Grossman, New York.

King, Franklin, A. 1984 Two Harbors: Minnesota's First Iron Ore Port. *The Nor'easter* 9(5):1-4.

Keel, Bennie 1979 A View from the Inside. *American Antiquity* 44(1):164-170.

1985 *White Paper: Disposition of Human Remains.* National Park Service, Washington, D.C.

Klein, L. 1841 Notes on the Steam Navigation Upon the Great Northern Lakes. *American Railroad Journal* 12.

Labadie, C. Patrick 1981 Inventory of Screw Steamers Built Upon the Great Lakes, 1840-1880. Ms. on file, C.P. Labadie Collection, Duluth.

1982a Preliminary Analysis of Great Lakes Lumber Steamers. Ms. on file, C.P. Labadie Collection, Duluth.

1982b Sketch and measurements of *Stanley,* Star Island, June 8, 1982. Document on file, National Park Service, Southwest Cultural Resources Center, Submerged Cultural Resources Unit, Santa Fe.

1984 Nineteenth Century Bulk Freighters on the Great Lakes System. Ms. on file, C.P. Labadie Collection, Duluth.

Labaree, Benjamin W. (editor) 1975 *The Atlantic World of Robert G. Albion.* Wesleyan University Press, Middletown.

Landon, Fred 1955 The End of Coastal Steamer Service on Georgian Bay. *Inland Seas* 11(1):68-70.

1970 Engines Salvaged from Lake Depths Powered the *Manitoba. Inland Seas* 26(4):313-315.

Lane, Alfred C. 1898 Geological Report on Isle Royale. *Michigan Geological Survey* 6(1). Michigan Geological Survey, Lansing.

Lapham, J.A. *1869 Disasters on the Lakes. Papers Relative to Losses of Vessels on the Lakes.* HR Doc. 10, 41st Congress, 2nd Session.

Laurent, Jerome K. 1983 Trade, Transport and Technology: The American Great Lakes, 1866-1910. *The Journal of Transport History* 4(1):1-24.

Lavelle, Omer 1974 *Van Horne's Road: An Illustrated Account of the Construction and First Years of Operation of the Canadian Pacific Transcontinental Railway.* Railfare Enterprises, Montreal.

Lavery, Brian 1984 *The Ship of the Line: Volume II: Design, Construction and Fittings.* Conway, London.

Lee, William E. 1983 Letter from Ontario Ministry of Tourism and Recreation, Old Fort William, Thunder Bay, re: Northwest Fur Company activities on Isle Royale, on file, Isle Royale National Park, Houghton.

Lenihan, Daniel J. 1983 Rethinking Shipwreck Archaeology: A History of Ideas and Considerations for New Directions. In *Shipwreck Anthropology,* edited by Richard A. Gould, pp. 37-64. University of New Mexico Press, Albuquerque.

1983 Managing Shipwrecks in Parks and Preserves. *Trends in Historic Preservation* 20(2):29-31.

1986 The *Cumberland/Chisholm* Site: The Results of a Non-destructive Archaeological Investigation at Isle Royale National Park. In *Underwater Archaeology: The Proceedings of the Fourteenth Conference on Underwater Archaeology,* edited by Calvin R. Cummings, pp. 105-106. Special Publication 7. Fathom Eight, San Marino.

Lenihan, Daniel J. (editor) 1974 *Underwater Archeology in the National Park Service: A Model for the Management of Submerged Cultural Resources.* National Park Service, Santa Fe.

1987 *Submerged Cultural Resources Study: Isle Royale National Park.* Southwest Cultural Resources Center Papers No. 8, National Park Service, Santa Fe.

Lenihan, Daniel J., Toni Carrell and Larry Murphy 1981 Report on a One-Week Field Trip to Test and Evaluate Underwater Archeological Research Approaches for Use at Isle Royale in the 1981 Field Season. Ms. on file, National Park Service, Southwest Cultural Resources Center, Submerged Cultural Resources Unit, Santa Fe.

Lidfors, Kate, Thom Holden, Ellen Maurer, Jerry Livingston and Larry Murphy
1982 Report of a Two-Day Underwater Survey of Selected Historical Sites at Apostle Islands National Lakeshore with Considerations for Future Research. Ms. on file, National Park Service, Submerged Cultural Resources Unit, Santa Fe.

Lindblad, A.F. 1924 *A Critical Analysis of the Factors Affecting Safety and Operation of the Bulk Freight Vessels of the Great Lakes.* Unpublished Ph.D. dissertation, University of Michigan. University Microfilms, Ann Arbor.

Little, John J. 1978 *Island Wilderness: A History of Isle Royale National Park.* Unpublished Ph.D. dissertation, University of Toledo. On file Isle Royale National Park, Houghton.

Log Chips 1983 Institute for Great Lakes Research, Bowling Green State University, Bowling Green, Ohio.

Luckenbach, Lewis 1945 American Bureau of Shipping 1862-1943. In *Historical Transactions 1893-1943.* Society of Naval Architects and Marine Engineers, New York.

Lumby, John R. 1974 *Historic Fort William.* Mika, Belleville, Ontario.

Lytle, William M. and Forrest R. Holdcamper 1952 *Merchant Steam Vessels of the United States, 1790-1868.* The Steamship Historical Society of America, Staten Island.

Maass, Carol 1982 Undesignated Cultural Sites Inventory Forms. Document on file, Isle Royale National Park, Houghton.

1984 Isle Royale Interim Cultural Sites Inventory. Document on file, Isle Royale National Park, Houghton.

MacElwee, Roger S. 1921 *Economic Aspects of the Great Lakes, St. Lawrence Ship Canal.* Ronald Press, New York.

MacLean, Harrison John 1974 *The Fate of the* Griffon. Sage/Swallow, Chicago.

Maginnis, Arthur J. 1892 *The Atlantic Ferry: Its Ships, Men, and Working.* London.

Mahan, John and Ann Mahan 1985 Return to Passage Island. *Lakeland Boating* June:47-50.

Malone, John M., Sr. 1986 Interview recorded by Dave Snyder on January 19, 1986, re: Isle Royale Lighthouse on file, Isle Royale National Park, Houghton, Michigan.

Manning, George C. 1943 *Manual of Ship Construction.* D. Van Nostrand, New York.

Mansfield, J.B. 1899 *History of the Great Lakes.* 2 vols. J.H. Beers, Chicago. 1972 reprint, Freshwater, Cleveland.

Marshall Cavendish Publications 1975 *The History of the Sailing Ship.* Arco, New York.

Martin, Patrick E. 1985 Report on Isle Royale prehistoric pot. Ms. on file, Isle Royale National Park, Houghton.

Mason, Philip P. 1956 *The Lumbering Era in Michigan History 1860-1900.* Michigan Historical Commission, Lansing.

1957 *The History of Great Lakes Transportation.* Brown-Branfield, Ann Arbor.

McCannel, R. 1932 *Shipping on Lake Superior: Shipping out of Collingwood.* Papers and Records, Number 28. Ontario Historical Society, Ontario.

McCarty, John Myron 1971 *Economic Aspects in the Evolution of the Great Lakes Freighter.* Unpublished Ph.D. dissertation, University of Southern California. University Microfilms, Ann Arbor.

McClellan, Stan 1979 Fathom-Five Provincial Park – A Working Example of an Underwater Park. In *Underwater Parks: Symposium Proceedings,* Extension Bulletin E-1350, edited by Charles A. Hulse, pp. 54-56. Michigan State University, East Lansing.

McDonald, W.A. 1959 Composite Steamers Built by Detroit Drydock Company. *Inland Seas* 15(2):114-116.

McDowell, W. 1961 *The Shapes of Ships.* Rev. Ed. Hutchinson, New York.

McLuckie, Jane A. 1976 Minong Mine Historic District. National Register of Historic Places Nomination. Washington, D.C.

McPhedran, Phillip 1952 *Cargoes on the Great Lakes.* MacMillan, Toronto.

McVey, T.J. 1938-41a Camp Inspection Report. NP-2, May 31, 1938; NP-1, June 1938; NP-1, August 17, 1939; NP-2, August 27, 1940; J.C. Reddock, Camp Inspection Report, NP-2, August 23,24, 1941; NP-3, August 24, 1941. Documents on file, National Park Service, Washington, D.C.

1938-41b CCC Camp Educational Report. May 31, 1938; June 1,1938; August 16, 1939; August 17, 1939; August 25, 1940; August 27, 1940; unsigned CCC Camp Educational Report, August 24, 1941. Documents on file, National Park Service, Washington, D.C.

McWilliam, Scott 1983 *The Gray Oak. A Report Covering Observations Made During Archaeological Investigations in 1982.* North Central Region Report 14. Heritage Branch, Ministry of Citizenship and Culture, Thunder Bay, Ontario.

1984 Record of Dive Form, Isle Royale National Park, September 29, McCargoe Cove. Document on file, Isle Royale National Park, Houghton.

1985 Record of Dive Form, Isle Royale National Park, August 11, Siskowit Mine. Document on file, Isle Royale National Park, Houghton.

Menz, Katherine B. 1983 *Historic Furnishings Report, Sleeping Bear Point Life-Saving Station, Sleeping Bear Dunes National Lakeshore, Frankfort, Michigan.* Branch of Historic Furnishings, Harpers Ferry Center, National Park Service, Harpers Ferry.

Merritt, Glenn 1965 Oral history tape recorded by Lawrence Rakestraw, September 28, 1965 on file, Isle Royale National Park, Houghton.

Meyer, John R., Merton J. Peck, John Stenason, Charles Zwick 1959 *The Economics of Competition in the Transportation Industries.* Harvard University Press, Cambridge.

Miller, Quenton M. 1986 Letter to Park Historian on file, Isle Royale National Park, Houghton.

Mills, James Cook 1908 Giant Ore Carriers on the Great Lakes, *Cassier's Magazine* 35:109-119.

1910 *Our Inland Seas: Their Shipping and Commerce for Three Centuries.* A.C. McClurg & Co., Chicago. 1976 reprint, Freshwater Press, Cleveland.

Mitchell, C. Bradford and Kenneth R. Hall 1975 *Merchant Steam Vessels of the United States 1790-1868, The Lytle-Holdcamper List.* Steamship Historical Society of America, Staten Island, New York.

Moe, Elvis 1987 Interview recorded by Toni Carrell and Ken Vrana, March 16, 1987. On file National Park Service, Southwest Cultural Resources Center, Submerged Cultural Resources Unit, Santa Fe.

Montreal Register 1839-50 Bureau of Marine Fisheries, Public Archives of Canada, Ottawa, Ontario.

Morehead, John M. 1981 Shipwrecks of Isle Royale: A Manager's Perspective. In *Underwater Archaeology: The Proceedings of the Eleventh Conference on Underwater Archeology,* edited by Calvin R. Cummings, pp. 63-67. Special Publication 4. Fathom Eight, San Marino

Morison, Elting E. 1966 *Men, Machines, and Modern Times.* MIT Press, Cambridge.

Morrison, John H. 1903 *History of American Steam Navigation.* Argosy-Antiquarian Ltd. New York.

1905 *Iron and Steel Hull Steam Vessels of the United States, 1825-1905.* Steamship Historical Society of America, Salem.

1958 *History of America's Steam Navigation.* Stephen Doyl Press, New York.

Muckelroy, Keith 1978 *Maritime Archaeology.* Cambridge University Press, Cambridge.

Murphy, Larry 1981 Isle Royale Shipwreck Management Program, Phase I: Preliminary Assessment. Paper presented at Twelfth Annual Conference on Underwater Archeology, New Orleans.

1982 Isle Royale Shipwreck Management Program: A Pilot Study. Paper presented at Thirteenth Conference on Underwater Archeology, Philadelphia.

1983 Shipwrecks as Data Base for Human Behavioral Studies. In *Shipwreck Anthropology* edited by Richard A. Gould, pp. 65-90. University of New Mexico Press, Albuquerque.

Murphy, Larry, Dan Lenihan and Toni Carrell 1982 *Underwater Archeology of Isle Royale National Park. An Interim Report Covering the 1981 Field Season.* National Park Service, Southwest Cultural Resources Center, Submerged Cultural Resources Unit, Santa Fe.

Murphy, Rowland W. 1966 The Four Welland Canals. In: *The Great Lakes Reader,* edited by W. Havighurst, pp. 391-396. Collier Macmillan, London.

Musham, H.A. 1946-60 Early Great Lakes Steamboats 1816-1830. *American Neptune* 6:1-18; 7:1-24; 8:1-24; 17:89-104; 20:79-103.

Neu, Irene 1953 The Building of the Sault Canal: 1952-1955. *Mississippi Valley Historical Review* 40(1): 25-46.

Nichols, John 1945 The Development of Marine Engineering. In *Historical Transactions 1893-1943.* Society of Naval Architects and Marine Engineers, New York.

Nimmo, Joseph 1885 *Report on the Internal Commerce of the United States.* U.S. Dept. of the Treasury, Bureau of Statistics, Washington, D.C..

Nordby, Larry V. 1987 Preliminary analysis of artifact clusters resulting from Star Island reconnaissance survey, June 1982. Ms. on file, National Park Service, Southwest Cultural Resources Center, Submerged Cultural Resources Unit, Santa Fe.

North, Douglass C. 1961 *The Economic Growth of the United States 1790-1860.* Prentice-Hall, New York.

Northern Michigan University 1978 Isle Royale Shipwreck Survey. Ms. on file, Isle Royale National Park, Houghton.

Nute, Grace Lee 1944 *Lake Superior.* Bobbs-Merrill, New York.

O'Brien, T. Michael 1976 *Guardians of the Eighth Sea: A History of the U.S. Coast Guard on the Great Lakes.* U.S. Government Printing Office, Washington, D.C.

Oldham, Joseph R. 1897 Shipbuilding and Transportation on the Great American Lakes. *Cassier's Magazine* August:499-512.

1907 American Lake and Ocean Steamship Models. *Cassier's Magazine* January:229-240.

Opheim, Lee Alfred 1972 *Twentieth Century Shipwrecks in Lake Superior.* Unpublished Ph.D. dissertation, Saint Louis University. University Microfilms, Ann Arbor.

Paasch, Captain H. 1890 *Illustrated Marine Encyclopedia.* W&J Mackay, Chatham, Great Britain. Nd. reprint, Argus Books, Watford, Herts, England.

Pankhurst, J.F. 1893 The Development of Shipbuilding on the Great Lakes. *Transactions of the Society of Naval Architects and Marine Engineers* 1:252-262.

Patterson, Susan S. 1976 *Canadian Great Lakes Shipping: An Annotated Bibliography.* University of Toronto, Ontario.

Pomeroy, Lawrence A. 1946 The Bulk Freight Vessel. *Inland Seas* 2(3):191-200.

Pred, Allan 1970 Toward a Typology of Manufacturing Flows. In: *Economic Geography: Selected Readings,* edited by Fred E. Dors and Lawrence M. Sommers, pp. 267-286.

Purdy, T.C. l883a *Report on Steam Navigation in the United States.* U.S. Tenth Census, vol. 8:655-724. Dept. of the Interior, Washington, D.C..

1883b *Report on the Canals of the United States.* U.S. Tenth Census, vol. 8:725-764. Dept. of the Interior, Washington, D.C.

Rakestraw, Lawrence 1964 Historical Background and Documentation for Historical Base Map of Isle Royale. Ms. on file, Isle Royale National Park, Houghton.

1965 *Historic Mining on Isle Royale.* Isle Royale Natural History Association in cooperation with the U.S. Department of Interior, National Park Service, Houghton.

1967a Post-Columbian History of Isle Royale, Part I: Mining. Ms. on file, Isle Royale National Park, Houghton.

1967b Post-Columbian History of Isle Royale, Part II: Fishing. Ms. on file, Isle Royale National Park, Houghton.

1968 *Commercial Fishing on Isle Royale 1800-1967.* Isle Royale Natural History Association in cooperation with the U.S. Department of Interior, National Park Service, Houghton.

Ratigan, William 1960 *Great Lakes Shipwrecks and Survivals.* Eerdmans, Grand Rapids.

Ridgley-Nevitt, Cedric 1981 *American Steamships on the Atlantic.* University of Delaware Press, Newark.

Robinson, Orrin W. 1938 *Early Days of the Lake Superior Copper Country.* Houghton.

Rogers, C.C. 1892 The Water Route from Chicago to the Ocean. *Scribner's Magazine.* March:287.

Rosenberg, Nathan 1972 *Technology and American Economic Growth.* Harper and Row, New York.

Rowland, K.T. 1970 *Steam at Sea. A History of Steam Navigation.* Praeger Publishers, New York.

Sadler, Herbert C. 1909 Some Points in Connection with Shipbuilding on the Great Lakes, U.S.A. *Transactions of the Institution of Naval Architects* 51:220-232.

Salmond, John A. 1967 *The Civilian Conservation Corps, 1933-1942: A New Deal Case Study.* Duke University Press, Durham.

Schiffer, Michael B. 1976 *Behavioral Archaeology.* Academic, New York.

Schuette, Katie 1979 *Kamloops* Goes Missing No Longer. *Anchor News.* May/June.

Scott, Emmett Hoyt 1924 Unpublished memoirs on file, Indiana University, Lilly Library, Bloomington.

Scovill, Douglas H., G.J. Gordon and K.M. Anderson 1977 Guidelines for the Preparation of Statements of Environmental Impact on Archeological Resources. In *Conservation Archaeology: A Guide for Cultural Resource Management Studies,* edited by Michael B. Schiffer and George J. Gumerman, pp. 43-62. Academic Press, New York.

See, Horace 1891 The Building of the Steamship in America. *Engineering Magazine* May.

Shaw, Cornelius G. 1847 Unpublished diary. C.G. Shaw Papers, Michigan Historical Collections, University of Michigan, Ann Arbor. On file Isle Royale National Park, Houghton.

Shelvin, Charles 1937 Report to the Director on Observations and Recommendations for Isle Royale National Park (Proposed), February 17, 1937. Document on file, National Park Service, Washington, D.C.

Sivertson, Stanley 1987 Interview recorded by Toni Carrell and Ken Vrana, February 2, 1987, re: Lake Superior small watercraft on file, National Park Service, Southwest Cultural Resources Center, Submerged Cultural Resources Unit, Santa Fe.

Slyker, Francis J. 1958 Reinforced Wooden Vessels on the Great Lakes. *Telescope Magazine,* Great Lakes Maritime Institute.

Smiley, E. Thomas and Donald F. Holecek (editors) 1982 *Aquatic Park Management: Symposium Proceedings.* Michigan Sea Grant, Ann Arbor.

Smith, Edgar C. 1938 *A Short History of Naval and Marine Engineering.* University Press, Cambridge.

Smith, William E. 1932 Letter dated October 2, to Superintendent Stoll, regarding burials at Cemetery Island, on file Isle Royale National Park, Houghton.

Spratt, H. Philip 1951 *Transatlantic Paddle Steamers.* Glasgow.

Standard, W.L. 1947 *Merchant Seamen: A Short History of Their Struggles.* International Publishers, New York.

Stanton, Samuel W. 1962 *Great Lakes Steam Vessels.* Meriden Gravure, Meriden, Connecticut.

Stonehouse, Frederick 1974 *Isle Royale Shipwrecks.* Harboridge Press, Marquette.

Storey, Dana A. 1971 *The Building of a Wooden Ship.* Barre Publishers, Barre, Massachusetts.

Superintendent's Orders 1986 Part I, Section 1.5 (a)(1). Document on file, Isle Royale National Park, Houghton.

Swineford, A.P. 1876 Early History and Review of the Copper, Iron, Silver, Slate and Other Material Interests of the South Shore of Lake Superior. *Mining Journal,* Marquette.

Tanner, Henry S. 1840 *A Description of the Canals and Railroads of the United States Comprehending Notices of all the Works of Internal Improvements throughout the Several States.* T.R. Tanner and J. Disturnell, New York.

Taylor, George R. 1951 *The Transportation Revolution 1815-1860.* Holt, Rinehart and Winston, New York.

Thompson, Douglas G. 1983 *The* Annie Falconer *Archaeological Survey and Salvage Project 1982.* P.O.W. Kingston Ltd. and Ontario Heritage Foundation, Toronto.

Towle, Edward L. 1964 *Bibliography on the Economic History and Geography of the Great Lakes-St. Lawrence Drainage Basin.* University of Rochester, Canadian Studies Program. Ms. on file, Michigan State Library, Detroit.

Trimble, George 1907 *The Rose Pilot's Handbook: Useful Pertaining to Great Lakes.* Riverside, Port Huron, Michigan.

True, Dwight 1956 *Sixty Years of Shipbuilding.* Society of Naval Architects and Marine Engineers, Great Lakes Section, Ann Arbor.

Tunell, George G. 1898 *Transportation on the Great Lakes.* House Document No. 277, 55th Congress, 2nd Session:1-106.

Tuttle, Charles R. 1873 *A General History of the State of Michigan.* Tyler, Detroit.

University of Michigan Archaeological Survey of Isle Royale National Park. Site Survey No. 20IR29. Ms. on file, University of Michigan, Ann Arbor.

U.S. Army Corps of Engineers 1975 *Final Environmental Impact Statement: Operation and Maintenance Activities Two Harbors, Minnesota, Lake Superior.* U.S. Army Corps of Engineers, St. Paul.

U.S. Bureau of the Census 1960 *Historical Statistics of the United States, Colonial Times to 1957.* Government Printing Office, Washington, D.C.

U.S. Coast Guard 1977 *Marine Casualty Report: SS* Edmund Fitzgerald: *sinking in Lake Superior on 10 November 1975 with loss of life.* U.S. Coast Guard Marine Board of Investigation Report and Commandant's Action, Washington, D.C..

U.S. Department of Commerce 1981 *United States Coast Pilot 6: Great Lakes.* National Oceanic and Atmospheric Administration, Washington, D.C.

U.S. Department of the Interior, Geologic Survey 1926 *The Geologic Story of Isle Royale National Park, Geological Survey Bulletin 1309.* Superintendent of Documents, No. I 19.3:1309, Washington, D.C.

U.S. Department of the Interior, National Park Service 1945 *Isle Royale Rules and Regulations, Fishing, Hunting and Trapping.* Title 36, Chapter I, Part 34 Sections 34.1-34.4. Washington, D.C.

U.S. Department of the Navy 1970 *Dictionary of American Naval Fighting Ships.* Vol. 5. Government Printing Office, Washington, D.C.

U.S. Engineer Department 1848 *Commerce of the Lakes and Western Rivers.* 30th Congress, 1st Session. House ex. doc. 19, vol. 3:516-51.

1930 *Transportation on the Great Lakes.* Transportation Series No. 1. The Board of Engineers for Rivers and Harbors, War Department. Government Printing Office, Washington, D.C.

U.S. Light-House Establishment 1789-1871 *Compilation of Public Documents and Extracts from Reports and Papers Relating to Light-Houses, Light-Vessels, and Illuminating Apparatus and to Beacons, Buoys and Fog Signals 1789-1871.* Government Printing Office, Washington, D.C.

1873 *Annual Report of the U.S. Light-House Establishment.* Government Printing Office, Washington, D.C.

1902 *Instructions to Light-Keepers and Masters of Light-House Vessels.* Government Printing Office, Washington, D.C.

U.S. Secretary of the Treasury 1872 *Steam Vessels in the United States.* HR Doc. 138, 42nd Congress 2nd Session.

U.S. Shipbuilding Color Adjustment Board 1918 *Decision as to Wages, Hours and other Conditions in Atlantic Coast, Gulf and Great Lakes Shipyards.* October 1, 1918. Washington, D.C.

Van der Linden, Peter J. 1984 *Great Lakes Ships We Remember.* Freshwater Press, Cleveland.

Van Riemsdijk, J.T. and Kenneth Brown 1980 *The Pictorial History of Steam Power.* Octopus Books, London.

Walker, Augustus 1902 Early Days on the Lakes. *Publications of the Buffalo Historical Society* 5:287-323.

Walker, Fred 1984 *Song of the Clyde: A History of Clyde Shipbuilding.* W.W. Norton, London.

Walsh, George Ethelbert 1899 American Lake Shipping and Casualties. *Cassier's Magazine* April:499-507.

Ward, Charles 1909 Shallow Draught River Steamers. *Transactions of the Society of Naval Architects and Marine Engineers* 17:79-106.

Warner, Thomas D. and Donald F. Holecek 1975 The Thunder Bay Shipwreck Survey Study Report. Ms. submitted for the Recreation Research and Planning Unit, Department of Park and Recreation Resources, Michigan State University.

Weber, Bruce E. 1981 Oral History Standards – Isle Royale National Park. Ms. on file, Isle Royale National Park, Houghton.

1982 Isle Royale's Submerged Resources. *The George Wright Forum* 2(4):52-54.

Wells, Homer Jr. 1938 *History of Accidents, Casualties and Wrecks on Lake Superior.* U.S. Army, Corps of Engineers, Duluth.

Wheeler, Robert C., Walter A. Kenyon, Alan R. Woolworth and Douglas A. Birk 1975 *Voices from the Rapids.* Minnesota Historical Society, St. Paul.

White, William H. 1899 The Progress in Steam Navigation. Presidential address before the Mechanical Section of the British Association for the Advancement of Science, 1899. Smithsonian Report on file, San Francisco Maritime Museum.

Whittier, Bob 1983 *Paddle Wheel Steamers and Their Giant Engines.* Seamaster Boats, Duxbury.

Williams, David 1909 Shipping on the Upper Lakes. In *Papers and Records of the Huron Institute* 1:43-59. Huron Institute, Collingwood.

Williams, E.B. 1962 The Great Lakes Iron Ore Carrier. Paper presented at the Spring Meeting of the Society of Naval Architects and Marine Engineers, 1962. Duluth, Minnesota.

Williams, Ralph D. 1907 Commerce of the Great Lakes in 1905. In: *The Saint Marys Falls Canal,* edited by Charles Moore, pp. 189-205. Semi-Centennial Commission, Detroit.

Williamson, Samuel H. 1977 The Growth of the Great Lakes as a Major Transportation Resource, 1870-1911. *Research in Economic History* 2:173-248.

Winkelmann, A. 1978 Ms. on file, National Park Service, Submerged Cultural Resources Unit, Santa Fe.

Wolbrink, Donald and George Walling 1937 Isle Royale Resorts: A Report Prepared at the Request of Chief Architect Thomas C. Vint Covering the Condition of Present Developments and Making Recommendations for their Future Development. In *Pre-Park Survey of Isle Royale.* Ms. on file, Isle Royale National Park, Houghton.

Wolff, Julius F. 1979 *The Shipwrecks of Lake Superior.* Lake Superior Marine Museum Association, Duluth.

Workman, James C. 1945 Shipping on the Great Lakes. In *Historical Transactions 1893-1943* pp. 363-388. The Society of Naval Architects and Marine Engineers, New York.

Wright, Richard J. 1970 *Freshwater Whales: A History of the American Ship Building Company and Its Predecessors.* Kent State University, Kent.

1973 *Inventory of Shipwrecks within Michigan Coastal Waters.* Michigan Department of Natural Resources and Northwest Ohio-Great Lakes Research Center, Bowling Green, Ohio.

Young, Anna G. 1957 Off Watch. Toronto.

Periodicals:

Ashland Press, Ashland, Wisconsin

Benton Harbor Daily Palladium, Benton Harbor, Michigan

Calumet News, Calumet, Michigan

Canadian Railway and Marine World

Cleveland Herald, Cleveland, Ohio

Cleveland Leader, Cleveland, Ohio

Cleveland News, Cleveland, Ohio

Cleveland Plain Dealer, Cleveland, Ohio

Cheboygan Tribune, Cheboygan, Michigan

Chicago Inter Ocean, Chicago, Illinois

Chicago Herald and Examiner, Chicago, Illinois

Chicago Tribune, Chicago, Illinois

Cobourg Star, Cobourg, Ontario

Daily Mining Gazette, Houghton, Michigan

Detroit Free Press, Detroit, Michigan

Detroit Daily News, Detroit, Michigan

Detroit Marine Historian, Detroit, Michigan

Detroit Telegram, Detroit, Michigan

Duluth Daily Tribune, Duluth, Minnesota

Duluth Evening Herald, Duluth, Minnesota

Duluth Minnesotian, Duluth, Minnesota

Duluth News Tribune, Duluth, Minnesota

Fort William Daily Times Journal, Fort William, Ontario

Glasgow Herald, Glasgow, Scotland

Holland City News, Holland City, Michigan

Houghton Daily Mining Gazette, Houghton, Michigan

Keweenaw Miner, Calumet, Michigan

Kingston Gazette, Kingston, Ontario

Lake Carriers Association, Cleveland, Ohio

London, Ontario, Free Press, London, Ontario

Manistee News Advocate, Manistee, Michigan

Marine Engineering, Cleveland, Ohio

Marquette Daily Mining Journal, Marquette, Michigan

Meaford Monitor, Meaford, Ontario

Minneapolis Star, Minneapolis, Minnesota

Montreal Gazette, Montreal, Canada

New Orleans Times-Picayune, New Orleans, Louisiana

New York Times, New York, New York

Nordic Diver, Inner Space Society, Duluth, Minnesota

Ontonagon Herald, Ontonagon, Michigan

Owen Sound Advertiser, Owen Sound, Ontario

Owen Sound Daily Sun Times, Owen Sound, Ontario

Owen Sound Times, Owen Sound, Ontario

Portage Lake Mining Gazette, Portage, Michigan

Port Arthur Daily News, Port Arthur, Ontario

Port Arthur Herald, Port Arthur, Ontario

Port Arthur News Chronicle, Port Arthur, Ontario

Port Arthur Sentinal, Port Arthur, Ontario

Port Huron Times, Port Huron, Michigan

Sarnia Observer, Sarnia, Ontario

Sault Daily Star, Sault Ste. Marie, Ontario

Scanner, Toronto Marine Historical Society, Toronto, Ontario

Skillings Mining Review, Duluth, Minnesota

Superior Evening Telegram, Superior, Wisconsin

Thunder Bay Sentinental, Thunder Bay, Ontario

Toledo Blade, Toledo, Ohio

Toronto Daily Star, Toronto, Ontario

Toronto Globe and Mail, Toronto, Ontario

Toronto Mail, Toronto, Ontario

Toronto World, Toronto, Ontario

Traverse City Record Eagle, Traverse City, Michigan

Winnipeg Free Press, Winnipeg, Manitoba

Wisconsin State Journal, Milwaukee, Wisconsin

Other publications of Lake Superior Port Cities Inc.

Julius F. Wolff Jr.'s Lake Superior Shipwrecks
    Hardcover: ISBN 0-942235-02-9
    Softcover: ISBN 0-942235-01-0

Shipwrecks of Lake Superior by James R. Marshall
    Softcover: ISBN 0-942235-00-2

Shipwreck of the Mesquite by Frederick Stonehouse
    Softcover: ISBN 0-942235-10-x

The Superior Way, Second Edition by Bonnie Dahl
    Spiralbound: ISBN 0-942235-14-2

Michigan Gold, Mining in the Upper Peninsula by Daniel Fountain
    Softcover: ISBN 0-942235-15-0

Wreck Ashore, The United States Life-Saving Service on the Great Lakes by Frederick Stonehouse
    Softcover: ISBN 0-942235-22-3

Lake Superior Magazine (Bimonthly)

Lake Superior Travel Guide (Annual)

Lake Superior Wall Calendar (Annual)

Lake Superior Wall Map

For a catalog of the entire Lake Superior Port Cities collection of books and merchandise, write or call:

Lake Superior Port Cities Inc.
P.O. Box 16417
Duluth, Minnesota 55816-0417
USA

218-722-5002
800-635-0544
FAX 218-722-4096